Translated for the first time into English, this memoir offers unique insights into the epic confrontation between the French and Russians in Poland during the winter of 1806–1807, including the terrible carnage at Eylau.

A Hanoverian by birth, General Levin von Bennigsen spent 45 years in the Russian army earning a reputation as a capable officer. Due to his father's connections at the Hanoverian court, Bennigsen began his service there at the tender age of 10 as a page and was commissioned as an ensign in the Hanoverian army at 14. In 1763, as a captain, he fought in the final campaign of the Seven Years War but then retired, deeply disillusioned with military service and widely regarded as an unpromising officer. After apparently squandering his inheritance, he sought a new career in Russia in 1773. Over the next four decades he fought against the Poles, Turks, and Persians, steadily advancing through the ranks and garnering a fistful of awards. A lieutenant general in 1798, he was caught up in Emperor Paul's purge of high-ranking officers and nurtured deep animosity towards the czar. He thus took an active part in the conspiracy that assassinated Paul in late March 1801. Despite his role in the conspiracy, Bennigsen's career did not suffer under the new emperor – promoted to general in 1802, he commanded a Russian corps sent to support Prussians during the War of the Fourth Coalition in 1806. It was then that his name became a household word as he took supreme command of the Russian army against Napoleon, at the height of his power and fresh from his thrashing of Prussia. The subsequent Polish campaign turned into a quagmire as the two sides clashed amidst one of Europe's poorest and most barren regions.

Bennigsen's memoirs offer unique insights into this war, revealing the extent of command dissension at the Russian headquarters, discussing operational and logistical challenges confronting the Russian army, and underscoring the heroism of the Russian soldiers. During a gruelling campaign, Bennigsen evaded Napoleon's enveloping manoeuvres during a five-day all-out pursuit that brought the two sides to the snow-covered fields of Eylau. Here over 140,000 French and Russian soldiers fought a terrible battle that claimed over 40,000 casualties and left thousands of dead and wounded littering the frozen slope.

Alexander Mikaberidze is Professor of European History at Louisiana State University at Shreveport, where he also holds the Ruth Herring Noel Endowed Chair for the Curatorship of the James Smith Noel Collection. He is the author of several books, including *The Napoleonic Wars: A Global History* (2020) and *Kutuzov: A Life in War and Peace* (2022).

Paul Strietelmeier is an independent scholar specializing in French history during the Revolutionary and Napoleonic era. He studied history at Valparaiso University and earned a master's degree in history from the University of North Texas.

Confronting Napoleon

Levin von Bennigsen's Memoir of the Campaign in Poland, 1806–1807

Volume 1 – Pultusk to Eylau

Translated by Paul Strietelmeier

Edited and Annotated by Alexander Mikaberidze

Helion & Company

Helion & Company Limited
Unit 8 Amherst Business Centre
Budbrooke Road
Warwick
CV34 5WE
England
Tel. 01926 499619
Email: info@helion.co.uk
Website: www.helion.co.uk
Twitter: @helionbooks
Visit our blog at http://blog.helion.co.uk/

Published by Helion & Company 2022
Designed and typeset by Mach 3 Solutions Ltd (www.mach3solutions.co.uk)
Cover designed by Paul Hewitt, Battlefield Design (www.battlefield-design.co.uk)

Text © Paul Strietelmeier, Alexander Mikaberidze 2022
Illustrations © as individually credited
Maps drawn by George Anderson © Helion & Company 2022
Cover: Levin von Bennigsen, oil on canvas by George Dawe (State Hermitage Museum). Bataille d'Eylau en Prusse, aquatint by Johann Rugendas (Anne S.K. Brown Military Collection).

Every reasonable effort has been made to trace copyright holders and to obtain their permission for the use of copyright material. The author and publisher apologise for any errors or omissions in this work, and would be grateful if notified of any corrections that should be incorporated in future reprints or editions of this book.

ISBN 978-1-915070-44-9

British Library Cataloguing-in-Publication Data.
A catalogue record for this book is available from the British Library.

All rights reserved. No part of this publication may be reproduced, stored in a retrieval system, or transmitted, in any form, or by any means, electronic, mechanical, photocopying, recording or otherwise, without the express written consent of Helion & Company Limited.

For details of other military history titles published by Helion & Company Limited, contact the above address, or visit our website: http://www.helion.co.uk

We always welcome receiving book proposals from prospective authors.

Contents

List of Maps and Illustrations		vi
Preface		viii
Acknowledgements		xvii
Editorial Note		xviii
1	The Situation of Russia in 1806	19
2	Russia, Turkey, and Austria	23
3	Russia, Sweden, and Prussia	32
4	Russia, England, and France	41
5	The Start of Hostilities – The Evacuation of Warsaw	53
6	Czarnowo and Pultusk	70
7	Golymin	88
8	Retreat of the Allied Armies – Plan of Operations	97
9	Bennigsen's Offensive – Mohrungen	111
10	Dirschau-Passenheim	127
11	Bergfried, Waltersdorf-Liebstadt, Hof and Heilsberg	141
12	Eylau	160
13	The Retreat to Königsberg	183
14	Return to the Offensive – Braunsberg	198
15	Launau – Winter Cantonments	213
Select Bibliography		225
Index		227

List of Maps and Illustrations

Levin von Bennigsen. (Courtesy of the James Smith Noel Collection)	ix
Mikhail Kamensky. (Public Domain)	x
Napoleon, the Emperor of the French and the Protector of the Confederation of the Rhine. Print, 1806. (Private Collection)	xi
Fedor (Friedrich Wilhelm) von Buxhöwden. (State Hermitage Museum)	xii
Alexander von Fock. (State Hermitage Museum)	xv
Ivan Michelson (Johann von Michelsohnen). (Public Domain)	54
'One Hero per Victory' – an early nineteenth-century French print showing the famed French commanders and their great victories. (Courtesy of Anne S.K. Brown Military Collection)	57
General View of the Theater of War in Poland.	61
Marshal Jean-Baptiste Bernadotte. (Courtesy of James Smith Noel Collection)	73
Situation as of late December 1806.	75
Karl Gustav von Baggehufvudt, commonly known as Baggovut. (State Hermitage Museum)	77
Khristophor (Christoph Hermann Karl) von Brevern. (State Hermitage Museum)	82
A British caricature, published in 1807, illustrating a battle between 'sturdy bears and skinny apes' at Pultusk on December 26, 1806. (Courtesy of Anne S.K. Brown Military Collection)	86
Cyprian Kreutz. (State Hermitage Museum)	90
Yefim Czaplic. (State Hermitage Museum)	91
Aleksey Scherbatov. (State Hermitage Museum)	93
General Aleksei Sherbatov, by Alexander von Kotzebue. (State History Museum (Russia))	95
Marshal Michel Ney in action. (Courtesy of James Smith Noel Collection)	99
Yegor Pillar (Georg Ludwig Pilar von Pilchau). (State Hermitage Museum)	112
Nikolai Vuich (Vujič). (State Hermitage Museum)	122
Roman (Heinrich Reinhold von) Anrep. (Public Domain)	123
Nikolai Tuchkov. (State Hermitage Museum)	130
Situation as of Late January 1807.	134
Karl Gersdorf. (State Hermitage Museum)	148
Situation as of 4-5 February 1807.	150
Lev Iachvill (Yashvil/Iashvili). (State Hermitage Museum)	152
The Battle of Eylau: Starting Positions.	161
Mikhail Balk. (State Hermitage Museum)	164
French cavalry charge about to pierce the first line of the Russian infantry at Eylau. Copper engraving by Pierre Adrien Le Beau after Thomas Charles Naudet, published in Paris in late 1807. (Courtesy of Anne S.K. Brown Military Collection)	168

Joseph O'Rourke. (State Hermitage Museum)	170
A superb engraving by Johann Lorenz Rugendas, published in 1820, showing the panoramic battle scene of the fighting at Eylau. (Courtesy of Anne S.K. Brown Military Collection)	172
'The Prussians at Eylau on February 8, 1807,' an early twentieth-century painting by Richard Knötel embellishing the Prussian involvement in the battle. (Courtesy of Anne S.K. Brown Military Collection)	174
General Jean-Joseph Ange d'Hautpoul leading the massive cavalry charge at Eylau. Engraving by J.J. Wolff after Carle Vernet, 1810. (Private collection)	176
The panoramic view of the epic charge of the French cavalry at Eylau on 8 February, painting by Jean-Antoine-Siméon Fort. (Public Domain)	179
Battle of Eylau: Situation at the end of the battle.	180
Jean-Antoine-Siméon Fort's painting conveys the misery of fighting amidst the frozen cemetery for control of Eylau on 7 February. (Public Domain)	182
Fedor von Korff. (State Hermitage Museum)	186
Karl Lambert. (State Hermitage Museum)	187
Area between Eylau and Königsberg.	193

Preface

Levin August Theophile (or Leontii Leontievich as he is known in Russia) von Bennigsen was born on 10 February 1745 into a Hanoverian family in Brunswick, where his father was a colonel in the guards. His family was of ancient nobility, originally residing in Saxony before his father, preferring a military career to the monotony of the ecclesiastical life of his ancestors, moved to Hanover. His service there was well rewarded, including with considerable estates at Banteln.

The young Bennigsen was destined for a military career – 'I have been raised at the camp and grew up to the sound of guns,' he once commented.[1] Due to his father's connections at the Hanoverian court, Bennigsen began his service there at the age of 10 as a page. Four years later he was commissioned as an ensign in the Hanoverian foot-guards and, in 1763, as a captain, participated in the final campaign of the Seven Years War. A year later, after the death of his father and his own marriage to the Baroness Steinberg, Bennigsen retired to his estate at Banteln, disillusioned with military service and widely regarded as an unpromising officer. He apparently squandered his inheritance and, after his wife's untimely death, briefly re-entered Hanoverian service before deciding to seek a career in Russia.

Bennigsen spent four decades in the Russian service. He was accepted with a rank of premier major and assigned to the Vyatskii (Vyatka) Musketeer Regiment in 1773. His first campaign was against the rebellious peasants who rose under the leadership of Emelyan Pugachev in 1773–1774. Bennigsen's regiment was among the troops sent to quell the uprising, which was accomplished by 1775. He was soon noticed by his superiors, including the famed Russian General Alexander Suvorov, and quickly advanced through the ranks. In January 1779, he became a lieutenant colonel in the Kievskii (Kiev) Light Cavalry Regiment where he remained for eight years until he was given command of the Izumskii (Izumsk) Light Cavalry Regiment. In 1787, he participated in another Russo-Ottoman war, distinguishing himself at Ochakov and Bender and earning a promotion to brigadier in 1788. His second marriage resulted in another heartbreak as his wife died after giving birth to his son, Adam (1776–1816), the future Russian major general and count of the Russian empire. Shortly thereafter he married for the third time, but this marriage proved childless, and his wife passed away in 1789.

In 1792–1794, Bennigsen participated in the Second Partition of Poland, commanding a flying corps that maintained communications between the Russian corps sent to defeat the

---

1 Levin August Theophil von Bennigsen, *Gedanken über einige dem Officier der leichten Cavalerie nothwendige...* (Leipzig: W. Rein et Comp., 1805), p.xv.

Polish forces. He participated in several actions against the Poles, including the capture of the Nesvizh castle and a combat near Zelwa, where he distinguished himself leading the decisive cavalry charge; when his advanced posts were attacked by the Poles and driven into the woods, Bennigsen rallied them and, through an accomplished manoeuvre, surrounded and defeated his enemy. After the start of the insurrection of Thaddeus Kosciusko in 1794, Bennigsen was again ordered into Poland and distinguished himself in several skirmishes, but more particularly in combats near Solami, Olita and Vilna, where, leading the charge of six squadrons of the Izumskii Light Horse Regiment, he captured a Polish artillery battery and seized seven cannon. For his service during the Polish campaigns, Bennigsen was promoted to major general on 9 July 1794, awarded the Order of St George (3rd class), the Order of St Vladimir (2nd class) and a golden sword (with diamonds) for bravery shown in combat. While in Poland, Bennigsen also married for the fourth time. His new wife Marie Leonarde (Ekaterina Fadeevna, in Russian parlance) Andrzejkowicz-Buttowt, who was 30 years younger than him. The couple's first and only son, Alexander, was born in 1809, destined to become an eminent Hanoverian statesman.

Levin von Bennigsen. (Courtesy of the James Smith Noel Collection)

After the Third Polish Partition, Bennigsen briefly commanded troops in cantonment before travelling to St Petersburg, where he formed a close association with Valerian Zubov, the brother of Empress Catherine II's favourite Platon Zubov. In 1796, he participated in the Persian Campaign, commanded by Zubov, and fought the Persian forces at Derbent, for which he garnered the Order of St Anna (1st class).

After Emperor Paul's accession to the throne in November 1796, Bennigsen was named chef[2] of the Rostovskii (Rostov) Dragoon Regiment (14 December 1796) and was promoted to lieutenant general (25 February 1798). However, during Paul's subsequent purge of high-ranking officers, Bennigsen was dismissed from service (11 October 1798) and developed

---

2   Chef, *shef*, was similar to a British regimental colonel, the formal and administrative head of the regiment, who, if present, superseded regimental commanders to a field command.

a deep animosity towards the Emperor. Thus, he took an active part in the conspiracy to overthrow him and, according to the memoirs of some conspirators, was chosen to lead the coup because of his reputation for audacity and courage.

Shortly after midnight on 24 March, as Paul retired to his private apartments, a group of about 60 accomplices, led by Bennigsen and the Zubov brothers, quietly entered the royal residence at the Mikhailovskii Castle. The men – fortified with alcohol to overcome their trepidations – overpowered the guards and rushed into the imperial bedroom, which they found empty. A momentary panic set in; some conspirators began to wail that the Emperor had escaped and was probably already rallying the guards to arrest them. But Bennigsen kept his composure. 'The wine is poured and must be drunk,' he was overheard saying.[3] The conspirators searched the room and saw the czar's bare feet beneath a screen in a corner of the room. They dragged Paul out and demanded that he sign an abdication document. He refused and in the ensuing scuffle was badly beaten. It took several men to overpower him, some banging his head on the floor while others threw a sash around his neck and strangled him; not content with killing the czar, the conspirators kicked and mangled his body.

Paul's murder paved paving the way for the accession of his son, Emperor Alexander, to the Russian throne. Despite his role in the conspiracy, Bennigsen's career did not suffer under the new emperor – he was appointed the Military Governor of Vilna and Inspector of the Lithuanian Inspection on 23 July 1801. Bennigsen was then promoted to general of cavalry on 23 June 1802 with seniority dating from 4 December 1799.

In the summer of 1805, at the start of the War of the Third Coalition against Napoleon, Bennigsen received command of the Army of the North of some 48,000 men arranged between Taurrogen and Grodno. He was tasked with nudging the Prussians out of their neutrality, forcibly if need be, but the war ended before Bennigsen could do anything. On 2 December, Napoleon routed the Russo-Austrian armies at Austerlitz. After a lull of 10 months, the war resumed in Europe as hostilities commenced in October 1806 between France and Prussia, the latter being aided by Russia.

The War of the Fourth Coalition, as the campaign of 1806–1807 eventually became known, began rather disastrously for the allies. Prussia, which could have had a decisive effect on the outcome of the war in 1805, had dithered until the autumn of 1806 when King Frederick William III was at last forced by his hawkish advisors

Mikhail Kamensky. (Public Domain)

---

3 Cited in Simon Sebag Montefiore, *The Romanovs, 1613-1918* (London: Weidenfeld & Nicolson, 2016), p.272.

Napoleon, the Emperor of the French and the Protector of the Confederation of the Rhine. Print, 1806. (Private Collection)

to confront Napoleon. Yet, the war was over just a month later. In early October Napoleon invaded Saxony and scored a brilliant victory at Jena and Auerstädt (14 October) where the Prussian army effectively collapsed. Less than two weeks later, Napoleon made a triumphant entry into the Prussian capital, Berlin. With his army in tatters, Frederick William was forced to leave his capital for East Prussia where he eagerly awaited news of the arrival of Russian force organized into two strong corps commanded by Bennigsen and Fedor (Friedrich Wilhelm) von Buxhöwden (Buxhoeveden). But Napoleon anticipated his enemies. In worsening weather, which turned the roads into mud, the Grande Armée marched into Poland, forcing the Russians to withdraw over the Vistula. By late November, the French emperor entered the former Polish capital city of Warsaw.

Confusion, meanwhile, reigned in the Russian army as the corps commanders quarrelled in the absence of an overall commander. 'It was difficult to find a commander-in-chief,' admitted one Russian officer.[4] A seemingly obvious choice to lead the army, General Mikhail Golenischev-Kutuzov - the veteran commander of the Russo-Ottoman Wars who commanded the Russian army against Napoleon and whose prudent advice of avoiding a decisive battle the czar chose to ignore at Austerlitz - was in disgrace. Unjustly blamed for the defeat on that December morning, 'Kutuzov was seen as undeserving in the eyes of the high society, and especially in the opinion of the Emperor, ever since that calamitous day of Austerlitz.'[5] Yet Alexander's reluctance to employ Kutuzov in the field army is all the more baffling when considering whom he nominated instead. Field Marshal Mikhail Kamensky was infamous for his abrasive character and, at nearly 70 years old, had long been retired from active service. It seemed everyone except for the czar knew that he was both senile and in poor health. 'I almost completely lost my vision and am unable to find any locations on the map,' the field marshal admitted after arriving to the army. 'I suffer from [excruciating] pains in the eyes and head and cannot mount the horse... I am signing papers without even knowing what they prescribe.'[6] But the public clamored for a new and experienced leader and cared not for Kamensky's reputation as a callous and harsh commander. 'He was perceived a strong leader and event his repute as a ruthless commander was looked upon as an evidence of his exactness and strength of character, making people to look at him as the only person who could

Fedor (Friedrich Wilhelm) von Buxhöwden. (State Hermitage Museum)

---

4 Alexander Benckendorff, 'Vospominaniya...', in M. Sidorova and A. Litvin (eds), *Rossiiskii arkhiv* (Moscow: TRITE, 2012), p.124.
5 Benckendorff, 'Vospominaniya...', p.124.
6 Kamenskii to Alexander, 22 December 1806, cited in Alexander Mikhailovskii-Danilevskii, *Opisanie vtoroi voini Imperatora Aleksandra s Napoleonom* (St. Petersburg: Tip. Schtaba Otd. Korpusa Vnut. Strazhi, 1846), p.76.

stand up to Napoleon and bring the much-needed unity in the army.'[7] And so it was that in November 1806, the czar appointed Kamensky to lead the Russian forces against Napoleon.

The absence of a strong leader did exacerbate quarrels between Bennigsen and Buxhöwden who clashed on the issues of authority and seniority, their squabbles hampering Russian operations. 'General Bennigsen had instructions not to be subordinate to General Buxhöwden, even though the latter enjoyed seniority in rank,' remembered one senior Russian officer, who also lamented the presence of other generals who further muddled the matters.[8] As far as the general's rank was concerned, General Bogdan von Knorring was senior to both Bennigsen and Buxhöwden but as the quartermaster-general he had only the authority to advise them. Emperor Alexander had also dispatched Count Peter Tolstoy to act as a general for special assignments and his personal delegate (*doverennoe litso*) with instructions to submit regular reports on what was happening in the army.[9]

The winter campaign thus turned into a quagmire of snow and mud. It started with the bloody battles at Golymin and Pultusk, where the Russians checked the enemy's advance. Bennigsen claimed both these battles as decisive Russian victories, received the Order of St George (2nd class) on 8 January 1807, and was appointed the commander-in-chief of the Russian army on the 13th. He was resolved not to wait for Napoleon's new offensive and chose to anticipate the attack. He concluded that with Napoleon cantoning his troops in winter-quarters scattered across wide area, the Russians ought to take the field again and surprise the enemy. The Russian army commenced an offensive that could have produced decisive results if not for weather, logistics, and bad luck. Napoleon quickly counterattacked and forced Bennigsen to fall back to Preussisch-Eylau, where on 7–8 February a battle was fought. This was a bloodbath that left some 40,000 killed and wounded on the frozen fields around this Polish town; one appalled eyewitness described it as 'the most horrible butchery of men.'[10]

As the army withdrew from Eylau, the Russian headquarters was embroiled in heated discussions over the battle and its outcome. Bennigsen claimed Eylau as a Russian victory and told the czar that 'the enemy has been completely beaten, near 2,000 prisoners made and 12 standards [captured].'[11] Russian society celebrated the news of the victory, albeit days later the reports of the enormous Russian losses and Bennigsen's subsequent retreat to Konigsberg raised questions of faithfulness of his earlier reporting. Moreover, many senior Russian officers came to loath Bennigsen and one of them went as far as to challenge him to a duel. British commissioner to the Russian army Sir Robert Wilson informed his colleague in London that 'Bennigsen is not popular in this army. His enemies do not form their opinion from a due appreciation of his qualities: but they are hurried into prejudice by the false feeling that their national glory is obscured by the success of a foreigner at the head of their armies.'[12] Bennigsen sent a letter to Alexander offering to resign his command,

---

7   Benckendorff, 'Vospominaniya...', p.124.
8   Benckendorff, 'Vospominaniya...', p.124. Benckendorff also complained that 'the army comprised of generals who were resentful of each other, young officers, and the largely inexperienced soldiers.'
9   Benckendorff, 'Vospominaniya...', p.123.
10 Jean Baptiste Barrès, *Memoirs of a Napoleonic Officer* (London: George Allen & Unwin, 1925), p.101.
11 Bennigsen to Alexander, 8 February 1807, in Robert Wilson, *Brief Remarks on the Character and Composition of the Russian Army...* (London: T. Egerton, 1810), p.238
12 Robert Wilson to Lord Hutchinson, 11 February 1807, in Herbert Randolph (ed.), *Life of General Sir Robert Wilson* (London: John Murray, 1862), vol.2, p.414.

but the Emperor demurred. He kept the general in charge of the army and awarded him the Order of St Andrew the First Called.

After Eylau, the French and Russian armies went to their winter quarters to recover, with the certain expectation of renewed fighting in the spring. They did in June 1807, fighting at Guttstadt, Heilsberg and Friedland, where Bennigsen made a fatal mistake that resulted in a heavy Russian defeat. Displeased with his actions, Alexander removed him from command in July 1807.

Bennigsen remained in semi-exile for the next five years, spending much of his time at his estates near Vilna. On the eve of Napoleon's invasion of Russia in 1812, he was ordered to join the Imperial Retinue and, once the Franco-Russian war commenced, was considered for the post of commander-in-chief before being rejected in favour of Mikhail Kutuzov. Instead, Bennigsen became the chief of staff of the united Russian armies and bickered with Kutuzov throughout the campaign. After Borodino, he advised the commander-in-chief against abandoning Moscow to the French but was overruled. The two men clashed again at Tarutino, where their squabbles prevented the Russians from gaining a major victory over the French advance guard. Their relations soon devolved into outright animosity, with Kutuzov admitting (in November) that he no longer allowed Bennigsen to visit him. Just days later, the field marshal issued a concise but blunt order informing Bennigsen that because of 'bouts of illness' he was to leave the army at once and proceed to Kaluga, there to await a new assignment from the czar.[13]

Bennigsen returned to the army in the spring of 1813, just as Kutuzov got sick and died in April. He received command of the Army of Poland and took active part in the War of the Sixth Coalition, fighting at Lutzen, Bautzen, and Leipzig before being diverted to besiege the fortresses of Torgau, Magdeburg and Hamburg; for his dedicated service, he was conferred the title of count of the Russian Empire and the Order of St George (1st class).

After the Napoleonic Wars, Bennigsen took charge of the 2nd Army but was criticized for poor administration and forced to retire in May 1818. He left Russia and settled in Hanover, where passed away on 3 October 1826.

'A pale, withered personage of high stature and cold appearance, with a scar across his face' – that is how Napoleon's aide-de-camp Philippe-Paul comte de Ségur saw Bennigsen in December 1806.[14] Bennigsen was a brave officer who showed his martial prowess when leading regiments and divisions but struggled at the operational and strategic level. Even Robert Wilson, who tended to like the Hanoverian, had to admit that he was 'a most gallant and good man in every sense of the word' but 'not, however, a great officer' and was often 'perplexed by the impediments thrown in his way by malice, ignorance, and idleness.'[15] Despite Bennigsen's claims to victories, the battles of Pultusk, Eylau, and Heilseberg were

---

13 Mikhail Golenischev-Kutuzov to Levin von Bennigsen, 15/27 November 1812, Russian State Historical Military Archive: fond VUA, delo 1078, list 168.
14 Philippe-Paul de Ségur, *An Aide-de-camp of Napoleon: Memoirs of General Count de Ségur, of the French Academy, 1800–1812* (New York: D. Appleton, 1895), p.328.
15 Robert Wilson to Lord Hutchinson, 11 February 1807, in *Life of General Sir Robert Wilson*, vol. 2, p.414. Wilson also noted that Bennigsen 'is frequently obliged, or thinks that he is obliged, to be superintending trifles, that he should not even be acquainted with if in the departments there was any method or capacity. The avidity to asperse and the habit of detraction is a fatal source of calamity'.

unimaginative defensive battles that claimed thousands of Russian casualties. At Friedland, Bennigsen's decision to cross the river and attack the French at rather disadvantageous positions led to a crushing defeat and an ignominious peace with France. General Louis-Alexandre Langeron, who served with Bennigsen in 1813, thought that he was 'an excellent general but weak when in charge for he knew nothing of how to make himself obeyed or how to repress the cabals and intrigues that formed against him.'[16] A French contemporary agreed that Bennigsen was 'an excellent officer and a man of firm character' who 'loved his trade and had studied it in the cabinet and on the battlefield'; but he was also quick to point out the general was 'new' to commanding army and lacked relevant experience.[17] Probably the best assessment of Bennigsen belongs to the quill of Faddei Bulgarin, the sharp-witted literary critic who had participated in the Polish Campaign of 1806–1807. Like many others, Bulgarin pointed out that prior to 1806 Bennigsen had never commanded a corps, not to mention an army, and his abilities as a military commander could not be properly judged by his previous service. 'He was brave and enterprising,' Bulgarin noted in his journal,

Alexander von Fock. (State Hermitage Museum)

> ... but if one considers that his main accomplishments came as a detachment commander against the Polish confederates, that is, the rebellious nobility and a small number of regular troops who were inexperienced, poorly armed and led by men with limited understanding of the art of war, then Bennigsen's former successes could not have served as sufficient guarantees of future victories, especially in a war against such a commander as Napoleon. Yet everyone recognised that Bennigsen had a broad knowledge and that although he had not had a classical education due to enlisting in the army at an early age, he had still acquired a thorough understanding of strategy through reading, thinking, and practicing. Nature created him as a warrior, endowing him with a passionate love for the art of war, quickness of mind, military eye, extraordinary courage, rare audacity and remarkable composure.

---

16 See Langeron's lengthy note in Alexandre Louis Andrault de Langeron, *Mémoires de Langeron: Général d'infanterie dans l'armée russe. Campagnes de 1812, 1813, 1814* (Paris: Picard, 1902), pp.17–18.

17 Armand d'Allonville, *Mémoires tires des papiers d'un homme d'Etat* (Paris: Michaud, 1835), vol.9, p.377.

Bennigsen was of tall stature but rather lean, and had expressive facial features and a quick glance. His imposing and dignified appearance, lordly manners and constant composure inspired respect and aroused instinctive confidence in his superiors, peers, and subordinates… Those who knew Bennigsen well claimed that he was a man of an extremely subtle mind and insinuating when he needed it, and that he nurtured inordinate ambition within himself, and therefore a great many feared him.[18]

While fighting in Poland in 1806–1807, Bennigsen befriended Alexander von Fock, who served as his staff officer and later duty general throughout that campaign.[19] The two men stayed close and continued to correspond for years to come. In 1807–1811, Bennigsen resided at his Zakret estate near Vilna, where he suffered greatly from dropsy and became so swelled with fluids that he could no longer wear his uniform. His physical turmoil was augmented by his intellectual angst at being held responsible for Russia's defeat. In response to numerous libellous pamphlets, Bennigsen decided to write his memoirs to explain what had transpired during the war.

Bennigsen spent over two years writing his reminiscences. They were based on his letters to Fock and incorporated dozens of captured French letters and reports. He completed the first draft by late 1810, when he began sharing lengthy excerpts with Fock, and continued to revise and expand the manuscript in later years; in his letters to Fock, Bennigsen claimed that he was not writing the memoirs to justify his own actions but rather to the extoll the Russian army and that he did not intend to publish the book in his lifetime. And so it happened. After his passing, his wife sold the manuscript to the Russian government which kept it under wraps for decades until Russian scholar Peter Maikov published an edited Russian translation in St Petersburg in 1900. Seven years later, Captain E. Cazalas of the French General Staff, produced a three-volume French edition (*Mémoires du General Bennigsen*) in Paris. Despite the appearance of a short pamphlet claiming to be 'Authentic Memoirs of the Baron of Bennigsen' in London in 1807, Bennigsen's memoirs had been largely unattainable to Anglophone audiences. This edition represents the first English edition of the general's memoirs.

Alexander Mikaberidze
Shreveport LA
November 2022

---

18   Faddei Bulgarin, *Vospominaniya…* (St. Petersburg: Izd. M. Olkhina, 1847), vol.3, pp.22–23.
19   Alexander Borisovich von Fock was Bennigsen's close friend and confidant. Born in 1763 in Oranienbaum, he was the son of Bernhardt Fock, chief gardener of Empress Catherine II. He began military service in 1780, participated in the Russo-Swedish War in 1788–1790 and the Second Partition of Poland. In 1795–1798, he was tasked with organizing horse artillery units and was promoted to major general in 1799. After retiring in 1800, Fock spent seven years at his estate before Bennigsen asked him to become his duty officer. Fock served with distinction during the Polish Campaign of 1806–1807 but was seriously wounded in the chest at Heilsberg. After recuperating, he was appointed a duty general to Minister of War Mikhail Barclay de Tolly in 1810 and later served as the chief of staff of the Finland Corps in 1812. He retired again (due to poor health) in early 1813 and settled at his estate at Oranienbaum, where he died on 15 April 1825. After the fateful events in Poland, Bennigsen began to write letters to Fock explaining what had transpired during the campaign and ultimately revised these letters into the first drafts of his memoirs.

Acknowledgements

I would like to thank Alexander Mikaberidze and Andrew Bamford, our editor at Helion, for this opportunity. Special thanks are also due to my high school French teacher, Debbie Olejniczek, and Dr Colleen Seguin, who taught the senior seminar on war and society at Valparaiso University. A huge debt of gratitude is due to Dr Michael Leggiere, who has done so much to shape me as a student of the Revolutionary and Napoleonic Wars. I would also like to thank my father, Charles, who started me down the path of military history. My children, Charles and Harper, were exceedingly bored while I completed my part in this project and watched far too much TV but were no less loving or sweet. My mother-in-law, Carolyn Wessell, was an extremely generous baby-sitter during the final months of this project. Above all, I must thank my wonderful wife, Katie, for her persistent love and support throughout. It is to her that I dedicate my share of this work.

Paul Strietelmeier
Arlington Heights, IL
2022

Editorial Note

Bennigsen's writing style varies considerably, from the economical and descriptive to the rhetorical, with a strong tendency to construct long, cumulative sentences that frequently obscure the argument that he was making. On such occasions, we felt it necessary to break sentences into shorter, more digestible units. The memoir refers to two primary measurements of length, the Russian *versta*, which equalled 1,066 metres, and the German *meile*, which Bennigsen referred to as mille, rather than French lieue. One *mille* equaled 7,416 metres.

Bennigsen frequently refers to 'corps' even when he discusses small detachments. To avoid any confusion, we tried to differentiate between French army corps, Russian temporary corps formations, and smaller detachments that Bennigsen designated for specific missions.

For stylistic purposes, we retained the names of French regiments as cited in the memoir but provided proper names for the Russian units mentioned in the narrative.

Until 1917, Russia continued to employ the Julian Old Style calendar that was progressively falling behind the Gregorian New Style calendar used in the West; in the eighteenth century, it was 11 days behind, and in the nineteenth, 12 days. We made sure to indicate dates in both calendars. It is worth pointing out that contrary to the enduring myth that in drafting their plans the allies had failed to account for the 12-day difference in their respective calendars (Gregorian vs. Julian), the allies (whether Prussians or Austrians) were well aware of the divergence and usually dated their documents under the Gregorian calendar, while the Russian documents were, as a rule, dated in both calendars.

1

The Situation of Russia in 1806[1]

I hasten, General,[2] to acknowledge the arrival of your letter. You reproach me for having neglected my correspondence with you since the Peace of Tilsit.[3] I was at fault, I admit; but the circumstances in which I found myself may well excuse me. I gave you successively, over the course of the war, my opinions concerning all of the major events that took place; but these dealt with just isolated events and after the peace, I promised to explain everything in full consequence and sequence, including the details of my military operations. I will, thus, do my best to keep my word and I am currently busy organizing all the papers that relate to that war. This occupation has contributed to the interruption of our correspondence, which I resume today with pleasure and interest.

I will not respond separately to the majority of the questions that you have posed to me, General, and that concern me personally, as the following correspondence should serve as a response. I will only repeat that, far from seeking command of the army, I requested on several occasions to be excused from it. If, on the one hand, my sense of pride was flattered to be a commander in chief in a fight upon which the eyes of Europe were fixed, because it could decide her fate, on the other hand, I had not lost view of the responsibility to which I had exposed myself toward my sovereign and the entirety of a great nation [the Russian Empire]. Reflecting on the circumstances in which we found ourselves and on the unforeseen catastrophes, which with a single blow had confounded all calculations, changed the plan and the theatre of war, as well as the operations, one could not deceive oneself concerning the great difficulties that I had to overcome during the glorious career that was mine to experience. The combination of experience and comparison proved that the least mistake would result in the immediate invasion of our frontiers. It was the moment when fortune and audacity seemed to be in action and to triumph over all wise and prudent measures with which one opposed them, and each

---

1 Bennigsen referred to the chapters as letters since they were in fact letters written to Fock. The first letter/chapter is dated 7 August 1807.
2 Bennigsen is referring to Alexander Borisovich von Fock, his comrade-in-arms and confidant.
3 The peace treaty was signed between Emperors Napoleon of France and Alexander of Russia at the town of Tilsit in July 1807. After the crushing defeat at Austerlitz in December 1805, Austria had signed the Treaty of Pressburg on 26 December 1805 that formally ended the Third Coalition, but Emperor Alexander I had refused to submit to the French emperor and Russia and France remained at war until the Treaty of Tilsit ended the Franco-Russian War and laid the ground for a political reorganization of Europe.

instant rendered these same measures more necessary, which alone could compensate for the too great disparity of means between the two sides, a disproportion that should not be attributed at all to the superiority of the enemy's resources, but to the new circumstances to which events had given rise and to the respective plans and intentions of the two adversaries.

Napoleon, having succeeded in crushing Prussia, kept his forces concentrated and announced his wish to invade Russia, and the latter had only prepared to bring aid to an ally in a distant theatre. I need not tell you, you will soon see it from our correspondence, that our court could not expect anything less than to fight with our forces alone a war for its defence. Nothing was prepared for this scenario; consequently, a single battle lost, a single event like the last campaign of 1805 in Austria had produced at Ulm and Austerlitz,[4] and as Prussia just offered at Auerstadt, Jena,[5] etc., in short the least reverse would have had incalculable consequences for Russia, especially because the war against the Turks was soon to ignite[6] and was becoming inevitable, a war whose outcome should also be decided on the Vistula.

Add to all of these considerations that I had to act against Napoleon, the greatest captain of our time, against all the marshals of France, the majority of which had already commanded armies with distinction and the greatest success, against an army that was always victorious and accustomed to deciding a war with a single battle, moreover an army infinitely superior in number, especially at the opening of the second campaign, as I have already told you and as you will be convinced, in the following correspondence, by original documents.

In the wars against France in which Russia had taken an active part, she had until this point only been an auxiliary power; the theatre of war was always so distant that defeats, as considerable as they were, could not have any dangerous consequences for her own lands.[7] Then, her task was limited to fighting with force and efficacy the communal enemy, so as to realize the goal of the coalition, to assure the independence and safety of the states of Europe. Today, forced to make war directly on her own frontiers against all the combined forces of France, the majority of the princes of Germany, Holland, Italy, etc., the task of her own conservation imposed on her altogether different duties.

How could one foresee, even believe that Russia, which in all the previous wars had so loyally helped her allies with formidable armies, would be abandoned by these same powers that she had helped? That Austria would remain neutral and allow to pass the best moment to put the French army in the worst predicament and reclaim the influence that she seemed to have lost irrevocably? That Russia would have nothing to hope for from diversions that England could have executed, and that Sweden, too weak and too disconnected from immediate events to be able to act effectively alone, would take

---

4   Bennigsen refers to the decisive victories Napoleon had scored over the Austrians and Russians during the War of the Third Coalition.
5   At the twin battles of Jena-Auerstädt on 14 October 1806, Napoleon routed the Prussian army, resulting in the collapse of the Prussian state two weeks later.
6   The Russo-Ottoman War commenced in October 1806.
7   Russia did not participate in the War of the First Coalition (1792–1797) but joined the Second and Third Coalitions. In 1799, the Russian army fought in Italy, Switzerland, and Holland. Six years later the Russian forces were involved in the operations in the Mediterranean, Hanover and, most famously, Austria.

a posture that was more fidgety [*remuante*] than active, more harmful to herself than advantageous to the common cause? That all of these Prussian forces, this great and beautiful army that seemed like it ought to serve for a long time as a bulwark against French forces, would virtually disappear in eight days? That all of the fortresses, even Magdeburg, Stettin, and Küstrin, which should have stopped the advance of the enemy or, at the least, greatly weakened [the French] army due to the forces it would have had to detach in order to besiege them, would surrender at the first sight of enemy troops, without the least resistance? That, with these fortresses fallen, the French Emperor, placing there weak garrisons, taken from auxiliary troops, and having nothing more to fear at the rear of his armies, would immediately be able to send not only all the national forces, but also a considerable number of allied troops against Russia, before she had had time to exploit her great resources and assemble commensurate forces on the frontier?

This state of affairs – in essence, the total abandonment in which Russia found herself – naturally had to change, or rather render unobtainable the primary goal of her preparations and conduct. It could not be a question of Russia reducing France by herself, to the point of being able to place limits on the preponderance that the latter had acquired over the rest of Europe. It was now only a matter of maintaining the integrity of the Russian Empire and conserving her influence in Europe, in order to preserve the means of being useful to her friends and allies. There were two ways to achieve this end; that of peace negotiations and that of the fortunes of war.

Emperor Alexander, judging Europe according to the purity of his intentions, was still hesitant to believe the passive resignation and pusillanimity that had overtaken the other relevant powers and preferred the fortunes of war. His troops fought battles could have reanimated the failing courage of his allies. But, finally seeing himself frustrated in his last hopes and unable to count on any foreign assistance, he thought it necessary that his brave nation sacrifice its initial disinterested designs that favoured its allies and decided to seize the first opportunity to negotiate.

Such was the true situation, especially at the beginning of the second campaign. I will have the occasion to convince you, in the following, that nothing is less founded than the widely accepted opinion that after the battle of Friedland[8] Russia found herself in such a critical position that she was obliged to make peace. The exaggerations of the French bulletins, about which I will speak to you one day at greater length, and the false rumours scattered about in this respect could only alter the truth for a moment. When the course of my correspondence with you leads me to the time of this action, you will make your own judgment about the importance that can be given to this battle and you will be convinced that the loss at Friedland, which only cost our army 4,830 men,[9] was too insignificant to weaken the Russian forces, to influence later operations and to be, as was briefly thought, the cause of the peace that shortly followed (I have sufficiently explained to you the reasons that motivated it), all the more so since the considerable reinforcements, which were forming in the

---

8 On 14 June 1807, Napoleon inflicted a heavy defeat on the Russian army, commanded by Bennigsen, at the small town of Friedland in East Prussia.
9 The Russian army, in fact, lost over 10,000 prisoners and some 12,000 killed and wounded, as well as 80 cannon and some 70 colours.

interior of the Empire, were already on the march, not far from our frontiers and ready to reach the theatre of war. I will speak to you in detail in my following correspondence about these reinforcements; you will see that the great resources and the forces of Russia were again spared for the defence of the country and you will learn at the same time the reasons that impeded the arrival of these reinforcements to the army, before the beginning of the second campaign.

2

Russia, Turkey, and Austria[1]

In my first chapter, I tasked myself to give a sense of some of the difficulties that I had to overcome and the changes in our position that had resulted from the success of Emperor Napoleon over our allies.

Before beginning the account of the military operations, it is, I think, necessary to make note of the basics that I gathered concerning the political relations of our court with the principal powers of Europe. One will see what our hopes could have been and how often they were illusory. The treaty of alliance of 1798 had determined the relations between Russia and the Ottoman Porte;[2] concluded at a difficult time for Turkey,[3] it was nonetheless advantageous for her, because it was this treaty that was principally responsible for the evacuation of several of her provinces that were overrun by the enemy at that time. By a return of sentiments of sincere amity that had dictated the stipulations by virtue of which Russia guaranteed the integrity of the Ottoman Empire, it was among other things agreed in the same treaty that the Princes of Moldavia and Wallachia could only be deprived of their rulers after a certain number of years and for some offense that was known and sufficiently verified by the Porte, in concert with our resident minister to it. This article was very important for Russia because it could, despite the fickleness of the Divan,[4] maintain peace in these neighbouring provinces. It certainly bothered the Porte a bit, but it did not prevent it nevertheless from expressly requesting around the year 1803 the renewal of the treaty of 1798. The Turkish government, as I just said, therefore recognized the advantages of this treaty, advantages that were in truth shared by the two Empires. The navigation by both naval vessels and merchant vessels on the Black Sea, the entry of the latter into the various ports for the purpose of commerce, the tariff on the products of the two respective countries, everything was stipulated therein with precision and fairness. Since the partition

---

1 The Russian edition omitted this chapter. The editor of the French edition, Captain E. Cazalas, noted that the letter must have been written or at least revised after 1812.
2 The treaty of defensive alliance, prompted by the French invasion of Egypt, was signed between Russia and the Ottoman Empire on 3 January 1799 (Gregorian calendar, 23 December 1798). This was complemented by the Anglo-Ottoman alliance formed later that month.
3 Bennigsen uses term 'Turkey' interchangeably with the 'Ottoman Empire' and 'Ottoman Porte'. The origins of the term (from Latin Turchia/Turquia) can be traced back to medieval era and it was widely used, though its spelling varied (Torke, Turkie, Turky, etc). The modern version, Turkey, dates back to late seventeenth century
4 The high government council in the Ottoman Empire.

of Poland, the frontier between these two Empires was formed along a length of more than 400 *verstas* [426 kilometres] by the river Dniester, which provided a good military frontier and shielded both states from any territorial disputes.

Russia in particular had no motive to wish to extend her frontiers into Europe at the expense of Turkey. The conquest of Moldavia and Wallachia could not tempt her, given the great sacrifices that it had required, which was already known from the experience of previous wars. I will only touch briefly here on the idea of a plan that was attributed for a long time to Russia, especially to Catherine II,[5] for the conquest of Constantinople, and consequently also of all Turkish territory in Europe, and the execution of which would certainly rouse a great deal of opposition from the other powers, especially Austria and England; and even if one managed to come to terms with them, in this respect, at the expense of Turkey, it would be yet to be seen if the Turkish population of Europe, of the Muslim faith, repressed in Asia, could not one day cause some trouble to Russia in the vicinity of the Caucasus, seeing that its attention, in this event, would no longer be split between Europe and Asia, and, her forces could be deployed from this latter part of the world, when she is threatened in Europe.

For that matter she could not ignore the fact that these aggrandizements would necessarily draw the jealousy of the great powers that she needed to treat with care, especially given the critical state of Europe as a whole, and at a time when one power had gained a preponderance so pronounced that every other state, however great and powerful it was, had to renounce any prospect of conquest so as to be able to dispose of all its forces for its defence and the conservation of its integrity.

In a word no consideration could move either party to stray from the desire to preserve peace and good harmony between their respective states. Unfortunately, a foreign influence made itself felt at this time. The Turkish government, giving into the insinuations of France, thought it could dispense with the obligations that were solemnly agreed to with Russia and soon appeared to no longer desire to display any moderation. Emperor Alexander, hoping to avoid a rupture with this power, responded to this wicked conduct with the most unflagging patience and restraint. Far from appreciating such conduct, the Ottoman ministry only accumulated grievances and crowned its violations by deposing the princes of Moldavia and Wallachia, the rule of which should have lasted three more years, according to the stipulations agreed to in the treaties.

The *Grand Seigneur*[6] sent a *firman* [decree] for the arrest of these two princes, with orders to bring them to Constantinople. Having been warned, that of Moldavia, Mourouzy,[7] whose gratitude and attachment to Russia had never been sincere, chose to leave, before the arrival of the envoy, for Constantinople, where he could rely on powerful friends; while that of Wallachia, Ypsilanti,[8] suspected by the Porte, thought it necessary for his preservation to go

---

5   Russia's empress from 1762 to 1796.
6   Ottoman Sultan Selim III (r. 1789–1807)
7   Alexander Mourouzis (Moruzi), Grand Dragoman of the Ottoman Empire and Prince of Moldavia in 1802–1807.
8   The son of Alexander Ypsilanti, Constantine Ypsilanti was a member of the influential Phanariote family. He served as a Grand Dragoman of the Porte (1796–1799), *hospodar* of Moldavia (1799–1802) and of Walachia (1802–1806).

with his family, his wealth and those persons closest to him, via Transylvanie, to Kamenetz-Podolsky, from whence he went to Saint Petersburg.

Peace had just been concluded between France and Austria:[9] the moment was favourable; all of the Russian troops had returned within the frontiers; but Emperor Alexander was true to his system and limited himself again to making amicable appeals to the Porte, asking only the reinstatement of Princes Mourouzy and Ypsilanti to their principalities. After having hesitated as long as possible to give a decisive response, the Porte consented;[10] but this response was not even sent quickly enough to Saint Petersburg to prevent hostilities. The nature of this concession and the circumstances in which the response was given no longer allowed one to believe in the sincerity of the pacific sentiments of the Sublime Porte and rendered a state of war preferable to the delays that it hoped to gain.

In the meantime, our minister, M. Italinsky,[11] had already had to leave of Constantinople and General Michelson[12] moved into Moldavia with an army.[13] The fortresses of Chotin and Bender surrendered at the first appearance of our troops.[14] Jassy was occupied immediately by a detachment of our army and Bucharest was too on 15/27 December after a small action between the Russian advance guard and a small Turkish corps, which had advanced to defend the capital of Wallachia. In this way the Russians were already, from the opening of the first campaign that was begun very late in the season, in possession of all of Moldavia and Wallachia, with the exception however of the fortresses that are on the left bank of the Danube.

A wish is not an act of violence; *en bon Russe*, I will therefore hold without scruple one that Moldavia and Wallachia will one day be entirely detached from Ottoman power. The political situation of Russia demands that her ambition not aim at the acquisition of these provinces, but that she try to have them entrusted to a Turkish prince as a realm for himself and his descendants. The reasons for this principle, which Russia must adopt, are evident; I will try to develop them here as much as the knowledge that I have acquired of the geographic position of this country and of the political interests of Russia in this respect permits me.

I begin by recalling that almost all of the wars between Russia and Turkey were caused by acts of violence that the Turkish government committed in these provinces, contrary to the stipulations in the peace treaties formally concluded with Russia. I will add here a very essential consideration, on which Russia must reflect well before beginning a war in this region; it is the enormous losses that she has always suffered in money, but especially in men. I will only note two of these wars that are known to me by experience. First, the initial war

---

9   The Peace of Pressburg, signed on 26 December 1805 between French Emperor Napoleon Bonaparte and Holy Roman Emperor Francis II, as a consequence of the French victory over the Third Coalition at the Battle of Austerlitz (2 December).
10   The Ottomans consented on 15 October 1806.
11   Andrei Italinskii, one of the most prominent Russian diplomats, serving as Russia's ambassador to Naples, Constantinople and Rome.
12   Ivan Michelson (Johann von Michelsohnen) (1740–1807), of Baltic-German origin, was a Russian military commander who distinguished himself during the suppression of the Pugachev's Rebellion in 1770s.
13   The invasion began in late November 1806.
14   The fortresses of Khotin and Bender fell between 23 and 28 November 1806.

of Catherine II,[15] led by Marshal Count Roumianzov,[16] whose army was never larger than 60,000 men; by the end of this war that only lasted five years, it was replenished twice over, by which one can estimate the casualties of war at 120,000 men. It is easy to believe, when one is willing to recall that at the Battle of Kagul[17] the Marshal only had 17,000 men under arms. I will also note a more recent war, during the reign of Emperor Alexander, which began in 1806 and ended in 1812. Among the casualties who died from illness were three senior commanders (generals *commandant en chef*) and 36 generals (generals) of various ranks. Imagine then what must have been the losses during this war amongst officers and rank-and-file!

A third reflection that supports my principle, that Russia should not incorporate these provinces into her Empire, is that she must avoid all contact in this area with Austria. Here I ask that the reader look at a map and examine whether or not Austria could watch with peaceful eyes and without jealousy as Russia came by a new conquest to flank her lands, by which I mean Transylvania, and, in establishing herself in the Bannat[18] of Craïowa or Little Wallachia, drawing closer to the Bannat of Temeswar and consequently to Hungary?

See also what a beautiful new frontier the Danube would form against Turkey, this considerable river that extends from the Black Sea into Austria. No scruple about this new order of things should stop its execution, seeing that it is in no way a question of tearing apart nations by throwing them against their will under different governments, since these provinces are only occupied by a single nation that has no connection, no relationship with those that surround it. It is known that Moldavia and Wallachia were in times past the Siberia of the Romans and that all of their malefactors were sent into exile there. Their language, which is a corrupt Italian, serves as proof of it. These nations became weak and idle; here it is only a matter of the lowest class of inhabitants [*la dernière classe des habitants*]. One sees therefore that everybody would win: Russia, Austria, and the Moldavian and Wallachian nations, who would then find themselves under a single government whereas they were ruled until the present by two governments, by that of the region and that of Constantinople. This salutary change for all parties, guaranteed by Austria and Russia, would become stable and even united powers would not be in a position to harm it.

Austria certainly recalls that she was twice already threatened with seeing Russia establish herself on this frontier, namely, the first time at the end of the first war of Catherine II, who requested Moldavia and Wallachia for 25 years as indemnification for the costs of this war: it is certain that after the 25 years Russia would really have found reasons to retain these provinces forever. Consider what Frederick II[19] said about it in his posthumous works. The second time, this was during the war of Emperor Alexander, from 1806 to 1812. This sovereign published a declaration in the form of a manifesto that Moldavia and Wallachia had

---

15　The Russo-Ottoman War of 1768–1774.
16　Count Peter Rumyantsev-Zadunaisky was one of the foremost Russian commanders of the eighteenth century. His victories over the Turks during the Russo-Ottoman War of 1768–1774 ensured continued Russian expansion to the Danubian principalities and secured him the title of Zadunaisky, meaning Trans-Danubian.
17　The decisive battle of the Russo-Ottoman War of 1768–1774 was fought at the Kagul River near the village of Frumoasa (now Cahul, Moldova) on 21 July/1 August 1770.
18　A frontier province led by a military governor who was called *ban*.
19　Frederick II the Great, King of Prussia between 1740 and 1786.

been incorporated into Russia. Austria, terrified by such prospects, immediately protested against any such occupation, first under Maria-Theresa[20] and the second time under Francis II.[21] Even the Sultan and his Divan would soon forget this loss, seeing the disinterest of these two neighbouring great powers, neither of which would have made the least conquest to round out their states in this area at the expense of Turkey.

Austria had been considerably weakened by the disasters of the last war;[22] she had to heal the wounds that the campaign of 1805 had inflicted on her.[23] Still a great power of the first order, she believed she had not recovered enough force and vigour to play the part. Shortly before the beginning of hostilities between France and Prussia [in 1806], the cabinet of Vienna did make, it is true, to that of Saint Petersburg propositions for an alliance by which could be observed some kind of arrangement with the court in London, whose ministry was simultaneously working toward the same end. But either because the Russian Emperor believed that by such engagements he would expose himself to undermining negotiations that were already underway or about to start, or because he believed he could better and more effectively play the role of mediator by remaining isolated, the Russian court did not pursue these propositions, which even the court of Vienna seemed only to have made for the case of war; barely had hostilities begun than this power, of which several provinces were at this time still occupied or surrounded by French troops, declared itself neutral and assembled an army of 70,000 men on the frontier of Bavaria, under the orders of Archduke Charles, in order to enforce her neutrality. All that could be obtained from this court were pointless assurances of friendship and good harmony; this was proof that if Austria would not actively support us, neither would she join France against us. Is that what was required? Russia, abandoned to herself, could certainly defend, as I said, her lands and her frontiers against all of the united forces of France and her allies, but all of these efforts could never have led to that state of things that all the rest of Europe and Austria in particular had an interest in desiring. The more Russia took care to fix the attention of the Austrian cabinet on its true position, the more the latter seemed to attach itself to its system of neutrality. All attempts to renew the negotiations were rebuffed; still less did they wish to hear of a new coalition.

How does one explain, after all the lessons of the past, the resigned blindness to the dangers that this power [Austria] was risking? Of course not, she did not have illusions about her true position. She continued to arm, to concentrate her troops; to establish considerable magazines and depots. But the court had been struck by the idea, it was even convinced that Russian arms would not be able to resist French forces, and, in this scenario, what was her duty? I do not speak of that duty imposed on her by the constant friendship of which Russia had never ceased to give her proof, but that imposed on her by the cares of her own conservation.

---

20 The ruler of the Habsburg domains between 1740–1780, Maria Theresa was Holy Roman Empress, Archduchess of Austria, and Queen of Hungary and Croatia.
21 Francis was Holy Roman Emperor between 1792–1806, and Emperor of Austria between 1804–1835.
22 Austrian armies suffered crushing defeats at Ulm and Austerlitz during the War of the Third Coalition in 1805.
23 Bennigsen is referring to the War of the Third Coalition when Napoleon scored a quick succession of victories of Austria, most notably at Ulm and Austerlitz.

Emperor Alexander only had for his benefit weak talking points with France while Austria no longer had then the means to repair the mistakes that too many events had forced her into. The full weight of French power could come down on her. While Emperor Francis formally declared to Russia that he would be unshakable in his neutrality, the court and city of Vienna, all the good patriots of Austria, more enlightened about the interests of their country, followed the armies with that interest that is naturally inspired by a fight as noble as that which Emperor Alexander was going to undertake for the sake and safety of their fatherland, as much as for the glory of his nation. The first clash was anxiously awaited; one sensed that it would have to be dreadful.

Then arrived the news of the Battle of Pultusk, fought on 14/26 December [1806]. The enemy had taken all precautions to manage the first impressions and spread the news that the Russian army had been completely beaten. To give this rumour more plausibility, he had placed at the public places of Warsaw all of the cannons that the Russian army had been obliged to abandon in the mud, at the time of its retreat from the Wkra River, the roads having become impassable. The truth was not long in coming out; the Austrian officers, who were at this time in Warsaw, at the French headquarters, sent their court detailed relations, the summary of which was that the French army had been repulsed at Pultusk with considerable losses and that the same had happened in the actions that occurred the same day at Golymin, etc. This news arrived at the same time as that of the unrest that had broken out in Hesse. The effect made itself felt; a sudden change took place in the dispositions of the court in Vienna. Its ministry became calmer, and one caught a glimpse of the possibility that Austria would stir from the profound lethargy to which she had condemned herself.

Negotiations began with great caution as a matter of fact, but much had already been gained by them lending an ear to each other.

The fear that the French government suspected Austria of hostile intentions was such that [the Austrian] ministry made the express request to only make verbal overtures relating to negotiations. At this juncture the battle of Preussisch-Eylau took place [on February 7–8]. It was no doubt for Austria the best moment to declare herself. The French Emperor had strained all his resources against Russia; all of his forces and those of his allies were concentrated on the Vistula and between this river and the Narew; the entire area that he had placed between France and the theatre of war was wide open. The great warrior no doubt sensed the difficulty of his position; but he knew how to skilfully parry the great blow that Austria could have struck against him at this time, an opportunity that probably would never arise again. Prompt and active cooperation from this power and diversions on the part of the English, especially in order to support the Swedes, would have turned all the odds of this war in favour of the cause of the powers oppressed by France. The opinion of Europe is not divided on this subject, but neither all of these considerations nor all of the wise counsel and approaches made by our ambassador to Vienna, Count Razoumovsky,[24] that respectable minister, nor even the advantageous effect made by the news of the battle of Preussisch-Eylau in Vienna were sufficient to produce that *élan* of feeling, which the court should have nourished instead of stunting it as it had done until that very time; continuing

---

24 Andrey Razoumovsky (Razumovskii) was a distinguished Russian diplomat who had served as a Russian ambassador to Vienna.

to give promises to declare herself, she postponed carrying it out, under various pretexts, from one moment to the next; it was quite necessary to resign oneself and convince oneself that Russia had nothing to hope for from Austria and should only count on her cooperation if the French armies suffered a general and total defeat. Such was the conduct of the court of Vienna toward Russia at a time that was as important as it was decisive. It is even more surprising since, in all respects, these two powers could only have the same interests in the wars against Napoleon, as the reverses that the one suffered must sooner or later, but without fail, impact the other, as we have already seen and as we could well see again.

The relations between England and Russia at the beginning of this war, for all the appearances of closeness, was no more settled or stable. Some time before this period, M. Fox[25] wrote to the ministry of Saint Petersburg that the cabinet of Saint-James thought that it would be necessary to bring together the powers of the continent, of which the latest events had more or less altered their relations, and declaring that Russia would find England ready to contribute all of her means to this salutary end and to furnish all of the help that one could expect from her. If the Emperor had had motives to avoid commitments with the court of Vienna, there was even more reason that he should not again make them with England, whose interests, naturally divergent from those of the continent, could carry him far from the goal that he should have in common with the other continental powers. Everything therefore remained on the former footing between Russia and England; they had common enemies, and that seemed sufficient for both to employ all the means of which they could dispose to mutually aid each other. The English minister, being frustrated in his designs by the refusal of Russia to again strengthen their contacts, there resulted some coolness on the part of England; this reflection can only be explained by her conduct over the course of the last war [1805]. This power, always the first to fan the flames of wars against France and the last to support them, remained throughout it a tranquil spectator and idle as though Russia had never been either her ally, or her friend. The coasts from Venice to Danzig offered her a line on which she could make her landings and stage diversions. Entirely inactive against France, her fleets in the Mediterranean and *l'Archipel* [the Aegean Islands] were not of any use to Russia either. It is known that on 6/18 February 1807 the English fleet forced the passage of the Dardanelles,[26] burned a ship of the line, four frigates, two corvettes and two launches; that it dropped anchor on 8/20 February in the environs of Constantinople and that at the moment when it could have delivered a great blow against the capital of the Ottoman Empire, it left the channel of Constantinople to go to Egypt and take Alexandria. This expedition was equally unsuccessful, and was generally disapproved of, even by the majority in England; it naturally irritated the court of Saint Petersburg. If England limited herself to complete inactivity, she was no less lavish with promises of diversions that she wished to make. To prove how many of these promises were illusory, I will cite a letter from *mylord* Hutchinson, the English minister to the court of Prussia.[27] This respectable man

---

25 Charles James Fox, British Whig statesman whose parliamentary career spanned over three decades. The arch-rival of William Pitt the Younger, Fox served as Secretary of State for Foreign Affairs in 1806 before dying on 13 September 1806.
26 Bennigsen is referring to the Dardanelles Operation of the British Royal Navy led by Vice Admiral John Duckworth in February 1807.
27 John Hely-Hutchinson, Anglo-Irish politician, and military commander.

in every respect, this famous soldier, who was certainly acting in good faith and had the best intentions, wrote the following on the date of 27 March from Memel to his brother, M. Hutchinson, who was with Colonel Wilson[28] in my headquarters since the month of January:

> To the Honorable Count Hély Hutchinson
> You will inform *Son Exc. M.* General Bennigsen that I ordered that all of the first English vessels of war, that arrive in this port, go at top speed to Danzig to aid in the defence of this city. As I had foreseen, a long time ago, the utility of having at my disposal such warships, I had in consequence, two months ago, sent the request to my government. I also wrote to M. Gartick,[29] minister from our court to Copenhagen, praying him to send at top speed to the harbour at Danzig all the warships that until the present are in the port of Elseneur. Moreover, you will inform *Son Excellence* that I proposed, some time ago, to our government sending a considerable body of English, Swedish and Hanoverian troops to land on the left bank of the Oder; it is in my opinion, given the extent to which French troops occupy the right bank of this river, one of the favourable points of attack. Moreover, this landing of our troops in Pomerania would be more advantageous as they would immediately be within range to act in concert with Swedish troops. The rigor of the season that has rendered navigation of the Baltic very difficult was without any doubt the sole cause, that could have delayed the real and very sincere measures that the cabinet of Saint-James had taken to cooperate in the events of the campaign. Nevertheless, I am quite persuaded that the same measures are currently so advanced that we can rest assured that, in very little time, the troops will be in a position to act. You can assure *Son Excellence* that I would consider myself quite happy, if I found myself in a position to contribute in some way to his amazing successes, to the glory and fame that his most wise conduct has already acquired for him throughout the whole of Europe. Full of this sentiment, I long to have the honour to be able to profess this to him personally. It is to this end that I am offering to go one of these days to his headquarters, which I would have done were I not awaiting at each moment the important arrival of a courier from my court.
> Hutchinson

Whoever knows the personal character of *mylord* Hutchinson and his manner of thinking certainly will not doubt his full belief, that the help of which he informed me was coming. He was convinced of its utility and its indispensable necessity. The consequences would

---

28 Robert Thomas Wilson, future British general and politician who had distinguished himself during the Napoleonic Wars, serving in Flanders, Egypt, Iberian Peninsula, Prussia, and Russia. Wilson was with the Russian army during the 1806–1807 campaign and later published an interesting account of his experiences, *Brief remarks on the Character and Composition of the Russian Army, and a Sketch of the Campaigns in Poland in the Years 1806 and 1807* (London: T. Egerton, 1810). His letters and journals were later published by his nephew, Reverend Herbert Randolph, *Life of General Sir Robert Wilson,... from Autobiographical Memoirs, Journals, narratives, Correspondence, etc.* (London: Murray, 1862).
29 Benjamin Garlike was a British diplomat and ambassador to Denmark in 1807.

have been incalculable. Stralsund and Danzig would have been able to stop the progress of the enemy and prevent the concentration of its army. I will return to this subject when discussing the events that took place around these cities. In fact some preparations were made in England for an expedition that was claimed to be destined for the Baltic, but it only appeared that way, to impress the Allies who were imprudent enough to believe it. It must be supposed that the English minister never had the intention of actually helping Russia and Sweden, but rather that he wished to take advantage of the latitude that his allies got for him to conquer some colonies from France and Spain.

Could these momentary advantages compensate for the loss of the confidence of a loyal and powerful ally? Should not England have expected that by thusly abandoning Russia in the middle of the most important war that she had to bear since the reign of Peter the Great, she would alienate her irrevocably and that the latter would remember this when she managed to make peace and make her rapprochement with France? Is there anything surprising if the Russian Emperor committed himself, at the Peace of Tilsit, to using all his means of negotiation or vigour to contribute to re-establishing the general peace in Europe and resort to hostilities against a power that had given him so many just causes for discontent, in the case where this power would never lend a hand to an arrangement?

3

Russia, Sweden, and Prussia[1]

The courts of Russia and Sweden had been sufficiently close, and their relations had become sufficiently intimate through the war even, to act in concert against France. A poorly thought-out way of doing things on Sweden's part, at a time when Russia was engaged in two wars, momentarily revived that natural mistrust between two powers, one of which regretted the loss of beautiful provinces and the other of which should always, and especially in such difficult moments, watch with an anxious eye a jealous neighbour too near her capital. This is what happened:

England, sending to Russia a sum of money that she owed her in arrears, delivered it to the Swedish port of Gothenburg to be transported from there to its final destination. The King of Sweden [Gustav IV Adolph] intercepted this money, on the pretext that he was still owed, by virtue of past treaties, a sum from Russia. The first news of this sequestration arrived at Saint Petersburg at the moment when the first division needed to be sent to the Prussian frontier and join the army, when the circumstances demanded it. The court of Petersburg, unable to reasonably explain this act of violence, thought it must be attributed to a change of system of the cabinet of Stockholm and consequently halted the march of these troops, which really had quite regrettable consequences, as this reinforcement of 20,000 men would have arrived, without this accident, if not for the battle of Preussisch-Eylau, then at least immediately afterwards. Those that know the positions of the two combatant armies at this time, and the circumstances in which they found themselves, will easily conceive of the dreadful influence of this contretemps and of the delay produced by such unsuitable conduct on the part of an ally, at a time when it was necessary to sacrifice all other considerations to the maintenance of harmony and reciprocal confidence. It is in this way that Emperor Alexander acted constantly and even on this occasion, in wisely suppressing his resentment and his discontent with the thoughtless conduct of the King of Sweden. He avoided all discussion, not even demanding for the moment the restitution of the money. In this way amicable and confidential communications about the operations of the war continued without noticeable interruption.

In April, during the siege of Danzig, I proposed sending a trustworthy person to Stockholm, in order to negotiate there the dispatch of some Swedish vessels to help this

---

1   Letter not dated, must have been written in the 1810–1812 period.

fortress. The Emperor approved this project and *chamberlain* Ribeaupierre,² one of the people who accompanied me to maintain foreign correspondence, was sent there to this end with a letter from *Sa Majesté Impériale*. The King of Sweden received this mission quite well, consented to this proposition with a great deal of good will and gave to M. Ribeaupierre, upon his departure, the following note:

> *Sa Majesté le Roi* having ordered a certain number of frigates and brigs to the coasts of Prussia before Pillau and the Frische-Nehrung, so that there results from this measure all of the proposed utility, it seems necessary that there be effective cooperation on the part of the combined armies.
> The principal object being to dislodge from the Nehrung the enemy, who took possession of this tongue of land, a crossfire must be established to achieve this end. The shallowness of the Frische-Haff does not permit any vessel of *Sa Majesté* to enter it; but there are two other equally practicable means to stage an attack from the interior coast:
> The first is to construct rafts in the ports of Pillau and Königsberg, and to place on them cannons of large calibre that would make of them so many floating batteries; the second, arm un-ballasted vessels, which are sufficient in the two aforementioned ports; then approach land and moor at a suitable distance the rafts or the vessels armed with large cannons, the fire of which will not delay in producing all of the desired effect. Even in the current state of things, the difficulties that seem to be against the execution of this project will be easily surmounted.
> Communications by water with Danzig being free, we will be able to seek out in this place the pieces of heavy artillery that there could be conveyed to the army and that might not be at Pillau and Königsberg. There are certainly still some carpenters at the building sites of these two cities; beams, necessary materials must be there and, in order to accelerate the simple but solid construction of a raft suitable to carry heavy artillery, the officers sent by *Sa Majesté le Roi* will not fail, if they are asked, to provide their counsel and their care for the direction of this work.
> Land operations only falling within my competence insofar as they are related to those of the sea, I must only observe that, in order to gain from the proposed measures all of the fruits expected from them, it is indispensably necessary that troops descend on the Nehrung, that they advance there in concert with the fire of the batteries and that they capture in its entirety this tongue of land, to try to open communications with Danzig from this direction, a truth that *Sa Majesté prussienne* will do well to adopt and that the urgency and the great interests of the moment and of the thing will no doubt lead *Ladite Majesté* to execute.
> Maloé, 23 April 1807
> Signed: De Gyllensweld
> *Premier aide de camp en fonctions de Sa Majesté le Roi pour la marine.*

---

2   Alexander Ribeaupierre (1781–1865), Russian diplomat of Swiss descent. He was the son of Brigadier Ivan Ribeaupierre who entered Russian military service and died during the Russian storming of Ismail in 1790. The young Ribeaupierre began his service in the Life Guard Semeyonovskii Regiment and quickly advanced through the ranks, becoming Emperor Paul's flugel-adjutant in 1799. He served at the Russian embassy in Vienna and was assigned as a diplomatic liaison to the Russian army in Poland in 1806–1807.

List of Swedish vessels sent by the King to the coasts of Prussia:

1 frigate of 44 cannons
1 (ditto) 36 cannons
1 (the same) 18 cannons
2 *grands bricks de guerre* each 18 cannons
1 cutter of 12 cannons
1 *petit brick* of 10 cannons

At the same time, the King of Sweden requested from that of Prussia the assistance of 6,000 men. As hard as it was for the combined army to detach troops at this time, it was nevertheless decided to immediately send, by water, to Stralsund Lieutenant General de Blücher,[3] with 4,000 men raised in part from the newly formed Prussian battalions and in part from the troops from General l'Estocq's[4] corps, which I replaced with Russian troops. There was also an intent to send 4,000 more men when the enemy moved away from Colberg.

We know that the Swedes had at this time, not far from Stralsund, a small success against Marshal Mortier's[5] corps, but then lost all of their gains shortly after and concluded an armistice in which it was stipulated, among other things, that they would give no help to Danzig or Colberg and that whoever would wish to recommence hostilities would be bound to inform the enemy four weeks in advance. This armistice, freeing Mortier's corps, permitted it to withdraw from Pomerania and march against us; it thus arrived in time to join the French *Grande Armée*, and participate in the last stages of the second campaign.

So you see, General, that Sweden, the sole power that still had an air of activity, quite far from being of some help to Russia, only deprived the combined army of the Prussian corps that was detached to help the Swedes in Pomerania, and augmented the French forces facing us because of the armistice, which sent Mortier's corps to the *Grande Armée*.

Now I will explain to you, General, our relations with the Prussian court. The personal friendship of the two sovereigns[6] formed the principal base of it, a friendship the likes of which history offers us few examples, steadfast amidst political discussions, unchanging despite all the vicissitudes of the chance and luck of war.

Discussions, entirely unknown to Russia and of which she did not even have official knowledge, were so advanced between France and Prussia, that the cabinet of Berlin thought that it was no longer able to choose between peace and war.

On the eve of breaking off relations, the King asked his ally, in the month of September 1806, for the help of 60,000 men. Forgetting all other considerations, Emperor Alexander I

---

3 Gebhard Leberecht von Blücher, Fürst von Wahlstatt (1742–1819), future Prussian *Generalfeldmarschall*, who earned recognition leading the Prussian army against Napoleon at Leipzig in 1813 and Waterloo in 1815.
4 Anton Wilhelm von L'Estocq (1738–1815), Prussian cavalry general, best known for eluding the French pursuit in 1806 and supporting the Russian army during the 1807 campaign. After the Battle of Friedland, L'Estocq was part of an investigative commission into the causes of Prussia's defeat in the Fourth Coalition. He served as the Governor of Berlin in 1808 and of Breslau in 1814.
5 Adolphe Édouard Casimir Joseph Mortier, 1st Duc de Trévise (1768–1835), French general and Marshal of France. In 1806 Napoleon entrusted him the command of the newly formed VIII Corps.
6 Emperor Alexander of Russia and King Frederick William III of Prussia.

not only did not hesitate for an instant to grant him this help, but moreover announced his full intention to help his friend and ally with all his forces. Despite all of the speed made to gather and send the requested help, this first army, 60,000 men strong and placed under my orders, had barely reached our frontiers when already the ruin of Prussia was complete.[7]

Just as the columns of this army were crossing the Niémen, with the intention of heading via Silesia to Saxony, the disasters of Auerstadt and Jena had taken place and their repercussions developed in a frightening manner. Military errors make up the sad painting of the destruction of Prussia, whose political errors had for a long time undermined the foundation. All mistakes that the history of wars present us with were, in a way, repeated in the disposition of the Prussian army. It would be difficult to enumerate them all; but the main reason that alone sufficed to decide the loss of the army was that, quite far from attacking the French army while it was still dispersed, the Prussians allowed Emperor Napoleon all the necessary time to concentrate his forces, and, without even giving some cohesion to their own forces, they committed the fate of the monarchy to corps posted separately, such that the most advanced could not even be supported, in their resistance, by corps that were on the same line or behind them in reserve. A successive and total tumbling effect necessarily had to be the fatal result of this unfortunate disposition, which one thought dictated by prudence, without considering that the ordinary measures of caution and wisdom, very insufficient for the systems of modern war, are much more so against the spirit of genius.

The military history of our time will judge with justice and impartiality the conduct of the captains to whom Prussia's fate had been confided; but would even the best efforts in the art of war have prevented the fall of the monarchy? Or could they only have delayed the end? I believe that the response ceases to be doubtful if Prussia remained isolated, as she was, on the eve of her rupture with France. Her previous conduct had alienated her from all the European courts, without consolidating her relations with Emperor Napoleon. The rupture with England and Sweden was recently announced; Austria retained painful memories and one could hardly believe that Emperor Alexander would find in his friendship for the King [of Prussia] and in his interest for the state of Europe sufficient motives to forget the fateful manner in which Prussia had, the year before, shattered his designs by her indecision and her tortuous politics, since she no longer dared to be frank.[8] Moreover even the final reasons for the rupture, France's intention to restore Hanover to the King of

---

7   Bennigsen refers to the French victory at Jena-Auerstädt and the subsequent French occupation of Prussia.
8   In the fall of 1805, Prussia remained uncertain at how assertive it should be with regard to the French Empire. Russia offered an alliance aimed at France but the Prussians hesitated to join it. The relations between the two powers worsened to such a degree that, while mobilizing forces for war in the summer of 1805, Alexander considered forcing the Prussian monarchy out of its neutrality either peacefully or forcibly, should the Hohenzollern king refuse to grant the Russians the right of passage through his realm. Only in November 1805, with Napoleon already in Vienna, was the Russian emperor able to convince King Frederick Wilhelm III to sign the Treaty of Potsdam and promise to support the coalition if Napoleon did not accept Prussian mediation, which seemed all but certain, considering the steep concessions the Allies expected from the French; within weeks, Prussia could commit over 100,000 troops for the Allied cause. The Prussian mediator, however, arrived after Napoleon had smashed the coalition at Austerlitz on 2 December.

England and the obstacles Prussia was presenting to the formation of the *ligue du Nord*[9] were not done to win over the friendship of the powers, whose assistance could have brought Prussia victoriously through the fight that she was going to undertake. This fight was no longer voluntary; it was only the dénouement, the last act of a tragedy the script for which had been written long ago, and the entire framework of which had escaped only the King [Frederick William III]. He had been surrounded by illusions to pull the wool over his eyes about his true situation. He did not see that he was moving into a labyrinth; he still believed that he could control events and held in his hands the thread that in actuality had already been broken by the exchange of his former provinces for the Electorate of Hanover. It is from the time that Prussia had attached herself to the system of neutrality that her decline dates. This system did not reflect the circumstances, nor did it fit with the spirit of the times. Amid these upheavals, while seeming to guarantee the prosperity of his state, the King had in fact undermined its strength and prepared its fall. The violent turmoil that affected all of Europe, the terrible shocks with which the continent was threatened from both sides alternately, furnished him from time to time with moments that were more or less favourable to regain the ascendance, which his position and his forces seemed to assure him; but due to the lack of foresight and inactivity, the Prussians failed to exploit these moments.

Without following the conduct of the Prussian cabinet prior to the campaign of 1805, it is sufficient to quickly survey the most recent period to have a clear idea of the role it could still play and to appreciate the consequences of that which it took upon itself.

When Russia, England and Austria had decided to wage the war against France, the King of Prussia was urged by these powers to join the coalition. Russia took it upon herself to lead these negotiations. Yet all attempts and endeavours failed against the strong resolve of the King to persist in that neutrality by which he hoped to guarantee the prosperity of his subjects, his crown, and the integrity of his states. Meanwhile, four Russian armies were assembling along the frontiers.[10] One, under the orders of General Kutuzov,[11] went directly, via Galicia, to help the Austrians; the other, led by General Buxhöwden, was intended to

---

9   The League of Armed Neutrality, or the League of the North, was an alliance of the northern European powers (Denmark–Norway, Prussia, Sweden, and Russia) during the War of the Second Coalition in 1800–1801. Initiated by Paul I of Russia, it was intended to displace British interests in the wider Baltic region.

10 In 1805, two Russian armies were formed in the western borderlands. Kutuzov commanded the Army of Podolia while General Ivan Mikhelson was given the task of supervising the second and much larger force – some 90,000 men – designed both to exert pressure on Prussia and to conduct operations against France. This force comprised of General Levin Bennigsen's Army of the North (almost 50,000 men), which was stationed between Taurrogen and Grodno in an effort to nudge the Prussians out of their neutrality (forcibly if the need be), and Friedrich Wilhelm Buxhowden's Army of Volhynia. There is a certain confusion on the designation of the forces commanded by Bennigsen and Essen, with some scholars referring to the 'Army of Lithuania' under Essen I and the 'Army of the North' led by Bennigsen. But both generals were subordinate to Ivan Mikhelson. Order of Battle of General Bennigsen's Corps, [n. d], Russian State Military Historical Archives (RGVIA): f. 846, op. 16. d. 3130, ll. 2-3.

11 Mikhail Golenischev-Kutuzov (1747–1813), the eminent Russian commander who spent five decades in the Russian military service and commanded the Russian armies during Napoleon's invasion of Russia in 1812. Bennigsen and Kutuzov were close friends in their youth but had an acrimonious fight that drove them apart in 1812. In 1805, Kutuzov commanded the Army of Podolia that was sent to support Austrians in their campaign against Napoleon in southern Germany.

reinforce the latter;[12] the third, the command of which was entrusted to me, under the name *armée du Nord*, was advancing via Lithuania toward the Prussian frontier and was supposed to be reinforced by the fourth, which was also already in movement in the area of Brest, under the orders of Lieutenant General Essen I.[13]

Assuming that Prussia would join the coalition, the last two armies had to cross it, so as to reach their destination. The Russian minister at Berlin[14] was charged with negotiating this passage. We soon had the occasion to believe that we would have no more success to expect from these negotiations than we had had from those that sought to obtain active cooperation. At any rate we had charged our minister with declaring that it was indispensable that the Russian army pass via Prussia and that our court, not having been able to foresee the possibility of a refusal on the part of the Prussian cabinet, had already ordered its army to cross into it at the fixed time, which was 16/28 September 1805, in order to follow the route that was indicated. This time was approaching and while gathering his troops to maintain his so-called neutrality, the King wrote to the Emperor [of Russia] immediately, before the last declaration of our minister to Berlin, M. Alopeus, a letter saying in substance that he was not expecting such a violation of his territory and that, far from suspecting it, he thought it necessary to be quite tranquil in this respect.

It is well known how much it cost Emperor Alexander I, always guided by his personal friendship for the King, to yield to this urgent necessity to obtain from Prussia a formal declaration concerning the side she wished to take. He gave new proof of his sentiments by stopping, following this letter, the march of his army and resuming amicable negotiations in Berlin. To this effect he sent his aide de camp, General Prince Dolgorouky.[15]

Despite the great armies that had been drawn up and could have with time opposed France, it was always understood that it was only with the active and pronounced assistance of Prussia that we could perfectly and with certitude attain the goal of the coalition and

---

12 Friedrich Wilhelm Buxhöwden's Army of Volhynia (40,000 men) was deployed around Brest-Litovsk and prepared for a campaign through Bohemia or Saxony, depending on how the war progressed. Order of Battle of Count Buxhöwden's Corps, [n.d], RGVIA: f. 846, op. 16. d. 3130, ll. 4-4b. Also see Article 12 in the Austro-Russian Protocole des Conférences, July 16, 1805, RGVIA: f.341/1, d.26, l.50.
13 Roman numerals after Russian officer names were used to identify officers with the same last names serving. For example, the Russian army included 12 Ilovaiskys, 18 Grekovs, four Tuchkovs and as many Essens. To differentiate them, numerals were attached to their last names, i.e. Essen I, Tuchkov II, Grekov XVIII, Ilovaisky IX.
14 Magnus Maximilian Graf von Alopaeus (1748–1822), Russian diplomat of Finnish extraction, ambassador to Prussia (1802–1806) and Britain (1806–1808). His brother, Frans David Alopaeus (1769–1831) was also a Russian diplomat and served as ambassador to Sweden, Württemberg, and, in 1813–1831, Prussia.
15 Peter Dolgorukov (1777–1806), a scion of a distinguished Russian family of princes, born with a deep sense of power and privilege. He was enrolled in the elite Life Guard Izmailovskii Regiment at the tender age of just three months and began actual service as a 15-year old captain, quickly rising through the ranks due to the family connections. At 21, he was already a major general and adjutant-general to Emperor Paul. His meteoric rise only accelerated after Alexander became the emperor in 1801. The young ruler became very fond of Dolgorukov, who espoused hawkish views in foreign policy and wanted Russia to be more assertive in Europe. In 1804–1805, Dolgorukov was one of the architects of the Russian confrontation with Napoleon and carried out several diplomatic missions, including one to sway the Hohenzollern court to join the Third Coalition. He later played a crucial role in the events leading up to the decisive battle at Austerlitz.

guarantee the safety, the integrity and the independence of the states of Europe, principally of Prussia itself.

The urgent elucidations, with which Prince Dolgorouky was charged, sought to enlighten the Prussian cabinet in this respect and concerning its true position, and at the same time to reassure it in the most solemn manner of the intentions of the united powers. He was nevertheless coldly received upon his arrival and there remained very little hope of succeeding when an extraordinary attack by France, one of those insults that the Emperor Napoleon, subsequently, took too far, showed the King a glimpse of what he had to expect.

The march of Marshal Bernadotte's *corps d'armée* through the Prussian provinces of Franconie was necessary to the clever scheme that was supposed to, on the first attempt, crush Austria and take the French armies to the gates of Vienna. The passage by force of the French troops across the territories of Anspach and Bayreuth, despite the protests of the authorities, finally convinced the King to concede to Russian propositions to grant passage to the army under my command and to take an attitude that, well advised as it was, he should have taken two months earlier.

Meanwhile, we had lost a great deal of time, always so precious in such enterprises and particularly against an adversary as active and vigilant as Emperor Napoleon. Our armies had been stopped in their march by the equivocations of Prussia, who, in the end, must be blamed for the lack of success in the campaign of 1805 and, consequently also, the disasters she herself suffered in the campaign of 1806 that were only the consequence and the development of her earlier dithering. With less weakness or with a little more wisdom and perceptiveness, the Prussian cabinet, without awaiting the violation of its territory, which was only an event of secondary importance, could have foreseen, based on the facts of the past, what it had to expect from its designs that were shattered in the space of three weeks at both ends of its monarchy.

Was it still necessary to await pretexts when from all directions one could only see invasions and upheavals? Our discussion would continue endlessly if we decided to review all the consequences of the behaviour of the cabinet in Berlin. The immediate consequence, however, was that the [coalition's] operations lacked cohesion and one could calculate from that moment, independently of the sad disaster of the Austrian army,[16] that the campaign of 1805 would no longer have the happy results that one could have expected from the coalition plans if Prussia supported them. I must add again that, when passage through Prussian realms was eventually granted to the army under my orders, it was specifically demanded that the army should cross the frontier only in the environs of Grodno. I had a column of 30,000 men at Jurburg.[17] So I was obliged to make these troops first march to Grodno, where I had to wait for them with the rest of the army. If the troops at Jurburg had been able to cross the frontier, my entire army could have arrived in this same time in Warsaw. This redeployment from Jurburg to Grodno cost me two weeks. If not for this delay, I would have been able to join General Koutouzov's army in Moravia and reinforce it with 50,000 men well before the Battle of Austerlitz.

---

16 Battle of Ulm where Napoleon routed the Austrian army in October 1806.
17 Modern-day Jurbarkas (Lithuania), located over 200 kilometres north from Grodno.

At long last, a treaty of alliance had been concluded between Austria, Russia and Prussia and the two sovereigns, Emperor Alexander and King Frederick William, personally cemented the stipulations with solemn promises. The Battle of Austerlitz, fought immediately thereafter, as unfortunate as it was, was by no means liable to destroy the basis of this convention. On the contrary, Prussia, after that day, could certainly have tipped the balance in favour of the cause that she had just espoused if, combining the forces she had at hand with the fresh Russian troops that were in her lands, she had decided to fall on the rear of the French army that was exhausted by the fatigue of forced marches and broken-down by battles that it had fought. But the evil genius of Prussia pushed this realm violently toward its unfortunate destiny.

The timid condescension that France momentarily showed to Prussia should have given Prussia the exact measure of her position at this time, but Prussia only saw chasms on the new path that she had chosen and believed she could only avoid them by returning to the narrow path of negotiations. The Treaty of Vienna was the result; a treaty concluded, as was quick to appear, with the intention, on the part of France, not to fulfil the stipulations, as much as they seemed to be favourable to Prussia, but to keep an eye on the execution of the principal point, the occupation of Hanover by Prussian troops, because this apparent seizure of the German states of the King of England was destined to break its ties with the cabinet in London and cool its relations with the other allied powers.[18]

Without following Prussian politics through the new labyrinth into which she went astray, Emperor Alexander, sensing the danger that the Prussian King was risking, declared to him, just as Austria made peace with France, that he was giving him his word, without taking back his;[19] that he was leaving at his disposal, either to support his negotiations, or to pursue hostilities, all of the troops that were still in Germany, that is to say an army of 45,000 men stationed in Silesia under my orders and the *corps de troupe* that still remained in Hanover,[20] and that he was going to prepare all the resources of his power to help his ally and friend. *Voilà*, this was the second time that Prussia, profiting from the great means that were being offered from all sides, could have joined the English and Swedish troops that arrived in the interval, as well as all of the forces of Russia, to its own power and shaken off the yolk that a deft hand was preparing for her, and, imposing the law on France, to assure her own independence and become the saviour of Germany.

---

18 The Treaty of Schönbrunn was a treaty of friendship signed between France and Prussia at the Schönbrunn Palace in Vienna on 15 December 1805, less than two weeks after the Battle of Austerlitz. Negotiated by Géraud Duroc for France and Christian Graf von Haugwitz for Prussia, the convention permitted the Prussian monarchy to annex Hanover but required it to cede Ansbach, the Duchy of Cleves and the Principality of Neuchâtel. Ansbach went to Bavaria, which gave up the Duchy of Berg to France. Berg was then joined with Cleves to form the Grand Duchy of Berg and Cleves, a French satellite state. Neuchâtel was given by Napoleon to Marshal Louis-Alexandre Berthier, his talented chief of staff. Prussia also agreed to accept the terms of the peace treaty between France and the Holy Roman Empire that was being negotiated then. The Treaty of Schönbrunn was superseded by the Treaty of Paris of 15 February 1806, which incorporated its key provisions.
19 Meaning that Alexander released Frederick William from his commitments but did not renege on his own.
20 Part of the expedition that General Peter Tolstoy led to Stralsund, where he expected to meet up with the Swedish army for a joint campaign to Hanover.

The indecision and pusillanimity of the Prussian cabinet again did not fail on this occasion. Half-measures again prevailed in the King's Council. Count Haugwitz[21] was sent to Paris to resume the negotiations that he himself had ended in Vienna by a treaty of which the Emperor Napoleon no longer wished to fulfil the commitments.

The Prussians consented to everything; not only did their troops drop the threatening posture that they had taken, but they served notice to the Russian troops to turn back to their frontiers, just as those of England and Sweden retreated as well. From then on, Prussia found herself all alone and her interests placed in contradiction with those of England and Sweden. The cabinet of Saint-Cloud [the French government] now dictated her policies. The Confederation of the Rhine, this profound transformation that eminently augmented France's position in Europe, occurred without any Prussian involvement. The Prussian monarchy, in struggling with the consequences of its errors, suffered that series of insults that is unfortunately set out only too truly in its subsequent manifesto against France. Neither recognition of the Confederation of the Rhine, nor the sacrifice of all of her commercial relations could any longer obtain for Prussia from the French government the concession that she believed she could still hope for, if not peace, at least the delay to the war that she needed, to fully comprehend the abyss in which she found herself and search for an escape from it. The region that Bavaria was supposed to cede to her in compensation for the region of Anspach was reduced in size. The regions of Essen and Verden were taken from her by force. The King wishing to form the *ligue du Nord* to counterbalance that of the Rhine found himself frustrated at every step that he took in this direction.

Finally, negotiations began between France and England. They began with France's offer to return Hanover to its former sovereign, the King of England. Such an offer constituted, in the Prussian king's opinion, an all-out attack on his realm. He could not reasonably count on any help. All previous considerations about the superiority of the French disappeared immediately. The King no longer took counsel from anyone, and was guided by his own deep sense of despair. He asked of his sole friend, Emperor Alexander, a reinforcement of 60,000 men, which was granted to him. I thus marched at the head of this army and you will find, General, in my following correspondence, the details of the military operations of this campaign. Rest assured that my account will be free of any exaggeration.

---

21 Christian August Heinrich Kurt Graf von Haugwitz (1752–1832), German statesman, best known for serving as foreign minister (*Kabinettsminister* in charge of foreign affairs) of Prussia during the Napoleonic Wars. His assistant was Johann Wilhelm Lombard (1767–1812), a member of the Prussian cabinet and one of the key architects of the Prussian foreign policy, known for his pro-French sentiments.

4

Russia, England, and France

For the time being the relations between Russia and France were almost imperceptible in the European political system. Separated by states of the first order, they could not reach each other, and all subjects of discussion seemed bound to get lost in the distance that separated the one from the other. In their direct communications they could discuss only commercial relations and, as the exchange of the respective products of the two countries was as advantageous as it was indispensable to both sides, it seemed that their accord should never be interrupted. However, no such thing existed and here is what the attitude of the two nations was, almost from the moment that Russia began to claim the place that belonged to her among the European powers.

From her very beginning, Russia proclaimed herself as a warrior and conquering nation; she pushed her authority everywhere on her periphery, among others toward Sweden, Poland, and Turkey. It is particularly the latter that France thought necessary to protect against Russia. The principal motive thereof was the domination of the Mediterranean Sea. Without ever supporting the ideas that the Russians would drive the Turks from Europe, France feared that if Russia managed to gain important conquests in the Black Sea region, weakened the Ottoman Empire and intimidated or influenced the Divan, France's own domination over the Mediterranean, which she firmly believed belonged to her and that she ought to be watchfully protecting, would be compromised. This protection on the part of France and the confidence accorded to her by the Turkish ministry could have had major consequences and hampered Russia a great deal more than they did, if during a long period – from the death of Louis XIV [in 1715] to that of Louis XVI [in 1793] – the French government had shown so little verve in its measures. Quite far from declaring herself in any way against Russia, France limited herself to spying on the wishes and plans of our court, to upset them as much as she could silently and without a stir, and to exasperate the Divan with her counsels and never-ending plans for offensive or defensive wars against Russia. It was considered the height of the French exertion and resolve when she sent from time to time a few officers to the Turkish army to serve against us. Such a timid march toward such an essential goal could scarcely produce decisive results. To compensate for the weakness and insufficiency of the means, the French augmented their diplomatic attacks in every direction and particularly where the predominance of Russia was the most visible.

Warsaw and Stockholm, therefore, served for a long time as the stage where the French ministry practiced its skill in upsetting Russian designs. France should have been the most concerned in the preservation of the independence of Poland but she failed to ensure this and there was not much for her celebrate at all. It was only by means of Sweden that she actually sometimes stopped the Russian expansion and obstructed the execution of the plans of the cabinet of Saint Petersburg.

Jealousy over even the smallest success and consequently of any territorial aggrandizement on either side;[1] anxiety about every step and mistrust of all insinuations – all of that paired with the most considerate forms and accompanied by professions of friendship, which one did not even claim to give sincerely – such were the distinctive characteristics of relations between France and Russia, until the time when the French Revolution, striving to give a new foundation to the social order, came to threaten to overturn the entire European political system. It was only noticed too soon the effect made on the minds of all the countries by this new doctrine and these principles proclaimed in the name of *liberté* and *égalité* – these revolutionary divinities that were already drenching in blood the steps of thrones and altars; that were anathematizing the fortunes of the rich and the virtues of the poor and that, after having devastated France, had established their terrible tribunal to overthrow the still surviving thrones or altars and destroy any remaining fortunes or virtues.

Catherine II, as imbued by her dignity as she was apprehensive for her authority, could not see without horror these attributes of sovereignty trampled underfoot by a nation that the Russians were still accustomed to viewing as the most enlightened. This painful feeling augmented other considerations that determined the Empress' attitudes towards the revolution. Despite the confidence that she could have in the devotion of her nation and in its attachment to the throne, she believed it her duty to take the most suitable measures to

---

1   Bennigsen's note: To give a precise idea of the way in which the cabinet at Versailles viewed the progress of Russia, it is sufficient to read the instructions given by Louis XV to the *marquis* de L'Hospital, who went in the year 1757 as the French minister to the Russian court. He was directed to study with care what were the true dispositions of the Russian ministry relative to Turkey, Sweden, and Poland. In one passage, these instructions read: 'Sound policy must not permit that we allow the court of Pétersbourg to profit from the advantages of its current state to augment its power and extend the limits of its Empire. A country almost as expansive as the realms of the greatest princes of Europe and that, only having need of a small number of men for its own defence, may have outside of its frontiers formidable armies,' etc. Later, it says: 'We can be certain without exaggeration that the power of Russia has grown by almost half since the death of Peter I [the Great] and one can judge by the role that she plays today what she would eventually do on the global stage, if new acquisitions brought her to a higher degree of greatness and power,' etc.

Further still one finds this remarkable section: 'The lack of fidelity that Russia has shown in the execution of her last treaty with the Turks, who protest that she established a fort and a colony on the land belonging to them and that she retains a great many subjects of the Ottoman Empire, to whom liberty was supposed to be given immediately after the peace of Belgrade [of 1739]; the authority that she has claimed to exercise on the internal government of Sweden; the manner in which she has conducted herself with the Poles for three years; the views that she has already expressed concerning a fixation of limits between the Russian Empire and Poland; finally the system and conduct of Russia, the form of her administration and her military situation must cause fear of the aggrandizement of this power amongst all princes who have at heart public security and tranquillity. This reason suffices to make the King desire that the Empress of Russia withdraw her claims on ducal Prussia,' etc. It was during the Seven Years War, after the conquest of *ancienne* Prussia by the Russians, that Empress Elizabeth formed a plan to incorporate this province into Russia. The intentions of France against Russia were already apparent in the year 1747, when the French court worked secretly to join Turkey, Poland, Sweden and Prussia into a perpetual alliance, a project in which she failed.

preserve her realm, as much as possible, from any seed of corruption. She knew well that ideas spread with the speed of thought, that the distance that separated Russia from France and put these two empires out of reach of each other was not a sufficient guarantee against the communication of the errors and fanaticism of democracy. She knew well that this all consuming fire, whose hearth [France] was ablaze with hateful passions spewed by demagogues, would find everywhere kindling for these same passions, for these hopes for spoils and in the confusion into which had been arbitrarily thrown all principles so as to mislead even the most honest of men.

She considered it her duty to break off all relations and restrict all communications with democratic France. While declaring herself openly against the Republic, she took no active part in the war that the other states, closer to France, waged because she judged that, given the geographic position of the two countries, the results could never match the sacrifices that the war would demand; and that, always guided by the love of her people and the genius of *gloire*, she only wished to shed the blood of her subjects for the good of her people or the safety of Europe. It is true that she proposed, in 1793, to furnish an army of 60,000 men that should act on the Rhine and another army of 15,000 men that, reinforced with at least as many English troops and placed under the command of the Comte d'Artois,[2] should disembark on the coasts of Normandy and support the counter-revolution in the Vendée, which, at this time, was at its height.[3] But she demanded that the united powers solemnly commit themselves by a manifesto to only wage war against the Revolution, to re-establish the former order of things, and that they would adopt for their foundation the peace of Westphalia. She did not find in the respective courts the same disinterested views. Austria was strongly attached to a plan that the Empress openly disapproved of, that of dismembering France and getting rich from the spoils. The English minister also declined this wise project and even presented difficulties to receiving the Comte d'Artois in England. Based on that it was quite clear that that power, far from wishing to suffocate the Revolution, wished to prolong it, to weaken France in Europe and win time to make conquests at her expense in other parts of the world.

Meanwhile, Poland had revolted and the Empress profited skilfully from the troubles that were shaking Europe to come an agreement with the concerned powers about the partition of this state and the means to put this plan into action. It is not my aim to discuss the effect that this great *coup de main* had on Russia's attitude towards the powers of Europe. You know that opinions are very divided on this subject. It has been said that Russia, in placing herself adjacent to the great powers, may, as the result of political designs that these powers may come up with, lose as much of her own security as she might gain preponderance in the affairs of the continent. I may return to this matter when the time comes to discuss the question of the Duchy of Warsaw. It is sufficient to remark here that, in the given circumstances, the partition of Poland was a measure that was as useful to Russia as it must have been displeasing to France. The revolutionary government must have comprehended the consequences of losing a sister republic that, having

---

2   Charles Philippe, Comte d'Artois (1757–1836) was the younger brother to reigning kings Louis XVI and Louis XVIII; he eventually acceded to the French throne as King Charles X in 1824.

3   The Vendée, a coastal region located immediately south of the river Loire in western France, was the centre of a counter-revolutionary movement from 1793 to 1796.

begun with acts of violence and massacres, promised to elevate itself to the height of the revolutionary principles and would hold in check northern Europe, while France would spread her revolutionary rage over the rest of Europe. It was to be expected that upon the return of a stable government in France, the destruction of Poland should provide a real and more immediate object of the jealousy, that, until the Revolution, had only dwelled on vague objects and only fed itself on distant designs. The active part that Emperor Paul decided to take in the war against France must have finally opened the French eyes in this respect. It became clear that Russia, despite her great means, could never have, before and without the partition of Poland, deployed them with as much vigour as she did and intended to do so again, if the differences of opinion of the allied powers had not dissolved the coalition just when success began to give hope of a happy outcome.[4] From this moment – the first time that Russia played a major and active role in the West – dates a new era in her relations with France, whose government passed at almost the same time into the hands of that illustrious captain who had recently returned from Africa to Europe and whose genius, first calming the civil war inside his country, had elevated him to the height of power, splendour and glory that struck the popular imagination and exacerbated the misfortunes of humanity. From this moment, I say, dates a new era in the relations between Russia and France. On the Russian side, this vague feeling of bitterness, expressed in various statements and manifestos, was replaced by a tenor of dignity and coolness, that matched the purity of her intentions and the awareness of her own strength, to which the personal qualities of Russian officials at times added an air of presumption. On the French side, a noble deference, which was often taken for timidity, seemed to preside over all her interactions with Russia.

Prudence dictated this secretive behaviour on the part of the First Consul [Bonaparte], who already then held alone, with a firm hand, the reins of government. In calculating with his wisdom and his perceptiveness all of the chances and not leaving anything to luck, he had to try to appease Russia in order to evade the great obstacles that she could place in the way of the execution of his vast projects – obstacles that would have, if not, prevented him from consolidating his government in the interior, at least delayed its organization and prevented the development of his plans for conquest.

The aims of the French government could not at that time – that is to say after the Peace of Lunéville – be the same as they are today. They changed progressively, as diplomatic and military successes forced the other powers to scale down their own. By the Peace of Lunéville and the forced mediation of Ratisbonne, France had managed not only to guarantee her own independence, but also acquire friends and allies that could be useful to her, if a new coalition formed against her. The Treaty of Presbourg and the creation of the Confederation of the Rhine assured her predominance. The Peace of Tilsit and the decline of Prussia laid the foundation for the system that the French diplomats today call *central*, a term that clearly points to France's aspirations while no one is mistaken as to the point taken as the centre. When this system reaches its fullest development, only then we will be able to judge the sincerity of the assurances that France made, every time the occasion

---

4 Bennigsen is referring to the Anglo-Russian-Austrian squabbling in the fall of 1799 which led to the collapse of the coalition.

presented itself, of her friendship to Russia. Meanwhile, France's greatest interest was to keep Russia out of the transformations in Europe that France herself was initiating.

The power and the great means of Russia could very certainly have tipped the balance in favour of the coalitions, if the plans had not always been so poorly conceived, still worse executed, and the wars often launched belatedly.

The result that we see today proves that Russia should have, as much out of interest for her allies as from concern for her own interests, followed with a vigilant eye the growth of France, her conquests and politics.

If the latter were managing to subjugate the powers that separate her from Russia, or only influencing them to the point of being able to dispose of their resources, against whom would she employ this mass of forces? This reflection should naturally have dispelled the prestige in which French politics surrounded itself and made visible to Russia that the care that had been taken towards her had no other purpose than to bring about earlier and with less difficulty a state of things that would render superfluous all caution.

Among the means employed by the current French government to win over Russia, there was one idea that merits closer examination, because it was repeated on every occasion and because it appeared, at first glance, to be great and generous. It suggested, in substance, that Russia and France, two great nations, that could not have between them any immediate subject of misunderstanding, getting on with each other and acting in concert, would easily manage to set themselves up as two great powers, that would imperiously and irresistibly dominate the rest of Europe and would be, as it were, the arbiters of Providence. The wisdom of the Russian government never permitted it to give in to the temptations of this plan, the true ambition of which was only to exclude Russia from any influence in the affairs of Europe. France would have reaped all the benefits, and the consequences could have become alarming, even fateful for Russia. This project would perhaps have been less susceptible to objections than it is by its nature, if at least the alternative had been proposed, either that the two empires partition the whole of Europe into two federative systems, of which the forces and advantages, calculated in all respects, would be exactly balanced, or else that France on the one hand and Russia on the other, isolating themselves from each other absolutely and solemnly renouncing any territorial aggrandizement at the expense of their neighbours, only unite to maintain the peace of the world and to combat those who would wish to trouble it.

This alternative, impracticable maybe, but truly generous, matched so little with France's designs for conquest, that she could never fully embrace the idea. If it had been in question, she would have evaded it under the quite reasonable pretext that it would require a century of war to realize it, a pretext that, in truth, could, with just as much foundation, have served Russia to reject the specious insinuations of France. What about if she had only taken as a base the *état de possession*, the position the continent is currently in? France, as is claimed, wanted to preserve the imperative influence that her successes and the fickleness of her adversaries and victims had procured for her over Spain, Portugal, Italy, Holland, Switzerland, and Germany. Russia would have had to guarantee these encroachments on the rights of other nations and freely gotten involved in the conspiracy against their independence! How would she answer the questions of the current generation and the cries of posterity, which would reproach her for having contributed to the destruction of the last glimmer of hope of the nations, that succumbed, but can throw off the foreign yolk?

She could not even, in her defence, allege some national interest, a notable aggrandizement of territory, or the prospect of extending her domination; because what would France offer to Russia to balance the advantages that the latter would guarantee for her? Perhaps the influence of France or even her domination would extend up to the Vistula? Is that proportionate? And anyway, Russia can do so without that. Finally, it seems to me that the slightest analysis shows that there is nothing in this idea that can for an instant captivate or give an illusion. Also, it must be supposed, the result of the reflections of our cabinet always were and always will be that above all, the peace of the two great empires demands that there be between them intermediary and independent states that, in separating them and maintaining the equilibrium, absorb the discussions that immediate contact would necessarily give rise to.

Moreover, disregarding all other considerations, we must emphasize one of utmost importance, that, quite far from admitting an absolute conformity of views of the two cabinets of Saint Petersburg and the Tuileries, underscores how highly problematic is the possibility of any stable alliance between France and Russia. Specifically, Russia, by necessity, must contribute [through trade and commerce] to the prosperity of England, the debasement of which has been an established maxim of the French politics for so many centuries. Russia certainly shares with all of the other nations of the continent an interest in combatting any superiority so pronounced that it can, by the abuse made of it, become prejudicial to her independence and her prosperity or to that of her allies. The same principle, which convinced her to fight with a great deal of effort and less success against the continental superiority, must today convince her to hinder the [British] despotism of the seas as it hinders her in her commercial relationships with the other nations; but she must not go further. Should she follow in a moment of blindness the impulse of France, then she would soon be thrown past her goal and, after having passed it, she could see herself dropped into a labyrinth, where it might be difficult to find her way out.

France being superior on land, Russia must religiously see to it that England maintains her maritime superiority over France, including those states that enter into her federative system.

Imagine for a moment the state of affairs if Fortune always the friend of the hero of the day, grants France that preponderance that England currently exercises at sea. What would the consequences be? They are incalculable. That catastrophe would bring about or rather complete this general upheaval, which a clever hand is preparing and that, judging from what we are seeing, may be the destiny of the world, but against which prudence demands straining all resources and arming oneself with a great energy. Certainly, this upheaval would not reach Russia immediately, but she would feel its shock. Let us pause at those that it would produce first.

What use would France make of the fleets and of the riches she would join, in this scenario, with the superiority that she has from her armies, alliances and influence? Would she not employ this same wealth, which England poured out to repulse the French yolk, to extend it and to strengthen it? Today the commerce of all nations suffers from the system adopted by the English cabinet, but the French government, having no need to show consideration, would impose on it far more arbitrary still and much more unbearable laws. Do not be mistaken, do not think that one nation will be more generous than the other; all governments have in mind only the maximum of national prosperity possible in the given circumstances. It is possible to be mistaken about the means, and this is the case where knowledge and ability have some hold over ignorance and clumsiness. But these cases are rare nowadays and with a much less lasting effect, since in each country there is always a mass of enlightened individuals, who soon enlighten the government as to its errors. Now, be it from Westminster or the Tuileries, what does it matter from which departs the bills or decrees, if the principles are the same? France, at the least misunderstanding between our nations, would impede our commerce as much as England does today; she would no less cut the communications between our ports and the squadrons that could be equipped there. Russia furnishes the entire world with maritime materials. Since she has ports, she must be a maritime power strong enough to protect her commerce from insults and humiliations. But, I believe, her geographic position demands that she not even aspire to become a maritime power of the first order, in the modern sense of the word. It must suffice for her to be preponderant in the Baltic Sea and, if possible, on the Black Sea. Our ports are situated on different seas and at vast distances from each other; by consequence our squadrons, not being and never needing to be strong enough to fight those of the premier maritime power of the world, would remain without [mutual support] and communication in the event of hostilities, as we see happening today. This consideration, although subordinate, nevertheless influenced the resolutions of our cabinet and convinced it to be cautious with England. Such an approach would become much more urgently necessary with France and would not be reciprocated as with a power that, in every respect, has equal need of seeking our friendship.

I said that Russia must take an interest in the prosperity of England, and I believe I have proved the necessity in respect to her independence and that of her neighbours. Add to that the reflections that are brought up by commercial relations, reflections that are within reach of everyone, and act strongly on the public spirit, because they concern the public and private bliss and they are intimately bound with the idea of the wealth of the state and the individual. Compare the balance sheet of commerce done by Russia. If it is true that in commerce the real advantage that a country like Russia gets from it is in proportion to the surplus in the hard cash that enters it, then it must be agreed that the commerce with England is as advantageous for the immense sums that it imports into the country, as that of France is disadvantageous for the considerable sums that it draws out. One could object, with some semblance of reason, that it is irrelevant which nation Russia sells her products to, provided that silver, which she cannot do without, reaches her and that supposing the extreme case, in which France would replace England, there would still be the same need of the articles furnished by our country. To this it must be observed that France, superior on the sea, would be at the same time more so on land than she is today; that she would support her maritime power with strong armies; that she would despotically buckle the commerce of the world under her arbitrary laws and would perhaps want to go as far as fixing the market prices. No longer having to fear on the continent these coalitions of which the idea itself would become non-existent and absurd, lacking the money that England alone is still in a state to furnish and lacking powers to unite, France would no longer self-impose any of the restraints of which her great continental superiority does not absolutely free her. England, on the contrary, would be more and more obliged to placate Russia, to favour her commerce and seek her alliance, as she has done thus far on every occasion. Because she does not have strong armies at her disposal, the English minister is sufficiently enlightened to understand that it is only by a natural and perfect harmony that England and Russia can together form a boulevard against this federative mass that has just been born, and to guarantee to British commerce the access to the markets for her merchant fleets and the goods they carry.

It was thought for a moment that England would be vanquished on the continent; that she would be forced to accept the peace and to somewhat moderate her maritime superiority, if one managed to close off the ports of Europe to her and ban her from its commerce.[5] The Emperor of the French, after having declared all of England in a state of blockade, to give some reality to this fanciful idea, wishes to hold the continent in a state of siege. Europe has now realized that this measure, be as it may be commensurate with the French government's other policies, does not correspond at all to that which serves as its pretext. England became richer and more formidable as the ports were closed to her, and the states that were swept along into this system, either by yielding to force, or through deference, are the victims, from the dilapidation of their finances and the penury to which they find themselves reduced. This fact is proof that if England draws a profit from the commerce that she does with the continent, through the output of her articles of manufacture, this benefit itself comes round, as a final result, to the profit of Europe, and that it is the other parts of the world that pay the price.

The attitude Russia must take in the case of war between France and England, the single attitude that assures her good fortune, is to remain neutral and to ensure respect for her neutrality, her flag, and that of her allies. Providence provided her with the means; it is for her wisdom to profit from them by avoiding taking an active part in discussions that already have been going on for 15 centuries, and that, given the respective positions of France and England, will likely do so indefinitely.

Following particularly the history of the progress of Russia, we see that it is basically to follow the history of her commerce, in which the English nation plays such an important role. It is only since the reign of Peter the Great that dates the first solid establishment of Russian commerce, with the acquisition of the Baltic ports and the development of water communications [canal/river systems] that he undertook in the realm and that were further improved under the following reigns. The inhabitants of this vast empire soon felt the happy effect. The products of the country, sought out by domestic and foreign merchants, increased in price and were paid for in hard cash. Industry was encouraged, the country became richer and the state, the revenues of which increased successively from 20 millions to double that and finally more than quadruple that, expended more for the good of the nation, to form a considerable navy and to increase her army little by little from 100,000 to 500,000 men.

At the same time, Russia gained in esteem and influence abroad; she became formidable to her neighbours. By means of the strong armies that she could maintain, she found herself in a state to make wonderful and important conquests. This state of grandeur, Russia owed to the wisdom of her government, which knew, from one era to another, to expand the commerce of the Empire by protecting it and to increase its revenues by developing national prosperity. Catherine II, so as not to increase debts contracted abroad and especially in Holland, found herself nevertheless obliged, during her first war against the Turks, which exhausted her wealth, to introduce *assignats*, pledging that the total sum would not exceed

---

5   Bennigsen is referring to the Continental Blockade that Napoleon initiated in late 1806.

100 millions, a quite modest sum relative to her revenues. This sum was put into circulation successively. It began with 25 millions and it was only in 1786 that the 100 millions circulated completely in the public. In 1794, Catherine II found herself obliged to increase the sum of *assignats* by 22 millions, her second war against the Turks and her campaigns in Poland having once again occasioned considerable expenses. As in all of the departments and in the imperial establishments there was always money belonging to the Crown, one could presume that only about 100 millions were in public circulation, which is why the *assignats* remained for a long time on par with hard cash; moreover, given the ease that they offered for transactions in the interior, they were even preferred to hard cash. Consequently, the sum of assignats gradually increased. The flourishing state of Russian commerce supported its value, even during the various wars that the Empire had to wage on the continent. But from the second that a war of another nature imposed constraints on the commerce of the country, the value of the *assignats* fell so precipitously that the Crown and private individuals lost a great deal. The excess produce stayed with the owners in the countryside; the circulation of specie was halted and the lack of hard cash was felt in a frightening manner. Such are and always will be the consequences of an alliance with France for Russia if she cannot conserve her neutrality with England.

As one can predict that all of the powers of Europe united will never manage or, to grant something to the current system, will only manage after very extended efforts to reduce England and that it is impossible that Russia can do without her commerce for long, it is also impossible that an alliance between her and France can be sincere, durable and national; it would always end by impoverishing the country and depriving the state of the means to maintain its power and its dignity.

After this digression, which is not as unrelated to our subject as it may seem, let us return to the relations between these two nations on the continent.

We have seen that, as much as France will seek to overextend her influence, no alliance, even were it sincere, could be stable. The security of our frontiers demands that our neighbours be more or less protected by us or in alliance with us, and that a foreign impulse is not able to trouble its repose. Taking this principle as a starting point, how does one reconcile France's [supposed] peaceful intentions with the fact of the establishment of the Duchy of Warsaw? It is not Poland, and neither is it a province of Saxony, whose King[6] is formally in charge but in reality stripped of all authority and free disposition, especially in relation to the army, and seeking only favours and rewards from France. The latter even left in Poland, after the pacification of Tilsit, a very considerable corps of troops. It is therefore a military frontier of France, just like the one the Romans used to establish while waiting for the favourable moment to push forward. The same goal here is obvious.

Is it not natural, then, that the inhabitants of the lands remaining to the powers that partitioned Poland[7] view this state as the core around which must be reassembled the fragments of the old [Polish] realm? Everyone knows the agitation into which the formation of

---

6   King Frederick Augustus I, the last Elector of Saxony from 1763 to 1806 (as Frederick Augustus III) and King of Saxony from 1806 to 1827. He held the formal title of the Duke of Warsaw from 1807 to 1815 but the actual management of the Duchy of Warsaw was in the hands of the French and Polish officials.

7   Russia, Prussia, and Austria participated in the three partitions of Poland.

the Duchy of Warsaw threw the spirits of the Poles, and some remain quite determined to nourish their hopes. From all the regions remaining under the control of the other powers the young men are running, without even asking the permission of their respective governments, to enlist in the troops that are already called the Army of Poland. Note the length of which this new state forms the frontier of Russia in an area that, whatever the government does, the numerous inhabitants will always be disposed to rebel and to join with its compatriots, and you will not deny that Russia must distrust such conduct as incompatible with the assurances of amity from France, done to give offence to our government.

If it was a question of rewarding Saxony for the sacrifices that she had made [to France] or to render her more powerful at the expense of Prussia, then it would have been better achieved by granting her other portions of the Prussian realm, for example Silesia. Let us say frankly – it is a gift – if one can even consider it as such – given only temporarily to Saxony, and one that could be taken away from her as easily as it was given; it only serves as a pretext to veil the true motive, that nevertheless has escaped no one. Emperor Napoleon sensed it so well that, yielding to the circumstances of the moment, he made a solemn declaration against the speculation concerning this subject, in proclaiming that he had never intended the re-establishment of Poland.[8] But such a declaration, however solemn it was, means nothing, for it is well known that it is one of those declarations like treaties of eternal peace, that is maintained only for as long as it is practical, and has no real strength except insofar as it has for its foundation mutual interest and security. If it is true that at the peace of Tilsit a secret article held that the Duchy of Warsaw would never be enlarged, this declaration was quite necessary to reassure the Russian government. It is not less true, that apart from the motives that the French government has to push back the frontiers of Russia to dispose more freely of the rest of Europe, there is also an ulterior motive, well expressed by a remark attributed to Napoleon. Following an interview, of which I would not be able to name the subject, nor guarantee the authenticity, he was supposed to have said: '*Je ne veux pas qu'on voie après moi les Capitaines d'Alexandre.*'[9]

Indeed, having managed to introduce great transformations in Europe and distribute thrones among his family, Napoleon must, as a great man, use all means to give stability to these states and to the governments he created. Russia is, without question, the power that, without being dangerous for France, could be so for the French external establishments and their federative system, insofar as she will easily be able to join her troops with those of Austria and Prussia, with whom she would have a common interest. To push back and weaken Russia, to separate her from these two states with whom she could act in concert, to impede or render infinitely more difficult her cooperation in the overthrow or the modification of the establishments Napoleon made in Europe – such are the future advantages that he would gain through the re-establishment of Poland, as she was before the first partition, especially if given a skilful and warlike sovereign who would be capable of organizing her army and putting it on a respectable footing. Poland would then have a population of 15 million inhabitants, which would give her the means to expand her army, when needed,

---

8   Bennigsen alludes to Napoleon's statement in June 1810 that he would 'never re-establish Poland.'
9   'I do not desire to see after me the captains of Alexander.' Napoleon is referring to the Diadochi, the rival generals of Alexander the Great who fought for control over his empire after his death in 323 BCE.

to 300,000 men. The interests of this realm and its safety would then forever be attached to those of France, whose immediate help and influence over Poland could well put her in a position to hold Russia in check and exclude her from any intervention in the affairs of Europe. In one of his declarations Napoleon says that 'the partition of Poland was never recognized by France and that it is contrary to her interests'; in a message to the Senate, of 29 January 1807, he expressed himself thusly: 'It required 15 years of victories to give France recompenses commensurate with those [Russia gained through] the partition of Poland, which a single campaign conducted in 1772 could have prevented.'[10] To the Polish deputation sent to Berlin to call for his protection in their favour, Emperor Napoleon responded: 'I will see if you are worthy of being a nation.' Since that time, these brave men spill their blood in great torrents to prove that their nation is worth something. It is a different matter, but the proof of their devotion is received quite well.

As much as France is and will be eager to support and reinforce the state that she has formed on our frontiers to serve as a barrier against us, so much must Russia be determined to destroy it. Political reasons may cause our court to conceal such an objective for the moment. But I ask you if, when dealing with an issue so fundamental and so innately connected with the [national] honour, dignity and security, can there be a perfect sincerity or even appearance of stability in the relations between the two great powers? Today we no longer need to engage in conjectures; the short time that has passed since the peace of Tilsit has shown us what we should expect from the friendship with France.

Russia must destroy the very idea of the rebirth of Poland in any form. Moreover, she cannot even constrain herself to that – she must seize the first opportunity that presents itself to establish her frontier on the Vistula River; no other consideration must divert her from this objective. Recall, General, what I explained in my correspondence from the year 1801 concerning this frontier. I said that with Catherine II having taken two steps, the first to the Dnieper, the second to the Niémen, Russia must now think of taking the third, to the Vistula.

If France has managed to execute the plans of Louis XIV by extending herself to the Rhine, which gives her a natural and solid frontier, how could Russia not manage to establish her own on the Vistula? Just look at the map and observe the length of our current frontier from Galicia to Courland. The disadvantages leap off the page, when one compares this frontier with that which the Vistula offers us. You will agree that it is the natural frontier of Russia; she will be able not only to defend it with more energy, but she will again be able to divert any influence, foreign and dangerous for her, emanating from the neighbouring states on the left bank of the river. These states would remain under her sole protection. She could easily assure that the tranquillity of Germany can no longer be perturbed and preempt any attempt to direct hostile forces against her own sovereignty. The whole of Europe would gain from the calmness and peace that would be ushered when Russia, having reached her natural frontiers, would be able to counterbalance French power.

The vast Russian Empire, whose population exceeds 40 million inhabitants and grows every year by several hundred thousand souls certainly has nothing to fear from any power,

---

10 Bennigsen mistakenly referred to the campaign in '1778.' The original text of Napoleon's message to the Senate is available in *Correspondance de Napoléon Ier, publ. par ordre de l'Empereur Napoléon III* (Paris: Imprimerie Impériale, 1863), vol.15, p.253.

if governed according to the principles of wise and sound politics. Russia must, no doubt, one day claim the preponderance to which she is destined. She must make use of it, as she has constantly done up to this moment, not to satisfy some immoderate ambition but to place on solid foundations the national prosperity, and to enjoy that respect to which she has already acquired so many rights, and that is due to the grandeur and energy of her nation.

Those who are unfamiliar with Russia express astonishment at the enormous length of her frontiers, and say that their defence will always absorb her forces, to the point that there will only remain to her very few troops available for offensive wars. That is an error. The greater part of our frontiers, from the Arctic Ocean to the Caspian Sea, do not require for their defence a single man from the regular army; this border is occupied and guarded by cordons raised from the local inhabitants. That leaves the European frontier that, if one takes the Vistula as a military line and extends it right up to the Black Sea, would not be more than 300 miles in length.[11] This line, along which Russia could be menaced, is rather exposed in the direction of Turkey and infinitely more advantageous for us in the direction of Poland or Germany. It is not disproportionate to the size of her army. There would always be enough troops to give cause for regret to any enemy whatsoever, who would dare to cross our frontiers, as well as to act offensively and prevent the powers, located between Russia and France and still enjoying an independent existence, from being subjugated by the latter, the sole case that could become alarming for the Russian interests, as I have already observed.

France does not enjoy the same advantages as us, relative to her frontiers. Her military line begins in Dalmatia[12] and goes up to the mouth of the Escaut (Scheldt)[13] and the Rhine; from there, France has to defend more than 300 *lieues* of coastline, on which she must maintain land and naval forces. Add to this that France is surrounded by nations that, although subjugated at this moment, need to be constantly watched by strong garrisons, while Russia only finds herself in the same situation at one place, where she must concentrate the greatest mass of her troops to be close at hand for any developments in Europe.

---

11 In actuality, the distance between the Vistula River and the Black Sea is over 500 miles, as the crow flies.
12 Dalmatia is a region on the eastern shore of the Adriatic Sea, a narrow territory stretching from the island of Rab in the north to the Bay of Kotor in the south. In 1805, when establishing the Kingdom of Italy, Napoleon annexed to it the former Venetian Dalmatia from Istria to Kotor. Three years later, he annexed the Republic of Ragusa. In 1809, he removed the Venetian Dalmatia from the Kingdom of Italy and created the Illyrian Provinces, which were directly annexed to France.
13 One of the crucial waterways in Western Europe, the Scheldt is a 220 mile long river that flows through northern France, western Belgium, and the southwestern part of the Netherlands, before joining the North Sea.

5

The Start of Hostilities – The Evacuation of Warsaw[1]

On 27 September/9 October 1806, finding myself at Medjiboje, in Podolia, 100 *verstas* from the Dniester River, and destined to lead an army against the Turks, I received, via *feldjäger*,[2] a decree from the Emperor, my master, dated the 23rd or 24th of the same month, in which His Majesty, in the most gracious and flattering terms, honoured me with the command of a *corps d'armée*, composed of four divisions: the 2nd Division under the orders of Lieutenant General Count [Alexander] Ostermann[-Tolstoy], the 3rd under Lieutenant General [Fabian von Osten-]Sacken, the 4th under Lieutenant General Prince [Dmitri] Golitsyn and the 6th under Major General [Alexander] Siedmioraczki. His Majesty ordered me at the same time to hasten as much as possible my arrival at Grodno. These four divisions totalled 60,000 men, both combatants and non-combatants,[3] with which I was destined to bring aid to the King of Prussia against Napoleon.

I left the next day, September 28/October 10, and arrived five days later at Grodno, where I already found the Prussian *commissaires*, Major General Chlebowski and Stein's[4] private advisor, who had been sent by the King to organize the march of my *corps d'armée*. I attached to them the *chef* of my *état-major*, General de Steinheil, and we worked diligently toward an agreement for the march of the Russian forces through the Prussian realms. According to this agreement, the soldiers should be nourished *à l'étape* [in stages], that is to say by their hosts at each resting point, and fodder also had to be supplied by the inhabitants, wherever

---

1 This letter is dated March 1808, Vilna.
2 A military courier.
3 For the new war against Napoleon, Russia mobilized three army corps (*corps d'armée*) for the campaign in Poland. Two of these, marching generally toward the area north of Warsaw, would form the principal force committed to contending with Napoleon's Grande Armée: Bennigsen (on paper, 71,680 men (2,443 officers and 69,237 other ranks) of whom some 60,000 were present, with 276 cannon) and General Friedrich Wilhelm (Fedor Fedorovich) von Buxhöwden (55,000 men with 216 guns). A smaller, third force under General Magnus Gustav (Ivan Nikolaevich) von Essen (37,000 men, 132 guns) was approaching from Moldavia to guard the Russian strategic left flank and shield Russian territory from any French forays to the east.
4 Heinrich Friedrich Karl vom und zum Stein (1757–1831), commonly known as Baron vom Stein, was a Prussian statesman who, in the wake of the Prussian defeat in 1806, advocated substantive reforms to modernize the Prussian state.

our troops passed, all at a fixed price. This agreement was sent to the two respective courts, for the confirmation of the two sovereigns. One could not foresee then the need for magazines on the right bank of the Vistula, because I was supposed to, without stopping, march via Silesia and cross the Elbe to reach the theatre of war.

I worked meanwhile at the necessary measures to have my *corps d'armée* cross our frontier and I received the order to accelerate my march as much as possible, without however excessively tiring the troops, and to follow all of the orders that H. M. the King of Prussia [Frederick William III] saw fit to give me. But the circumstances soon changed completely: instead of the long march that I had expected to reach the theatre of war, the disasters that befell the Prussian army and the defeats that it suffered required not

Ivan Michelson (Johann von Michelsohnen). (Public Domain)

only a complete change in the projected plan of operations, but precautions and the greatest activity in armament on our part for the security and defence of our own frontiers; circumstances that we certainly were not expecting and for which we were still less prepared. We shall see on this occasion the resources of Russia, when it is a matter of a war that can threaten her frontiers, and the extent of the help that a beloved sovereign can expect, by all of the sacrifices that the Russian nation made then with the greatest enthusiasm.

A few days before leaving Grodno, I received news of the unfortunate actions at Auerstadt, Jena and Halle, that occurred on the 2/14 and 5/17 October. This vexing news was not slow in reaching Petersburg either, and I was soon sent the orders to keep the army concentrated and not to cross the Vistula so as to not uselessly expose our brave troops. At the same time, General Buxhöwden received the order to assemble in Lithuania four other divisions, the 5th Division under the orders of Lieutenant General Tuchkov,[5] the 7th under Lieutenant General Dokhturov,[6] the 8th under Lieutenant General Essen III[7] and the 14th under Lieutenant General Anrep.[8] These four divisions amounted to about 40,000 men. General Michelson, who had already commenced hostilities against the Turks,[9] received the

---

5   Nikolai Alekseevich Tuchkov I (1765–1812).
6   Dmitri Sergeevich Dokhturov (1759–1816).
7   Peter Kirillovich von Essen III (1772–1844).
8   Roman Karlovich (Heinrich Reinhold von) Anrep (1756–1807).
9   The Russo-Ottoman War commenced on November 23, 1806 when the Russian forces crossed the Dniester and took control of the Ottoman fortresses of Khotin, Bender, Akkerman and Kilia.

order to send immediately from his army Lieutenant General Essen I[10] with two divisions,[11] which nevertheless only amounted to 17,000 men, having been obliged to leave several troops detachments behind. This General was ordered to march on Brest to cover there our frontiers.

Such were the first arrangements made on the part of Russia. Before going further, it seems necessary that I say something about the enemy forces, which were advancing toward our frontiers. According to the more precise intelligence, the forces of the various *corps* of the French army, while crossing the Rhine, were as follows:[12]

The Guard under Marshal Bessières	12,000
Augereau's 7th Corps	11,400
Bernadotte's 1st Corps	16,800
Lefebvre's 9th Corps	12,000
Davout's 3rd Corps	34,000
Soult's 4th Corps	30,600
Lannes' 5th Corps	23,400
Ney's 6th Corps	22,200

---

10   Ivan Nikolaevich (Magnus Gustav) von Essen I (1758–1813).
11   These were the 9th Division of Volkonsky and the 10th Division of Zakomelsky.
12   Following the victory at Jena–Auerstedt in mid-October 1806, Napoleon split the Grande Armée into two large, *ad hoc* groups. The first, consisting of 1st, 4th and 6th Corps with much of the Reserve Cavalry, remained preoccupied with the pursuit and destruction of the Prussian units that had escaped Jena–Auerstedt; 6th Corps besieged the fortress of Magdeburg while 1st and 4th Corps with the Reserve Cavalry pursued Prussian forces under General Gebhard Leberecht von Blücher north toward the Baltic coast. The second part of the French army moved into cantonments: Marshal Jean Lannes's 5th Corps in and around Stettin, Marshal Louis Nicolas Davout's 3rd Corps at Frankfurt-an-der-Oder, and Marshal Pierre Augereau's 7th Corps, the Imperial Guard, and the remainder of the Reserve Cavalry billeted in Berlin; the Bavarian corps camped near Crossen. As soon as the first group completed the task of subduing the remaining Prussians, Napoleon intended to concentrate his army and march east to face the approaching Russians. By the second week of November, the remnants of the Prussian army had surrendered, with Blücher capitulating near Lübeck on 7 November and the fortress of Magdeburg falling the following day. Napoleon thus regained additional corps to send eastward to support Davout against the slowly advancing Russians. In accordance with the new imperial instructions, Davout moved his headquarters to Posen and pushed his light cavalry outposts further east, with some French scouts venturing as far as Kalisch and Thorn. As the Russians were still far away, Napoleon ordered 3rd, 5th and 7th Corps to converge on Thorn, which the French occupied on 18 November. By the end of the month, Napoleon had concentrated most of the Grande Armée around Posen, where the emperor himself arrived on 27 November. For a general discussion of the operations in late 1806, see Eduard von Höpfner, *Der Krieg von 1806 und 1807* (Berlin: S. Schropp, 1850), vol.3, pp.1–157; Mathieu Dumas, *Précis des événemens militaires, ou, Essais historiques sur les campagnes de 1799 à 1814* (Paris: Treutell, 1826), vol.27, pp.99–205; Karl Ritter von Landmann, *Der Krieg von 1806 und 1807: auf Grund urkundlichen Materials sowie der neuesten Forschungen und Quellen* (Berlin: Voss, 1909), pp.300–327; Carl von Plotho, *Tagebuch während des Krieges zwischen Russland und Preussen einerseits, und Frankreich andrerseits, in den Jahren 1806 und 1807* (Berlin: Braunes, 1811), pp. 1–43; F. Lorraine Petre, *Napoleon's Campaign in Poland, 1806–7* (London: Low & Marston, 1901), pp. 59–118.

Total:	*162,400*
Cavalry Reserve under the *grand-duc* de Berg	20,400
Guard Reserve under Oudinot	8,000
Total French National Forces:	*190, 800*[13]

It is with this force that the French began the war against Prussia in the first days of October 1806.

Let us now examine, without embellishment, the losses of the French army against the Prussians.

At Jena and Auerstadt:
killed   4,500
wounded   8,000
[total]   12,500

At Saalfeld and other engagements before the battle:
killed   500
wounded   1,500
[total]   2,000

At Halle:
killed   300
wounded   900
[total]   1,200

In the various engagements of Nordhausen, Wanzleben, Zehdenick, and Prenzlow:
killed   200
wounded   500
[total]   700

In the engagements with General Blücher in the Mecklembourg and at Lübeck:
killed   1,500
wounded   2,600
[total]   4,100

At Magdebourg, killed and wounded 160
Total   20,660

I will also add here that the French army had some 14,000 sick men in the hospitals up to the Vistula. The total, therefore, is 34,660. Subtracting it from the total strength of 190,800 gives us the remaining balance of 156,140 men.

---

13   The effective strength of the French army was, in fact, about 165,000 men.

'One Hero per Victory' – an early nineteenth-century French print showing the famed French commanders and their great victories. The notable figures include Marshals Jean Lannes (2), Louis-Nicolas Davout (4), Alexander Berthier (6), Édouard Mortier (8) Pierre Augéreau (20) and Joachim Murat (23). (Courtesy of Anne S.K. Brown Military Collection)

After the actions against the Prussians, a Bavarian *corps* of 16,000 men joined the French army, bringing the total to 172,140 men.

From these troops were detached:

In Silesia (the Bavarians)	16,000
In the *pays* of Hesse	2,000
At Hameln	800
At Hambourg	1,500
At Magdebourg remained	3,000
At Berlin	2,000
At Lübeck	800
At Stettin and Küstrin	3,000
Total:	*29,100*
Subtracted from	172,140
Remaining	143,040

And so it was with these 143,040 soldiers that the French army, after having crossed the Oder, launched a winter campaign against the Russian army and the remainder of the Prussian army. When the French reached the Vistula River, the Russians only had 60,000 men to oppose them, while the Prussians fielded just 10,000 men.

On 22 October/3 November, my *corps d'armée* began to cross our frontiers in four columns, at Jalowka, Grodno, Olitta and Jurburg. I myself departed on 27 October/8 November. Two days later I arrived with my headquarters headquarters at Ostrolenka, where I found the Emperor's aide-de-camp, Benkendorf,[14] who had been sent from Petersburg to the King of Prussia and whom the latter had sent from Graudenz to me with dispatches dated 25 October/6 November; in these letters His Majesty [Frederick William III of Prussia] deigned to give me news of the various unfortunate events that his army had suffered, of the loss of the fortresses of Stettin and Küstrin; finally that the French were marching quickly towards the Vistula, in two columns, of which one was marching via southern Prussia and the second via Pomerania and western Prussia. His Majesty made known to me his desire to concentrate the Russian and Prussian troops behind the Drewenz River between Osterode and Soldau, where we could find an advantageous position to oppose the progress of the enemy into Old Prussia or if the enemy tried crossing the Vistula, to even attack and force it back.[15]

---

14 Alexander Karl Wilhelm Christoph Graf von Benckendorff (1781–1844), Russian military commander and political leader. He served as the czar's aide-de-camp and later commanded a flying detachment in 1812–1813. He is, however, remembered more for his role in reorganizing and leading the Russian secret police, the infamous Third Section of the Imperial Chancellery, under Emperor Nicholas I.

15 While in Graudentz with the Prussian royal family, Benckendorff did his best to bolster Prussian spirits in the wake of the crushing defeat at Jena-Auerstädt. He urged King Frederick William III to remain steadfast and trust in his alliance with Russia, whose armies were already moving through Poland to support Prussia. He was, however, displeased with the Prussian response. '[The Prussians] tried to conceal from me that Napoleon's army was at Kalisch and the King, without informing me, sent individual orders to our division commanders instructing them to turn to Osterode. I considered

His Majesty invited me at the same time to enter into correspondence with his General of Cavalry Count de Kalkreuth,[16] who commanded the Prussian troops at that time, so as to act in concert with him in our operations. Given the distance that separated from the four divisions commanded by General Buxhöwden and those of General Essen from our frontiers then bereft of any defence, I thought it my duty to explain to the [Prussian] King that if I moved my *corps d'armée* between Osterode and Soldau, the enemy column that was directing its march on Warsaw could cross our frontiers without the least obstacle. As I principally had to protect [the Russian] frontiers against invasion, and as the orders of the Emperor, my master, called for me to never lose sight of that object in my operations, I begged the King to authorize the measures that I found indispensable in my position, and according to which I had already given the necessary direction for the march of my columns. The orders that I had given in this respect were as follows:

> One division under the orders of General Siedmioraczki to Praga. He will send via Warsaw a detachment under the orders of Colonel Yurkovskii, composed of five squadrons of the regiment of the Aleksandriiskii Hussars, a regiment of Cossacks, a battalion of jagers and two cannon to take up a position at Blonie, on the road from Posen, and at Kazun on the road from Petrokow or that from Breslau.[17] Colonel Yurkovskii will extend his line of light troops on the Bzura River. This detachment will serve to observe the enemy column, which is directing its march on Warsaw and at the same time must prevent the insurgents from being able to approach Warsaw before the arrival of the French army.
>
> General Siedmioraczki will have occupied by a detachment the right bank of the Bug, from the Austrian border to the Narew; he will establish a chain of light troops on his right along the length of the Vistula, [halfway up the road from Plock – *jusqu'à moitié chemin de Plock*].
>
> Major General Barclay de Tolly, commanding the advance guard, will himself go to Plock; he will have under his orders his regiment of jagers, a regiment of infantry, five squadrons of the regiment of *chevau-légers polonais*, two regiments of Cossacks and the company of horse artillery [*artillerie à cheval*] under Prince

---

it my duty to hasten to meet General Bennigsen and warn him about everything, as I was convinced that the Prussians would try to conceal from him actual situation on the ground and, consequently, Bennigsen, being unable to receive in timely fashion instructions from St. Petersburg, might find himself in a serious predicament. I asked the [Prussian] king permission to leave and sought out his aide-de-camp to learn where I could find General Bennigsen. When he perceived my intentions, he sought to gain time by not giving me directions and instead assuring me that the leading elements of our forces were already in Warsaw. Because of this untruthful statement he forced me to undertake a rather lengthy journey, hoping that by the time of my belated arrival our columns would have already changed their direction in accordance to the [Prussian] king's orders. But he had failed in his enterprise because none of our division commanders followed these orders since they only obeyed orders coming from the commander-in-chief.' Benckendorff, 'Vospominaniya...', pp.120-122.

16   Friedrich Adolf Graf von Kalckreuth (1737–1818), Prussian military commander and future *Generalfeldmarschall*. After the Prussian defeat at Jena-Auerstädt in October 1806, Kalckreuth did his best to rally the surviving Prussian forces. He later defended Danzig against the French.

17   Bennigsen's note: in Petrokow as in Posen and in several other towns in *grande Pologne*, the insurrection fomented by the enemy had already broken out.

Iachvill.[18] The majority of his detachment will occupy the area between Plock and Plonsk; his chain of Cossacks on his left will take over there where that of General Siedmioraczki's ends. On his right, in the area of Thorn, it will go as far as the chain of Prussian troops. To coordinate the cordon on this side, he will immediately communicate with General L'Estocq.

General Barclay de Tolly will send parties of light troops across the Vistula to patrol there and to try to gain news of the enemy.

Lieutenant General Sacken with the 3rd division will occupy the distance from Mlawa to Soldau and Gilgenburg.

Lieutenant General Count Ostermann will occupy with the 2nd division the environs of Ciechanow.

Lieutenant General Prince Golitsyn with the 4th division will occupy the environs of Pultusk, where my headquarters will be established.

In this position I could concentrate my four divisions in two days and move in force wheresoever the circumstances required. I made my report to the Emperor, my master, on these arrangements that the King deigned to approve. The Prussian corps, under the orders of General Count Kalkreuth, found itself in tight cantonments between Saalfeld and the Soldowka River, with the chain of advance-posts deployed along the Vistula from Danzig to the environs of Plock. General L'Estocq, who was then commanding these advance-posts, sent out detachments on the left bank of the Vistula, to gather reliable news of the march and approach of the enemy; one of these detachments, led by Major Mutius, encountered in the small town of Bromberg two enemy officers from the [French] état-major, sent with an escort on reconnaissance; these two officers were taken prisoner and the escort dispersed. Two days later, the approach of the advance guard of Lannes' corps forced all of these [Prussian] detachments to re-cross the Vistula; General L'Estocq ordered the destruction of the bridge that was on this river below Thorn, which was fulfilled on 4/16 November.

With the report that I sent to the Emperor from Ostrolenka, I wrote a letter to the minister, M. de Budberg, on the date of 30 October/11 November concerning a matter, which subsequently and almost throughout the war caused me the greatest difficulty and that often presented obstacles to my plans for operations. It concerned the measures to be taken for the provision of the army. My experiences can serve as an example that the arms of the enemy are not as terrifying to a commanding general as is the anxiety that he experiences from the lack of the means to sustain an army in the field; such hindrances make you lose precious moments irrevocably while the public, unaware of these circumstances, always imputes the unfortunate consequences to the error or inaction of the general. I will have another occasion to emphasize this truth when I will recount the siege of Danzig where the lack of supplies held me at all times nailed, so to speak, to the same position. When I wrote my letter to the minister, it was hardly just about provisioning the army, but it will be seen subsequently that it is not in the sole respect of supplies and magazines that Russia found herself to be unprepared in this unexpected war. It will be seen that she lacked, at this end of

---

18 Leo Iashvili (1768–1836), Georgian prince and graduate of the Artillery and Engineer Cadet Corps; he commanded Russian artillery units in 1805–1812 and served as the commander of the main Russian army's artillery in 1813–1814.

THE EVACUATION OF WARSAW 61

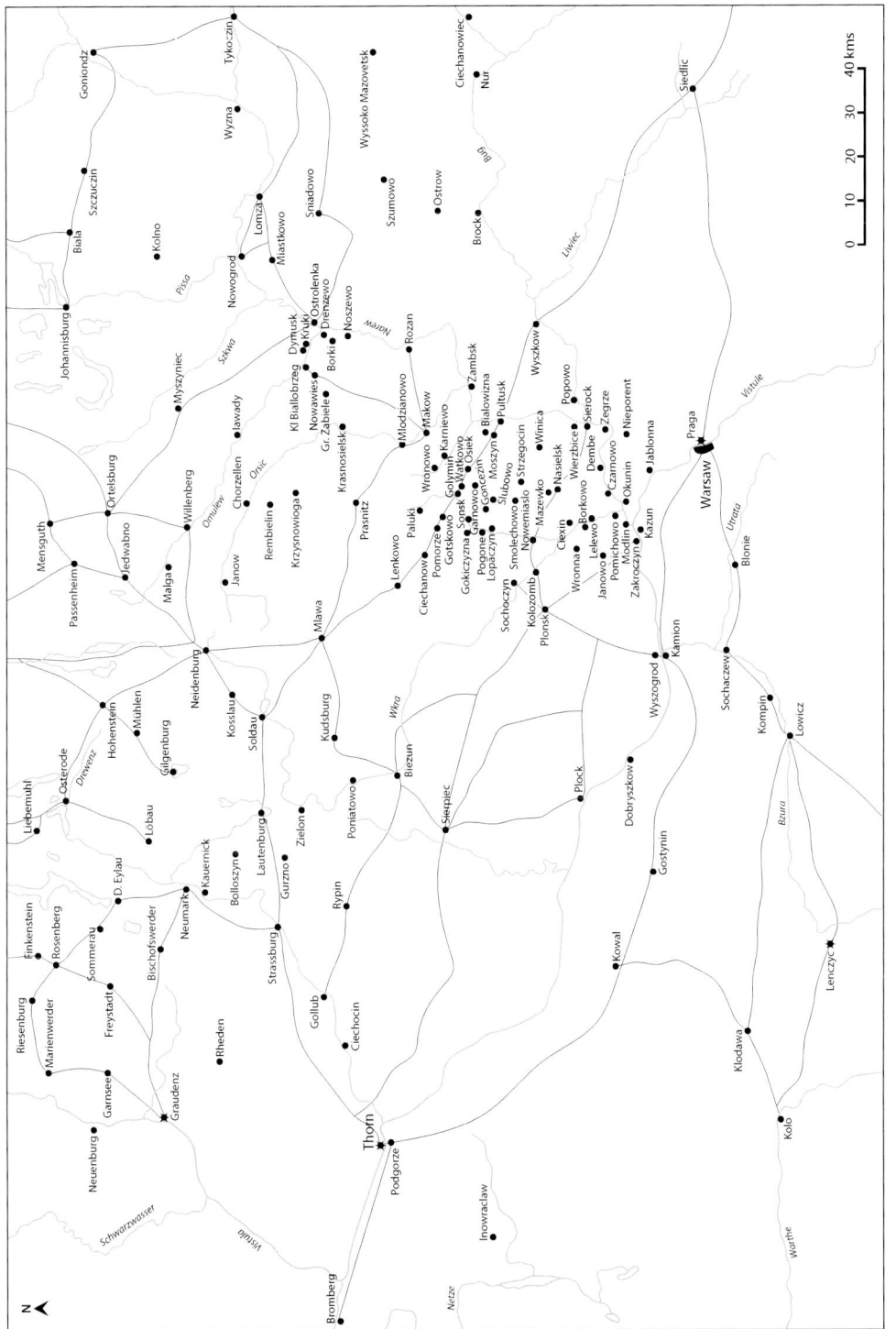

General View of the Theater of War in Poland.

the Empire, all the means that must be prepared in advance and that an active war urgently demands such that a general can act vigorously in his operations.[19]

At the end of my letter I attempted to fix the minister's attention on the critical state of the forces that we had to oppose the torrent [Napoleon] that was threatening us. I insisted in particular on the necessity of taking, in a timely fashion, the measures that would render us capable of a vigorous resistance. The situation was all the more urgent as all of the reports assured us that the forces of the French army, that was moving against us quickly, greatly surpassed not only those that were placed at my disposition, but even those that we would be able to assemble in the nearest future. Determined by these circumstances, the government addressed the nation, which acted with the greatest haste, and even with enthusiasm, to raise 612,000 militiamen, not to mention the numerous donations individuals offered in cash, horses, wheat, arms, etc., for the defence of the fatherland. In the manifesto published in St Petersburg, you will find exposed the manner in which this militia *levée* was conducted and how these troops were distributed in the various provinces of the Empire. Subsequently, it was found that this number was too high and, in dismissing a part of the *levée* already raised, the militia force was reduced to 215,000 men that the nation actually furnished. Yet the great distances of the empire hindered the timely arrival of these troops to the army.

On 31 October/12 November, I arrived at Pultusk with my headquarters; my first care was that of searching for the means to provision the army. Not finding a magazine anywhere, having no means to procure one, no wagons attached to the army to transport supplies, the roads additionally being so bad as to be impassable, the peasants' horses already either worn out or too weak to carry the necessary load, I received daily complaints about the lack of supplies from which various units were suffering and that the regiments found it necessary to send troops into villages to take the necessary supplies by force.[20] In this extreme difficulty, I addressed myself to the governor of Warsaw, the baron de Köhler, asking him to send me the necessary supplies from the Warsaw magazines or from the area, if only for the division that was occupying Praga and its environs; but his response was that he found

---

19   Throughout the 1806–1807 campaign, Bennigsen had been criticized for the mismanagement of military funds. One participant lamented his 'poor management of subordinates and other malpractices' which left the army poorly supplied. In June 1807 one senior Russian diplomat told Dowager Empress Maria Fedorovna about meeting officers who accused Bennigsen of 'making a fortune at the expense of the army coffers' by engaging in fraudulent transactions with suppliers. One officer 'could not understand how Bennigsen could enjoy such a high opinion in the capital when he was perceived so differently in the army where everyone found him weak and lacking energy in commanding.' A. Kurakin to Dowager Empress Maria Fedorovna, 10/22 June 1807, in *Russkii arkhiv* (1869), pp.178-179. Writing in his diary, General Fabian von der Osten-Sacken scathingly noted that 'the Jews are plundering our army; they ruin the local population and leave our troops in complete misery and hardship. Bennigsen protects them as if they were his own children. His actions only raise suspicions that he shares in their profits.' 'Iz zapisok fel'dmarshal Sakena' in *Russkii arkhiv* (1900), p.168 (hereafter cited as Osten-Sacken, *Diary*).
20   Mikhail Petrov, serving in the Yeletskii Musketeer Regiment, recalled 'extreme circumstances' that he and his comrades experienced as they awaited 'deliveries of provisions and other necessities from the Jewish suppliers.' Mikhail Petrov, 'Rasskazy sluzhivshego v 1-m egerskom polku polkovnika Mikhaila Petrova o voennoi sluzhbe i zhizni svoei i trekh rodnykh brat'ev ego, zachavsheisya s 1789 goda,' in F. Petrov, A. Afanasyev, et al. (eds), *1812 god. Vospominaniya voinov russkoi armii*, (Moscow: Mysl', 1991), p.142.

himself unable to acquiesce to my request and that all that he would be able to do would be to supply at most for one or two days the sole division of General Siedmioraczki. I sent the original letter to the minister, M. de Budberg, in Petersburg, depicting the quandary in which the army found itself and praying he could work toward the means by which we could escape this critical state.

You see therefore, General, that even the aid of provisions in an allied country, for which we going to fight, was entirely lacking. As of my arrival in Warsaw, I offered to send out large detachments to collect as much as possible the considerable magazines that were in several places not far from Warsaw, on the left bank of the Vistula, before the arrival of the enemy; but this proposition was evaded on the pretext that one could not consent to it without the express permission of the King, and yet there was not enough time to wait for a response from His Majesty, a response that certainly would not have been in the negative. In this way, all of these magazines fell into the hands of the French and augmented our suffering. The bad intentions of the officials in charge of these magazines revealed themselves again even more so at Plock, where they hid from General Barclay de Tolly the amount of provisions that was actually there, at a moment when it was very difficult to supply his troops, and it was only when we were about to quit the Vistula that they opened the magazine and we found such a great amount of provisions that we could not transport them all for lack of time and wagons. In the end, our predicament regarding provisions grew daily in an allied country, a country abundant enough in every kind of supplies.

In an interview that I had with the Prince de Neuchâtel,[21] during the peace negotiations at Tilsit, he said to me: 'We enjoyed fifty percent greater advantages in this war because for us it was a war of invasion and permitted us to make requisitions in all of the conquered states.' I felt the weight of this truth throughout the war.

On 4/16 November, I went to Warsaw to get in touch with the military governor of this town, the baron de Köhler. He greatly feared an uprising by the inhabitants of Warsaw, which contained 60,000 souls and which one could already regard as the heart of insurrection, as soon as the French made themselves the masters.[22] We agreed to remove all military munitions from the city to the Vistula, then to the Bug and then the Narew for use by the Russian army. We still found in the shops of the merchants from Danzig lead and musket balls [dragé] in large-enough quantities; I commandeered and carried away those as well. The Prussian artillery, which was in Warsaw, was split up amongst different units in the city and deployed in the open squares while the rest was near the bridge over the Vistula; the entire garrison had to be assembled every night in different houses so as to be able to leave the city at the first signal

---

21 Louis-Alexandre Berthier (1753–1815), Prince of Neuchâtel and Valangin, Prince of Wagram, was twice Minister of War of France and served as Napoleon's chief of staff throughout the Napoleonic Wars.
22 Alexander Benckendorff also noted that 'upon arriving in Warsaw, I found the Prussian commandant in a rather strange state of mind. He was fearful of everything and was afraid to leave his furniture, his cellar and did not have the courage to order the evacuation of neither the gunpowder that the Poles coveted nor the weapons that [the Poles] desired to capture and use against us.' Benckendorff, 'Vospominaniya…', p.122.

General Siedmioraczki was ordered to quickly build batteries on the right bank of the Vistula below Praga, the better to defend that passage from the French. A very gracious letter, which His Majesty the King of Prussia wrote to Prince Joseph Poniatowski[23] and by which he charged him to organize a bourgeois guard to maintain order in the city, contributed greatly to the tranquillity that reined during the evacuation by the Prussians and the French occupation. Prince Poniatowski, nephew of the last King of Poland, knew how to profit from the consideration which he was shown and handled it with great prudence and wisdom.

On 5/17 November, the advance guard of Lannes' corps arrived at Podgorze, across from Thorn, where General L'Estocq had his headquarters; the commanding general sent a representative with a letter to the magistrate, by which he summoned the town [officials] and demanded that they quickly deliver all the ships then located on the right bank of the Vistula, as well as several thousand servings of bread and meat, and other supplies; if these were not provided, he threatened to bombard the city and reduce it to ashes. General Lestocq sent the emissary away with the response that he could not permit the city to fulfil the least demand of the French general. The envoy had not even departed from the town when the enemy already fired several explosive rounds.

The next day, all of Marshal Lannes' corps, 18,000 men strong, arrived at Thorn, which was bombarded again, but without effect. The French again tried to convince General L'Estocq to surrender the town; he rejected all these propositions with dignity and firmness. There were even discussions between General L'Estocq and General Victor,[24] and later with Marshal Lannes on a small island in the Vistula; the French generals employed all of their eloquence to encourage L'Estocq to withdraw his troops from the town and from the Vistula, but he remained firm in the resolution to defend his position. The generals therefore parted ways and Marshal Lannes subsequently bombarded the town again; the effect was of no consequence. Meanwhile, the enemy cut down trees and transported ships from the Brahe to the Vistula, for the construction of a bridge. L'Estocq devised a plan to take as many as possible of these boats from the enemy. Bülow's battalion of fusiliers acquitted itself well in this task, taking and destroying 26 boats. Fatigued by L'Estocq's resistance, the French gave up on their plans to cross the Vistula in the environs of Thorn and continued their march on Warsaw along the left bank of the river. Shortly after the departure of Marshal Lannes' corps, that of Marshal Augereau passed by the same road near Thorn; at this time, the town was again bombarded, however weakly.

On 6/18 November, I returned to Pultusk, where I received a letter from His Majesty the King of Prussia from Osterode, dated 10/22 November, in which His Majesty deigned to

---

23 Prince Józef Antoni Poniatowski (1763–1813) was a Polish general, minister of war and army commander who began his military career in the Austrian army but later transferred to the Polish army at the request of his uncle, King Stanislaus Augustus. A talented and intelligent commander, Poniatowski took part in the Polish–Russian War of 1792 and the Kościuszko Uprising in 1794 but withdrew into private life after the Third Partition of Poland. He returned to politics in the autumn of 1806 when the Prussian king Frederick William III asked him to assume the governorship of Warsaw and form the city's municipal guard and citizen militia forces. Poniatowski later rallied to the French and loyally served Napoleon until 1813 when he perished during the Battle of Leipzig.
24 Claude Victor-Perrin (1764–1841), French military commander, future marshal of the Empire.

inform me that General Duroc[25] had reached him on behalf of Emperor Napoleon, with propositions for an armistice, but the conditions were of such a nature that His Majesty was not certain if he should consent, and as for the rest, it was withheld from me until the King could personally convey them to me. Duroc had to return the next day to his master. The King added that he thought it his duty to inform me immediately of these circumstances, so that, supposing that in the wake of this refusal, the enemy could quicken his march, I could take the time to take the necessary measures. General Duroc left Osterode on 11/23 November, and the King arrived at my headquarters in Pultusk the following day. The conditions of the armistice that Duroc had proposed were that the King yield all fortresses still occupied by Prussian troops on the Oder and the Vistula until the peace, the foundations of which were not mentioned; that he abandon his alliance with Russia; that he close his ports to the English; and that he arranged that Russia also, whether she liked it or not, close her ports to the navigation and commerce of Great Britain.

In your last letter, General, you judged, as a true soldier and as the person whose wisdom I value, my decision to not defend the passage of the Vistula. Let me forgo all the criticism that has already been voiced; it would be useless to refute it all here. The temerity to judge with haste and without understanding the [true] causes of things, about which many do not even possess basic knowledge, is, alas, all too common and we should not be surprised to hear mistaken opinions voiced all around us. If originating from a soldier, such opinions sometimes can be trusted, but even then, in the eyes of an enlightened man, such opinions prove only that person's ignorance, which, on occasion, is made worse by the fact that these opinions are expressed in bad faith. But if these views belong to a lay person, one cannot but laugh at them, for it is the best reaction that one can have in such circumstances. It is sufficient to remember that the war was barely over when there appeared countless essays, accounts, even entire histories of this campaign, all testifying to the fact that their authors were simply determined to be the first to comment on this subject but had no intention to speak the truth or carefully examine the circumstances that caused and shaped these events.

A soldier, who wishes to closely examine, with map in hand, the respective positions of the two armies, will find only one development that special considerations rendered inescapable. As I have already stated, the *corps d'armée* under my orders was then only 60,000 men strong, including non-combatants; that of the Prussians, under the orders of Lieutenant General L'Estocq, counted just 10,000 men. The course of the Vistula, from the Austrian frontier to Graudenz, extends over a distance of about 45 German *lieues* [~338 kilometres]. Would I not have committed an inexcusable fault, if I had risked scattering my forces to defend the passage of this river against an army twice as strong, and still on such an extended line, even if one wished to suppose that the fortresses of Graudenz and Danzig defended the lower Vistula? Observe that neither General Buxhöwden nor General Essen had arrived at their destinations with their corps. The French army, so numerically superior and so favoured by the inhabitants of the country, had already arrived in Warsaw in force and could only have the goal of forcing the passage of the Vistula, scoring a victory between

---

25 Géraud Christophe Michel Duroc (1772–1813), French general and diplomat, known for his close friendship with Napoleon Bonaparte, who appointed him as the first Grand Marshal of the Palace and the head of the Emperor's military household.

this river and the Narew, then inciting an insurrection of the previously Polish provinces and obliging the army of General Michelson to depart from the Ottoman domain.

Add to this that in defending the Vistula I would have had to occupy in force the principal points, where the enemy would have tried to effect the passage and especially those that the enemy was already probing; the latter being principally Warsaw and Thorn but the French prepared at the same time the necessary wood for the construction of a bridge on the Netze, and could deliver this [bridging] material to the Vistula, where they could move them up or downstream depending on where they needed to construct the crossing. In defending these two points, separated by some 30 *milles* [58 kilometres], I risked not having sufficient forces to oppose the French crossing at any point between Thorn and Warsaw. In order to effect it, the French only needed three days; two for the construction of the bridge and one for the passage. They would not have had a great deal of trouble hiding from me for 48 hours the march of their troops either from Warsaw, or from Thorn, or from some other place already occupied by them. Continuing to threaten both Warsaw and Thorn, they could have gained another day or two and not only built a bridge, but have made one or two marches, without me being able to take the necessary measures to defend against a passage. I was therefore exposed to the danger of my army being cut in half and suffering a decisive defeat. Moreover, this passage could be easily forced at Warsaw, across from Praga, under the protection of several heavy-calibre batteries; I therefore had to retain a large force concentrated on this bank.

Everything I have just said is without doubt more than enough for me to have renounced the defence of the Vistula, but there was also another factor that always had to enter into my consideration. The events that occurred at Ulm [in October 1805] were too fresh to escape my memory: the left wing of the Austrians having rested on the regions of Anspach and Beyreuth, it was thought perfectly secure, while the French, far from respecting this neutral country, crossed it and in turning the left wing of the Austrians managed to destroy it, which gave rise to the such unexpected results.[26] Here, my left wing was resting on Galicia. Should I not have feared that the French, if I stretched out too far on my right, would traverse Galicia to turn my left wing? Should I not have taken measures against this eventuality that could have ruined everything? Look at the map and look at the open path the French would have had and say what must have happened. No help would have been able to reach me; all available forces would had been obliged to rush to the defence of our own country. If therefore I needed to preserve the principal part of my forces at the extremity of my left wing, how could I stretch myself on my right and defend so enormous a distance as was discussed above?

It was during the King's stay at Pultusk that His Majesty gave me the overall command of his troops, at the head of which he replaced General of cavalry Count Kalkreuth with Lieutenant General L'Estocq, a soldier of the greatest merit, who, in the preceding wars, had already served with brilliant distinction. In this war, having always commanded a separate corps, composed of Prussian and Russian troops, he managed to achieve the greatest reputation. I must further add that L'Estocq, by noble and just conduct, knew above all how to gain the confidence of the Russian troops, such that all of those who found themselves under

---

26   The Austrian army was forced to surrender at Ulm in late October 1805.

his orders felt honoured and still speak of this brave general with the greatest attachment and with gratitude. The King informed me that he had sent Major de Goltz to Silesia with orders to form a corps that would be composed of the troops that were still in fortresses, of men who, dispersed after the various engagements, had gone to that province, and of new recruits being raised there. This corps, which could have retreated into the fortresses and constituted a considerable force, certainly would have been able to create some powerful diversions, which would have forced the French to divert considerable bodies of troops. Yet this did not happen and I do not know who prevented the execution of this wisely conceived plan. We had assembled so few forces that the Bavarian corps, which went to Silesia, beat them, and forced the rest to seek refuge in Bohemia. The majority of fortresses gave themselves up one after the other; on 1 December, the enemy began to weakly bombard Glogau and the very next day, the fortress had surrendered. Breslau fell on 6 January, after a defence of just four weeks. On 10 January, the French arrived before Schweidnitz; this fortress only held out until the 16th, when it also capitulated. I will speak to you at the appropriate time about the events that took place in Silesia. His Majesty, after having conferred with me about future operations, left Pultusk on 14/26 November for Osterode.

The Prussian troops were already in the positions that I indicated above; the entirety, excepting the garrisons in various fortresses and those still in Warsaw, consisted of six battalions of fusiliers, eight regiments of regular [line] infantry, 50 squadrons, and nine battalions of artillery. The combined army remained for some time in these positions. General Barclay de Tolly had several parties of Cossacks swim across the Vistula; they ran into some scraps [petites affaires] that all ended up well enough for them and each time they brought back prisoners, which included as many officers as soldiers, from whom we learned that Prince Murat, with a portion of the [French] cavalry reserve, and Marshals Davout and Lannes, with their corps, were marching on Warsaw. We then learned that Davout's headquarters had arrived on 9 November (new style) in Posen and that he had continued, on 16 November, his march to Warsaw.

Colonel Yurkovskii also sent us several prisoners taken in skirmishes at the advance posts. On 12/24 November, the French arrived at Sochaczew and the detachment under his orders was obliged to retreat to Blonie, where on the 13/25 November there was another advance-post skirmish, which cost about 10 men on both sides, upon which Colonel Yurkovskii retreated to Warsaw. This city was evacuated on 14/26 November by the Prussian troops in the greatest order and the bridge over the Vistula was burned. On 15/27 November, a detachment of French cavalry entered Warsaw. On this occasion the inhabitants were peaceful, which one must attribute, as I said before, to the wise dispositions of Prince Poniatowski. General Siedmioraczki had already received the order to hold fast at Praga and defend the passage of the Vistula there. The Prussian garrison that left Warsaw was still 4,000 men strong; but as the regiments that composed it were made up of Poles, the majority deserted in Galicia, as soon as they arrived on the Bug, which formed the frontier between Austria and Prussia in this area.

At first I did nothing to change my position and I would have been able to hold there some time longer if Siedmioraczki, to whom I had confided the left wing of my position and at the same time the defence of the passage of the Vistula at Praga, the suburbs of Warsaw, had not suddenly left this position on 19 November/1 December against my precise orders; he retreated on the incorrect understanding that the French were already passing through Galicia to turn his flank. The French in Warsaw were immediately informed of it by the inhabitants of Praga, and they did not hesitate to exploit our general's misunderstanding and cross the Vistula. When I received General Siedmioraczki's report at Pultusk, the French had already occupied Praga in force, which I could no longer retake without a useless effusion of blood.[27]

At Warsaw at that time were Prince Murat and the *corps d'armée* of Marshals Davout and Lannes, whose forces greatly outnumbered my own; we also knew that all the other *corps d'armée* were already approaching the Vistula. As a consequence, the passage of the Vistula at the extremity of my left wing became a real possibility, and I had to fear that the French would take advantage of the situation and attack my isolated forces before I had time to concentrate my corps. Therefore, I could no longer hold my position on the Vistula and had identify, without any further loss of time, the means by which we could cover our frontiers in the direction of Brest, where our General Essen had not yet arrived. Hoping that the French had not yet been informed of the approach of General Buxhöwden with his corps and expecting that they would be following me with the intensity they usually put into their operations, I opted to retreat toward the reinforcements that the afore-mentioned general was leading. To this effect, I directed the march of different detachments from their cantonments, on 20 November/2 December, to Rozan and from there to Ostrolenka, where I hoped General Buxhöwden could join me with at least a portion of his corps; I planned on luring the enemy to the plains in the area and where the Prussian corps under the orders of General L'Estocq was also supposed to go. But this strategy did not succeed.

On 24 November/6 December I received the news that the enemy was pushing no further and that the French had contented themselves by fortifying the bridge at Praga with works on which they employed a certain number of local inhabitants.[28] I therefore resolved to

---

27 Alexey Yermolov, who participated in this campaign and went on to make a distinguished career in the Russian army, commented that 'General Siedmioraczki belonged to a group known as the Gatchina officers and he had learned his art under Kannabich, who taught the kind of tactics someone shrewdly described as the science of rolling up your coat.' Siedmioraczki, argued Yermolov, should have either evacuated the vast supply stores or, 'if there was no time, set them alight to deny the enemy their use. However, he did not consider himself authorized to act and had awaited specific instructions.' Alexander Mikaberidze (trans. & ed.), *The Czar's General: The Memoirs of a Russian General of the Napoleonic Wars* (Welwyn Garden City: Ravenhall Books, 2005), p.65.
28 Napoleon learned of the Russian retreat on 5 December and urged his corps commanders to reach the Vistula River. Assuming that the Russians would continue to fall back, Napoleon directed 6th Corps to Thorn and ordered 3rd Corps to seize Sierock (north of Warsaw), where it would control the confluence of the Narew and Vistula Rivers and thus safeguard the northern approaches to Warsaw. He sent 7th Corps to Zakroczin and Wyszogrod while tasking 5th Corps with occupying Warsaw and its suburbs. Surprised that his forces encountered only modest resistance while crossing the Vistula, the emperor sent letters to his marshals explaining his operational concept in the event of a Russian counteroffensive. If the Russians counterattacked along the Pultusk–Sierock route, 5th and 7th Corps would maintain positions around Zakroczin and support 3rd Corps as it conducted a holding action near Sierock, where Davout would 'defend with all his strength a bridgehead on the Narew.' Believing that 3rd Corps would halt the Russian advance near Sierock, Napoleon planned to move 5th and 7th Corps in a flanking maneuver against the Russian right flank while Murat would sweep behind the enemy lines with all of the army's cavalry. Should the Russians move north and threaten Ney's 6th Corps, the emperor instructed the marshal to avoid a pitched battle, move across the Vistula, and hold his ground long enough to allow the Grande Armée's right flank (three army corps strong) to

return to Pultusk at once. On the map you will see the position my corps took in two lines in tight cantonments [cantonments serrés], so that the troops could be concentrated promptly within 24 hours near Pultusk, on the right bank of the Narew. A reserve of 12 battalions was placed along the river near Pultusk.

Lieutenant General Count Ostermann, to whom I had given command of the left wing of the army, in place of General Siedmioraczki, occupied the environs of Sierock and Czarnowo to defend the passage of the Wkra River, where it flows into the Narew, and to stop the enemy, for the time that was necessary to concentrate the army at Pultusk.

General Barclay de Tolly was sent to Nowe Miasto with the advance guard to occupy positions on the Wkra River; his advance posts connected on his left with those of General Count Ostermann and on his right with those of General L'Estocq, whom I had ordered to retreat from Thorn to Strassburg on the Drewenz River. This general arrived with his headquarters on 24 November/6 December at Gollub and the next day at Strassburg. Renouncing the defence of the Vistula, I could no longer hold Thorn; I had to save the troops, and those that I would have left there for its defence would have been irrevocably lost, as this place was not sufficiently fortified for a garrison to hold for long.

On 25 November/7 December, Colonel Roussanov of the Aleksandriiskii Hussar Regiment was sent with his squadron and a company of the 4th Jager Regiment under the orders of Captain Koulich to reconnoitre the enemy positions from Pomichowo via Modlin up to Zakroczyn. On his return, he found that the enemy had cut off the road to him with infantry. He decided to break through and charged with infantry, personally leading the attack with a sabre in his hand. He succeeded without too many losses; the French managed to surround the company of jagers and it could not escape. In this critical situation, Captain Koulich did not lose his cool; He [rallied his men] and pushed back the French threatening his front, then took two small batteries and forced the enemy to fall back to the Vistula, where the French jumped into boats to escape but lost more men from the fire of our jagers. The enemy, meanwhile, had occupied the road from Pomichowo, a place where our jager company had to recross. Captain Koulich was informed of it. This enterprising officer, having already fought from dawn to three o'clock that afternoon and seeing that he only had a few cartridges remaining, decided to retreat through the woods. He passed through the village of Wronna and fortunately reached Kolozomb, where he crossed the Wkra River and joined General Dorokhov's detachment. In this affair, which brought great honour to Captain Koulich, we only lost 26 men killed, wounded, or missing. Due to the report I made on the conduct of this officer, the Emperor, sent him the Order of Vladimir (4th class), while the Prussian king granted him the Prussian Order Pour le Mérite. Sadly, this brave officer was never able to enjoy these distinguished decorations, as he had the misfortune of being killed at the battle of Czarnowo, where he once again distinguished himself.

On 29 November/11 December, Colonel Grekov XVIII with his regiment of Cossacks went on reconnaissance to Zakroczyn, where he found an enemy detachment waiting in ambush to fall unexpectedly on General Dorokhov's detachment. Grekov surprised the enemy, killed a few men, captured one officer and 15 *chasseurs à cheval,* and dispersed the rest.

---

make a flanking maneuver against the Russian left. For Napoleon's instructions, see *Correspondance de Napoleon I*, Nos 11422 and 11430, vol.14, pp.55–56, 61–62.

6

Czarnowo and Pultusk[1]

About eight days after my return to Pultusk, General Buxhöwden deployed his corps in the environs of Wyssoko-Mazovetsk, where he established his headquarters. I dispatched Lieutenant General Count Tolstoy[2] to instruct him to use one of his divisions to relieve my troops along the left bank of the Narew, to occupy the distance on the Bug from the Austrian frontier to the mouth of the Narew, so that I could concentrate my four divisions entirely on the right bank of the Narew. Moreover, it was agreed that Buxhöwden would bring up his three other divisions close enough to the left bank to be able, if needed, to rejoin me at Pultusk within two marches. In this manner we were strong enough to accept battle, which the enemy, consistent with the information that we had received, would not be long in offering with all of his forces. L'Estocq made a few attempts to retake Thorn, but, upon learning that the enemy had already occupied this town with considerable forces, he wisely renounced his intention and contented himself with establishing a chain of advance posts from Bischofswerder to Strassburg, the left wing of which was connected to the Russian right flank; at the same time he occupied the area between Danzig and Bischofswerder with a *corps volant* [flying detachment]. Soon after we learned that Emperor Napoleon had arrived at Posen on 15/27 November, and thereafter expected every day to receive the news of his arrival to Warsaw, which, we anticipated, would mark that start of great military events.[3]

---

1 Letter written in February 1808.
2 Peter Tolstoy (1769–1844) was an experienced officer and veteran of the Russo-Swedish and Russo-Polish Wars, as well as the Russian campaign in Italy and Switzerland. In 1805, Tolstoy commanded an expeditionary corps sent to Hanover. Benckendorff recalled that in late 1806 'Count Tolstoy joined the army in capacity of a general for special assignments [general po osobym porucheniyam] and the Emperor's delegate [doverennoe litso].' Benckendorff, 'Vospominaniya…', p.123.
3 On entering Poland, Napoleon's central objective was to occupy a position on the Vistula with suitable bridgeheads at Thorn and Warsaw from which he could launch a spring offensive. Thus ensconced, he could rest his weary army, reduce the Prussian fortresses in his rear, and rally the restive Poles to his side. In total, the emperor could count on more than 120,000 men in six corps, the reserve cavalry (now split into two formations), and his elite Guard. Additional forces, mainly from his German allies of the Confederation of the Rhine, conducted rear-area duties such as blockading and besieging Prussian fortresses. Given the absence of intelligence regarding Russian movements and the surprising ease with which the French had seized the crossings over the Vistula, Napoleon soon continued to press forward. For details see Paul-Jean Foucart, *Campagne de Pologne. Pultusk et Golymin* (Paris: L. Militaire Berger-Levrault, 1882), vol.1, pp.241–438.

Meanwhile, I received a writ from the Emperor, my master, in which he notified me that the [military] necessity compelled him to combine the two *corps d'armée*, of which one was confided to me and the other to General Buxhöwden, into a single force, more formidable in its unity and more capable of presenting a barrier to the enemy's progress, and to appoint Field Marshal Count Kamensky to lead forces against the French. This choice had been motivated by the desire and by the virtually unanimous voice of the public and the nation. The long and distinguished service that Count Kamensky had rendered to his sovereigns and his nation gained him this confidence, the most beautiful recompense that a general can enjoy at the end of his career. Kamensky was a colonel [at the start of] the Seven Years War and served as a volunteer in the French army during the campaign of 1759. In the wars against the Turks, during the reign of [Empress] Catherine II, he commanded detached corps with distinction. He combined with this great experience all of the knowledge and education necessary for a good general. In his youth he had often been enjoined to serve the functions of a quartermaster-general and he later studied thoroughly the sciences relative to that role. The Empire would certainly have benefited from the same good and distinguished service that this man had once given, if only his advanced age, his infirmities and the diverse ailments that he suffered had allowed him to exercise that level of activity that is indispensable in a commanding general so that he is able to observe with his own eyes the enemy's movements and to judge those of his own troops.[4]

---

4 Faddei (Jan Tadeusz) Bulgarin, the veteran of the 1806–1807 campaign and later a literary figure, left an interesting portrait of Kamensky: 'He undoubtedly was a learned man and a skilled tactician. The great Suvorov, with whom Kamensky had an eternal and implacable enmity, used to say: "Kamensky knows tactics, but I know the practice." Kamensky's personal courage bordered on insanity and even his enemies confirmed the truth of his words when he stated that he would be glad to know how it feels to fear death! His mind was deep and insightful, but all his laudable qualities were overshadowed by his extraordinary temper and intemperance in anger that drove him to cruelty, extraordinary pride, recklessness, perversity, and impatience in dealing with people, whom he frequently insulted for no reason. Neither comrades nor subordinates liked Kamensky, and all feared meeting him. During my last year at the [Cadet Corps] I met [Kamensky] on several occasions. He came to observe us during training and recreation, and talked, joked, and even played with the cadets. He was of rather small stature, lean and covered with wrinkles; he wore a Prussian style uniform, with which he was dismissed by Emperor Paul I. Unusually thick and heavy eyebrows, with eyes shining like burning coals underneath them, added certain ferocity to his face. He was abrupt in his conversation and had rather quaint manners, whether because he was imitating his archenemy, Suvorov, or by nature; despite his advanced age, he seemed vigorous and agile in all his movements. What made the Emperor appoint him commander-in-chief? Everyone was lost guessing, but the more experienced people were saying that it was done to excite the national spirit, to revive the memories of the glorious time of Catherine the Great, which was sacred to the people. It was in this spirit that the great [poet Gregory] Derzhavin praised the appointment of Kamensky, whom he described in his verses as "the sword bequeathed [to us] by Catherine." So one can say that Kamensky was employed in the same way that the Turks use the banner of [the Prophet] Muhammad – just for its appearance… could Kamensky, a 78-year-old man who had never commanded armies and who earned his reputation commanding small detachments during wars against the unlearned Orientals, resist the genius of Napoleon? At that time I heard from many that, due to his intensity of character and impatience, Kamensky was unsuitable to the post of commander-in-chief, for which one of the most important qualities must be unshakable composure.' *Vospominaniya Faddeya Bulgarina* (St Petersburg: M. Olkhin, 1847) part 3, pp.7–17.

Upon learning that our Field Marshal had arrived in Lithuania, I sent him a very detailed report on the state of my *corps d'armée*, accompanied by a map on which I marked precisely the position of my troops and by an exact analysis of the available intelligence about the position of the different French corps as well as the latest news concerning the enemy's intentions. The Field Marshal arrived at Pultusk on 7/19 December; two days later we received news that Napoleon had arrived during the night of the 19th (new style) in Warsaw. Lieutenant General Count Ostermann reported at the same time that the enemy was reinforcing himself considerably against our left wing, across from him; that the French were preparing the necessary materials for the construction of a bridge on the Bug, and that using a small island at the junction of the Wkra and Bug Rivers, at a small distance from the village of Czarnowo, the enemy could easily organize a river crossing.[5] In consequence we could expect, at any moment, to see our left wing driven back and Count Ostermann obliged to retreat to Pultusk, toward the position I had prepared for battle.

However, the Field Marshal did not approve of my position or the arrangements I had made. The day after his arrival, he dispatched 12 battalions that I had placed in reserve on the Narew to Nowe Miasto, on the Wkra River, to join there the advance guard. He then ordered me to go there myself so as to take command of these troops. His intention was to cross with a strong corps the Wkra River, at Nowe Miasto, to force the enemy to re-cross the Vistula at Plock and then to march from there to Graudenz, which the French had already blockaded. On 10/22 December, as I prepared to leave for Nowe Miasto, I went to the Field Marshal's quarters to request his final orders, when a report arrived from Lieutenant General Count Ostermann that the small island, of which I already made mention, had been attacked and taken by Marshal Davout's corps on 7/19 December and that it was already occupied by considerable forces; that the enemy was working on batteries, under the protection of which the passage of the small river, which still separated us from the enemy, would

---

Discussing Kamensky's appointment to lead the army, Alexander Benckendorff also noted that 'the army was thrilled [v vostorge] by this choice, even though it did not fully understand what was behind it. The field marshal was better known only by the cruelties that he had done in Moldavia, Poland, and Finland. But he was always known as firm and harsh man, and such a reputation, deemed to be a sign of rigour and strength of character, compelled [many] to consider him as the only individual who was capable of standing up to Napoleon and ensure the-much needed unity of the army that included generals envious of each other, young officers, and barely experienced [neobstrelyannykh] soldiers.' Robert Wilson, the British commissioner to the Russian army, commented, in December 1806, that 'General Kamensky who commands the Russians, is a very distinguished officer; and active, notwithstanding that he is seventy-two years of age. He affects to imitate [Alexander] Suvorov, and plays the antics of a semi-savage; but he has the confidence and regard of officers and men.' Benckendorff, 'Vospominaniya …', pp.124–125.

5 By mid-December, Napoleon deployed the Grande Armée along a one hundred mile frontline extending from Strasburg to Warsaw. With 1st Corps and the Guard remaining at Thorn, Napoleon split the rest of the army into two groups: the right wing consisted of Augereau's 7th Corps at Zakroczin, Davout's 3rd Corps near Nowy Dwor at the confluence of the Narew and the Vistula, and Lannes' 5th Corps at Warsaw; the left wing included Ney's 6th Corps at Strasburg and Marshal Nicolas Jean-de-Dieu Soult's 4th Corps stretched between Rippin and Dobrzyn. Murat's cavalry maintained communication between the two wings. The French deployment underscores the simple yet effective nature of Napoleon's operations. If the Russians decided to move toward Warsaw, 3rd and 5th Corps, supported by 7th Corps, would pin them down while the rest of the army attacked from the northwest; if the enemy chose a northern route toward Thorn (via Soldau/Strasburg), 4th and 6th Corps would pin them down while the right wing attacked from the south. For analysis see Foucart, *Campagne de Pologne*, vol.1, pp.342–457.

by all appearances be forced the next night and that then it would be impossible to hold against the considerable forces facing him.

Tolstoy reported at the same time that, according to the unanimous testimony of prisoners, Napoleon himself was present at the site and that there had been heard on various occasions cries of '*Vive l'Empereur!*' Marshal Soult with his corps had already crossed the Vistula near Wyszogrod and with him a portion of the *réserve de cavalerie* under the *grand-duc de Berg* [Marshal Murat]. Marshal Lannes's corps had crossed the Vistula at Warsaw and was following Marshal Davout's corps on the road to Pultusk, also with a portion of the *cavalerie de réserve*. The *corps* of Marshals Ney and Bernadotte had crossed the Vistula at Thorn; the former was at Rypin and the latter – on the extreme left wing of the French army.

Marshal Jean-Baptiste Bernadotte.
(Courtesy of James Smith Noel Collection)

Major General Count [Peter] de Pahlen, who maintained with his hussar regiment,[6] the chain of our advance posts over a certain distance in front of our right wing on the Wkra River, reported that the enemy, reinforced, was getting closer to him too. At the same time, we received a warning from Warsaw, which reached us via Galicia, that the enemy would attack us on 12/24 December at all points to force the passage of the Wkra.[7]

Our Field Marshal, either because he did not believe all of these reports, or because he supposed that the enemy would halt the movement that he seemed to be making on our right, did not stop me at Pultusk. He not only changed nothing about his dispositions, but

---

6   Pahlen served as the chef of the Sumskii Hussar Regiment.
7   In worsening winter weather, the Grande Armée marched deeper into Poland in late December. This advance resulted in two bloody yet inconclusive engagements as the French, slogging north between the Wkra and the Narew, intersected with the Russians retreating east. With no time to establish a reliable spy network, and cavalry reconnaissance hampered by bad roads and Cossack patrols, Napoleon had misread the situation and assumed that the Russian main body was withdrawing north through Golymin. In fact, Bennigsen and the bulk of his command were intending to move east to Pultusk, while French pressure forced only a disparate collection of Russian detachments to retreat via Golymin.

moreover he reinforced the advance guard with some troops from the first line and all of the infantry from the right wing of the second line. The next day, the 11th/23rd, he sent the order to Lieutenant General Prince Golitsyn to go with the two cavalry regiments that remained with him to Nowe Miasto.

On the 11th/23rd, I arrived in the morning at Nowe Miasto just as the enemy made a reconnaissance there, which produced a fairly serious skirmish. That same evening our Field Marshal [Kamensky] arrived at Nowe Miasto. All of these troops, which I have mentioned, were moving on our centre and on our right wing, when Napoleon actually attacked Count Ostermann during the night of the 11th/23rd to the 12th/24th and by means of that small island, of which I made mention earlier, forced the passage of the Bug River. As soon as the fighting commenced, Count Ostermann sent us Colonel and *aide de camp* to the Emperor, Uvarov, with a report, in which he explained the absolute impossibility of holding out against the considerable enemy forces that were attacking him. Colonel Uvarov was sent back with orders from the Field Marshal, but *en route* this officer was captured by the enemy. By then, Count Ostermann had already commenced his retreat after a fight of six hours and a beautiful defence that earned him the marks of satisfaction from his sovereign and the admiration of the entire army. As soon as day broke, our Field Marshal travelled in a small carriage to Czarnowo, but about an hour and a half later he returned, on horseback. He had not been able to reach it, finding the enemy already in possession of this location. At the same time, we received reports that our entire line of advance posts had been attacked, and, shortly thereafter, that our principal post, located about four *verstas* [4.3 kilometres] away on the Wkra River to cover Nowe Miasto, had been attacked and taken; the four cannon that were placed in a battery there had been taken and the enemy was advancing quickly and in force. Our Field Marshal decided to join units that were on the march on our right wing and he expressed his trust in me by charging me with the command of the remaining forces.[8]

We had good reason to fear that the enemy might beat us to Pultusk, where there only remained a small detachment, and that we would be cut off from the two divisions that were on the left bank of the Narew. Therefore, I ordered all of the troops of the advance guard to retire on the road to Strzegocin, the town that Kamensky had designated as our concentration point instead of Pultusk. I travelled four *verstas* from there to General Titov, who was, with his brigade, at a village some four *verstas* behind Nowe Miasto, and marched with these troops along the road to Strzegocin. Before leaving, I wrote orders to all of the generals, who had been earlier commanded to advance on our right,

---

8   Benckendorff: 'The Field Marshal moved to Nowe Miasto, where General Bennigsen gathered the larger part of his army [corps] while its forward elements were already in direct contact with the enemy. A report from an outpost deployed in Czarnowo informed Bennigsen that Count Ostermann bravely defended himself and was forced to fall back in the face of superior enemy forces only after a battle that lasted late into the night. The following day the Field Marshal [Kamensky] arrived at Czarnowo, where he was greeted by the rapturous shouts of "hurrah" by a part of Count Osterman's division that, having displayed an unmatched gallantry in action, demonstrated a superb poise in the ranks. Returning to Nowe Miasto in the afternoon, the Field Marshal soon had to leave it and, after a hard fight, the enemy troops occupied this town in the evening. An order was issued instructing General Bennigsen's corps to withdraw and concentrate at Pultusk and take up a position there while General Buxhöwden's corps was to gather at Makow.' Benckendorff, 'Vospominaniya…', pp.124–125.

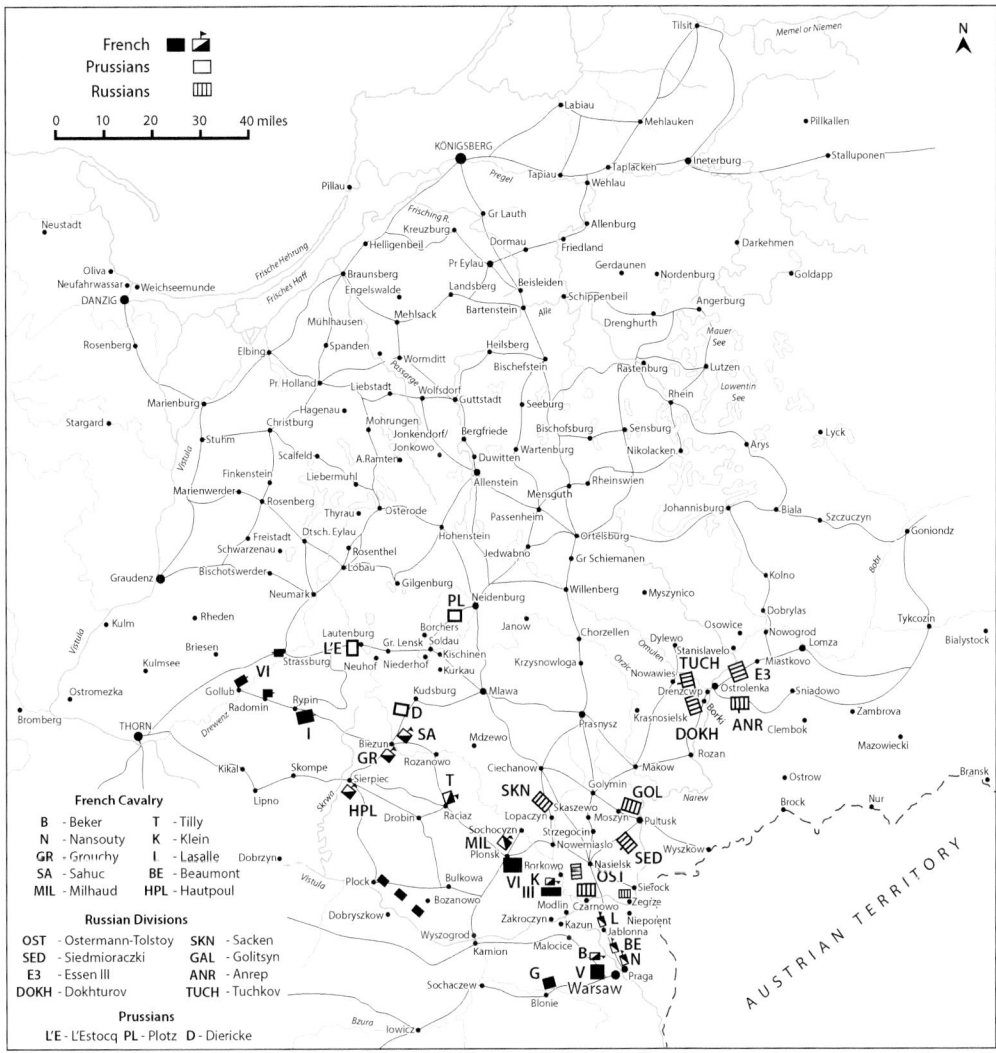

Situation as of late December 1806.

to leave immediately the road on which they were, to proceed on the road to Pultusk and to maintain all possible diligence while marching. At 10 o'clock in the evening, I arrived at Strzegocin, where I found Count Ostermann rallying his retreating corps and Major General Count Lambert with a detachment of cavalry that arrived there at that same time; around one hour after midnight, General Barclay de Tolly arrived with the advance guard from Nowe Miasto and then General Sacken with the right wing of the first line. Lieutenant General Prince Golitsyn – with his two cavalry regiments and various other detachments (in total, 12 battalions, 35 squadrons), and almost all of the Cossacks and a certain number of cannons were no longer able to make it either to Strzegocin or to Pultusk, as the enemy had cut off the road.

My first concern was that of arranging forces that had arrived at Strzegocin in *ordre de bataille* as much as the darkness of the night permitted it. After having rested the troops a little, I had them leave for Pultusk in the following order: General Count Lambert, forming the advance guard with light troops, left at two hours after midnight; at three o'clock, Count Ostermann departed with the troops under his command; an hour later, General Sacken was supposed to leave with some regiments from his division and then General Barclay de Tolly, commanded the rear guard, at five o'clock. Yet, General Sacken did not execute this order as faithfully as did the others;[9] needlessly and contrary to the orders that I had given him, he remained at Strzegocin until six o'clock and thus he prevented General Barclay de Tolly from setting off with the rear guard before daybreak. Because of this loss of time we were obliged to abandon on the roads, which had become impassable due to incessant rains, more cannons than we would have had to leave behind without General Sacken's blunder. The various detachments of the Russian army lost during this withdrawal 52 cannons, which got sunken in the mud so deep that despite all the extreme efforts we employed, it proved impossible to remove them.[10] The enemy was not following us closely and the marching, executed in accordance to these dispositions, remained orderly.

After having given all of the necessary orders for this march, I left to rejoin the advance guard, with which I arrived at nine o'clock in the morning at Pultusk, where fortunately I already found General Baggehufvudt,[11] whose troops occupied the distance from Sierock to Dembe. Upon learning of the retreat of our troops from the Wkra River, he had wisely moved with his detachment to Pultusk and had occupied the heights from which he covered the roads coming from Sierock and Nasielsk.

---

9 This brief comment hides a deeper issue that Bennigsen had with General Fabian von der Osten-Sacken, who loathed him; their relations quickly escalated during this campaign and eventually led to Bennigsen charging Sacken with alleged insubordination. Sacken maintained a diary throughout his service in the Napoleonic Wars. The original, which is presumably lost since Sacken left no direct offspring, was written in German, although Russian and French translations of it had been circulating in private circles in the mid-nineteenth century. A French translation of the diary was at one point owned by the Vorontsov family that allowed excerpts, in a heavily edited form, to be published in a Russian journal in 1900. In the surviving diary excerpts Sacken is, unsurprisingly, critical of Bennigsen's arrangements. He also records difficult conditions that his troops had to fight, including 'the roads so poor that one part of the artillery was stuck in mud [and left behind].' Osten-Sacken, *Diary*, pp.168–172.

10 Discussing conditions of this retreat, Sergei Volkonsky, who served as a lieutenant in the Chevalier Guard regiment, commented, 'Our retreat from Naselsk to Pultusk was incredibly difficult on account of mud: cannon, caissons and supply wagons stuck up to their axles in mud and, as I recall, over 100 guns were abandoned without a fight.' *Zapiski Sergeya Grigorievicha Volkonskago (dekabrista)* (St. Petersburg: Sinodalnaya Tip., 1902), pp.14–15. 'Snow, rain and thaw … we sunk down to our knees … and our shoes would stick in the wet mud,' recalled French soldier Jean-Roch Coignet, in *The Narrative of Captain Coignet, Soldier of the Empire, 1776–1850* (New York: Crowell, 1890), p.138. For the Russian perspective, see Alexander Mikaberidze (ed.), *Russian Eyewitness Accounts of the Campaign of 1807* (London: Frontline Books, 2015), pp.27–108.

11 Karl Gustav von Baggehufvudt (1761–1812), more commonly known as Baggovut/Baggowouth, was a Russian general whose Norwegian ancestors settled in Estonia in the seventeenth century and later found themselves Russian subjects. Born in September 1761, Baggehufvudt began his career in the service of the margrave of Ansbach-Bayeruth before transferring to the Russian army and advancing through the ranks. In 1800, he became a major general and the chef of the 4th Jager Regiment.

Around 11 o'clock, Baggehufvudt informed me that the enemy was advancing against him on the road from Nasielsk and that his advance posts were already engaged. We were later assured that it was General Suchet[12] who had arrived with a division either to reconnoitre Pultusk or to occupy it if we still had not returned there. General Baggehufvudt knew so well how to make the most of terrain that the enemy, despite his superiority in forces, was forced to retreat, as he had had the disadvantage of being unable to bring up his artillery on the impassable roads while Baggehufvudt had already deployed six 6-pounder cannon. The Tatar Light Horse Regiment, under Lieutenant-Colonel Knorring,[13] distinguished itself a great deal on this occasion; it overran an enemy cavalry regiment and took 17 prisoners. The enemy lost more men from our artillery fire as well. Our losses amounted to just two men killed and three wounded. I could not reinforce General Baggehufvudt, as I had only arrived with a handful of troops that barely sufficed to cover the main artillery that was kept near Pultusk. Moreover, I had no information about the size of the enemy force. As our troops arrived, I placed them in the position that I had selected before then. Fortunately for us, the day passed without a serious engagement.

That evening, at 10 o'clock, Field Marshal Kamensky returned to Pultusk.[14] I immediately went to see him and deliver report on everything that had transpired since his departure to

Karl Gustav von Baggehufvudt, commonly known as Baggovut. (State Hermitage Museum)

---

12 Louis-Gabriel Suchet (1770–1826), French general and future Marshal of the Empire. Suchet commanded the 1st Division of the 5th Corps.
13 Karl Bogdanovich von Knorring took command of the Tatar Light Cavalry Regiment on June 24, 1806; he earned the colonel's epaulettes on December 24, 1807.
14 Benckendorff: 'The Field Marshal spent the night at the outposts, despite the dangers of being captured by the enemy's forward detachments. The following day he travelled to Golymin: terrible mud slowed down the movement of our columns, and especially the artillery. Kamensky could see that horses could no longer haul cannon and even the efforts of 300 men were not sufficient to drag everything that got stuck in the mud; during this march we lost more than seventy cannon that had to be abandoned in the mud.' Aleksey Sherbatov, commanding the Kostromskoi Infantry Regiment in Barclay de Tolly's brigade, provides interesting perspective as well: 'Prior to Kamensky's arrival to the headquarters [glavnaia kvartira], the troops had already began to move in accordance with Bennigsen's orders, but

Nowe Miasto. I also shared my opinion that we should consider the appearance of the enemy that day as a reconnaissance rather than an attack, and that we should expect as far more serious attack the following day, probably led by Napoleon himself. Count Kamensky agreed to accept the battle and asked me if everything were ready for it.[15] I responded that I made arrangements to take up positions as troops arrived but a great many of them was still not there, though I expected that they would reach us during the night. Upon hearing this, the Field Marshal wrote, in my presence, to General Buxhöwden, whose one division was at Makow, about two *milles* [15 kilometres][16] from Pultusk, and second, under the orders of General Dokhturov, at Golymin[17] on the right bank of the Narew, and to Generals Essen III and Anrep, who were on the left bank of the Narew, to immediately set in march to help us at Pultusk. These orders were dispatched [at once] and all these troops could have actually arrived in time to participate in the battle that fought the following day. Meanwhile, I returned quite peacefully to the quarters that I had taken near the position where our troops were bivouacked.

Unfortunately, that night the Field Marshal became so ill that he expected not being able to mount a horse to oversee the impending battle in person. Consequently, he felt compelled to change dispositions that he had approved the day before.[18] To this end, about three hours before sunrise, he asked me to see him and gave me a written order in which he ordered me to retire immediately with all of the forces under my command toward our frontiers.[19]

---

     as soon as he arrived at Pultusk, Count Kamensky, as it befits anyone taking over authority and due to his quick temper [zapalchivii] and impulsive [oprometchivii] character, found all of his predecessor's orders erroneous and, without carefully considering circumstances, he began to issue new instructions to the regiments, thereby creating a bigger mess… Napoleon, inspired by his miraculous [chudesnii] victory over the Prussians, advanced rapidly in two columns against us: the lead column under his personal command encountered our army on the fields of Pultusk, where General Bennigsen was already expecting the enemy in battle formation, while the second column, also dispatched to Polustusk, marched via Golymin where it accidentally encountered two detachments [otryad] of our troops, which, under Count Kamensky's orders, wandered [brodili naudachu] in the countryside following unsuccessful clashes with the enemy advance troops and also accidentally joined at Golymin. These two detachments – one under command of General Dokhturov, and another led by Lieutenant-General Prince D. V. Golitsyn, which also included my regiment – observed the enemy movement and sought to stop it in order to prevent the enemy from participating in the battle at Pultusk, which saved our army from a complete defeat.' Benckendorff, 'Vospominaniya…', pp.125–126.

15 Benckendorff: 'The approach of the enemy forces compelled the Field Marshal to proceed to Pultusk. In the evening he passed amidst the bonfires of our bivouacs and the joy which his presence induced among the rank-and-file, seemed to have inspired him to fight and engendered the most alluring aspirations in us.' Benckendorff, 'Vospominaniya…', p.125.

16 Actual distance between Pultusk and Makow Mazowiecki is 21 kilometres.

17 Golymin is located 30 kilometres from Pultusk.

18 Scherbatov: '[On the eve of the battle] Count Kamensky personally went to the advance guard, commanded by Major-General Barclay de Tolly but before reaching it he became disheartened [poteryal golovu] upon encountering our advance troops that were disordered due to strong enemy pressure [natisk] and immediately returned to Pultusk. He was furious, on the verge of madness, telling Bennigsen that there is nothing he could do now to correct the wrongs of his predecessor and therefore he instructed him to operate according to circumstances, while he himself packed up and left for Grodno to supervise new preparations for war.' Aleksey Sherbatov (A. Shiryaeva (ed.), *Moi vospominaniya*, (St. Petersburg: Nestor-Istoria, 2006), p.45.

19 Benckendorff provides interesting details on what transpired in Kamensky's quarters that night. 'At four o'clock in the morning Colonel [Semen] Stavrakov suddenly woke us all up and informed us

Considering how widely our army was scattered, it was easy to foresee the dire consequences that such precipitous retreat would have produced. It would have been tantamount to losing an entire battle. Yet, in confronting the enemy I could at least hope to halt his advance and gain sufficient time for the other troops, that were already cut off from me, to reach the Narew further upstream. I therefore resolved to remain that day still in my position at Pultusk and to accept battle rather than risk the safety of the army and the interests of the state by retreating, the consequences of which could only have been dreadful. I must also state that I remained unaware that orders had been sent to Generals Buxhöwden, Essen III, and Anrep countermanding those of the previous day and commanding them to no longer come to my aid at Pultusk and instead to retreat immediately toward our frontiers. These generals received these orders while marching and not that far from the battlefield; examining the map, you will see that these three divisions could have arrived to support me during the battle [at Pultusk] and [our victory] that day would have invariably decided in our favour the fate of that entire campaign, for despite all these unfortunate circumstances, our troops fought gallantly and withstood the repeated attacks that the enemy launched at diverse points.

---

that the Field Marshal had seemingly lost his mind and was about to leave the army. Count Tolstoy rushed to see Kamensky, and all of us followed him. [We found] the Field Marshal restlessly pacing around the room. Tolstoy asked him whether he had received any news of the enemy. Kamensky answered in the negative but declared that he had no confidence in inexperienced generals and untrained army; that he was, therefore, departing and washing his hands of the whole matter; that he had already issued necessary orders on the retreat of our corps to the Russian border; and, finally, that he had allowed the abandonment of cannon and wagons in order to save the troops. These words struck us like a bolt of lightning; tears streamed down our faces and we could not understand such a sudden change of mind. Count Ostermann and General Bennigsen, who had also been forewarned, tried expressing their objections to the impractical plan [Kamensky] had proposed but the Field Marshal became so furious that he abruptly bid farewell to all of us, rushed to his carriage and left us all dumbfounded by what we had just seen and heard. No one was able to explain what precisely caused such a shameless clouding of the mind and compelled a man, so jealously protective of his own name, to betray his duty and abandon his command after orders had already been issued to fight a battle, in which success was completely assured. This unparalleled event can be considered as one of the greatest turns of good fortune for Napoleon: it seemed that Heaven itself safeguarded his plans and undermined all the virtues of the force that opposed him. The gallantry of our troops, the trust they felt towards their commander-in-chief, his prudent dispositions and especially the outcome of that day served as unequivocal evidence of the defeat that Napoleon would have suffered. The limited amount of artillery that he could commit to this battle, the wretched state of his cavalry and the fine condition of ours – all of this would have assured our complete victory. Pultusk should have marked the limit of Napoleon's military victories and become the triumph of Field Marshal Kamensky.' Benckendorff, 'Vospominaniya...', p.126. In his journal entry for 31 December, Robert Wilson noted that 'Kamensky is truly mad. In the streets of Pultusk he gave too painful evidences of his malady.' *Life of General Sir Robert Wilson*, vol. 2, p.42. Serving as the British chargé d'affaires to the Court of Prussia, George Jackson followed King Frederick William and Queen Louise to Königsberg, where he maintained close relations with many senior Prussian and Russian civil and military officials, who kept him appraised of most recent developments. On 2 January, he recorded in his diary that 'a letter from Buxhöwden, brought here today by a Russian officer, says that Kamensky had gone off *sans dire gare*, that he had ordered Lestocq to retreat to Johannisburg, and that he himself intended gaining the Bug. This has caused as much consternation as displeasure...' *Diaries and Letters of Sir George Jackson, KCH*, edited by Lady Jackson (London: R. Bentley, 1872), vol.2, p.71.

I will refrain from communicating to you the accounts that reached me from the detachments that were separated from me and attacked while they were on the march that same day. Instead, I will limit myself to relating to you the course of the battle of Pultusk and clarifying the great consequences of that memorable day. You will agree that, although the battle was not as bloody as that of Preussich-Eylau, its consequences were no less important for Russia, especially after the events that occurred on the Wkra River and of which I spoke to you. It is certain that, without the changes that took place relative to the measures that I had taken, the battle of Pultusk could have become' much more decisive than it was, as the enemy would have found there seven, rather than four, divisions.

I already told you, General, that I had chosen the position of Pultusk upon my arrival with the army in that region. It was supposed to cover the main road that leads to Ostrolenka, as well as the bridges that I had had built on the Narew River below Pultusk and Zamsk; at the same time it was supposed to assure free communications with General Buxhöwden's corps. From this position I could also move with celerity to protect our frontier wherever it might have been threatened, and I could as easily execute the plan that I had formed before the arrival of our Field Marshal, namely, to move, after a decisive victory near Pultusk, my principal forces toward the lower Vistula, liberate Graudenz and assure direct communications with Danzig. To this end I even made preparations to set up small supply stores at Soldau, Mlawa, Prasnitz, etc., that eventually fell into the hands of the enemy.

As you can see on the map, the terrain that I occupied formed a plain that offered no marked advantage to either side. Victory in the battle depended on gallantry, which the troops of both armies demonstrated throughout this war, and proper deployment and manoeuvring of troops. My left wing rested on the small town of Pultusk while my right wing – on scrubland adjoining the village of Moszyn. To cover the Narew River and the main road that leads from Sierock to Pultusk, I had to move four *verstas* [4.3 kilometres] in front of my left wing a detachment under General Baggehufvudt, composed of the Starooskolskii and Vilenskii Musketeer Regiments (each unit having three battalions), a battalion of the Revelskii Musketeer Regiment, the 4th Jager Regiment, the Tatar Light Horse Regiment, two squadrons of the Kievskii Dragoon Regiment, and a Cossack regiment. The advance guard – led by General Barclay de Tolly and comprised of the 1st, 3rd, and 20th Jagers (totalling nine battalions), the Tenginskii Musketeer Regiment (three battalions), and five squadrons of the Polish Light Horse Regiment – was deployed amidst the brushwood in front of the right wing and supported by six cannon to prevent the enemy from turning that wing.[20]

On 14/26 December, around nine o'clock in the morning, having inspected the troops that had arrived during the night, I received a report from General Baggehufvudt concerning the approach of the enemy.[21] We knew that Emperor Napoleon was with the army that

---

20   Sergei Volkonsky, a lieutenant in the Chevalier Guard Regiment who served as an aide-de-camp to Count Osterman, thought 'the position at Pultusk was chosen quite skilfully: the heights, which we occupied, had no other approach than across an open rolling plain. Our flanks could not be turned because the left was anchored onto the town and the river while the right flank was protected by the woods that were strongly protected by Barclay de Tolly.' Volkonsky, *Zapiski...*, p.15.

21   Bennigsen later did much to exaggerate the size of the French army. *The Journal of Military Operations of the Imperial Russian Army*, the official account of the Russian army's movements, operations, and

comprised of the *corps d'armée* of Marshals Davout and Lannes and part of the cavalry reserve of the *grand-duc* of Berg [Marshal Murat]. Based on this report, I moved my entire cavalry into the plain, about 1,000 paces in front of the infantry forming my first line, to prevent the enemy from being able to reconnoitre my position before his remaining forces arrived. Marshal Davout moved with his *corps d'armée* against our left wing; he impetuously attacked General Baggehufvudt's advance detachment, which was too weak to resist and was forced to fall back slightly. I considered it paramount not to allow the enemy to seize the town [of Pultusk], anticipating that the enemy could have no other end in attacking our left wing than to take control of it, I reinforced Baggehufvudt with three infantry battalions. Yet this reinforcement proved insufficient, and I soon had to dispatch there Lieutenant General Count Ostermann with the Tulskii Musketeer Regiment and the grenadier battalion of the Pavlogradskii Grenadier Regiment;[22] I also diverted there a cuirassier regiment, the Izumskii Hussar Regiment, and the Kargopolskii Dragoon Regiment.

From that moment on, the fighting intensified and both sides fought for a long time with the utmost determination. The grenadier battalion of the Starooskolskii Musketeer Regiment and a battalion of the 4th Jagers launched a bayonet attack against the enemy's centre column; at the same time, General Kozhin,[23] leading His Majesty's Leib-Cuirassier Regiment and two squadrons of the Kargopolskii Dragoons, successfully attacked the left flank of the [French] columns, smashed a column of about 2,000 men, of whom the greater part was killed and about 300 men taken prisoner.[24] Meanwhile, a strong enemy column attempted to force the left flank of Baggehufvudt's detachment by passing between the Narew River and the hill located on its bank; but it was, in its turn, attacked by two battalions of our

---

battle reports, thus, contains the following entry: 'On 14 [26] December, when our troops were in the process of being deployed in order of battle, at 11 a.m., they were attacked by a French army of 60,000 men, commanded by Napoleon in person, and consisting of the corps of Marshals Davout and Lannes, and the detachment of General Suchet.' Anon (ed.), *Zhurnal voennykh deistvii imperatorskoi Rossiiskoi armii s nachal do okonchaniya kampanii* (St. Petersburg: Imperial Academy of Sciences, 1807), p.38.

22 Volkonsky: 'The key to our position was on the left flank so the French assaults were primarily directed there. The Navarinskii and Tulskii Infantry Regiment, defending this flank against the superior enemy forces, began to waver [at one point] but the watchful and prudent Ostermann quickly noticed this problem: he set up a strong battery at the edge of the town and deployed the Pavlovskii Grenadier Regiment to defend it, telling these soldiers, "Here is the spot where you must prove that you are worthy of bearing the name of our late Emperor. Fight to the very last man but defend this battery! I have brought you to a dangerous place but you will earn [eternal] glory here. And since this place is perilous, I will stay with you." The French soon launched a fierce assault at this location. Despite the hail storm of grape-shot and bullets, we held on to this position. During this fighting Ostermann noticed that the grenadiers, who were standing like an impregnable wall, had suffered heavy losses so he ordered them to lay down on ground while he continued to sit on his horse like as a medieval knight. The mitres [shapki] of the Pavlovskii [Grenadier] Regiment still bear bullet holes that they sustained at this battle, where the regiment received its baptism of fire.' Volkonsky, *Zapiski...*, p.16.

23 Sergei Kozhin (Kogine in French sources) was a major general and chef of His Majesty's Leib-Cuirassier Regiment.

24 Volkonsky: 'The charges of the Leib-Cuirassier Regiment, commanded by Major-General Kozhin, of the Kievskii Dragoon Regiment led by Colonel Emmanuel, and of two squadrons of the Kargopolskii Dragoon Regiment led by Major Stahl, remain the most splendid episodes of that battle.' Volkonsky, *Zapiski...*, pp.15–16.

infantry. A battalion, under the command of Major Brevern[25] and accompanied with two cannon, arrived from General Anrep's division to the left bank of the Narew and flanked this enemy column, which was soon repulsed with losses. General Dokhturov, with the Izumskii Hussar Regiment, skilfully lured an enemy column toward one of our batteries with a feigned retreat; the enemy suffered grievously from the artillery fire of this battery. These counterattacks were so well coordinated that the enemy was forced to fall back and, for the moment, to abandon his initial plan to turn our left flank.

Nevertheless, the [French] still attached great importance to occupying Pultusk. Having received reinforcements, they renewed their attacks at all points against Baggehufvudt's detachment which was forced to yield a second time to superior numbers and to withdraw to a ravine that was behind it. But then arrived Lieutenant General Count Ostermann, with his detachment; he hastily formed a battery with several cannon on a hill behind the ravine. The fire from this battery had a great effect on the enemy and allowed Baggehufvudt's detachment to rally and charge the enemy, who was forced to retreat. Baggehufvudt had the enemy vigorously pursued for more than four *verstas* by all of his cavalry, supported by the jagers and the Tulskii Musketeer Regiment under the orders of Major General Somov.[26] We took about 500 prisoners in these attacks and during the pursuit of the enemy on our left wing. The success that we gained here was due expressly to the good conduct of General Baggehufvudt and to the wise dispositions of Lieutenant General Count Ostermann.

While this resolute fighting raged on our left wing, a large enemy column advanced upon our centre, causing me to order our cavalry to slowly retreat, pass through the two lines of infantry and place itself in a third line behind my right wing, close enough so it could be recalled if indeed the enemy had wanted to strike at our centre. But after our heavy artillery fired several rounds, this enemy column veered off to the left and joined the troops with which Marshal Lannes advanced, in several columns, against our right wing.[27] Lannes

Khristophor (Christoph Hermann Karl) von Brevern. (State Hermitage Museum)

---

25   Khristophor Logginovich (Christoph Hermann Karl) von Brevern (1779–1863), who served as a major of the Koporskii Infantry Regiment and later commanded the 33rd Jager Regiment (1812–1813); he became lieutenant colonel in April 1813 and major general in 1824.
26   Major General Andrei Somov, the chef of the Tulskii Musketeer Regiment in 1803–1809.
27   *Journal of Military Operations of the Imperial Russian Army*: 'During this furious attack upon our left flank, a numerous body of the enemy's infantry, divided into six columns under the command of Marshal Lannes, attempted, by penetrating through the brushwood, to flank our advance guard under

marched through brushwood and struck with a great deal of impetuosity our advance guard under the command of General Barclay de Tolly, who was covering our right wing; Barclay de Tolly was too weak to contain the enemy's superior forces so he was forced to concede some ground. I had had set up in this brushwood a concealed battery whose grapeshot salvoes cooled the enemy's ardour for a moment; but soon enough the French flanked this battery and Barclay de Tolly found himself forced to retreat again. He sent one of his aides de camp to General Sacken, who commanded our right wing, asking for help. Being unable to obtain support, as he desired and as he should have expected, even after asking for it for the second time, Barclay de Tolly sent this same aide de camp, M. Bartholomé, directly to me with the request to come in person to the right wing. Although my presence was still necessary on the left wing, where I then was, I felt it necessary to concede to Barclay de Tolly's request. Just as I arrived at our centre, I perceived that the enemy had already taken the brushwood adjacent to our right wing.[28] Afraid therefore of soon being flanked, I immediately commanded to change the battle line by withdrawing the right wing to the centre, as you will see from my second position on the map of the battle. At the same time, I reinforced Barclay de Tolly with three battalions of the Chernigovskii Musketeer Regiment, under the command of Prince Dolgorouky V,[29] that were all taken from the second line. This decision produced the greatest success, as all of the batteries deployed in the front of our right wing fired into the flank of the enemy columns that stood in the thicket. When I realized that the enemy had stopped, I sent the Litovskii Muskteer Regiment to General Barclay de Tolly, who, upon rallying his troops, rushed forward with bayonets drawn against the enemy columns. Just then I moved forward a battery, protected by several cavalry squadrons, which directed, with a great deal of success, its fire at the thickets; I then called the rest of the cavalry back and moved it in front of the centre of my first line to contain the enemy cavalry. By then I had already sent the order to General Count Ostermann to send forward all of the infantry of the left wing. These attacks succeeded everywhere; the enemy was forced to yield and retreated from the battlefield.

Both sides fought with the utmost bravery from 11 o'clock in the morning until seven o'clock in the evening.[30] The musket fire, especially on our right wing, remained intense and unrelenting

---

the command of Major-General Barclay de Tolly, which had taken up position to cover our right flank. The object of the enemy on this side was to break, or at least to push back our right flank, and by this means to cut off our communication with a part of the corps of Count Buxhöwden that was deployed at the villages of Makow and Ostrolenka. The attack of the French on this side was extremely violent and impetuous.' *Zhurnal voennykh deistvii imperatorskoi Rossiiskoi armii*, pp.42–43.

28 By afternoon, Lannes faced the real possibility of a major defeat. He was saved by the unexpected arrival of the 3rd Division of Davout's 3rd Corps under General Joseph Augustin Daultane (Gudin, its regular commander, was ill). Davout had sent Daultane south toward Pultusk while the rest of his corps slogged north to Golymin on the morning of the 26th. Daultane, hearing the rumble of battle to his front late in the afternoon, marched to the sound of the guns to appear on Lannes's left flank in the nick of time with his 5,000 men. He attacked at once. Such a small force could not turn the tide of the struggle in favor of the French but, by surprising Bennigsen and forestalling a Russian counterstroke against Lannes, he was able to gain enough time for night to bring the fighting to an end.

29 Major General Vasilii Yurievich Dolgoruky V, served as the chef of the Chernigovskii Musketeer Regiment in 1802–1809.

30 'In all my years of war, I have never seen a more bitter combat.' Lannes to Napoleon, 27 December 1806, in Foucart, *Campagne de Pologne*, vol.4, p.465.

throughout the six hours of fighting. On several occasions, the fronts of the infantry came so close to each other that they seemed to intermix. It was obvious throughout that day that our infantry was determined to justify the high regard for bravery that it has always enjoyed in Europe but that some unfortunate engagements of the preceding campaigns had momentarily undermined in the minds of only those who did not come to know the Russian soldier first-hand. The French, for their part, had become so accustomed under the direction of their great captain to crushing any enemy before them that they yielded with difficulty for the first time at Pultusk, and only after making the greatest efforts and demonstrating uncommon valour.

The darkness, the bad weather, and hail accompanied by a biting cold wind kept us from pursuing the enemy for very long and from profiting from our victory as we would have been able to do if the engagement had ended before nightfall.

It is my duty to render here to General Barclay de Tolly the justice that is due to him. By his distinguished conduct in this action, he again and even more so affirmed the reputation that he already enjoyed in the army. I must again render justice to my chief of staff, General de Steinheil,[31] who by his talents and enterprise on that day, as throughout the entire course of this war, helped me greatly in the execution of the dispositions I had ordered. Staff Colonels de Berg and d'Aderkas also distinguished themselves in this action. I would very much like to name all of those who contributed to the victory of that day, but the number is too great. I will limit myself therefore to expressing to all of them my contentment and the admiration that I felt in general regarding the conduct and bravery of the troops that were in that action under my orders. I need not tell you of the part that our artillery played in the victory of that day, nor of the conduct of the officers that commanded it, as my relation serves as their praise.

It was impossible for me to precisely indicate our losses in my first official report, but they actually amounted to about 7,000 killed and wounded.[32] The French losses can be evaluated, without exaggeration, at 10,000 men, including the 700 men we took prisoner on the battlefield.

I want to reiterate that I was not informed of the orders that General Buxhöwden's divisions had already received not to come to my aid. Throughout the battle I therefore felt a great sense of security with regards to the outcome of the battle, all the more so as a battalion from General Anrep's division appeared in the afternoon on the left bank of the Narew, near the bridge below Pultusk, while a Prussian *chasseur*, arriving at the same time, assured me that he had seen with his own eyes Buxhöwden, with General Tuchkov's division, marching on the road from Makow to Pultusk and that the cavalry would shortly reach the battlefield. I had all the more reason to expect the arrival of these troops as Lieutenant General Count Tolstoy had travelled to General Buxhöwden, while General Baggehufvudt's detachment was already in action and the fighting was about to escalate into a general battle.[33] It was

---

31 Faddei (Fabian Gothard) von Steinheil (1762–1831) was a major general in 1806.
32 *Journal of Military Operations of the Imperial Russian Army:* 'In this battle we made about 700 prisoners; and, according to the statement of some who were taken the day after, the enemy, besides three generals who fell in the action, lost in killed and wounded about ten thousand men. The total of the loss on our side amounts in killed and wounded to between two and three thousand.' *Zhurnal voennykh deistvii imperatorskoi Rossiiskoi armii*, p.46.
33 Benckendorff, whom Bennigsen dispatched along with Count Tolstoy to Buxhöwden, recalled: 'Bennigsen offered Tolstoy to travel at once to Buxhöwden and to assure him with regards to the field marshal's orders that had caused such anxiety. He was to suggest joint operations in the battle

only during the night, when everything was already over and I had rallied the majority of my troops at their first position, that I formally learned that all the forces that I had expected to join me were in fact retreating toward our frontiers.

Under these circumstances, what else could I do? Certainly, nothing other than to execute the orders given by the Field Marshal, for what would I have accomplished by remaining alone at the position near Pultusk? All the enemy *corps* that had been detached to attack our various detachments would not have hesitated to regroup, retrace their steps, and renew an engagement in which the disproportion of forces would have been too great for me to be able to resist successfully. Therefore, I most regretfully resolved to leave the position of Pultusk so as to be able to more easily draw toward Lieutenant General Golitsyn and his troops, who had been cut off from me and from whom I had no news. To this end, I ordered my heavy artillery to cross, with a suitable escort, the Narew River early in the morning of 15/27 December, with orders to march on the left bank of this river to Ostrolenka and to await me there. The road on the left bank was sandy and not so impracticable as on the right side of the river; moreover, I was quite sure that the enemy would not pursue me immediately [after such bloody battle] and that I could afford remaining for a while without my heavy artillery. Having sent off those of our wounded who were still capable of being transported, I directed the troops to proceed on the road to Rozan, on the right bank of the Narew. The last troops of the rear guard left Pultusk at 11 o'clock in the morning, without having seen the enemy.

The position in which I found myself that day was certainly rather awkward and difficult. I had received a clear order to retreat swiftly toward our frontiers, and, by consequence, not to give battle; to what personal responsibility was I exposing myself if I had had the misfortune to suffer a notable loss? The unfortunate consequences would have been blamed entirely on me; no amount of valid arguments I could cite to explain my decision to await the enemy and stop his advance, if only for a single day, to buy time for the rest of our army, scattered as it was across the right bank of the Narew, would have sufficed to avoid accusations of disobedience that would have been made against me, all the more so as it would have been possible to demonstrate to me that I still had time to send my troops across the Narew, on the bridges that I had built on that river. But as the day turned to our advantage, I was applauded as much as I would have been condemned had the contrary occurred. My gracious sovereign, in order to show me his satisfaction, granted me the Order of St George of the second class and added to it a generous gift of 5,000 *ducats* [gold coins].

Now, General, I pray that you will open the map and consider what the result would have been if I had acted differently, that is to say if I had decided to retreat. Firstly, which road was I supposed to take? I would have exposed my heavy artillery if I had had it cross to the left

---

as it was agreed in the initial dispositions. I accompanied the Count on this trip. We found General Buxhöwden's corps still at Makow. He was marching to Pultusk to arrive by the time specified by the Field Marshal in original instructions but upon receiving his second order, he turned his men back. [We found him] at noon and General Buxhöwden, citing the fatigue of his troops, refused to move any further even though the distance from Makow to Pultusk was no more than two [German] miles. At the same time, General Anrep, having received the startling order from the Field Marshal, had already destroyed the bridges [on the Narew River] and could no longer participate in the battle… One wonders what would have been left of the French army if the Field Marshal commanded that day and carried out the converging movements of corps of Generals Buxhöwden and Anrep.' Benckendorff, 'Vospominaniya…', pp.126–127.

A British caricature, published in 1807, illustrating a battle between 'sturdy bears and skinny apes' at Pultusk on December 26, 1806. The Russians, with their standard of a double eagle, advance with fixed bayonets under the leadership of 'spirited Benn-in-gin' who is encased from waist to ankles in a cask. Behind him, another Russian officer shovels French apes into 'Bux-oven" (Buxhöwden). On the French side, 'Mew-rat' with the head of a cat and the body of a rat, is leading an attack while Napoleon, an ape wearing a feathered bicorne astride the tree branch is proclaiming 'I am determined to beat these brutes in spite their teeth!' Above the battle hovers 'Angel Guardian Kamensky' with feathered wings and raised sword.
(Courtesy of Anne S.K. Brown Military Collection)

bank of the Narew, as I did after the battle, accompanied by a mere escort, as the enemy that was already near Pultusk would have soon reached it; if I had taken it with me on the right bank, I would invariably still have lost it, the roads there being impassable at the time; the enemy would have followed me closely, and that which happened to us, during our retreat from the Wkra River to Pultusk, would have happened to me once more. Let us now examine the consequences of my retreat by crossing the Narew with my entire corps. This would have been the easiest manoeuvre to execute and also the safest for the troops. But the consequences would nevertheless have been most unfortunate. Bear in mind that General Buxhöwden was, with two divisions, retreating from Makow and that General Prince Golitsyn, with more than a division, was cut off from me on the road from Golymin to Ostrolenka. Napoleon, present in person and at head of considerable forces, was also on the right side of the Narew, near Pultusk. He would have been doubtlessly soon informed of the scattered march of our troops that I have just described. He, who never failed to take advantage of mistakes that his enemies committed, would have only had to simply move alongside the Narew by the same road that I had taken to Rozan and Ostrolenka, and do it with celerity so our troops, whose march would have been slowed by the artillery on the bad roads, would have had a great deal of trouble of crossing the Narew in time to escape this adroit enemy.

The consequences of a decisive defeat and a considerable loss of our troops on the right bank of the Narew, under the circumstances in which we found ourselves, would have been calamitous. They would not have been limited to the sole failure of one day but would have produced far more ruinous results as the enemy would have crossed our frontiers and entered Lithuania. I would no longer have been in a state to resist the French army, all the more so as no reserve was close enough to support me. The formation of the imperial militia force had barely begun. I would not, therefore, have dared to risk a second engagement so as to not compromise the destiny of the State by yet another, and probably final, loss, and I would have been forced to abandon these neighbouring provinces to the enemy until I had sufficient forces to confront him.

Although the inhabitants of Russian Poland behaved agreeably and prudently during this war against the French, they would, however, have been forced or enticed to make a common cause with Prussian Poland against us.[34] This spirit of insurrection would not have failed to spread like wildfire through all of the formerly Polish provinces. The entry of a strong French army would invariably have served as the signal for insurrection and hardly anyone can deny that it would have been very difficult to re-conquer these beautiful provinces, certainly not without a great effusion of blood. Therefore, General, it becomes evident that the victory that Providence granted our arms at Pultusk prevented all of these misfortunes and gave us time to gather our forces to be able to resist again with vigour the formidable forces of the enemy.[35]

---

34   Bennigsen is referring to the Polish territories that Russia and Prussia acquired as the result of the Second and Third Partitions of Poland in 1792–1795.
35   Upon learning of the outcome of the battle at Pultusk, Field Marshal Kamensky turned back and tried to resume his command at Ostrolenka. However, senior Russian officers confronted him. Volkonsky remembered the field marshal returning to headquarters and 'attempting to reclaim the command of the army but because of his sudden and completely unjustified departure, the generals agreed not to let him resume command and to await the Emperor's new orders from St. Petersburg.' Volkonskii, *Zapiski...*, pp.18–19. According to Benckendorff, 'Count Ostermann was the first to declare that Kamensky was no longer worthy of this honour [of commanding an army] and that he must beseech for the mercy of the Emperor and conceal his shame in the provincial wilderness. Despairing, the Field Marshal departed once more, taking with him the scorn of the entire army.' Benckendorff, 'Vospominaniya,' p.127. Wilson noted in his journal on 9 January that 'the news from the Russian army is confirmed, that Kamensky has been declared mad by a council of officers. His acts of insanity indeed were so unhappily patent, that no sane man, hearing the evidence, could come to any other conclusion.' *Life of General Sir Robert Wilson*, vol. 2, pp.54, 56.

7

Golymin

I promised you, General, at the end of my previous letter, to convey to you reports of the generals who, on the day of the battle of Pultusk, were attacked separately during their marches. To avoid repetition, I will only offer extracts from these reports.

Major General Count Pahlen commanded the chain of advance posts in front of our right wing on the Wkra River, his forces comprising of the 21st Jager Regiment, eight squadrons of the Sumskii Hussar Regiment, and Major Pirogov's horse artillery company. Having received the order to retreat, he was attacked, on 13/25 December, before reaching the village of Lopaczyn, toward which he was directing his march. The enemy first appeared on the right side of the road around one o'clock in the afternoon and soon after, appeared in force, with a great deal of cavalry, marching through the village of Pogone. Count Pahlen, finding himself held up close by superior forces, was obliged to halt, deploy his small troop for battle and accept a fairly lively engagement, all the more so as he had behind him a swampy barrier, that he would not have been able to cross during the day in the enemy's presence, without excessive risk. Count Pahlen's good dispositions stopped the enemy, who was repulsed despite several attempts to break through our detachment at diverse points. The nightfall put an end to hostilities and the enemy withdrew a certain distance. Count Pahlen profited wisely from the time he gained; he continued his march, covering his retreat with a battalion of jagers and five squadrons of hussars.[1] In his report concerning this affair,

---

1   Eduard von Löwenstern, the younger brother of Waldemar von Löwenstern, the distinguished Russian major-general and author of insightful memoirs, enlisted in the army at the tender age of 14 and, in 1806, found himself as a young officer candidate in the Sumskii Hussar Regiment. In his memoirs, he provides further details on Pahlen's engagement: 'On 13 [25] December, the Sumskii Hussars and the 21st Light Infantry Regiment under Colonel Laptyev and Colonel Pirogov with his horse [artillery] company marched to Łopacin. As the sun was going down, we passed the village of Gołotczyzna [10 kilometres from Lopacin]. Not far from it we observed our baggage and pack horses running wildly and soon afterwards we recognised enemy riders harassing our servants any way they wished. Count Pahlen immediately deployed several Hussars and Cossacks to save the fleeing supply train. Our people were completely successful, denying the French dragoons their booty. We immediately turned around and passed Gołotczyzna in a sharp trot and in order to lighten out load, we threw away the large bundles of hay that [the village of] Ciechanow had provided us with. Before we reached the fields on the other side of the village, we were surrounded on all sides. The manor of the nobleman who had given us false information was immediately set on fire over his head. Soon also most of the village was burning brightly. The French positioned 16 cannon near a windmill and began firing specifically at the Hussars. For the first time, I heard the thunder of the cannon and the whistle of their balls. That imposing and

the Count highly praised the conduct of General Laptev, commander of the 21st Jager Regiment, and spoke with a great deal of praise for Colonel Kulikowski, commanding a jager battalion, and Major Potapov, who led a hussar squadron.[2]

Count Pahlen took the road to Ciechanow, where he found Major General Czaplic, with his detachment, which had received the order to go to Golymin, where General Dokhturov was with the 7th Division, belonging to General Buxhöwden's corps, with which he continued his march. Pahlen was however obliged to abandon three cannons that could not be pulled from the mud into which they had sunk during the march.[3]

On 14/26 December, these two generals joined, in the environs of Golymin, the forces of Lieutenant-Generals Dokhturov and Prince Golitsyn. The latter, as I already noted in my previous letter, had received an order from Field Marshal Count Kamensky to move to Ostrolenka with the troops that were still on the right wing of the second line near the Wkra River. These troops had occupied the distance between the villages of Lenkowo and Ciechanow: they were composed of two cavalry regiments (the Military Order Cuirassier Regiment and the Pskovskii Dragoon Regiment), the Kostromskoi Musketeer Regiment, and one and a half companies of field artillery. Prince Golitsyn received this order in the afternoon of December 12/24; a few hours later, he set off on his march, not knowing of what had transpired on the banks of the Wkra River that same day. He marched off intending to request further instructions concerning his detachment. At nine o'clock in the evening, he arrived at Nowe Miasto, where he only found some soldiers wounded too seriously to be transported, who informed him of the precipitous retreat of all of our troops that were then scattered on the banks of the Wkra. Prince Golitsyn then halted his detachment at Slubowo.

The orders that I had sent to all the generals upon my departure from Nowe Miasto and, among others, to Prince Golitsyn, to march with haste to Pultusk, had not reached him; the officer that he had sent to me at Strzegocin no longer found me there. Golitsyn had had a great deal of trouble transporting 18 pieces of artillery that he had been ordered to take with him. The roads were very muddy and impassable in that season. In this state of

---

    horrible play of battle awakened in me a feeling unknown up to then. It was not of horror. It was not of joy. It was not of fear. Maidan, a young Hussar in the Second Platoon, was shot next to me. He was the first man I saw dashed to pieces. His brains and blood splattered me in the face. After our squadron had retreated from the continued cannon fire, we stopped on a small elevation that was quite bushy. From there we clearly recognised the enemy squadrons chasing down the road. A few moments later, we also went on the attack. Several chasseurs à cheval surrounded Major Potapov. Before we could get to him, he had taken seven sabre blows to the head, luckily none fatal. As I saw my major in danger for his life, without thinking, I leapt into the thick pack and my good [stroke of] genius protected me. I do not know what happened after that. I rode around with the others without knowing what I was doing or what was happening around me. It was pitch black night when that dogged, bloody battle ended. Three dismounted light cannon and several carts with pelisses fell into enemy hands. The Sumskii Hussars' bravery and Count Pahlen's expertise saved the rest. In the middle of the night, we returned over almost impassable roads to our bivouac in Ciechanow where several dragoon regiments sent as reinforcements were waiting for us.' *Mit Graf Pahlens Reiterei gegen Napoleon: Denkwürdigkeiten des russischen Generals Eduard von Löwenstern*, 1790-1837 (Berlin: Mittler, 1910), pp.7–8.

2   Vasilii Danilovich Laptev served as the chef of the 21st Jager Regiment in 1806–1808. The regiment was commanded by Colonel Iosif Andreevich Kulikowski.

3   Eduard von Löwenstern: 'The night was dark, with the terrible rain and snow drifts. We were standing in soft mud that seemed to reach our stirrups.' *Mit Graf Pahlens Reiterei gegen Napoleon*, p.9.

ignorance concerning what was going on and uncertain as to how he should proceed so as not to upset the general operations of the army, Lieutenant General Prince Golitsyn decided to remain in the position he had chosen near the village of Slubowo and await further orders. At the same time, he sent reconnaissance parties down the road from Nowe Miasto to his right toward Lopaczyn and his left toward Strzegocin. At nine o'clock in the morning, his advance-posts informed him of the approach of a column of enemy cavalry on the road from Nowe Miasto. Golitsyn dispatched three squadrons to reinforce the main outpost [*grand'garde*] that he had deployed on this road.

Cyprian Kreutz. (State Hermitage Museum)

At that moment, rather fortuitously, arrived the Dneprovskii Musketeer Regiment, which was marching from the banks of the Wkra toward Strzegocin. Golitsyn halted the march of this regiment and ordered it to join his detachment. Shortly thereafter the enemy deployed some infantry, and the fighting commenced, lasting about two hours at which point the French turned back along the road from Nowe Miasto, by which they had arrived. It was soon determined that Marshal Augereau, with a corps of some 20,000 men and 6,000 cavalrymen from the *grand-duc* de Berg's [Murat's] cavalry reserve, had attacked the day before all outposts of our advance guard near Nowe Miasto and, having crossed the Wkra River at Kolozomb, about six *verstas* from Nowe Miasto, followed Prince Golitsyn in order to cut him off from Pultusk.

At noon, Prince Golitsyn was informed that two squadrons of the Sumskii Hussar Regiment, under the orders of Colonel Baron Kreutz,[4] which had been cut off from the rest of the army on the Wkra River and were seeking to cut their way out of the encirclement, were marching very rapidly on the road to Lopaczyn, closely pursued by a large detachment of enemy cavalry. In order to facilitate the retreat of these squadrons, Prince Golitsyn sent two squadrons from the Military Order Cuirassier Regiment and a battalion of infantry to support them. At the approach of these reinforcements, the French halted their pursuit and Colonel Kreutz, with his two squadrons, joined his regiment without considerable losses.

---

4 Cyprian Belzig von Kreutz (1777–1850) served in the Sumskii Hussar Regiment, which he commanded in 1808–1810. He later served as the chef of the Sibirskii Dragoon Regiment and distinguished himself during Napoleon's invasion of Russia, earning promotion to major general in December 1812.

At three o'clock in the afternoon, Prince Golitsyn joined to his detachment the Tavricheskii Grenadier Regiment and the Malorossiiskii Cuirassier Regiment, which were moving from the Wkra to Strzegocin. The enemy limited himself to occasional skirmishing along the advance posts, which lasted until nightfall. That evening, Prince Golitsyn was informed that considerable enemy forces were approaching the area of Ciechanow. He therefore resolved to abandon his position and, hoping to avoid being cut off, he marched to his right following the road to Pultusk. But hardly had he moved four or five *verstas* that dark winter night that he had to halt because his heavy artillery pieces had sunk so deeply in the mud on

Yefim Czaplic. (State Hermitage Museum)

those ghastly roads that after 10 hours of back-breaking labour only some pieces had been extricated. Recognizing the impossibility of saving his artillery and not wishing to expose his entire detachment to a greater loss by further delaying his march, Golitsyn spiked the cannon that could not be pulled from the mud and distributed among his cavalry as much as possible of the charges from the artillery caissons that were also impossible to move over those abominable roads. Having accomplished this, the Prince then took the road to Golymin, where he arrived on 14/26 December, at eight o'clock in the morning. In this place he found Lieutenant General Dokhturov with three regiments of the 7th Division of General Buxhöwden's corps. General Dokhturov, as the most senior officer, took command of all the troops gathered at Golymin.

I have previously mentioned that Field Marshal Kamensky had sent General Buxhöwden with two divisions to the right bank of the Narew, while he himself remained at Makow with the 5th Division, commanded by General Tuchkov. Dokhturov arrived with the 7th Division on 11/23 December at the village of Orguéchowka(?), where, in compliance with the orders received, he detached Major General Czaplic to Ciechanow, along with the Pavlogradskii Hussar Regiment, the Ingermanlandskii Dragoon Regiment and half of the Malakhov's Cossack Regiment. In compliance with the same orders, he directed Major General Zapolsky,[5] with the Ekaterinoslavskii Grenadier Regiment, the Vladimirskii Musketeer Regiment, and Colonel Yermolov's[6] horse artillery company to proceed to Golymin on 12/24 December, and, the following day, to Ciechanow, where he was supposed to join General Czaplic's cavalry. Dokhturov himself – with the Moskovskii Musketeer Regiment, the Moskovskii Dragoon Regiment, and the remainder of the Malakhov's Cossack Regiment – arrived at Golymin at eight o'clock in the morning. Having received the order for the general retreat that same day, Dokhturov ordered the troops of his division, which were still on the march, to halt and return to Makow. Just as Dokhturov was preparing to execute this order with the troops he had on hand, Golitsyn informed him that he was retreating on Golymin, followed very closely by a strong French corps. Dokhturov responded at once, dispatching all available troops to support him; shortly thereafter Golitsyn arrived with his detachment. General Dokhturov then placed all these troops in two lines in a position before Golymin. His forces, gathered from different units and divisions, consisted of 45 cavalry squadrons, one Cossack regiment, 27 infantry battalions, two companies of horse artillery, and one company of field artillery, totalling some 16,500 men. General Czaplic's detachment was deployed on an open plain to cover the right wing.

In front of the left wing, there was a fairly dense wood, traversed by three roads coming: one from the village of Osiek-Gorny, another from the village of Osiek-Stary, and a third from the village of Garnowo; the first two were main roads [*grandes routes*] and the enemy was advancing along them. This wood therefore required the greatest attention for the security of the left wing of our position. Major General Prince Scherbatov[7] was charged with occupying it

---

5   Major General Andrei Vasilievich Zapolsky, served as the chef of the Ekaterinoslavskii Grenadier Regiment in 1804–1813.
6   Aleksei (Alexis) Yermolov (1777–1861), prominent Russian artillery commander, who served as the chief of staff of the 1st Western Army in 1812.
7   Aleksei Scherbatov was the chef of the Kostromskoi Musketeer Regiment in 1805–1814. In his memoirs, he explained: 'Two days prior to the battle, I followed the Field Marshal's order and marched with my Kostromskoi Infantry Regiment to reinforce the advance guard; along the way, two artillery companies were supposed to join me and move under my protection. This junction, however, greatly complicated the movement of my regiment since throughout the night, I had to commit my men to the exhausting task of hauling guns and carriages that got stuck in the mud at every step. After tremendous efforts, I finally reached the destination point N [place not indicated], where my divisional commander Prince Golitsyn also arrived. I was just preparing to rest after such an exhausting march when I learned about the arrival of Count Kamensky and his staff, who, I mentioned above, were returning from the defeated advance guard. After Count Kamensky's departure, Prince Golitsyn remained at this location for the entire day, linking up with several regiments from other divisions that had retreated from various forward points. During the night this unintentionally-created detachment retreated to the town of Golymin, already pursued by the enemy cavalry and abandoning two or three cannon that got stuck in mud and proved to be impossible to remove despite our best efforts. At dawn, this detachment arrived at Golymin and was soon joined by the enemy. At the same time, Lieutenant-General Dokhturov, with his division being pursued by the French, happened to be passing through this location. He joined our detachment to repel the enemy attacks. I received the order to occupy the woods on the left flank of our position and my regiment was supported by the Denprovskii Infantry Regiment and one battalion of the Tavricheskii Grenadier Regiment, and later by two squadrons of the Pskovskii Dragoon Regiment.' Scherbatov, *Moi vospominaniya*, pp.45–46.

with the Kostromskoi Musketeer Regiment and the Tavricheskii Grenadier Regiment, which was commanded by Colonel Tuchkov.⁸ Three squadrons from the Pskovskii Dragoon Regiment were placed under the orders of Lieutenant-Colonel Vasil'chikov⁹ in a small plain near the woods, to serve as support for Prince Scherbatov in case the enemy forced him to leave the wood.

The enemy, which had closely followed Prince Golitsyn's rear guard, did not hestitate to appear at the wood and to start there a fairly lively fusillade, which lasted until two o'clock in the afternoon. Prince Scherbatov held his post and stopped the enemy. But the French having reinforced the troops in the wood, Prince Scherbatov was obliged to yield and to abandon the latter.¹⁰ The enemy, still following him closely, deployed almost at the

Aleksey Scherbatov. (State Hermitage Museum)

---

8   The Tavricheskii Grenadier Regiment was commanded by Major General Karl Ivanovich d'Anzas but he was suffering from poor health and the actual commanding officer was Colonel Alexander Tuchkov IV, who earned his major general's epaulettes in December 1808.
9   Nikolai Vasili̇evich Vasil'chikov, commanded the Pskovskii Dragoon Regiment in 1806–1810.
10 Scherbatov: 'This was my first battle and, despite having no prior military experience, I was given command of the position where the enemy directed his main attack, seeking to turn our position and cut off our line of retreat to the main army. During the battle my dispositions somewhat reflected my inexperience – at first I occupied the woods as only a novice would do but upon seeing that the enemy anticipated me with his skirmishers and thereby greatly threatened me, I made the fortunate decision to abandon the woods and take up position in the open plain. I must also note that my entire regiment consisted of young and previously untested soldiers and that like me, not a single staff or junior officer had experienced war before. Coming out of the woods with its left flank, one of the battalions … moving at the head of the column came under fire from the enemy skirmishers, who had managed to get through the woods, became disordered and began to retreat in disorder, veering to the side. This disorder soon spread through my entire detachment because fear, like electricity [elektrism], spread in instant from the head of the column to its end, and my own regiment became disordered as well. Observing the shameless retreat of this disordered crowd, I galloped to the fleeing standard-bearers of my regiment, jumped off the horse, grabbed a flag and rushed with it to the spot where the detachment had to be rallied. All the other standard-bearers followed me and, in turn, the disordered battalions followed them. Upon reaching the rallying line, I ordered my adjutants to place flags at battalion distances so the soldiers could rally accordingly. This was accomplished at once and

same time a great number of skirmishers [*tirailleurs*] and a column of cavalry, which acted as though it wanted to turn our left wing. When General Dokhturov realized this, he sent Lieutenant-Colonel Baron Rosen with six squadrons of the Pavlogradskii Hussar Regiment and two squadrons of the Sumskii Hussars; these attacked the enemy cavalry and forced it to retreat via the wood.[11] Another column of enemy cavalry, which had gotten close to our centre, was repulsed by Colonel Bucholtz, at the head of the Moskovskii Dragoon Regiment,[12] supported by the Pskovskii Dragoon Regiment, under the orders of General Baron Korff,[13] and two squadrons from the Military Order Cuirassier Regiment. While all of this was happening on our left wing and centre, the enemy advanced with large forces toward our right flank. General Dokhturov ordered General Czaplic to attack it, which he did so well that the enemy was repulsed and forced to retreat with losses.

This battle had commenced around nine o'clock in the morning and, at seven o'clock in the evening, the enemy finally abandoned the battlefield and retreated through the woods. Prince Golitsyn's detachment had lost on that day: three officers and 80 non-commissioned officers and soldiers killed; four officers, 13 junior officers and 473 non-commissioned officers and soldiers wounded; General Dokhturov's division lost 493 killed and wounded. In total, our losses amounted to 1,066 men. The enemy's losses remained unknown to us but they must have been considerable and, according to the testimony of prisoners, far greater than ours. In the various charges, our cavalry had captured two officers and 64 troopers.[14]

---

    other regiments followed this example and disordered was thus extinguished. This incident showed that it was inexperience, rather than cowardice, that was at the root of this momentary disarray and I considered myself fortunate that in my very first battle I was able to save myself and the troops entrusted to me from shameful behaviour. As the result of my dispositions, the enemy was contained until the nightfall.' Sherbatov, *Moi vospominaniya*, pp.46–47.

11 Eduard von Löwenstern offers more details on this engagement. 'The [French] 4th and 7th Dragoon Regiments attacked our Hussars in the midst of a terrible din. We were thrown into the first line and driven back quite in disorder, colliding with the Ingermanlandskii Dragoon Regiment that formed the second line. The dragoons did not let us pass and, as we did not want to halt, they even looked as if they wanted to battle us. But soon the fleeing hussars came together: "Hurrah Sumskii! Hurrah Sumskii!" they yelled from all sides and sabres and broadswords clattered. Now and then the fires in Golymin, when the flames were driven high by the storm wind, illuminated the bloody battlefield. The trooper from the Second Platoon next to me was stabbed through and through. The head of an enemy rider's horse when turning hit me in the face with his snaffle bit full of foam. I imagined I had been hit by a cannonball, at least to have lost my entire head. I began to fall from the saddle and only held myself on with one leg. You can imagine how desperate my situation was. Danger makes one brave – barely in my saddle again, I swung desperately around me and luckily my little saddle sustained several heavy blows. As soon as I caught my breath, I retreated from that tight pack. Only then did I notice I was bleeding. Looking more closely, I realised that I had a head wound that was, however, superficial and did not even need to be bandaged.' *Mit Graf Pahlens Reiterei gegen*, pp.10–11.

12 Moskovskii Dragoon regiment was commanded by Colonel Ivan Khruschev until October 1806. Colonel Karl Bucholtz was a commanding officer, having previously served as the chef of the Severskii Dragoon Regiment.

13 Major General Fedor Korff was chef of the Pskovskii Dragoon Regiment in 1801–1814. In 1806, he commanded a cavalry brigade comprising of the Military Order Cuirassier and Pskovskii Dragoon Regiments.

14 Eduard von Löwenstern: 'Several French prisoners were mercilessly massacred during the march. Most cruelly, a dragoon officer killed one [Frenchman] who had already been captured and had shot at him. Even I – may the Lord forgive me for my sin – let myself go so far that I took after a French

In this painting by Alexander von Kotzebue, General Aleksei Sherbatov, holding the banner, is rallying battalions of the Kostromskoi Musketeer Regiment before launching a crucial counterattack to protect the left flank of the Russian positions. The general's valorous conduct was recognized with the Order of St George of 4th Class in February 1807 (State History Museum (Russia))

After this battle, Dokhturov rested his troops and, the following morning, he followed orders that he had received to retreat to Makow. Prince Golitsyn marched from Makow to Ostrolenka, as I already mentioned above.[15] I must note here that the lost cannons, which I have mentioned earlier, are included in the number of 52 pieces, of which I already spoke to you in my previous letter.

---

    officer who only collapsed with the sixth or seventh blow to his face and head. You can hardly imagine how bloodthirsty a man can become when he has seen streams of blood for several hours in a row. You become an irritated animal and could at that moment of insanity rip your opponent to pieces with your teeth.' *Mit Graf Pahlens Reiterei gegen Napoleon*, pp.10–11.

15 Eduard von Löwenstern: 'After an unbearable two-day march, we finally reached Ostrolenka. I was utterly exhausted, could barely stay on my horse ever since the battle of Łopacin, I had almost never dismounted. The little bit of sleep I got while riding could not refresh me or strengthen me after those trials and tribulations. It was my bad luck that my coat had been stolen, the only one that protected me against wind and weather. I was truly very unhappy. The cold December night, wind and snow drifts increased my nasty situation. Only clothed in my uniform, shivering with cold, I followed the regiment… A large part of the army came together under the walls of Ostrolenka; hundreds of battalions and squadrons united and lay there helter-skelter. Munition wagons, field equipment, cannon, soldiers with all kinds of weapons camped on the plain together.' *Mit Graf Pahlens Reiterei gegen Napoleon*, pp.10–11.

The account given in this and previous letters shows the critical state in which our army found itself during the days of 12–14/24–26 December as the result of the wide dispersal of troops. The enemy dispositions demonstrate that [Napoleon] was perfectly aware of our circumstances. Marshals Bernadotte and Ney turned our right by moving against the Prussian corps under the orders of Lieutenant General L'Estocq. Marshal Augereau, with about 30,000 men, crossed the Wkra River at Kolozomb, six *verstas* from Nowe Miasto, to intercept our isolated detachments that I mentioned earlier, while Emperor Napoleon himself moved with about 50,000 men directly on Pultusk to deliver a decisive blow there. Yet, thanks to the prudent actions of our generals and the bravery of our troops, the enemy had failed in every respect and we pulled ourselves quite fortunately from that dangerous situation, losing only part of our artillery, which fell into the hands of the French, not by force of their arms, but merely because of impassable roads.

8

Retreat of the Allied Armies – Plan of Operations

At the end of my sixth letter, I told you that on 15/27 December, I marched from Pultusk to Rozan, a distance of three and half [German] *milles*. On 16/28 December, I continued my march to Ostrolenka (another three *milles*), where I remained on 17–18/29–30 December to rest my troops and to draw towards myself Lieutenant General Prince Golitsyn's detachment, which indeed arrived on December 30 with the 12 infantry battalions, 36 squadrons, and a handful of Cossack regiments. The enemy had not followed him at all.[1]

The order that I had received from Field Marshal Count Kamensky to retreat back to our frontiers stated, among other things, that as soon I arrived with my *corps d'armée* at Tykoczin, I had to place myself under the command of General Buxhöwden, as the most senior officer after the field marshal himself.[2] This was supposed to be a temporary arrangement until relevant orders arrived from the Emperor. General Buxhöwden had written me a letter – which he sent in the evening of 14/26 December and that reached me at night

---

1   Sacken's diary offers a starker assessment of the Russian retreat: '15th [27 December]: Contrary to common sense, we retreated during the night, abandoning wounded and sick on the battlefield and [some] cannon [still] stuck in the mud. Complete chaos spread among the troops; everyone, literally, fled headlong as if after a complete defeat. The soldiers had not received bread for two days in a row. Falling from exhaustion, covered in mud, we [finally] reached Rozan. 16 [28] December: Even here [at Rozan] Bennigsen did not feel himself safe. At dawn, he ordered everyone to retreat in utter disorder, and so we marched – without halting anywhere or receiving any food, pillaging villages, and noblemen's estates – to Ostrolenka. We were finally given a break on 17 [29] December. The troops were deployed in a rather astonishing manner – as if [prepared] for slaughter. Everything done or said is completely devoid of common sense. There is a genuine chaos of Babylon.' Volkonsky later remembered that 'Bennigsen first moved to Ostrolenka and then to Nowogrod, where, no longer pursued by the French, he had halted. Yet, the army found neither rest nor supplies at this place. Even the main headquarters lacked bread for 10 days; meat and potatoes, procured through foraging, satisfied our needs. I recall as on one occasion my batman Vasilii Zverev returned from foraging some distance away with two bags of communion bread that was prepared for church services but was not blessed yet; I shared it with my comrades-in-arms.' Osten-Sacken, *Diary*, p.171.
2   In his memoirs, Scherbatov noted that some in the Russian army were displeased that 'Buxhöwden, despite hearing a powerful cannonade, did not consider necessary or possible – precise reasons remain unknown to me – to advance with his corps to support Bennigsen which could have resulted in a different outcome of the battle. It is possible that this was occasioned by the thorny issue of seniority since Buxhöwden was senior in rank to Bennigsen and therefore was unwilling to be subordinated to him, but he could not take charge of the army either.' Sherbatov, *Moi vospominaniya*, p.47.

on the battlefield of Pultusk – in which he expressed himself among other things in the following terms, 'We cannot do better than to retreat in order to gain time and to put our heads together, etc.' At the same time, he wrote to me officially (and in compliance with the orders from the Field Marshal) and instructed me to dispatch my artillery park back to our frontiers. I replied the following day, 15/27 December, from Rozan:

> Your Excellency has informed me that I must return my artillery park to our frontiers. I confess, General, that I do not think that such an order can be fulfilled. Moreover, the unfortunate consequences of such an action would be incalculable for the common cause and just as devastating as those resulting from a defeat in battle. Insofar as I know the feelings of His Majesty the Emperor, [I am certain that] he will not approve of it. Our current lack of supplies can be rectified as soon as we move to the right, where we will be able to draw our subsistence from Old Prussia, Königsberg, etc.

Having remained for two days at Ostrolenka and receiving no news about changes in our dispositions from the Field Marshal, I decided, on 19/31 December, to cross the Narew and proceed, as ordered by Count Kamensky, to Tykoczin. The enemy followed us at a distance with small parties, only to gather intelligence about our movement. But it also seemed as if [Napoleon] wished to extend the *corps d'armée* of Marshals Bernadotte and Ney into Old Prussia and push them closer to Königsberg.[3] Meanwhile, I had sent Prussian Major General Chlebowski, who knew my intentions for future operations, to General Buxhöwden.

My first march from Ostrolenka to Miastkowo was of two and half *milles* and the second, on 20 December/1 January, to Nowogrod covered another one and half *mille*.[4] Here I received the second letter from General Buxhöwden, who invited me to re-cross the Narew and join him. That is precisely what I had proposed via General Chlebowski, so we could move our operations to Old Prussia and save Königsberg. But it was quite unfortunate that I had not received this letter while I was still at Ostrolenka, because there was no bridge at Nowogrod; the one at Ostrolenka had been destroyed. Moreover, strong frost had set in and the river was full of ice flow, so it was only with great difficulty that I managed to construct a bridge of boats [*pont de bateaux*]. But barely had some troops marched across it that the

---

3   With the Russians retreating northward, Napoleon decided to move his army into winter quarters. After the grueling start to the campaign, he hoped to rest the troops and improve his overstretched and inadequate logistical system. For a discussion of the operations in late 1806, see Höpfner, *Der Krieg von 1806 und 1807*, vol.3, pp.1–157; Dumas, *Précis des événemens militaires*, vol.17, pp.99–205; Landmann, *Der Krieg von 1806 und 1807*, pp.300–327; Plotho, *Tagebuch*, vol.1, p.43; Petre, *Napoleon's Campaign in Poland*, pp.59–118. For descriptions of the privations endured by both sides, see the collection of memoir extracts in Natalia Griffon de Pleineville and Vladimir Chikanov, *Napoléon en Pologne: la campagne de 1806–1807* (Paris: Le livre Chez Vous, 2008), pp.133–158; for a analysis of the Grande Armée's logistics during these campaigns, see Georges Germain Félix Lechartier, *Les services de l'arrière à la Grande Armée en 1806–1807* (Paris: Chapelot, 1910).

4   Sacken: 'On the 19th [31 December], the corps moved in one column towards Miastkowo, where the tail [the rear units] finally arrived at night. [Local] houses are devastated, soldiers spread around and pillage neighbouring villages. Anticipating the enemy, we always place our soldiers in houses. But now, with the [French] at long distance from us, the soldiers were billeted in their tents in the fields; they are not given any food.' Osten-Sacken, *Diary*, p.171.

bridge was damaged by the ice flow and most of the boats destroyed. On 23 December/4 January, colder weather set in and the river froze solid at Nowogrod.⁵ Quartermaster General de Steinheil worked diligently to arrange a crossing on the ice and, using planks, straw, and other material, he managed to get across, in the evening of 25 December/6 January, some troops from General Essen III's division (from General Buxhöwden's corps). Alas, that night, the weather changed once again – a mild thaw set in and the ice broke up. Seeing the impossibility of crossing the Narew at Nowogrod and having already spent five days there, I departed with my corps on 26 December/7 January and marched to Lomza (about two *milles* away), from whence I still had six *milles* to reach Tykoczin, which I covered in two marches on 27–28 December/8–9 January. At Tykoczin, I had earlier ordered to set up a magazine, so upon arriving there my troops were able to receive several-days' worth of provisions and then crossed the Narew on the bridges that were located there.⁶

Marshal Michel Ney in action.
(Courtesy of James Smith Noel Collection)

---

5   Sacken: '23rd [December, 4 January 1807]. Bennigsen informs us about rumours that the enemy had crossed the Narew... We remain idle. Expecting news from Barclay. We are constantly short of bread. Our actions have become not only hardly comprehensible but straight-out nonsensical. The weather is befitting the autumn and winter has not set in yet. 25 [December, 6 January 1807]. Attempts are being made to construct pontoons near Nowograd but the ice creates serious hurdles to this; a pontoon bridge fails as well. The winter begins at last.' Osten-Sacken, *Diary*, p.171.

6   Volkonsky remembered that 'our army remained idle for some two weeks, continuing to suffer from poor supply services, although the [relative] prosperity of that region and our foraging provided us with sufficient provisions. I must note, however, that foraging is a rather ruinous practice: it completely devastates the area and facilitates numerous abuses, especially the weakening of discipline, among the troops.' Volkonsky, *Zapiski*, p.19.

We then continued our march to Goniondz, where we intended to cross the Bobr River and enter the Old Prussia.

In the meanwhile, the French worked on repairing a bridge on the Vistula below Thorn while Marshal Ney directed his march against the Prussian corps of General L'Estocq, who, in those circumstances, should have had no other duty but to avoid a confrontation and resort to demonstrations to delay for as long as possible the enemy's approach to Königsberg. L'Estocq, despite the meagre forces that he commanded, retreated slowly and only by short marches, each time withdrawing only when pressed by superior forces. He executed this movement with so much prudence that it cost him only few casualties. He then directed his march from Strassburg to Lautenburg; from there to Soldau, Neidenburg, Jedwabno, Sensburg, Rastenburg and it was only on 22 December/3 January that he managed to arrive in the environs of Angerburg, where he occupied with his corps an advantageous position between the lakes; he remained there until 27 December/8 January. At the news that a detachment from Ney's corps was approaching on the road to Königsberg, L'Estocq resolved to go to Barthen so he can be within reach to protect this city. Having arrived at Barthen on 30 December/11 January, he sent General Prittwitz, with a strong detachment, to conduct reconnaissance toward Schippenbeil. This general acquitted himself perfectly of his commission; at Löwenstein, he encountered a detachment of the enemy troops from the *6e régiment d'infanterie*, which he defeated, and returned that evening to Barthen with 50 prisoners. The following day Marshal Ney issued an *ordre du jour* that reads as follows:

Order of the Day
Allenstein, 12 January.
It is with the greatest regret that I announce to the army that the *6e régiment d'infanterie légère* has allowed itself to lose half a company, with officers and *sous-officiers*, to the enemy on the 11th of this month, an hour before daybreak, in a village before Schippenbeil. Officers are guilty when, forgetting their responsibilities, they neglect to act with caution and to place soldiers under arms at the morning break, as has been the order since the beginning of the campaign. The generals deserve being reprimanded when they stray from the dispositions that have been given to them. The order of [January] 6th concerning the deployment of the troops stated that the 1st Battalion of the *6e régiment* would occupy Schippenbeil and not the surrounding villages. Needless to say, a fully concentrated battalion would never have suffered the fate of this half-company. The brave men who were captured are thus victims of double mistake. Provisions are lacking nowhere; therefore, there is no reason that the troops should not be concentrated when they are near the enemy.

Cavalry patrols are committing countless extortions everywhere, demanding heavy sums [from the populace]; I have in my hands indisputable evidence. The natural effect of these abuses is to exasperate the inhabitants and make them willing to support, with everything they have, the enemy. Therefore I declare that at the first complaint I will have arrested and judged by a military commission whosoever would demand such cash contributions. I once again order the execution of the order of [January] 6th, relative to the precautions that must be taken to protect cantonments from further surprises.
Marshal Ney

By the way, General, I will often cite orders and missives from Marshal Ney or those who wrote to him. These papers were taken at the Battle of Guttstadt on 24 May/5 June, 1807, as you will see when I start to discuss the opening acts of the second campaign.

On 30 December/11 January, just as I was about to depart from Tykoczin a courier arrived from Saint Pétersbourg with a rescript from the Emperor, my master, by which he deigned to confide in me the supreme command of the army operating against Emperor Napoleon. His Majesty added a gracious letter in his own hand, which read as follows:

> Mon Général,
> Although I have already conveyed the official letter of notification to you, I cannot refuse myself the satisfaction of expressing to you my deep gratitude for the [successful] engagement of 14/26 December. The superior talents you have demonstrated there give you new claim to all the confidence that you have already inspired in me. I can only give you the greatest proof of it by naming you commander of the entire army that was under the orders of the Field Marshal, including General Essen I's *corps* at Brest. I have no doubt that you will entirely justify the choice that I am making for you and that you will offer me further occasions to prove to you all of my gratitude.
> Receive, *Général*, the assurance of my esteem,
> Alexander

I went that same day again to Goniondz, four *milles* from Tykoczin, to speed up the passage of the Bobr by our troops there. I expected to find a great many difficulties still there, but fortunately the freeze deepened and the river froze over so the passage of this river was completed in two days.

On 1/13 January, I marched with my *corps d'armée* three *milles* to Szczuczin and, on 2/14 January, two more *milles* to Biala, where I took command of the entire army, which comprised of two corps: the one under my orders and the other under General Buxhöwden; each corps was composed of four divisions. As you will have observed in my fifth letter, upon crossing our imperial borders these eight divisions had 100,000 men so it remains to calculate the losses that I had already suffered, *savoir*:

1) 3,500 men – in the various engagements on the Wkra River, during the retreat to Pultusk, in the engagements of Czarnowo, Golymin, etc.
2) 7,000 men – at the Battle of Pultusk
3) 5,600 men – the ailing soldiers sent to the hospitals
4) In the units previously commanded by General Buxhöwden, I found 3,200 men ailing.

Thus, our losses amounted to 19,300 men. I was also obliged to detach the following units: the Tatar Light Cavalry regiment, some 600 men strong led by Lieutenant Colonel [Karl von] Knorring, was sent to Bialystok to maintain order there on the main road from Grodno and to facilitate the movement of army transports from our frontiers. Three squadrons, about 360 men, remained at Tykoczin under the orders of Colonel Manuel, to guard the magazines there. General Siedmioraczki, with four regiments of infantry, six pieces of field artillery and two regiments of Cossacks, totalling altogether 8,000 men, was detached to Goniondz to cover the Bobr River and to prevent an enemy *corps volant* [flying detachment] from being able to trouble our frontiers in the vicinity of Grodno and to assure free communications between the main army and General Essen I's corps, of which I will speak soon. General Siedmioraczki was also advised to cooperate with General Essen I and to execute the orders that he received in this regard from him. A battalion of infantry and a Cossack sotnya, altogether 1,000 men, were sent to occupy Johannisburg, so as to cover behind us the main road from our frontier via Biala and our direct communications with General Siedmioraczki's force. These detachments amounted to 10,000 men, which, when added to the 19,300 loses mentioned above, total 29,300 men that the army was missing. Thus, there remained only 70,690 men,[7] both combatants and noncombatants, with which I began the winter campaign in Old Prussia.

Lieutenant General Essen I had already arrived with his corps of 17,000 men from our frontiers and took up a position between Brest and the Narew. He was advised to move his headquarters to Wyssoko-Mazovetsk as it was the best point to cover our frontiers and to repulse the enemy if he had wished to cross the Narew in force.

The news I received of the enemy was that after the Battle of Pultusk, Emperor Napoleon had once again gone in person to Warsaw, where his headquarters remained. The enemy had actually mistaken my retrograde march for a retreat toward our frontiers; maybe also he had had news of the orders given in this respect by Field Marshal Count Kamensky, as the French army seemed intent on taking winter quarters. The *corps d'armée* of Marshals Soult, Davout, Lannes, Augereau, Bessières; the reserves under the orders of Prince Murat and Oudinot spread out in the environs of Neidenburg, Chorzellen, Mlawa, Pultusk, all the way to the Vistula, partially even on the left bank of this river, so assured were the French that the Russian army was retreating within its frontiers.[8]

Subsequently I discovered among the intercepted papers a report in which Marshal Berthier was given the following news: 'We are assured that General Bennigsen sent 16,000 men to the aid of Königsberg and that he is retreating with the rest of his army into Russia.' Marshal Bernadotte's *corps d'armée* occupied Elbing, Preussich-Holland, Mohrungen, Liebstadt, etc., etc. You will find the march of Marshal Ney's corps on Königsberg in the reports from the Marshal to the Minister of War the *Prince de Neuchâtel* [Berthier]. Emperor Napoleon was already sending considerable reinforcements of auxiliary troops and conscripts that were arriving one after another. Among the first was General Werner with 2,500 men from Hesse-Darmstadt; this general received, on 31 December, the order from Marshal Ney to occupy the upper Drewenz, from Strassburg, Neumark and Löbau up to Osterode and to deploy his cavalry along the lines of communications to Graudenz and Marienwerder. Furthermore,

---

7 Bennigsen's note: What a difference this makes from the number that several books, newspapers, etc., have cited for the Russian army. They all evaluated the army at no less than 200,000 men!
8 A quick glance at the map of French cantonments indicates that Napoleon employed his preferred operational formation, the *bataillon carré*, which underpinned French strategic flexibility and mobility. In case of a Russian attack, 6th Corps was instructed to concentrate at Mlawa, 4th Corps at Golymin, 3rd Corps at Pultusk, 5th Corps at Sierock, and 7th Corps at Plonsk. Thus, these five corps would form a diamond-shaped formation, with two forward corps separated by a distance of less than 25 kilometers while the rear corps remained one day's march away, allowing Napoleon to concentrate his forces wherever the enemy threatened.

Saxony sent 6,000 men, and Baden 2,500; In Poland, [the French] were forming a *corps* of 30,000 men through forced levies. From Italy, Holland, Spain, in short from all of the countries that found themselves under Napoleon's domination, troops were marching to reinforce the French army. In addition, some 20,000 recruits from the conscription of the year 1807 had crossed the Rhine in November and began to arrive successively.

In these circumstances, I did not have a moment to lose. I had to prevent the enemy from occupying the entirety of Old Prussia and taking Königsberg, the loss of which would have had the most unfortunate consequences. The fall of this city before the start of the second campaign would invariably have led to the fall of Pillau during the winter and the French then would have been in possession of the Frische-Haff and the Frische-Nehrung. All communication with Danzig by land would have been interrupted – no help would have been able to arrive there; the city's garrison, meanwhile, was not strong enough for its prolonged defence and neither was there sufficient amount of gunpowder to endure a siege of several months. With Königsberg in French hands, who would have been able to stop them from taking the Kurische-Haff and the Kurische Nehrung? They would have been the masters of the Baltic coast up to Memel itself. Moreover, Königsberg held riches of all kinds, especially provisions and munitions that the army needed. Look at the map and see with what huge advantages the French would have begun the second campaign if they had captured this city.

Among the intercepted papers of which I already spoke to you, there was an order from Marshal Ney to General Colbert, dated from Wartenburg, on 28 December/9 January, which proves that Königsberg was for a moment then already in danger and highlights the importance the French attached to the possession of this city. This order was written word for word in the following terms:

> Marshal Ney to General Colbert
> Wartenburg, 9 January
> My intention being to know positively if the Prussians are strong enough at Königsberg to defend that city, I have just given the necessary orders for all of the companies of *voltigeurs* and *grenadiers* of the army, formed in six battalions, according to the following table, to assemble along the Alle River from Schippenbeil, Bartenstein and Heilsberg, and to remain prepared to execute the dispositions that I am giving to you to this effect. The battalions of *voltigeurs* will assemble at Bartenstein; they will arrive in sleighs [*traineaux*] tomorrow, the 10th of this month. This means that you will march on Königsberg from the morning of the 12th to the 13th of this month.
>
> The companies of *grenadiers* will form a reserve under the orders of Colonel Lamartinière, with four pieces of artillery commanded by Captain Martin. They will occupy the following positions: the first battalion – Schippenbeil; the second – Bartenstein, where the artillery will take up position; the third battalion – Heilsberg; the remainder of the *3e hussards* and the *10e de chasseurs* should be placed in such a manner that they can observe Domnau and Friedland, while you will march on Preussisch-Eylau. The [commanding] colonels of these regiments must inform you promptly if the enemy advances in force to flank you or threaten your [line of] retreat.

You will leave with 200 horse of the *3e hussards* and *10e chasseurs*, commanded by the *chefs d'escadrons* Schöny and Saint-Léger, followed by two 4-pounders and your three battalions of *voltigeurs*, and will attempt to take up the following dispositions: the first day – behind Kreuzburg, leaving the 3rd battalion of *voltigeurs* in reserve at Preussisch-Eylau, along with a *brigadier* and four *chasseurs à cheval*. The second day, if it is possible, you will advance on Königsberg, leaving the second battalion of *voltigeurs* at Kreuzburg, unless you are certain that you will only have to fight small forces. In this case you will bring up the 3rd battalion; half will take up positions behind the Frisching at Gross-Lauth, the other half at Kreuzburg, behind the Pasmar, marching forward with the 1st and 2nd battalions of *voltigeurs*. Upon your approach to Königsberg, you will send on my behalf a trumpeter [*trompette*] to summon the military commander of this city and demand to evacuate it, threatening to burn it if they oppose placing it at the disposal of the French Army; otherwise, all property will be respected

If you find enemy forces ready to fight, which will render this attempt fruitless due to weak means at your disposal, you must consider retreating so as not to compromise your troops. Consequently, you will direct your withdrawal to Preussisch-Eylau and will invite Colonel Lamartinière to move in support to the right of this town with the 2nd battalion of *grenadiers* and two artillery pieces; the 3rd battalion of *grenadiers*, positioned at Heilsberg, should receive from Colonel Lamartinière the order to come and replace him at Bartenstein, just as the 3rd battalion of the *25e régiment d'infanterie légère*, positioned at Seeburg, will come to replace the 3rd battalion at Heilsberg, according to Colonel Lamartinière's suggestion, the orders being given to this effect.

I am sending you *chef de bataillon* Regnard, my *aide de camp*, M. Dalbignac, to follow your operations. Every day you will send me either officers from your *état-major* [headquarters] or *estafettes* [dispatch riders] who are knowledgeable of the country, to inform me of anything that might be of interest concerning this important mission. I think that it will be useful during your march to direct patrols of light cavalry on Elbing and principally on Tapiau, going back up the left bank of the Prégel. General L'Estocq's corps took this direction to reach Insterburg.'9

---

9   Bennigsen interpreted this order as a clear indication of the French intent to take Königsberg. In actually, it was a reflection of the dire conditions that the French troops were experiencing. By early January 1807, Bernadotte's 1st Corps and Ney's 6th Corps were in a precarious position, stretched too far north and separated from the rest of the army. Marshal Ney had exacerbated his vulnerability by extending elements of his corps toward Königsberg in search of rations and fodder despite Napoleon's orders prohibiting any forward movement that could provoke the Russians. Although sufficient provisions were available in Prussia, bad weather and terrible roads complicated their transport to the front and compelled Ney to disperse his troops over a vast territory between Bartenstein, Bischofsburg, and Guttstadt, and to look even as far as Königsberg. Upon learning on 18 January of Ney's units moving closer to Königsberg, Napoleon sent the marshal a sharp rebuke: 'Such individual measures interfere with the general plan of operations, and are capable of compromising an entire army.' Berthier to Ney, 18 January 1807, in Dumas, *Précis des évènements militaires*, vol.3, pp.324–325. See also Victor-Bernard Derrécagaix, *Le maréchal Berthier, prince de Wagram et de Neuchâtel* (Paris, 1905), vol. 2, pp.193–194. For details on challenges facing Ney, see Henri Bonnal, *La vie militaire du Maréchal Ney, duc d'Elchingen, prince de la Moskowa* (Paris: Chapelot, 1910), vol.2, pp.365–366;

The plan of operations that I therefore proposed for the moment was to enter into Old Prussia by passing between the lakes and to conceal as much as possible this march from the enemy; to intercept the enemy in his march on Königsberg; to make myself master of the Niedrigung, a province rich in provisions, and to establish free and assured communications with Danzig; to raise the blockade of Graudenz; then to move the army into winter quarters in Old Prussia and to await there the necessary reinforcements from Russia; upon their arrival, to reinforce the Danzig garrison with General L'Estocq's entire *corps*, which would have been strong enough to stop the enemy from approaching this fortress, unless he had wished to employ there very considerable forces, which would have weakened forces directed against the Russian army. If the enemy had not sent then substantial forces against Danzig, General L'Estocq would have been able for his part to stage diversions and disturb the enemy on the left bank of the Vistula. The map will make clear the rest of the advantages that we would have been able to reap from this plan at the beginning of the second campaign, which we would have been able to commence with vigor and success. You will soon see, General, that after having repulsed the two *corps d'armée* of Ney and Bernadotte I had partially succeeded in this plan and I had already drawn a formidable cordon that was supposed to cover the winter quarters of the remaining [French] forces; but as this plan was just as detrimental to the French as it would have been advantageous for us, the enemy resisted it with all his forces; [Napoleon] failed in his designs while I only partially succeeded in the execution of mine. The devastating battle of Preussisch-Eylau then stopped us both from completely achieving our respective goals.

In the new order of battle that I made before leaving Biala, Major General Markov was named commander of the advance guard of the right wing, composed of two infantry regiments, three regiments of jagers, two regiments of Cossacks, one regiment of hussars and a company of horse artillery, altogether about 6,000 men. Major General Barclay de Tolly was named commander of the left wing, composed of three regiments of jagers, an infantry regiment, two regiments of Cossacks, a regiment of *hussars* and a company of horse artillery, also about 6,000 men strong.

Major General Baggehufvudt was given command of a flying detachment composed of two regiments of jagers, an infantry regiment, a hussar regiment, and a regiment of Cossacks.

Lieutenant General Anrep commanded the cavalry on the right wing, composed of six regiments and two squadrons of dragoons, a regiment of Polish light cavalry from Lithuania and two regiments of Cossacks.

Marquis de Colbert-Chabanais, *Le général Auguste Colbert (1793–1809): traditions, souvenirs et documents touchant sa vie et son temps* (Paris: Berger-Leverault, 1888), vol.3, pp.1–11; Colbert to Mme. de Colbert, Colbert to Josephine de Colbert, 15–18 January 1807, in Jeanne A. Ojala, *Auguste de Colbert: Aristocratic Survival in an Era of Upheaval, 1793–1809* (Salt Lake City: University of Utah Press, 1979), pp.132–133; Raymond-Aymery-Philippe-Joseph de Montesquiou Fezensac, *Souvenirs militaires de 1804 à 1814* (Paris: Dumaine, 1863), pp.133–134. A key factor in this crisis arose because of poor communications, specifically the long delay in delivering Napoleon's instructions to Ney; for two different interpretations, see James R. Arnold and Ralph R. Reinertsen, *Crisis in the Snows. Russia Confronts Napoleon: The Eylau Campaign 1806–1807* (Lexington: Napoleon Books, 2007),), pp. 198–206, and Frédéric Naulet, *Eylau: La campagne de Pologne, des boues de Pultusk aux neiges d'Eylau* (Paris: Economica, 2007), pp.112–117.

The cavalry of the left wing, commanded by Lieutenant General Prince Golitsyn, comprised of three regiments of cuirassiers, three regiments of dragoons, two hussar regiments, a regiment of Polish light cavalry, a regiment of Cossacks and a company of horse artillery.

Lieutenant General Tuchkov was given command of the right wing, Lieutenant General Count Ostermann of the left wing, and Lieutenant General Dokhturov of the centre. The 4th and 14th Divisions, composed of 10 infantry regiments, a hussar regiment, four companies of field artillery, a company of horse artillery and two companies of Prussian artillery, formed the reserves under Major Generals Count Kamensky and Somov.

On 4/16 January 1807, after having occupied Johannisburg, as I already said, I had the army make a march of three *milles*. The headquarters was established at Arys; the advance guard of the right wing at Rhein; the cavalry of the right wing at Dombrowken, Kossinowen, Lötzen and Paprotken. The advance guard of the left wing was still behind at Stawisky; the cavalry of the left wing at Lyck, Schwiddern and Schimenke; General Baggehufvudt's detachment at Kolno. The army occupied Dombrowken, Kossinowen, Lötzen, Gopratken and the environs.

On 5/17 January, the advance guard of the left wing arrived at Biala. The right wing of the army remained in its quarters from the previous day and the left wing took up its cantonments in the environs of Odene, Gutten, near Arys, and Baranen.

On 6/18 January, the headquarters arrived at Rhein; the advance guard of the right wing at Zondern, the cavalry at Rastenburg. The advance guard of the left wing at Arys; the cavalry of the left wing at Krzysahnen and Budzisken. General Baggehufvudt's detachment at Dombrowken. The army's right wing occupied the cantonments of Gross-Partsch, Mertenheim, Doben and the left wing in the environs of Odene, Gutten, near Arys, and Baranen.

The enemy received frequent reports of the march of a Russian *corps* to aid Königsberg, without however yet knowing precisely that it was the entire army that was approaching. Marshal Ney, perhaps finding his *corps d'armée* too exposed if it continued its march on Königsberg or too weak to be able to achieve this end, authorized General Colbert, commander of his advance guard, to propose an armistice to the Prussian generals de Rüchel and L'Estocq. There was in fact a meeting on 5/17 January at Preussisch-Eylau between generals Rüchel and Colbert in this respect, as you will see from the letter with which the King of Prussia honoured me and by the adjoining pieces.

> Frederick-William, King of Prussia, to General Bennigsen.
> *Monsieur général* Bennigsen. You must be already informed about a meeting that Lieutenant General de Rüchel had on the 17th at Preussisch-Eylau with General Colbert. It could not be refused, but neither could it have produced any consequences. You can judge by the response attached here, that I have just issued to Rüchel and that I am sending today to your court. I naturally rejected General Colbert's armistice, of which you will be pleased to find attached here the proposal, because it would have hindered your operations and given rise to improper interpretations. I want to dismiss any step that would not be in unison with our relations with my ally. This matters the most! In addition, the current effort by the French reveals their predicament. They would like to gain a little rest during a season to

which their troops are not accustomed and to prepare for the resumption of their operations as soon as they can hope to do better. They would have liked to make the armistice more palatable by seeking to reassure us with regard to the safety of Königsberg, but since you have already pushed forward and are currently acting in concert with the brave General L'Estocq, who managed to resist alone until this point forces greatly superior to his own, I much prefer to entrust the safety of my capital to the care of an allied army than to the dubious and uncertain promises of the enemy. My hopes are buttressed by the letter that you wrote to me from Rhein dated the 19th of this month. The decisive moment approaches and you will know how to fully profit from it. I flatter myself therefore that you will soon inform me of good news, such as one can expect from your great talents and the great means that are at your disposal. You will justify my confidence and increase my gratitude to you. For this I pray to the Lord that he keep you, Monsieur General Bennigsen, in his holy and worthy care.
Memel, 22 January 1807
Frederick-William'

The letter was accompanied by the proposed armistice between the French troops under the orders of M. Marshal Ney and the Prussian troops under the orders of Lieutenant Generals Rüchel and L'Estocq. Here is what it entailed:

M. *général* Colbert, according to the powers granted to him by M. Marshal Ney, proposes, in his name, to MM. lieutenant-generals Rüchel and L'Estocq to make an armistice by which the troops of the two powers would be able to take the much-needed rest amidst so cruel a season and that would spare the blood uselessly spilled in skirmishes without purpose and without result.

Article 1 – An armistice will be concluded verbally on *parole d'honneur* or in a written form and signed by the generals, pending the approval of the respective sovereigns.
Article 2 – A demarcation line will be established that neither French nor Prussian patrols will cross.
Article 3 – The following points would compose this line: Peitschendorf, Sensburg, Drengfurth, Barthen, Gerdauen, Friedland, Domnau, Preussisch-Eylau, Landsberg, Mehlsack, Heiligenbeil.
Article 4 – M. Marshal Ney will be able to occupy with his troops all of the cantonments situated one *lieue* beyond the left bank of the Alle, from Schippenbeil and upstream to Guttstadt, as well as those that are on the right bank of the Passarge up to its confluence.
Article 5 – The cantonments will be considered only as posts; the Prussian troops would incidentally also be able to establish them, just as they would like, behind the demarcation line.
Article 6 – MM. the French and Prussian generals, being in agreement on this distribution of places to occupy, would agree to initiate no hostilities without a proper notification given four days in advance.'

There was also General Rüchel's response to General Colbert:

> *Monsieur Général*! As a mark of my kindness and my respect to you, I decided to accept, without hesitation and without even giving myself the time to request the authorization of the King, the request for negotiation that you did me the honour of conveying to me. At the end of our conference at Preussisch-Eylau, I sent to His Majesty [the King of Prussia] a faithful account of all that which passed there, and I placed before his eyes the plan for an armistice that you have proposed. I have just received his response and I hasten, *mon Général*, to transmit it to you.
>
> The King certainly desires peace. He expressed that wish in front of the entire Europe. He talked it over with your Emperor. He seeks to inspire the same sentiment in Russia and in England. At this very moment, he is employing again to this end his most assiduous cares, after His Imperial Majesty [Napoleon] expressly declared that it is only through these two powers and in conjunction with them that He wished to make peace. But it must be also noted that by this declaration the Emperor of the French has rendered the Prussian cause inseparable from that of the courts of St Petersburg and of London and, in such situation, it no longer depends on the King alone to allow himself to take any unilateral steps
>
> The armistice that you suggested, *mon Général*, must be extended also to the *corps* of Lieutenant General L'Estocq; but the operations of the latter are too closely intertwined with those of General Bennigsen for it to be possible to detach them and consequently we are unable to take any measure that would naturally influence the Russian army of which, at the moment, the King is no longer the master. Incidentally look at the map and you will see that the demarcation line indicated in your plans would have us lose part of our current positions and would move them even further back.
>
> An armistice is only desirable insofar as it can alleviate the evils of war, spare us a useless effusion of blood and lead to an imminent peace; but that of which you have conceived the notion, *mon Général*, would be limited to just single and rather limited points and would offer no real benefits to anyone, as the principal operations would continue as before. Let us therefore leave to our sovereigns the care of more effectively seeking ways to restore public order and tranquillity. May all of the powers join their efforts to heal the wounds of humanity and may they support in this respect the wishes and efforts of my August Master!
>
> May it be, *mon Général*, that I am soon in a position to share with you the joy of seeing this desire accomplished and in the more fortunate circumstances, to cultivate the interesting acquaintance with you that our meeting at Preussisch-Eylau has provided me.
>
> *J'ai l'honneur d'être avec la considération la plus distinguée, etc…*
> Rüchel
> Königsberg, [no date given] January 1807

We see that this proposal for an armistice had no other goal than to buy the necessary time to determine the movements of the Russian army; we see this especially in the short timeframe of just four days that was set for giving advance warning for the resumption of hostilities. It is difficult to reconcile the news that the King conveyed to me with regards to armistice proposal with the report that Marshal Ney sent to the Minister of War, Prince de Neuchâtel, on 16 January 1807, which I also cite here in its entirety:

Marshal Ney to the Minister of War
Bartenstein, 16 January
I have the honour of informing you that the enemy seems generally limiting himself to staying on the defensive against the majority of my posts. The skirmishes – that we have not ceased to have with the Prussians for the last 15 days and which, despite producing little consequence for either side, have nevertheless greatly fatigued the enemy – gave way to negotiations. The Prussians desire rest and for my part I desire it also in order to allow the troops to resupply and to work on repairing shoes, weapons and clothes.

Consequently, the Prussian generals Rüchel and L'Estocq granted a meeting to General Colbert tomorrow at noon, at Preussisch-Eylau, to arrange an armistice – with a promise to notify about the resumption of hostilities four days in advance – either verbally, on *parole d'honneur*, or in writing pending the approval of our respective sovereigns. I ordered General Colbert to request as points of the demarcation line, which would be considered as neutral by our patrols, the following places: Sensburg, Rastenburg, Barthen, Gerdauen, Friedland, Domnau, Preussisch-Eylau, Landsberg, Mehlsack, and from this point drawing a straight line on Heiligenbeil, such that there would remain to us a large part of the Alle and all of the Passarge. I do not know if the Prussians will consent to this demarcation, but I will not be moved from this demand.

I just wrote to Marshal Soult to inform him of my position; I am also giving him that of the enemy and I am asking him which dispositions he will be able to make to link his left to my right, in concordance with the general operations of the *Grande Armée*.

The King of Prussia is still at Memel; he has just divided the troops that remain available to him into two *corps d'armée*: the 1st *corps* will be commanded by General Rüchel, whose headquarters is at Königsberg, occupying with his advance posts Mehlsack, Landsberg, Preussisch-Eylau and Domnau; the 2nd by General L'Estocq, whose headquarters is at Angerburg and that occupies with its advance posts Friedland, Gerdauen, Barthen, Rastenburg and Sensburg; he has with him a few regiments (pulks) of Cossacks and a few Russian infantry.

Prince William of Prussia, wounded at the battle of Jena, is expected at Königsberg; he is supposed to take up the overall command of the two *corps d'armée*, whose force is estimated at 18,000 men. There are 10,000 Russians concentrated at Tilsit and Insterburg on the Pregel; the English must have furnished muskets and artillery to the King of Prussia to put this small army in a state to act at the opening of the next campaign.

There are no Russian troops at Königsberg, nor on the upper Pregel; there is no longer a question of a landing of English or Swedish troops on the Baltic shore: we attribute this change to the imminent arrival of Emperor Alexander at Memel, where he is expected any moment now and we conclude that the peace will not be long in being negotiated.

On 19 January, the Marshal wrote the following in another report to the Minister of War, concerning the same subject:

> Marshal Ney to the Minister of War
> 19 January
> As soon as the dispatches from Your Excellency designating my winter quarters reached me, I gave the order to General Colbert, who on the 17th was at Preussisch-Eylau, to break off the conference with General Rüchel. Nevertheless, this Prussian general ordered General L'Estocq not to initiate hostilities against our troops except if he was forced to do it. Here is what General Colbert was able to learn from General Rüchel over the course of the negotiations:
>
> The Prussian army completed its junction with the Russians, that is to say, that the latter have advanced their right up to Rastenburg. A corps of 20,000 English is supposed to land shortly, and some Swedish troops are expected too. General Rüchel sought to dispel an impression that we had of him as one of the driving forces behind this war. Whatever happens to Prussia, he told us, he has already made a firm decision – *resolution* – to travel to America where he expects – to situate himself honourably and advantageously.
>
> General Rüchel also promised that M. de Krüsemarck was expected at any moment to return from the mission with which he had been charged to Emperor Alexander; he added that he believed that the King [of Prussia] desires peace, but that harsh conditions would delay reaching an agreement.
>
> The Russians have considerable reserves.

9

Bennigsen's Offensive – Mohrungen

On 7/19 January, the advance guard of the right wing moved on Schesten, the cavalry on Rastenburg; the advance guard of the left wing to Rudowken, the cavalry to Prangenau; General Baggehufvudt's detachment to Wolka; the headquarters remained at Rhein. The right wing of the army had its cantonments at Gross-Blaustein, Rosengarten, Gross-Partsch and Kamionken; the left wing at Budzisken, Mertenheim and Krzysahnen. The same day, Lieutenant-Colonel Vlassov was sent with two companies of the 24th Jager Regiment and 200 Cossacks to Fürstwitten, to surprise a small enemy party that was quartered there; we took 18 prisoners and killed and wounded a few more.

On 8/20 January, the headquarters moved to Heilige-Linde. The advance guard of the right wing arrived at Molditten; the cavalry at Paaris; the advance guard of the left wing reached Langenbrück, the cavalry was at Langheim, General Baggehufvudt's detachment at Legeinen; the right wing of the army at Klein-Komlack, Lumienen, Dublienen, Podlacken and Tolksdorf; the left-wing at Gross-Moënsdorf, Klawsdorf and Pültz.

Lieutenant General Prince Golitsyn reported that upon learning that an enemy squadron was still in the environs of Langheim, he had dispatched there Colonel Grekov XVIII with his regiment of Cossacks; that this man had found means to surround the enemy squadron, which belonged to the *3e régiment de hussards français*; that he had killed some of them and that Captain Saint-Aubin-le-Brun, two junior officers [*officiers subalternes*] and 83 hussars had been taken prisoner. Colonel Grekov spoke highly of the bravery and good conduct of the French officers and in particular of their captain.

I must add again that the French were taken by complete surprise, which serves as a proof that the enemy was not well informed about our movement. Yet this incident, along with another one that occurred the day before, caused alarm along his entire line in Old Prussia.

I reinforced the Prussian *corps*, under the orders of Lieutenant General L'Estocq, with three battalions of the Vyborgskii Musketeer Regiment, under the orders of Colonel Pillar,[1] and a regiment of Cossacks, inviting him to attack the next day at Schippenbeil.

In the afternoon of 9/21 January, the army entered the quarters that the enemy had evacuated that same morning. The headquarters was established at Bischofstein; the advance guard of the right wing at Gallingen; the cavalry at Schwansfeld; the advance guard of

---

1 Yegor Pillar (Georg Ludwig Pilar von Pilchau, 1767–1830) commanded the Vyborgskii Musketeer Regiment in 1803–1809. He later served as the chef of the Vilenskii Musketeer Regiment in 1809–1810 and of the 34th Jager Regiment in 1810–1814; he became a major general in December 1812.

the left wing at Voigtsdorf, the cavalry at Frankenau; General Baggehufvudt's detachment at Thegsten. The army billeted the right wing in the environs of Plaussen, Wusslack, Sturmhübel and Molditten; the left wing, in the environs of Prossitten, Schulen and Santoppen.

General Markov sent to the headquarters a French officer and seven soldiers taken prisoner in a village. General Barclay de Tolly reported that, during his march, the Ilovaisky IX Cossack Regiment had encountered a small enemy party near the village of Bansen and that it had taken prisoner one non-commissioned officer [*sous-officer*] and 17 soldiers.

Yegor Pillar (Georg Ludwig Pilar von Pilchau). (State Hermitage Museum)

Lieutenant General l'Estocq, having concentrated his *corps* near Dönhoistadt, advanced up to Schippenbeil, but the enemy had burned the bridge on the Alle and evacuated the town. Concerning this movement, Marshal Ney made the following report to the Minister of War:

> Marshal Ney to the Minister of War
> Allenstein, 22 January 1807, six o'clock in the evening
> I have the honour of informing you that the retrograde movement of my *corps d'armée* began on the 20th. The *voltigeurs* and *grenadiers* that were deployed along the Alle, fell back under cover of two squadrons of the *10e chasseurs*, and retired, by echelons, from Schippenbeil, Bartenstein and Heilsberg; they will arrive tonight at Guttstadt. This same day, the 3rd battalion of *voltigeurs*, which was at Langheim, retired with the *3e de hussards* on Bischofstein, where the *25e légère* was earlier located. The *25e légère* and the *27e de ligne* withdrew, on the 21st, the former on Seeburg and the latter on Allenstein, where the *59e* already was. The *69e* and the *76e* and General Grouchy's four regiments of dragoons withdrew, on the 20th and 21st, from Bischofsburg on Passenheim; this column will arrive today at Neidenburg, where the *39e* is as well; the *6e d'infanterie légère* will be at Hohenstein on the 22nd.
>
> The dragoons are covering the lines of communications to Willenberg and are connected on the left with General Colbert, who has established himself at Wartenburg since this morning with a battalion of *voltigeurs*, one of *grenadiers*, two cannon and the *25e régiment d'infanterie légère*.
>
> Tomorrow, at four o'clock in the morning, the remainder of the *voltigeurs* and *grenadiers*, the *10e de chasseurs*, a company of light artillery and the *50e régiment*

will depart from Guttstadt to take up positions at Allenstein; at eight o'clock in the morning, the *27e* and *59e* will leave Allenstein to go to Hohenstein.

By means of these dispositions I will have, on the 24th, all of my troops concentrated between Hohenstein and Neidenburg: there I will wait for one day to discern the enemy's intentions; but I do not believe he is strong enough to dare attacking me seriously, as he has only shown to this moment a great deal of cavalry, but little infantry and no artillery.[2] Starting on the 19th, the enemy had made a general reconnaissance from Langheim, Leunenburg on the Zaine and the Barthen, up to Schippenbeil; his attempts were repulsed everywhere; at Leunenburg particularly, the enemy suffered great losses in killed, wounded and prisoners; among the wounded we found Colonel de Stutterheim;[3] at Langheim and at Schippenbeil, we were similarly successful.[4]

On the 20th, my columns were followed by Russian and Prussian cavalry and also by a few infantry that travelled in sleighs; that evening and during the night, the enemy harassed all the positions our troops occupied but it approached our infantry regiments with great circumspection; [after skirmishes] the enemy cavalry left behind a few wounded men and horses. But a squadron of the *3e régiment de hussards* got carried away during a charge and was sharply repulsed by the infantry, losing a few men.

Here is the testimony gathered from prisoners and deserters: 'A column of Russian and Prussian infantry, about 4,000 men strong, is marching from Sensburg to Willenberg. Another column of ten Russian cavalry regiments, each one 800 to 900 men strong, is marching on Guttstadt, Allenstein, Hohenstein and Neidenburg. The Russian infantry, which must be following this cavalry, is still several marches behind it; we do not know its strength. General Bennigsen is at Rastenburg. The Prussians, under the orders of General L'Estocq, are moving on Liebstadt and Elbing via the left bank of the Alle. I am informing the Prince de Ponte-Corvo [Bernadotte] and Marshal Soult of my retrograde movements and of the intelligence that I have on the enemy.

On 10/22 January, I ordered General Markov to march with the advance guard to Kerwienen and to dispatch parties to the vicinity of Heilsberg and Guttstadt to gather news of the enemy retreat and of the routes it was taking. A second order was sent to Lieutenant General Count Ostermann-Tolstoy to march with the 2nd Division, General Baggehufvudt's detachment, and two regiments of cavalry from the left wing to Seeburg in pursuit of the enemy. Lieutenant General L'Estocq, being unable to cross the Alle at Schippenbeil, was obliged to march on to Friedland, where he crossed the river and arrived the same day at Preussisch-Eylau.

---

2   Bennigsen's note: As you can see, *Général*, these words show how often the enemy was little informed, on the 10th/22nd, about the march that I was attempting with my entire army.
3   Bennigsen's note: Prussian.
4   Bennigsen's note: It was a march in advance that I made on the 7th/19th, and that the enemy took for a general reconnaissance. I have no knowledge of the actions listed here.

The headquarters remained that day at Bischofstein and the remainder of the troops in the quarters of the previous day.

On 11/23 January, I received General Markov's report that he found no enemy forces at Kerwienen; Lieutenant General Count Ostermann similarly reported that the enemy had evacuated Seeburg, shortly before his arrival in this place. Lieutenant General L'Estocq arrived with his *corps* at Landsberg. Meanwhile, on January 11/23, Marshal Ney made the following report to the Minister of War:

> Marshal Ney to the Minister of War
> Hohenstein, 23 January 1807, eight o'clock in the evening
> I have the honour of informing you that my retrograde movement continued today without the enemy attempting to disturb the march of my columns. Yesterday, at two o'clock in the morning, the enemy tried to conduct a reconnaissance at Wartenburg but retired after the first gunshots. General Grouchy wrote me from Jedwabno, yesterday, that since his departure with General Marcognet's brigade from Bischofsburg, the enemy no longer followed him; that the Russians and Prussians are leaning to the right and seem to be moving on Guttstadt, and finally that a dragoon regiment that he had at Ortelsburg and that he brought back to himself, has no new information on the enemy: that would seem to contradict the report that had been made to me of the march of a column moving from Sensburg on Willenberg.
>
> General Colbert informs me, this morning, that the Russian cavalry had provisions prepared at Bischofsburg and that Seeburg was occupied by several cavalry regiments.
>
> The troops of my *corps d'armée* will occupy, on the 25th of this month, the following positions: Neidenburg, Gilgenburg, Soldau, Lautenburg, Kuczbrack, Mlawa, Janow and Chorzellen.
>
> General Grouchy's dragoon division, maintaining advance-posts at Mühlen, on the road from Hohenstein to Gilgenburg, will occupy the cantonments from Neidenburg halfway up the road to Gilgenburg, with two regiments; the other two will be placed in the villages between Neidenburg and Soldau.
>
> General Colbert's light cavalry will occupy Janow; it will place one squadron at Chorzellen and another before Neidenburg, so as to cover communications with Willenberg, Jedwabno and Hohenstein.
>
> By means of these dispositions, I can completely assemble my *corps d'armée* in less than two days, be it on Neidenburg, Gilgenburg, Soldau or Mlawa.
>
> Tomorrow I will go to Neidenburg, where I will stay until I get better understanding what the intentions of the enemy are.
>
> I found Hohenstein occupied by Sahuc's[5] dragoon division from the Prince de Ponte-Corvo's *corps*; it is of paramount importance to retain this position because it ensures communications with Osterode.

---

5   Louis Michel Antoine Sahuc (1755–1813), French general, commanding a cavalry brigade in 1805 and a dragoon division in 1806–1807.

I am writing to the Prince de Ponte-Corvo and to Marshal Soult to inform them of my dispositions and of the direction that the enemy seems to have taken on Guttstadt.

That same evening Marshal Ney wrote to the Prince de Ponte-Corvo the following letter:

Marshal Ney to the Prince de Ponte-Corvo
23 January 1807, eight o'clock in the evening
Just this minute I received a letter that General Grouchy wrote to me from Jedwabno, dated today, and by which he informs me that the enemy is advancing rapidly from all sides on my right flank; that the enemy occupied Ortelsburg, Mensguth and Passenheim, immediately after we had evacuated these different points, and finally that the enemy is commonly employing infantry. I instructed General Grouchy to write to you tonight or tomorrow at daybreak and to convey to you all the information that he may come across. We are assured that the enemy has moved a great portion of his left wing from Ostrolenka, Johannisburg and Nikolaïken to direct his forces on to the Passarge, marching primarily by way of Rastenburg.

General Maison informed me of the position of your troops; he also warned General Dutaillis that tomorrow he would move Sahuc's dragoon division closer, and that an officer from your *corps d'armée*, coming from Liebstadt, has heard the sound of gunfire there. As it is probable that the enemy will march on Osterode, I am countermanding part of my dispositions. I will therefore strongly occupy Hohenstein and further back Mühlen so as to be able to support your right and turn the enemy's flank if he wishes to throw himself between my left and your right. Rest assured, Monseigneur, that whatever the circumstances, you will find me always ready to prove my zeal for the glory of the arms of the Emperor and of my affection for you.[6]

On 12/24 January, my headquarters arrived at Heilsberg, the advance guard of the right wing reached Elditten, and the cavalry was at Freymarkt. The divisions and the reserve of the right wing occupied Amt-Heilsberg, Lawden, Grossendorf and Kerwienen. The advance guard of the left wing at Lemkendorf; the cavalry at Schönwiese; General Baggehufvudt's detachment at Tollack. The divisions of the left wing occupied Guttstadt, Heidenberg and

---

6   Although receiving reports on the Russian movements, Napoleon refused to believe that Bennigsen would undertake a winter campaign so soon after Pultusk and Golymin. He dismissed these reports, insisting that the Russians were simply redeploying their forces in response to Ney's movements. The emperor remained convinced that the Russians would take winter quarters as soon as they completed this repositioning. Yet, reports from Ney, Soult, and others all claimed that a large number of Russian troops were concentrating to the north in preparation for an advance between Mühlhausen and Liebstadt. According to Ney, 'trustworthy information derived from merchants agrees with the stories of deserters and prisoners in stating that there is a considerable mass of Russian troops assembled at this moment between Mühlhausen and Preußisch Eylau, and that the united army under the command of General Bennigsen is 80,000 men strong'. It took the whole week of 20–27 January to convince the emperor that the Russians had in fact launched a general offensive. Ney to Berthier, 24 January 1807, in Colbert-Chabanais, *Général Auguste Colbert*, vol.3, pp.257–258.

Seeburg. Major General Barclay de Tolly reported that he had detached a squadron of the Izumskii Hussar Regiment, with 60 Cossacks, under the command of Lieutenant-Colonel Verigin, to Passenheim, where this officer encountered two enemy squadrons of the *6e régiment de dragons*; he defeated them, killed a few of their men and took prisoner two captains, Derivaux and Cachelot, with 29 dragoons.

Major General Markov reported that, upon arriving with the advance guard of the right wing at Elditten, he had learned that the enemy, who was occupying the small town of Liebstadt with an infantry detachment and some squadrons of dragoons and hussars under the orders of General Pacthod,[7] was gathering the peasants' wagons to commence his retreat. Upon receiving this news, General Markov marched with his advance guard to engage the enemy before their departure from Liebstadt, which worked perfectly for him. Despite the enemy's resistance inside the town, Markov had dislodged him with considerable losses in killed and wounded. As prisoners, he sent to the headquarters a lieutenant-colonel, a major, 16 junior officers [*officiers subalternes*] and 270 soldiers. Our losses were 27 men killed and wounded.[8]

Lieutenant General L'Estocq, with his corps, took up position between Wormditt and Mehlsack and pushed his advance posts up to the Passarge.

Receiving the news that Prussian General Rouquette, who had been with a detachment in the Niedrigung, was repulsed by troops from Marshal Bernadotte's *corps d'armée* and forced to retreat via Preussisch-Holland and even to abandon Braunsberg, General L'Estocq decided to push forward with his right wing to Mühlhausen, so as to anticipate the enemy's retreat.

Marshal Ney sent, on this date, the following letter to Marshal Bernadotte:

Marshal Ney to the Prince de Ponte-Corvo
24 January, six o'clock in the evening
The enemy limited himself today to mere reconnaissances; he sent infantry and cavalry in the direction of Ortelsburg and Passenheim, and it would seem enough

---

7   French brigadier general Michel-Marie Pacthod (1764–1830).
8   Yermolov, who commanded the artillery in Markov's advance guard: 'On 12 [24] January, the vanguard arrived at Elditten and learned from the residents that a French detachment lay at Liebstadt and its patrol had been inquiring about Russians just half an hour ago. We made a rather long march that day and General Markov had to call for volunteers from the less-fatigued troops. A large number volunteered but when the 5th Jager Regiment was ordered up and the others heard that Colonel Gogel himself would lead the regiment, everyone declared that they would join him and off they marched without a break. I asked for permission to take two guns and join them to witness the action. Some two *verstas* from Liebstadt, the enemy caught sight of us from some heights and began deploying troops on the city walls and gates, preparing for defence. We could see, however, that there were few of them. Our jagers occupied a cemetery adjacent to the town and engaged the enemy, while the line infantry went against the city gates that led to the main street. Colonel Yurkovskii with two squadrons of the Elisavetgradskii Hussars rushed into the town from a side gate and the infantry made a bayonet attack. The enemy was routed and pushed into narrow and twisted streets, suffering heavy casualties. Those who fled from the town were pursued by the Cossacks of courageous Colonel Sisoev. Our guns did not fire a single shot. We captured 22 officers and over 300 rank and file. The red hussar regiment, for some reason referred to simply as the Parisian, was almost destroyed here. Leaving some cavalry in the town, Markov returned to Elditten, where the exhausted troops found food and shelter. That day we had marched and fought for 16 hours.' Yermolov, *The Czar's General*, p.71.

to indicate by that his movement on Danzig. Deserters and prisoners made the following reports: 'There is occurring at this moment a considerable concentration of Russian troops between Mühlhausen and Preussisch-Eylau; the army under the orders of General Bennigsen is 80,000 men strong. This General had a conference with the English General Hutchinson, who is supposed to join him with 10,000 men, which are supposed to land at Danzig, as well as a similar number of Swedish troops. Marshal Kamensky was disgraced and replaced by General Bennigsen, who [is the commander in chief – *commande en chef*]. It is said openly that the French army will be forced to evacuate the right bank of the Vistula before 10 days have passed. General Courbière, the *commandant* of Graudenz, was informed by the Russian General, that he would be unblocked at the same time as they were masters of Thorn and that all preparations had been made to cross the Vistula, immediately after this first operation, and so to force the French army, which is at Warsaw, to retreat promptly.' Finally [they go as far as to say that – *on va jusqu'à dire que*] upon the first victory that the Russians score on us, and of which, given their superiority, they have no doubt, the Austrian army will make a diversion in Moravia and will penetrate into Silesia.

    I will add to that that the Russian and Prussian officers, who came to negotiate, on the 22nd, at the advance-posts, before Allenstein, said that they were very much in a position to chase us beyond the Vistula.

On 13/25 January, the headquarters moved to the village of Arensdorf. The advance guard of the right wing received the order, if the enemy was retreating, to march on Mohrungen, and the cavalry of the right wing was supposed to take up cantonments in the environs of that town. The advance guard of the left wing received orders to march on Digitten while General Baggehufvudt's detachment to Jankendorf. The direction of these two detachments had a twin purpose: that of observing Marshal Ney's corps and that of leaving the enemy uncertain as to our intentions. To this end, General Barclay de Tolly was charged with spreading on his march the rumour that the majority of the Russian army was following that route and that it was moving on Osterode. The cavalry of the left wing at Alt-Ramten; the right wing of the army, at Vogtsdorf, Schwenkitten, Sommerfeld and Launau; the left wing at Chenenthal, Elditten and Guttstadt. Lieutenant General L'Estocq, having learned that the enemy had already retired from Braunsberg via Mühlhausen on Preussisch-Holland, decided to march on Mehlsack, from whence he went to Wormditt. Marshal Ney's reports on that day, dated from Hohenstein, to the Minister of War were as follows:

Marshal Ney to the Minister of War
Hohenstein, 25 January, five o'clock in the morning
I have the honour of relaying to Your Excellency the copy of two letters, that I have just received from the Prince de Ponte-Corvo and General Maison, his *chef d'état-major*, dated yesterday. I will keep my position at Hohenstein, Mühlen and Neidenburg until new orders from the Emperor.

    The enemy is limiting himself to observing me with patrols; he still occupies Allenstein, Wartenburg, Seeburg, Bischofsburg and Passenheim. His march on Danzig with superior forces must have another purpose than that of lifting the blockade of that place. Yesterday a reconnaissance conducted by dragoons from General Grouchy's division was sharply pushed back from Passenheim on Jedwabno. The road from Willenberg via Chorzellen and Prasnitz is not troubled by the enemy. Marshal Soult, even better placed than myself to be precisely informed of all enemy movements in this direction, will no doubt inform Your Excellency.

The Same to the Same[9]
25 January, nine o'clock in the morning
I have just received a letter from General Maison, of which I have the honour of sending you the copy.[10] I do not think it necessary to move on Osterode, because that would pull me away from communications from Neidenburg, which are extremely necessary to retain to cover the left flank of the *Grande Armée*: I will therefore remain in my positions at Hohenstein, Mühlen and Neidenburg. The circumstances seem pressing; it seems to me that it would be quite essential that His Majesty, should he judge it unsuitable to march on the enemy, send at least one of his *aides de camp* to be on the spot, to check the state of affairs and inform him of it.

Marshal Ney to General Maison:
Hohenstein, 25 January, 11 o'clock in the morning
I received, my dear General, your letter from today. I am pained by what happened to General Pacthod at Liebstadt. The enemy, who is moving on Mohrungen, seems to have the intention of making you to evacuate Elbing and Marienwerder, so as to establish his communications with Danzig; this movement will leave time for the *1er corps d'armée* to concentrate at Osterode, which it would not have been able to do if the enemy had marched rapidly on Preussisch-Holland; my position is such, that I cannot leave it without compromising the communications of the *Grande Armée* via Neidenburg; it is therefore impossible for me to support your right any more so.

The Minister, whom I have informed exactly of all events, has still not responded to me and the last orders that I have from him are to take up my winter quarters at Mlawa.

I await with great impatience for news from the imperial headquarters.

The same to General Grouchy[11]
Hohenstein, 25 January
Yesterday I received, my dear General, your report on the action that took place at Passenheim; I hope that this lesson, which the dragoons just received from the

---

9 Bennigsen's note: These letters are not among the intercepted papers.
10 Bennigsen's note: This letter is not among the captured papers.
11 Bennigsen's note: *Général* L'Estocq directed his march on Preussich-Holland, but he would never have been able to cut off Marshal Bernadotte's corps from Osterode there; it was by the rapid march of the Russian army on Mohrungen and above all by the direction that I gave to the column of the left wing on Alt-Ramten, where the cavalry arrived at the moment the action began quite close to Mohrungen, [which could no longer have any consequence – *ce qui ne pouvait non plus tirer à conséquence*]. The retreat on Thorn still remained open to him and he took it, in fact, upon the approach of the Russian army on Mohrungen. By the arrival of our troops at Liebemühl, the road from Osterode was entirely cut off to Bernadotte's corps.

enemy, will encourage them henceforth to have outposts outside towns and to mount up with the first light of day [*à l'heure de la diane*]; express to the officer who was commanding at Passenheim the full extent of my discontent concerning such a shameful manner of service.

I also received your letter from today. Continue to be in contact with Chorzellen, until General Colbert's arrival in that position. The Prince de Ponte-Corvo was obliged to retire on Mohrungen [and Osterode]; we are both awaiting orders from the Emperor.

Marshal Ney to the Prince de Ponte-Corvo
25 January, four o'clock in the evening
I received the letter that Your Excellency did me the honour of writing to me today on the 25th, at two o'clock in the morning. General Maison, your *chef d'état-major*, had already informed me of the action that took place at Liebstadt. I told him that I considered the concentration of your entire *corps d'armée* at Mohrungen as the surest way to ensure its safety because of this location's proximity to Osterode as well as defensive capabilities that I would be able to add there, so as to give one major battle to the enemy instead of several minor actions. Your Excellency was so well aware of the necessity of this movement that you have instructed me to carry it out, as it is evident from your letter.

I believe this to be the enemy's intentions: in retaking the offensive, his goal is undoubtedly to restore land-based communications with Danzig. The sole means to achieve this objective was to direct columns via Rastenburg directly on Guttstadt, which the enemy did with a great deal of cavalry, keeping his left and right wing back until his arrival on the Passarge. As soon as he is at Preussisch-Holland, I presume that the enemy will send down a column from Braunsberg onto the same point; in that case Elbing would remain exposed and the enemy will probably remain peacefully there, unless his initial dispositions indicate a far greater plan of military operations.

In the first case, we should concentrate in very tight defensive positions; that is what I did with my *corps d'armée*, finding myself in a position to rest on Osterode, which His Majesty [Napoleon] has designated for your *corps d'armée*. I conclude that the enemy will only make a weak demonstration on Mohrungen, just as he did on the entirety of my right wing, as I refused it from Guttstadt to Allenstein and Passenheim. The interior of this line has been occupied by enemy cavalry, placed in echelons, from Rastenburg to Bischofsburg, Bischofstein, Seeburg and Guttstadt.

Your Excellency invites me to make a movement on his right wing and to move on Allenstein. However, it seems to me that this disposition would be contrary to the general plan of operations that we should adopt against the enemy. [By following your order] I would expose my right flank to the enemy but by remaining at Hohenstein, where the main forces of my *corps d'armée* are currently located, I am in a position to support you in direction of Osterode and to march anywhere as circumstances might necessitate it; I can also stray away the points I am currently occupying, without compromising my communications with the *Grande Armée*, until His Imperial Majesty has made a new decision.

If I had any advice for Your Excellency, I would advise you to avoid a separate battle against superior enemy forces until we achieve a junction and if, at that time, we are so hard-pressed that it must come to this extremity [fighting a battle] without orders from the Emperor, then we will fulfil our duty.

General Markov reported that he had left, on the 25th, with his advance guard from Elditten, in order to pursue the enemy, and that he had made a march of one and a half *milles*, partially through defiles and forests, without having seen the enemy. But having reached the plain near the village of Georgenthal, he received from the small detachment that preceded him the report that it had engaged the enemy advance posts, and that it had initially forced them back until the enemy received reinforcements and that several columns composed of cavalry and infantry were moving on their left flank, seemingly to cut off our men from the defiles. At the same time, the Cossack Colonel Malakhov reported that considerable [enemy] columns were still arriving on the road to Mohrungen; it was Marshal Bernadotte himself, who was marching with his entire corps from Elbing and who advanced with the remaining forces to the aid of those who were already engaged.

Major General Markov formed his small detachment not far from the village of Georgenthal, in a fairly advantageous position on the hills; the Pskovskii Musketeer Regiment formed his right wing, the 25th Jagers his left wing, and the Ekaterinoslavskii Grenadier Regiment took up position in the second line. Two battalions from the 5th Jagers scattered as skirmishers to cover his front while a battalion from the same regiment formed the reserve. Two battalions from the 7th Jagers along with two companies of the Ekaterinoslavskii Grenadiers occupied the village of Georgenthal and the roads that could be used to move around it; a battalion of the 7th Jagers occupied the woods near the left flank, where the action began very hotly one hour after noon.

The Elisavetgradskii Hussar Regiment, commanded by General Yurkovskii,[12] was placed in a ravine; for some time, this unit contained, with a great deal of skill and bravery, the enemy cavalry that was actively supported by horse artillery. Seeing that he could no longer resist superior enemy forces, Yurkovskii decided to fall back and pass through a defile that was behind him. The enemy cavalry pressed him vigorously, and Colonel Gogel,[13] upon seeing this, threw himself into the defile with a battalion of the 5th Jagers. Supported by the company of horse artillery, under the orders of Colonel Yermolov, they stopped the enemy, which gave time to General Yurkovskii to complete this difficult withdrawal without considerable losses.[14]

---

12 Colonel Anastasii Antonovich Yurkovskii served as the commander of the Aleksandriiskii Hussar Regiment until 13 January 1807, when he was appointed the chef of the Elisavetgradskii Hussar Regiment. He was also promoted to a major general on that same date.
13 Colonel Fedor Grigorievich Gogel, commander of the 5th Jager Regiment until December 1804 and the chef of the same regiment between 1804 and 1814.
14 Yermolov: 'The disposition of 13 [25] January instructed the vanguard to bivouac at Mohrungen so we marched at dawn. Colonel Yurkovskii led the way with the Elisavetgradskii Hussars and two Cossack regiments and drove the enemy pickets back; as he climbed the nearby heights, that surrounded the vast Mohrungen valley, he observed large enemy forces deployed for battle. Yurkovskii then made the mistake of descending into the valley and the enemy engaged him with its cavalry. Moving by forced marches, the vanguard arrived on the battlefield only to find Yurkovskii hard pressed by the

Just as the fighting commenced, General Markov sent a message about the circumstances in which he found himself to Lieutenant General Anrep, who was marching with the cavalry of the right wing, but was still too far off to be able arrive in time to help our advance guard. Anrep nevertheless ordered the regiments forming the head of his column to march with the greatest speed while he himself rushed forward accompanied by just two *aides de camp* and a small escort.

The situation, meanwhile, became ever more serious, and the disproportion in forces was rather great. Marshal Bernadotte's *corps d'armée* was 16,000 men strong while General Markov's advance guard did not have even 6,000 men; Markov held an advantageous position but could not reinforce or safeguard his wings to avoid being flanked. As the French opened fire with their artillery, Markov observed a strong infantry column advancing against on his left flank. Colonel Vuich,[15] leading the 25th Jager Regiment, made a bayonet charge; at first he had some success but this newly raised regiment was, after a certain time, routed. Lieutenant-Colonel Panchulidzev saw this – he rushed with two companies of the 5th Jagers to help this regiment. The enemy was stopped and Captain Reitzenstein, serving in one of these two companies, took during the melee the flag of the *9e régiment d'infanterie*,[16] but its Eagle had already been broken off;[17] at the same time this brave officer was gravely wounded. General Markov then pushed forward two battalions of the Ekaterinoslavskii regiment, which attacked with the bayonet and, demonstrating that gallantry that has always distinguished this regiment, forced the enemy column to yield. Major Fischer, who commanded

---

enemy and falling back to a small village, the main street of which was being bombarded by enemy artillery. I immediately brought my horse artillery company up and, taking advantage of my elevated position and numbers, I drove the enemy guns back and covered our cavalry's retreat. They took up positions behind our troops while part of the Cossacks engaged the enemy. Major General Markov deployed his troops on the nearby heights. The enemy attacked our left flank; its infantry column moving against the village. To protect itself from our artillery, it went towards the frozen lake located on the right. Having captured the village, the infantry deployed in some gardens enclosed by high fences and ditches. Since the trees had no leaves, our skirmishers were easily detected and driven out and enemy musket fire caused us considerable harm. Colonel Vuich was ordered to charge with the 25th Jäger Regiment. This unit had been established just before the start of the campaign and was not accustomed to the dangers of war; it became disordered while crossing the ditch and could not hold its ground. Some courageous lads climbed the fence but were not supported and remained isolated. Six companies of the Ekaterinoslavskii Grenadier Regiment, led by the gallant Major Fisher, and two companies of the 5th Jägers rushed forward and, without firing a shot, broke through and exterminated virtually everyone in the gardens and the village. We captured the flag of the 9th Légère, while a few survivors fled to the lake.' Yermolov, *The Czar's General*, pp.71–72.

In his memoir, written decades after the event, Volkonsky recalled one particular incident of the battle of Mohrungen: 'The battle was marked by a splendid charge of the Sumskii Hussar Regiment and a bayonet melee between the infantry forces. Although, I am wrong to call this a bayonet melee. Eyewitnesses told me that Ekaterinoslavskii Grenadier Regiment was surprised that a column of the French voltigeurs dared to accept our bayonet melee. "These underlings are not worthy of our bayonets," the grenadiers said and, reversing their muskets, they drove off the French column with their musket-butts.' Volkonsky, *Zapiski*, p.23.

15 Colonel Nikolai Vuich (Vujič) (1765–1836), Russian officer of the Serbian origin. He served as the chef of the 25th Jager Regiment in 1806–1808.
16 For French perspective see T.E. Crowdy, *Incomparable: Napoleon's 9th Light Infantry Regiment* (Oxford: Osprey Publishing, 2012), pp.199–201.
17 Crowdy, *Incomparable*, p.201.

one of these battalions, was gravely wounded.[18]

Another French infantry column moved to turn General Markov's right flank. The latter sent Colonel Gogel with a battalion of the 5th Jagers and Lieutenant-Colonel Loshkarev[19] with a battalion of the Pskovskii Musketeer Regiment, with orders to halt the march of this column, which these officers executed with a great deal of intelligence and bravery.

General Markov, seeing that the French were reinforcing the columns that were supposed to turn his flanks and understanding the impossibility of resisting for long against such superior enemy forces, ordered a retrograde movement, beginning with his right wing that he thought was most exposed. The enemy continued to press him with alacrity; but the steel composure and bravery of the troops that were covering his retreat stopped the enemy.

Nikolai Vuich (Vujič). (State Hermitage Museum)

---

18 Yermolov: 'we saw the enemy issuing from a forest on to the road to the village of Holland. Covered by cavalry, the enemy formed up for battle and advanced against our right flank. Captured flanqueurs told us that these troops belonged to Bernadotte's corps and he was in command. We could have disengaged an hour earlier, but now could not hope to escape without heavy losses. Our forces were exposed and we could not deceive the enemy in respect of our strength or force him to act cautiously. The French could see at once that they outnumbered our forces by at least three to one. The enemy advanced against the heights we occupied and, although our canister fire and bayonets defeated several columns, fresh enemy forces immediately resumed the offensive, forcing us back. Several battalions on the right, not far from the road, moved towards Georgiental, which the enemy seized with skirmishers from the infantry that Malakhov had detected earlier; we could not allow them to hold this place and General Markov led our battalions as they advanced. The enemy infantry was supported by fierce artillery fire and punished the rest of our rearguard, forcing us to retreat. Our artillery fired only canister. It was already dark when we entered the forest and the enemy ceased its pursuit, probably hoping to capture us the next day. After General Markov's departure, there were no other generals left, so Colonels Turchaninov and Vuich and I took orders from Senior Colonel Yurkovskii. Our first goal was to find an escape route, and I was concerned not to abandon some 20 artillery pieces; however, we encountered either deep snow or swamps all through the forest and could not escape. The gallant Sisoev, commander of the Don Cossack regiment, finally found a place where artillery could reach the main road, but it had to pass very close to the enemy bivouac near Georgiental. Of course, this was a very risky way of saving our guns, but we had no other choice and decided to do it. While passing the French camp, they opened up with musket fire and we had a few wounded, but we made it through.' Yermolov, *The Czar's General*, p.73.
19 Pavel Loshkarev (1776–1857) Russian officer of Georgian origin. He was promoted to a colonel in 1811 and commanded the Volynskii Musketeer Regiment in 1806–1811.

Roman (Heinrich Reinhold von) Anrep. (Public Domain)

Just then, as the sun set, Lieutenant General Anrep arrived. After taking note of the details of this action, he ordered General Markov to continue his retreat, and then, in order to be able to see with his own eyes the enemy's strength and the direction that his columns were taking, he went in person to the rear guard. His zeal for service carried him too far – this brave general approached some brushwood that the enemy *tirailleurs* had already occupied and he was killed there on the spot by a ball that went through his head; his two *aides de camp* were wounded.[20] This loss hurt us and made a profound impression on the entire army due to the distinguished manner in which this general had always served. He enjoyed the confidence

---

20 Yermolov: 'Although he received this order late in the day, Anrep decided to make up for lost time and moved his cavalry at the trot. A mile and half away from the battlefield, he met General Markov, who assured him that the battle had ended, our troops were retreating and nothing else could be done. Anrep did not accept General Markov's assurances because of the audible artillery fire and he ordered his regiments to speed up. At Georgiental, he encountered enemy infantry and his flanqueurs opened fire: just as he was climbing a nearby hill, Anrep was killed by a bullet that hit him in the head. It might still have been possible to attempt something but it would not have helped us and therefore his reconnaissance was ultimately futile.' Yermolov, *The Czar's General*, p.74.

of his sovereign. Demonstrating gentle character in private life and unshakeable firmness in most difficult occasions of the war, he had gained the general confidence of our troops.

General Markov retreated with his advance guard to a *lieue* from Liebstadt. Our losses in this action amounted to five hundred men and, to judge after the number of dead that the enemy left and that we found on the battlefield two days later, in going to Mohrungen, his losses must have been a great deal more considerable. We captured two officers and 53 soldiers.[21]

It is certain that General Markov would have done better to not engage at all in this action with such disproportionate forces.[22] From the prisoners taken the day before and from those captured at the beginning of the action, he would have been able to learn that Marshal Bernadotte had concentrated his corps at Mohrungen and, in this case, Markov ought to have passed back through the defile, defended only the exit from it, and [immediately] made his report on these events. It is safe to presume that the enemy would not initially have left his positions; several of our divisions, which were very close to the area, would have been able to reinforce our advance guard the next day and assure us of a resounding and unquestionable victory (if the enemy did not retreat during the night); this all the more so as the column that was marching on the road from Alt-Ramten would have been able to take him in the flank and rear, as will be seen soon by the appearance of a detachment of our cavalry that appeared during the action at Mohrungen in the rear of the enemy by marching along the road from Alt-Ramten. Yet General Markov, emboldened by his success of the previous day, consulted only his confidence and ignored the risks that he was going to take.

---

21 Arriving at Mohrungen on 1 February, Wilson heard from the Russians that the French had lost about 1,500 men two days before. 'Their bodies were lying to the right and left of the road by which we passed.' *Life of General Sir Robert Wilson*, vol.2, p.82. In a letter written to Lord Hutchinson, Wilson spoke of never witnessing 'so many dismal objects as the field of battle yesterday presented. It was indeed truly terrible: and at this moment hundreds of wretches are lying on the ground without help.' He was rather surprised by the abject misery of the Russian soldiers. 'The want of provisions has been attended with fatal consequences to their discipline. They now plunder without discrimination, and some severe examples must be made. The hardships which they have gone through may plead some excuse for their desire of food, stores, &c.; but this is now rushing into licentiousness. If I had been told that men could live as the poor Russians have been doing, now for six weeks, I could not have believed it. Black bread, snow for water, and snow only to lie on, is tremendous suffering. However, officers have not been at their ease; and we have generally been eighteen hours out of twenty-four on horseback. We literally had no food all day yesterday. I wonder General Bennigsen with the oppression of responsibility can bear the fatigue.' Robert Wilson to Lord Hutchinson [not dated, circa January 1807], in *Life of General Sir Robert Wilson*, vol. 2, p.399.
22 Yermolov was critical of Markov's leadership. 'We found Markov at Amtmann's house at Liebstadt and he was already asleep, having enjoyed a nice dinner; his companions had devoured everything as though we were not supposed to return. To console ourselves, we could have instead admired the beautiful breasts and gorgeous eyes of Amtmann's wife, but since I was a defeated hero who had just completed a retreat, I was not granted even a glance, which, I was told, a victor would have claimed together with her heart. Well, the vanquished have no claim to any booty! Shrewd General Markov did not look surprised to see us, as though we had simply carried out his orders. We paid him back with the same indifference… It must be mentioned that our troops were just three miles away from Mohrungen but still no one came to our rescue. The sound of the guns was heard at the main headquarters as well but only Anrep moved towards us, and only because he had orders to bivouac at Georgiental.' Yermolov, *The Czar's General*, p.74.

While Major General Markov was fighting against Prince de Ponte-Corvo's *corps d'armée* in the environs of the village of Georgenthal, Major General Count Pahlen and the Emperor's *aide de camp*, Colonel Prince Dolgorouky, executed a *coup de main* on the town of Mohrungen, located one *lieue* behind the enemy's battlefield. This *coup de main* was executed with as much courage as prudence, as we will see in the following:

Lieutenant General Prince Golitsyn, having arrived with the cavalry of the left wing at Alt-Ramten and hearing a cannonade from the vicinity of Mohrungen, ordered Major General Count Pahlen,[23] commander of the Sumskii Hussars, and Colonel Prince Dolgorouky,[24] commanding the Kurlyandskii Dragoon Regiment, to approach that place with their regiments, so as to investigate what was happening there.

Following this order, Count Pahlen marched with his regiment, which comprised of 10 squadrons. After passing through the village of Eckersdorf, he approached a forest with a narrow winding road, which convinced him to leave seven squadrons in front of the defile, so that they could serve him either as succour or as a place to fall back on. Accompanied by the remaining three squadrons, he continued his march with all possible haste. Two *verstas* from Mohrungen, around six and seven o'clock in the afternoon, he rejoined Prince Dolgorouky who was leading three squadrons of dragoons. There, to the right, they observed the bivouac of the troops of the Prince de Ponte-Corvo, who were then fighting not far off against our advance guard of the right wing. Prince Dolgorouky, with one squadron, rode down the outposts, which he found before Mohrungen and rushed into the town. Major General Pahlen followed him closely with a squadron; some enemy soldiers were cut down in the streets and two officers were taken prisoner along with 183 soldiers; a great deal of transports, including the Prince de Ponte-Corvo's own possessions, were taken, as well as a fairly considerable sum in a military chest [*caisse militaire*], which became the spoils of the brave troops employed in this daring attack.[25] All of it was shortly sent under a good escort down the road to Alt-Ramten. Count Pahlen had taken the precaution to send, as soon as he arrived at Mohrungen, two squadrons via the town down the road to Georgenthal, so as to be able to be warned in time of the approach of the troops that would return from Bernadotte's *corps* to reclaim this place. Indeed, the enemy did not hesitate to rush over there, but our men had the time to retire with everything they had taken in the town.

---

23 Peter von der Pahlen III, the chef of the Sumskii Hussar Regiment in 1801–1814.
24 Mikhail Petrovich Dolgorouky III was the regimental chef, replacing Karl Johann Löschern von Herzfeld; he formally served the chef of the Kurlyandskii Dragoon Regiment in April 1807–May 1808. The commanding officer was Lieutenant Colonel Matvei Argamakov III.
25 Yermolov: 'Count Pahlen rushed into Mohrungen, seizing Marshal Bernadotte's headquarters and capturing his entire train, chancellery, and the contribution he had levied on various Prussian cities; a dinner cooked for the victorious Marshal was even found.' Yermolov, *The Czar's General*, p.75.
The British commissioner to the Russian army, Sir Robert Wilson, claimed 'in General Bernadotte's baggage, the money levied on the town of Elbing for his own private use, 10,000 ducats, exclusive of 2,500 for his staff, was recovered; and there were found, to a great amount, various pieces of plate, candlesticks, &c. bearing the arms of almost all the states of Germany. The Marshal's servant was so ashamed of this plunder, that he would not claim it when purposely desired to point out his master's property; but as the articles were taken in the Marshal's own quarter, and in his trunks, and were in such quantity, they must have been there with his knowledge.' Wilson, *Brief Remarks*, p.85

Colonel Kreutz[26] was charged with covering the retreat with a squadron of the Sumskii Hussar Regiment. At the moment of his departure from the town, he was cut off and surrounded by the enemy, but resolved to break out, leading his men with a sabre in hand; fortunately, the squadron broke through, although Colonel Kreutz, this brave officer, fell from his horse gravely wounded and unconscious and remained in enemy hands; this was the sole loss of consequence that these squadrons suffered.[27]

---

26 Cyprian Belzig von Kreutz (1777–1850) assumed command of the Sumskii Hussar Regiment in February 1808 and became a major general in 1812.
27 Kreutz was released after Tilsit. Eduard von Löwenstern offers more vivid description of this attack: 'The deep snow and the cold aggravated our forced marches to Osterode that we had to undertake in order to join Prince Bagration's advance guard that was awaiting us there. Not far from Preusissch-Eylau, I assumed the duties of an orderly for Count Pahlen, who did not have me do anything important the entire day. The innkeeper's daughter, a cute girl, tried all kinds of tricks to seduce me, but chaste and inexperienced I stayed brave, and was berated as a dumb kid by the girl and not worth the trouble of staying with. Theodor brought me a roasted goose he had stolen from somewhere, since he knew only too well that being an orderly and hunger meant the same thing. After marching back and forth several times, after innumerable encounters and engagements, we approached the little town of Mohrungen. Through deserters and spies, we had learned that Marshal Bernadotte with his headquarters, suspecting no danger, were spending time in that town unguarded and busy levying contributions. In the dark of the night the Sumskii Hussar Regiment and the Kurlandskii (Courland) Dragoons slipped in as quietly as possible. Exploiting the incomprehensible carelessness of the French, we galloped into the middle of the town, shouting wildly, without finding a single guard post. You can imagine the shock and the horror of the enemy quietly resting there. Because our Colonel Shishkin was slow, our squadron arrived a little too late to hew in. We only got the gleanings of the rich booty. Nevertheless, we had our hands full to capture or cut down the half-clothed French pouring out of the houses. I myself captured 14 men that night. Yelling 'Pardon,' clinging to my stirrups, several of them escaped from me in the throng. Three squadrons led by Colonel of Cavalry Kreutz did not spend much time plundering and taking prisoners but galloped through the other town gate to spread death and destruction in the bivouac out there. Our brave hussars emphatically exploited the initial surprise. In the dark they cut down everyone who resisted them; but soon they were attacked by several hurriedly-pulled together squadrons and driven back. They lost their brave leader Colonel of Cavalry Kreutz, whose horse fell on the ice. He was immediately surrounded and, covered with many wounds, taken prisoner. During that bloody night, we took over 1,000 prisoners, captured Marshal Bernadotte's entire equipage, consisting of four well-packed coaches as well as pack horses and captured all of the contribution money, packed into barrels and loaded on wagons. Not far from Mohrungen, we bivouacked near an isolated mill. We all had more than enough money but nothing to eat. For two days, I had not had even a piece of bread to eat. The hussars were paying a ducat for a piece of bread. Especially because of the booty from Mohrungen, the value of money had fallen. Exhausted from hunger, wrapped in my coat, I lay down and certainly would have died if Lieutenant Obosenko had not found me and revived me with strengthening soup. The only thing we had plenty of was pork fat, that the hussars hungrily devoured without any bread or salt.' *Mit Graf Pahlens Reiterei gegen Napoleon*, pp.13–14.

10

Dirschau-Passenheim

On 14/26 January, having received news that Marshal the Prince de Ponte-Corvo, whose *corps d'armée* was supposed to have received considerable reinforcements, intended to attack our advance guard, I directed the march of the columns of the right wing and centre on Liebstadt; the left wing and its cavalry continued in the direction of Alt-Ramten. General Markov received the order to remain in his position on the other side of Liebstadt and to await there the above-mentioned reinforcements. At 11 o'clock in the morning, I arrived with my headquarters at Liebstadt. An hour later, our advance posts reported that the enemy was retreating in haste.

Lieutenant General Prince [Peter] Bagration having just arrived at the army from St Petersburg, I gave him the command of the two advance guards, including General Baggehufvudt's detachment. Prince Bagration received the order to advance with the advance guard of the right wing, to which I had added some more cavalry, to occupy Mohrungen directly and to push that same day still to Alt-Bestendorf. So as to better execute my first plan of operations, in entering into Old Prussia, and so as to be able to better support the cordon that I intended to draw up for the rest of the winter, I divided the entire combined army into four corps: the first or that of the right wing under the orders of Lieutenant General L'Estocq, who commanded the Prussian corps, which I had reinforced, as I already mentioned, with Russian troops. The second corps, under the orders of Lieutenant General Tuchkov, composed of the advance guard of the right wing, the 5th, 7th, 8th Divisions and the cavalry of the right wing. The third corps, under the orders of Lieutenant General Prince Golitsyn, included the advance guard of the left wing, the cavalry of this wing, General Baggehufvudt's detachment, and the 2nd Division. Finally, the fourth corps, which was supposed to serve as a reserve under the orders of Lieutenant General Sacken, comprised of the 3rd, 4th, and 14th Divisions.

Lieutenant General Tuchkov received the order to depart that same day from Liebstadt with his corps, to follow the enemy, and attack him on the other side of Mohrungen, if he could manage it. He was also to see to it that the advance guard was not exposed and that he could support it in time; for this purpose, the advance guard was supposed to move a half-*mille* ahead of the rest of the corps.

The march of Lieutenant General Prince Golitsyn's corps was directed to Alt-Ramten, along the main road from Mohrungen, with the orders to occupy with his right the village of Klein-Luzeinen, situated between the lakes Narien and Mahrung; with his centre, Horn and Schwenkendorf, and with his left, Reussen, situated on the main road from Osterode to Mohrungen, so that there was no more direct communication on that road between the corps of Marshals Bernadotte and Ney. To this order was added another one – at the first cannon shot fired by General Tuchkov's corps, Golitsyn was supposed to march directly to his aid, taking the direction of Gross-Gottswalde and attempting to turn the enemy's right wing; he was also to keep upon his departure Reussen occupied and dispatch strong parties to Osterode.

Lieutenant General Sacken was ordered to march the next day with the reserve, to occupy the environs of Mohrungen and to keep himself at a distance of two *milles* behind Tuchkov's corps. General Barclay de Tolly delivered to the headquarters a non-commissioned officer [*bas-officier*] and some French soldiers, which his Cossacks had captured.

Lieutenant General L'Estocq marched that same day, with that eagerness that he had displayed throughout the war, via Preussisch-Holland, supporting his right on Hirschfeld and his left on Samrodt. By this movement, our communications with Elbing were opened and consequently also those with Danzig.

Lieutenant General Prince Golitsyn reported that that same day an officer of Grekov XII's Cossack Regiment, who was commanding this regiment in the absence of his colonel, finding himself marching toward the quarters indicated, had been informed by his advance guard that there was still an enemy detachment near the village of Lioko. He moved at once toward that place with a party from his regiment and found there a detachment of enemy cavalry, supported by infantry; he attacked them vigorously, killed a few of them and took prisoner two officers and 42 soldiers.

The communications that Marshal Ney offered that day, January 26 (new style), on my operations were as follows:

> Marshal Ney to the Prince de Ponte-Corvo
> 26 January, seven o'clock in the evening
> I just received your letter of the 25th. I am instructing General d'Hautpoul to extend his left, and to be ready to march to your aid on Deutsch-Eylau or Löbau, depending on how the enemy's movements unfold over the next few days. I am also advising him to establish communications with Osterode, so as to correspond directly with you.
>
> I ordered the *27e régiment de ligne* to leave today from Mühlen with General Roguet, who is marching at its head, to go and take up positions at Osterode, with orders to return to its initial position as soon as your retrograde movement on this point begins.
>
> I informed Marshal Soult of all that happened since the resumption of hostilities by the Russians up to this point; I am going to share with him the last paragraph of your letter in which you tell him to take the necessary precautions. His Majesty [Napoleon], who cannot fail to be informed at this time of the pressing circumstances in which we find ourselves, will no doubt determine to make the enemy repent of his [absurd] [*sic!*] undertaking.
>
> I am writing to General Dulauloy, commandant at Thorn, to make him aware of what is happening, so as to be ready to evacuate everything that is in Thorn, either to the left bank of the Vistula, if that is possible, or by directing to Plock the baggage trains and anything else that is unnecessary for the army. As for the

artillery and the park, I am inviting him to move to Mlawa that which belongs to the *6e corps d'armée*; to Strassburg, that which belongs to General d'Hautpoul, and to Gilgenburg that which might belong to Your Excellency's corps.

I am also telling General Dulauloy to inform General Dombrowski to take up a position at Bromberg, unless there are contrary orders from His Majesty, until we execute all the movements that He [Napoleon] will surely order.

I am also telling General Dulauloy that, if he is obliged to evacuate Thorn, he should fall back toward Marshal Augereau's corps and engage General Dombrowski to place a *corps d'observation* before Thorn with some cannon in position. If Your Excellency thinks that there is something to change in these precautionary measures, I pray he make his intentions known to General Dulauloy.

Marshal Ney to General Dulauloy, Governor of Thorn
26 January, seven o'clock in the evening
I believe I must inform you, *Monsieur le Gouverneur*, that a Russian army vigorously attacked the Prince de Ponte-Corvo and that after having forced him from some positions, it has succeeded in its initial ambitions, which must have been to re-establish its communications with Danzig. The Prince de Ponte-Corvo, having recaptured yesterday the important post of Mohrungen, is going to concentrate his *corps d'armée* at Osterode, which is the point that His Majesty designated for him in general dispositions.

The Prince informs me that the enemy is marching on our left and, in this case, he will move first to Graudenz to raise the siege and from there to Thorn… Following are the instructions that he had mentioned in the letter to the Prince de Ponte-Corvo.

Marshal Ney to Marshal Soult
Hohenstein, 26 January
His Majesty's instructions, my dear Marshal, being that the Marshals should tell each other about any and all attacks that the enemy may make, I urge you to share news of what is happening with your corps to Marshals Davout, Lannes, and Augereau, and to invite the latter to establish a cordon of light cavalry along the Drewenz River in order to observe the enemy whose detachments might penetrate to Thorn.

I am writing to General Dulauloy, the governor of Thorn, that I believe it prudent to evacuate that place, unless he has received contrary orders from His Majesty.

I have just received your letter of the 26th, my dear Marshal; it is impossible for me to send my light troops to Willenberg – my two regiments hardly have 400 horses and, harassed as I am by the Cossacks, you must sense how vulnerable I already am. To the contrary, I entreat you to return to Neidenburg, via Mlawa, the 25 *chasseurs* from the *10e* [regiment]…

Marshal Ney to the Minister of War
26 January, seven o'clock in the evening
I received Your Excellency's letter, dated January 24 from Warsaw and which was brought to me by your *aide de camp* Montholon, by whom you engaged me to supply His Majesty with precise news of what has been happening. In the last three or four days I have already dispatched seven or eight officers with relevant reports and at this time you must be informed as to the events that have befallen *1er corps*.

I have the honour of sending here to Your Excellency a copy of the letter I received from the Prince de Ponte-Corvo and a copy of my response. You will find therein the precautionary measures that I thought necessary to suggest to the governor of Thorn. Please repeat them to him, if you approve, or send him such others as you deem necessary according to the circumstances.

Here we are harassed by the Cossacks who, day and night, attack our advance-posts; they have captured a few of our hussars. This afternoon, they came extremely near the town; I had the call to arms beaten and I cannot praise highly enough the ardour of the brave troops who are under my orders and of the speed with which they went to their positions.

On 15/27 January, I moved with my headquarters to Mohrungen, determined to wait there and see how the enemy reacted to the operations I had already executed; I then intended to advance with my right wing, that is to say with Lieutenant General L'Estocq's corps, to raise the blockade of the fortress of Graudenz.

Lieutenant General Tuchkov took up position near the villages of Klein and Gross-Gottswalde. General Prince Golitsyn received orders to remain that day in his position from the previous day, unless General Tuchkov needed his help. Lieutenant General Sacken, with the reserve and the heavy artillery, was placed in tight cantonments in the environs of Mohrungen.

Upon the news that Marshal the Prince de Ponte-Corvo had stopped with his corps in a position near Sonnenborn, I ordered Lieutenant General Tuchkov to attack him the next day, around eight o'clock

Nikolai Tuchkov. (State Hermitage Museum)

in the morning. At the same time, I commanded Lieutenant General Prince Golitsyn to send forth his cavalry so that it could arrive, by eight o'clock in the morning, at Gross-Gottswalde and to dispatch Lieutenant General Count Ostermann with the 2nd Division to Liebemühl in order to get around Osterode and to intercept all communications to the Prince de Ponte-Corvo's *corps d'armée*. Prince Golitsyn was again told to keep Reussen heavily occupied.

General Barclay de Tolly reported that Captain Loshkarev, with a party of the Izumskii Hussar Regiment and a few Cossacks, had captured nine men from an enemy outpost near Osterode. That day Lieutenant General L'Estocq occupied Saalfeld; his advance guard took as a prisoner General Lasseur, who was wounded the previous day. From a secret agent in Warsaw, we received news that all of the enemy corps that were on this side [of the Vistula] had received orders to march on Chorzellen and Mlawa, and that Emperor Napoleon was going to leave immediately from Warsaw and go in person to the army. Following are the communications from Marshal Ney on 15/27 January from Hohenstein.

> Marshal Ney to the Prince de Ponte-Corvo
> Hohenstein, 27 January
> I am addressing to Your Excellency some letters from S. A. the Minister of War, which just reached me by the return of one of my *aides de camp*, whom I had dispatched to Warsaw. Your Excellency knows the position of my troops; it conforms to the intentions of His Majesty. I think the enemy has renounced his intention to push further with his advance posts to Graudenz and Thorn. I will give no order for the evacuation of this place [Thorn], unless you inform me of such necessity as a result of the enemy's dispositions. I pray Your Excellency to cover with General Sahuc's dragoons the position of Wittigwalde, which the *27e d'infanterie de ligne* will occupy today. Marshal Soult informs me that he is currently occupying Willenberg with the advance guard of his *corps d'armée*. My officers tell me that the Russians, before moving their troops from the left wing to advance against us, launched a Cossack raid on Marshals Soult and Davout. We lost a few squadrons of hussars and chasseurs who allowed themselves to be taken by surprise. The forward outposts of these two *corps d'armée* extend to Kolno, which the enemy has evacuated.
>
> The Emperor has prepared some transports on the road from Pultusk and Prasnitz. Your Excellency's reports will probably prompt a major offensive movement, which will avenge us of the enemy's enterprise.

> Marshal Ney to the Minister of War
> Hohenstein, 27 January
> I have just received Your Excellency's letter from yesterday, six o'clock in the morning, via my returning *aide de camp*. The positions I occupy conform to the intentions of His Majesty and I will make no other movement until the enemy's intentions are apparent. I do not have news today from His Excellency the Prince de Ponte-Corvo. I am addressing to him the letters and packets emanating from the headquarters at Warsaw. Our communications with Osterode have never been interrupted, nor those with Neidenburg and Chorzellen. I have not ceased to inform

M. Marshal Soult of all that has passed on my front since the 20th of this month, when General Bennigsen's undertaking began…

P.S. – I have just received a letter from today from General Maison, of which I am sending you a copy and by which he informs me that the Prince de Ponte-Corvo who is at Liebemühl has received news that the enemy wished to attack him; I am therefore making the decision to give orders to Thorn to evacuate the artillery and other objects belonging to the army, which are in that place.

On 16/28 January, at five o'clock in the morning, Lieutenant General Tuchkov reported that the enemy had suddenly retired from Sonnenborn during the night, taking the road from Thorn, which motivated the order to this general to move directly on Liebemühl and to Lieutenant General Prince Golitsyn to send without delay General Barclay de Tolly, with the advance guard of the left wing, to make himself master of Osterode, to hold this post with all the necessary precautions, and to push strong reconnaissance parties down the road to Gilgenburg. At the same time, Prince Golitsyn received orders to march with the rest of his corps, to which I added the 4th Division, to Hohenstein, to dislodge the enemy there if he still occupied it, and also to send out strong reconnaissance forces in one direction toward Gilgenburg and on the other down the road to Neidenburg. This was the first movement I made to extend the army on the left, no longer having need of considerable forces on my right flank.

Lieutenant General Tuchkov sent to the headquarters two officers and 44 French soldiers, whom the light troops of the advance guard, under the orders of Prince Bagration, had taken from the Prince de Ponte-Corvo's rear guard.

Lieutenant General L'Estocq's corps rested for a day. Nevertheless, the general ordered, during the night, another march by his advance guard, which arrived the next day at dawn at Marienwerder, at the same time that the enemy was preparing to leave it; they captured General Faultrier, his *aide de camp*, two officers and 27 soldiers.

Marshal Ney to the Minister of War
Hohenstein, 28 January, four o'clock in the morning
I have the honour of addressing to Your Excellency a copy of the letter written to me by General Maison concerning the retrograde movements of *1er corps d'armée*, which will begin today behind Osterode. Consequently, I am also giving orders to make a minor movement to be in a position to fight with better concentrated forces and to support the Prince de Ponte-Corvo. I am only leaving a cavalry picket on the heights of Hohenstein, and a battalion of line infantry at Lichteinen. The *27e régiment*, which occupies Wittigwalde, will come to take up positions at Kirchsteindorf; the *25e de ligne*, General Roguet's brigade, at Mühlen. General Labassée's brigade, in the second line behind Mühlen. The *6e d'infanterie légère*, which I had momentarily moved closer to Mühlen, is returning to Gilgenburg. The *cavalerie de ligne* of General Colbert is at Thymau and its environs. General Colbert, who was at Wittigwalde informed me, tonight, that he had heard a strong cannonade, on the 27th in the afternoon, around Osterode. General Maison, however, does not speak of it in his letter. The enemy continues to envelop the Prince de Ponte-Corvo's left. I pray to the Lord that the Russians have 60,000 men

there, because not one of them would see Muscovy again, if His Majesty marches on them with all of his forces.

I establish myself today at Mühlen, to be within reach of the Prince de Ponte-Corvo. The enemy remains in the same positions before me. The Cossacks are moving in diverse directions but do not approach our infantry.

On 17/29 January, Lieutenant General Prince Bagration received orders to occupy, with the advance guard of the right wing, Deutsch-Eylau, and Lieutenant General Tuchkov – to remain with the remainder of his detachment at Liebemühl. These dispositions were undertaken to contain the Prince de Ponte-Corvo's *corps d'armée* and to remove any obstacles that Lieutenant General L'Estocq may have faced in his march to Graudenz. The same day, at three o'clock in the morning, General Baggehufvudt was sent to Bogounschowen, down the road to Löbau, to harass the enemy's march. Having arrived at the Drewenz, he found the bridge there burned but, after a few hours of work, he managed, with the help of some peasants of the village of Bergfriede, to rebuild the crossing and, at eight o'clock, he crossed the river; the Cossacks, meanwhile, swam across it. At Grabau, he reached the enemy rear guard, which retired in haste, but we captured one captain and 17 hussars from the *4e régiment français*. General Baggehufvudt continued his march but as soon as he realized that the Prince de Ponte-Corvo was in position with his entire corps near Löbau, he halted and limited himself to observing the enemy. The next day, General Baggehufvudt's detachment was directed to Deutsch-Holland; he made this march without enemy interference.

Receiving reports that the enemy had moved away from Osterode, taking the road to Neidenburg via Hohenstein, I commanded General Prince Golitsyn to send General Barclay de Tolly from Osterode down the road to Neidenburg with instructions to send in advance a strong reconnaissance party to Neidenburg and to gather news of the enemy's march. Prince Golitsyn himself, with the rest of his detachment, was supposed to occupy Allenstein, Passenheim and in front, on his right, Hohenstein and, on his left Ortelsburg, so that the detachment placed at Passenheim could serve cover or support the troops at Hohenstein and Ortelsburg. Golitsyn was also supposed to send a strong reconnaissance toward Willenberg to verify what had just been learned from our secret agents, namely, that the enemy was gathering troops at Mlawa and Chorzellen.

Lieutenant General L'Estocq had taken the following position that day: his right wing at Marienwerder, six *milles* from Graudenz, anchoring himself on the Vistula; his centre at Riesenburg, and his left at Rosenberg, from which he established communications with Prince Bagration's advance guard, posted at Deutsch-Eylau. His advanced posts were established at Neuenburg and Garnsee. General L'Estocq had sent Captain Rawen with 30 Cossacks onto the left bank of the Vistula, to reconnoitre between Mewe and Neuenburg and at the same time to observe the corps[1] of Polish General Dombrowski, which was in cantonments in this area. This general had previously advanced as far as Dirschau but he was attacked there by a detachment from the Danzig garrison, which repulsed him and took from him, beyond several prisoners, a few cannon and a military chest [*caisse militaire*].

---

1   In actuality, a division.

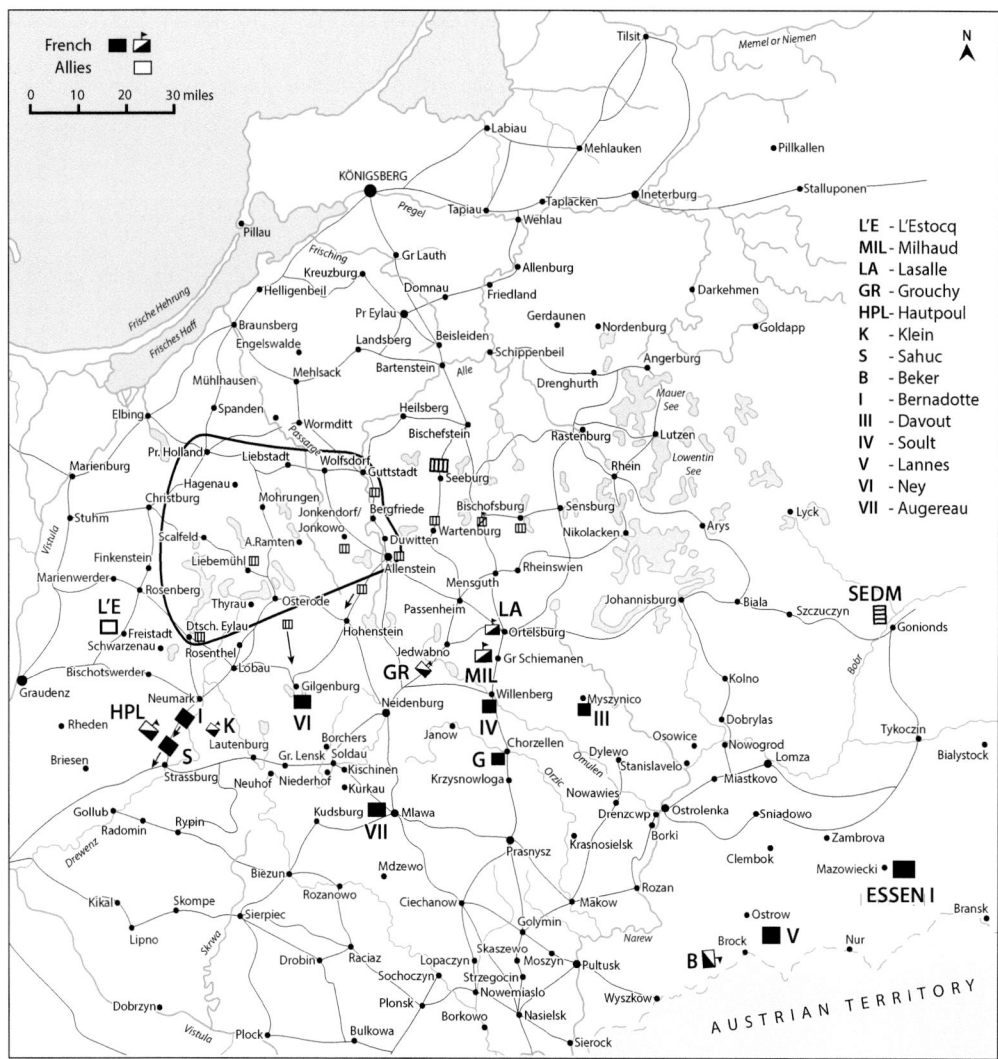

Situation as of Late January 1807.

The right wing of the army having arrived at these points, the enemy raised the blockade on Graudenz and our communications with this fortress reopened.

> Marshal Ney to the Minister of War
> Gilgenburg, 29 January, four o'clock in the evening.
> I have the honour of addressing to Your Excellency a copy of the letter from the Prince de Ponte-Corvo, which he wrote to me from Liebemühl on the 27th. General Maison, his *chef d'état-major*, had already informed me yesterday of the retrograde movement that *1er corps* was making on Osterode and even to Rœschken. Having left no one at Osterode, I, for my part, made, on the 28th, a minor movement

backward to the heights of Mühlen, where I had concentrated three regiments, one at Kirchsteindorf, on the road from Osterode, and a few squadrons at Lichteinen and Drobing with some *voltigeurs* to observe Hohenstein and the road from Osterode via Platteinen.

Today knowing that the Prince de Ponte-Corvo is taking up position with his entire corps at Löbau, I sent orders so that tomorrow at daybreak the majority of my troops will be concentrated at Gilgenburg. But if the enemy appears in force on the flank of my position at Mühlen, then the retrograde movement will begin at midnight. I am keeping nevertheless an outpost at Neidenburg, with two infantry regiments and two of dragoons; another infantry regiment will be at Soldau and two dragoon regiments – between Soldau and Gilgenburg.

I thought it necessary to keep the position at Mühlen and the observation posts toward Hohenstein, so as to menace the enemy's left flank, if he had dared to follow the Prince de Ponte-Corvo. My *aide de camp*, who was with this Prince, told me verbally that the blockade of Graudenz would only be lifted tomorrow, that the enemy still seemed to be directing his forces there, that Marshal Lefebvre had arrived at Thorn and that he was awaiting there the Polish division of General Dombrowski. Nevertheless, the Thorn bridge, according to what I have been told by General Leroux, commander of my artillery, will only be completed by 1 February.

The Prince de Ponte-Corvo did not wish to take it upon himself to preserve our artillery supplies at Thorn; consequently I ordered that everything belonging to *6e corps* should move to the area between Soldau and Gilgenburg, crossing the Drewenz at Ciechocin and proceeding from there via Rypin to Zielona. By the disposition of my troops Your Excellency will note that I am in line with the Prince de Ponte-Corvo, and that in one day I can direct the totality of my corps to Hohenstein. The Gilgenburg position is excellent for the defensive, and I cannot believe, according to the movements that His Majesty is making on Willenberg, that the enemy would be daring enough to come and give battle. I do not believe that he has the time to retire from whence he came.

Second Report from Marshal Ney to the Minister of War on the Same Day
Gilgenburg, seven o'clock in the evening
I have just received the letter included from General Maison, *chef de l'état-major* of *1er corps*. Your Excellency will note that the enemy continues to pursue the Prince de Ponte-Corvo with all of his forces, and it seems, according to the unfortunate events that keep unfolding so quickly, that there is not a moment to lose to disengage him. Despite the most active correspondence, I was never able to truly know the situation of *1er corps*, nor the enemy forces that were pursuing it. I now fear that Thorn will be threatened and that I am too far away to support it. I will hold the position of Gilgenburg tomorrow, and if the enemy attacks me there with more forces than I have at my disposition, I will avoid an inconclusive action by directing my march to Neidenburg while informing the Prince de Ponte-Corvo of it.

On 18/30 January, to continue extending forces on our left, the enemy made no movements or concentration of troops that could reveal his intentions to aid his left wing. Receiving to the contrary news that the troops coming from Mlawa and Prasnitz were advancing against our left, and in order to be able to concentrate imposing forces on all points, I ordered General Sacken, with the reserve composed of the 3rd and 14th Divisions, to depart in such a manner as to arrive the first day at Liebstadt, the second day – at Schönwiese and the third day – at Seeburg, where he was to place his troops in tight cantonments. Lieutenant General Prince Golitsyn received orders to place his forces as follows: the 2nd Division at Allenstein; the 4th Division – between Allenstein and Guttstadt; to occupy with a cavalry detachment the distance from Wartenburg to Bischofsburg and to form the cordon in front of the reserve placed at Seeburg; to occupy Wartenburg in force with a detachment of troops drawn from the 4th Division; to place pickets before Wartenburg, at Schidlitz, Pattricken, Preylowo and Gillau, who could send out frequent patrols on the roads from Ortelsburg and Willenberg, and to place General Baggehufvudt's detachment at Bischofsburg, so that the enemy could not turn our left wing without us being able to know first.

Lieutenant General Tuchkov received orders to replace in short order at Osterode the detachment under the orders of General Barclay de Tolly, which belonged to Prince Golitsyn's *corps*, and to send there Lieutenant General Dokhturov with his division and order him to hold the vicinity of Gilgenburg, given that according to new reports, the enemy was there in force; to leave a division at Liebemühl, as much to be able to support this place as to reinforce, should it be necessary, the detachment at Osterode or even our advance guard at Deutsch-Eylau; and lastly, to add to his 3rd Division a [detachment comprised of] a regiment of jagers, along with a regiment of cavalry and a regiment of Cossacks; this detachment would occupy Jonkowo, with orders for its commander to link up his advance posts on his right with those of the division placed at Osterode and on his left – with those of General Prince Golitsyn.

Prince Golitsyn's *corps* was next supposed to establish, if circumstances permitted, direct communications from Johannisburg to Goniondz with General Siedmioraczki's *corps*, left on the Bobr River, who maintained his communications with General Essen I's *corps* on the Narew. Lieutenant General L'Estocq pushed forward his advance posts that day up to Freystadt, Sommerau, etc., to establish more solidly his communications with Graudenz.

In this position I ordered the generals, commanders of the different *corps*, to correspond among themselves and to communicate to each other all that they learned of enemy movements and to support each other in case of need; I particularly instructed Prince Golitsyn to request help from the reserve placed behind him at Seeburg, and sent the necessary orders to General Sacken in this respect and to General Tuchkov, who was on his right; and, finally, to the commanding generals I sent orders to make the necessary changes to this disposition based on local circumstances, their own military experiences, and acquired intelligence about the enemy movements.

Following are the enemy communications of the day.

> Marshal Ney to the Prince de Ponte-Corvo
> Gilgenburg, 30 January 1807, noon
> I have just received the letter from Your Excellency, dated today from Löbau. The retrograde movement that I completed this morning to Gilgenburg encountered no resistance on the part of the enemy, which only has some observation posts near Hohenstein; yesterday evening, the enemy came close to us and engaged in a

skirmish at Kirchsteindorf. The posts of the *27e de ligne* were pushed back sharply to Reichenau and even beyond it; but henceforth I received no further news of enemy movements.

I currently have five regiments of infantry; the sixth regiment guards the gap from here to Neidenburg; another is in this latter town, and the eighth regiment is at Soldau. The Emperor must direct the columns of Marshals Augereau and Soult and we cannot wait any longer for orders concerning the offensive movement. If Your Excellency is convinced that General Bennigsen could attack you today with considerable forces, I would certainly arrive too late to support because I will have to march with troops that have already covered six *lieues*. It seems to me that it would be better to refuse battle and concentrate your troops between Kauernick and Neumark rather than receive battle in the vast plains of Löbau, principally due to the superiority that the enemy cavalry would have over our own. My opinion should however in no way influence the decision that Your Excellency will judge suitable to undertake in these pressing circumstances. If I receive no order from the minister before tomorrow, I will concentrate here the entirety of my troops and extend my left to Rumienitza and Guttowo.

The Same to the Same
Gilgenburg, 30 January, five o'clock in the evening
I reflected a great deal on your situation and mine as they relate to the general operations and with the objective of the movements that the Emperor is making for the other corps of the *Grande Armée*. Permit me to express to you once again the desire to see you avoid a decisive battle in your current position at Löbau. Can we not suppose that the enemy is attempting to mislead you in threatening your front by coming out from Osterode, in order to manoeuvre by his right, march on your rear via Deutsch-Eylau and thus beat you to Neumark. I consider this latter position as the real point of defence; it renders you master of the junction of the two roads from Osterode and Marienwerder, of which the enemy may use either because he has the initiative of movement. This area covers Thorn; you are moving closer to forces that are going to debouch via this town and you retain the freedom of manoeuvre on either bank of the Drewenz, which is always good to keep.

If the conjecture that I just made is correct and you were cut off from Neumark, you would be forced to retire to Gilgenburg or Lautenburg, and Thorn would be abandoned. Without dwelling any longer on this supposition, I must remind you that the Emperor's intention is to draw to his left the enemy forces so as to be able to turn them by his right and cut them off from any possible retreat. I will now examine what influence that a battle at Löbau could have on the execution of that overall plan. The outcome of such a battle against a superior enemy, equipped with a more numerous cavalry, may seem doubtful. Even if the combat were favourable to you, as I hope it would be, you would still not dare to vigorously pursue this success for fear of compromising yourself and moving yourself too far away from Thorn. If the enemy was battered badly enough to make a hasty retreat, he might manage to escape the pursuit of our right wing forces and his defeat would actually become his salvation. If the battle remained indecisive and you were obliged to retreat the next day on Neumark, the losses that you had suffered in this fight would be a useless sacrifice. And if, contrary to all expectations, you suffered a defeat, this event, although not decisive to the overall plan of operations, would still be rather disastrous. Thus, in all of these scenarios, it is reasonable to believe that by accepting a battle Löbau we would digress from the objectives that the Emperor set for us, whereas if we fall back and lure the enemy toward the upper Drewenz, we would make him more and more entangled in our designs.

I feel much less restraint, *Monseigneur*, in giving you my opinion on this question as, given the circumstances, it would be impossible for my *corps d'armée* to be able take a serious part in the action at Löbau. If you were attacked by strong enemy forces at seven o'clock in the morning, I would only receive news of it at 10; the assembly of my troops would finish around 11, and, however diligent I might be, I could not arrive with large enough forces before five o'clock in the evening, that is to say when the battle would have already been decided. My *corps d'armée's* movement would thus be needless, have no consequences for you, and no impact on the course of events if the battle were indeed fought at Löbau. Therefore, I can without any regret follow the orders of the minister, which state expressly that 'if the superiority of the enemy forces will constrain your manoeuvring to cover Thorn, I should retire with my *corps d'armée* to Neidenburg.' Consequently, I just revoked the orders that I had given to concentrate the entirety of my *corps d'armée* at Gilgenburg and occupy Klein-Nappern with an infantry brigade.

I hereby submit to you my ideas, *Monseigneur*, with all the confidence inspired by an old friendship, formed in war, persuaded that you will see in them only the desire to contribute to the success of the Emperor's vision and to that of your own operations. *Je vous renouvelle l'assurance de ma haute considération et de mon attachement inalterable* [Please accept, once again, the assurance of my highest esteem and unwavering support].

Marshal Ney to the Minister of War
Gilgenburg, 31 January 1807, 10 o'clock in the morning
I just received the letter from Your Excellency dated from Warsaw on the 28th of this month, by which I have been ordered to concentrate my *corps d'armée* at Hohenstein, on the assumption that the Prince de Ponte-Corvo would be able to hold at Osterode. The events that have occurred since this time, which I already reported, have obliged me, so as not to allow *1er corps* to be destroyed, to lean slowly to the right so as to divide the enemy forces. That is what made me retire from Hohenstein to Mühlen, and from this latter position to Gilgenburg. The Prince de Ponte-Corvo is withdrawing to Neumark today so as to avoid a general battle in a bad position the results of which could only be unfortunate for the general operations of His Majesty and might deliver Thorn to the enemy. I will therefore remain here in hopes of receiving new orders in response to my letter from yesterday evening. In the meantime, I am informing the troops at Soldau and Neidenburg to be prepared to join me as soon as Marshal Augereau arrives in this latter town. If, before the arrival of *7e corps* at Neidenburg, Your Excellency orders me to go to Hohenstein, as I expect it to happen, then my offensive movement will allow the

Prince de Ponte-Corvo to slowly follow the enemy rear guard, and will permit the columns on the right to cut off all retreat to it.

I am attaching here the copies of two letters written to me by His Excellency the Prince de Ponte-Corvo. The first is dated January 30th while the second is not dated. I assume it is due to a clerical error [*erreur du secrétaire*] that he assures me that an enemy corps of 8,000 to 10,000 men is moving on Mlawa; but what makes me think that the Prince really believes it, is that he added in his own hand the following postscript: 'This *corps* is entirely independent of that which I have in front of me; it has been detached for a long time.' Only after completely losing a mind can one give any credence to such a manoeuvre.'

On 19/31 January, Lieutenant General Prince Golitsyn received orders to send a large detachment and, taking all the necessary precautions, to attempt to take Hohenstein. General Meller-Zakomelsky was tasked with this operation, which involved His Majesty's Cuirassier Regiment, the Kargopolskii Dragoon Regiment, and the Ilovaisky IX's Cossack Regiment. Upon his arrival at Hohenstein, this general found this place already evacuated by the enemy. The occupation of this location was important for us in order to safeguard the centre of our position and so that the enemy, of whom all of the *corps d'armée* were in movement, which we already knew, could not move his forces quickly on Gilgenburg and Neidenburg, and arrive at the heights of Hohenstein without us being forewarned and able to concentrate ourselves to meet him in force.

By an order of the day, I returned command of the cavalry of the right wing, previously under the orders of Lieutenant General Anrep, to Major General Count Pahlen. Lieutenant General Prince Golitsyn reported that, following the orders he had received the day before, he had occupied Allenstein and then sent the Emperor's *aide de camp*, Colonel Prince Michel Dolgorouky, with the Kurlandskii Dragoon Regiment, a battalion of the Rostovskii Musketeer Regiment, and Yefremov III's Cossack Regiment to occupy Passenheim. Prince Dolgorouky, approaching this place, found the enemy there in force. He therefore kept his infantry battalion at the village of Scheufelsdorf on the road to Allenstein to serve as a rallying point in case of a retreat. He then marched with the dragoon regiment and the Cossacks and attacked and routed the enemy below Passenheim. According to the prisoner statements, the French lost in killed a colonel, several officers, and a considerable number of soldiers; as prisoners, Prince Dolgorouky sent to the headquarters a major, two officers, and 97 cavalrymen. He occupied Passenheim taking all those precautionary measures that this young and brave officer had manifested on every occasion throughout this war. Our losses were only 15 men killed and wounded.

That same day, however, the enemy made an attempt to retake Passenheim but Prince Dolgorouky, reinforced by Colonel Kakhovsky, who brought five hussar squadrons, held out there and forced the enemy to retreat.

On our right wing, there was no change in our position; everything there remained quiet after the retreat of the enemy to Neumark.

In my following letter you will find, General, events far more serious than those that I have discussed until now, but before finishing this one, I cannot go without telling you a bit more about Prince Michel Dolgorouky, whom I already mentioned several times in the account of my operations and of whom I will often speak again. This is the same person who was unfortunately recently killed in a battle against the Swedes;[2] this was a manifest and real loss for the army. This young man possessed all the essential qualities of a good soldier. He paired constant diligence with a great deal of innate spirit, sound judgment, judicious wisdom, poised character; he was serious when it was necessary, and full of life and effervescent when his men needed encouragement; he was enterprising but prudent, daring without excessive recklessness. I often employed him in this war and he always acquitted himself with forethought and success. The whole army recognized his talents and future prospects. His Majesty the Emperor [Alexander] promoted him to a major general and made him his *aide de camp general*. In the war against Sweden, where Dolgorouky once again distinguished himself, he was promoted to the rank of lieutenant general.

This Prince Dolgorouky was the brother of Prince Peter Dolgorouky, *aide de camp general* to the Emperor, who died at St Petersburg at the end of 1806, returning from the army that was operating against the Turks and on the point of coming to join me at the army in Prussia. The death of this general in the prime of life was again a huge loss, not only for the army but for the empire as well. He had a lively and penetrating spirit and had demonstrated a rare level of enterprise in his service. Our Sovereign, whose confidence he gained completely, often employed him for both military and political commissions. It was Dolgorouky whom, as I noted in my third letter, the Emperor dispatched to Berlin to persuade the Prussian cabinet to declare itself for the coalition in 1805.[3] We know that he acquitted himself of this mission with skill. The loss of these two young, distinguished soldiers, of whose services the empire has been deprived too early, will be mourned for a long time by the army and by all of Russia. They owed their reputation to their great merits, their excellent qualities, and to the favour of their Sovereign.

---

2   Dolgorouky was killed by a cannonball in the battle of Idensalmi (Koljonvirta) on 27 October 1808.
3   Bennigsen makes no mention of the role Peter Dolgorouky played in the Russian defeat at Austerlitz. A scion of a distinguished Russian family of princes, Dolgorouky (Dolgorukov) was born with a deep sense of power and privilege. He had been enrolled in the elite Life Guard Izmailovskii Regiment at the tender age of just three months and began actual service as a 15-year-old captain, quickly rising through the ranks due to family connections. At 21, he was already a major general and adjutant-general to Emperor Paul. His meteoric rise only accelerated after Alexander ascended the Russian throne in 1801. The young czar became very fond of Dolgorukov, who espoused hawkish views in foreign policy and wanted Russia to be more assertive in Europe. In 1804–1805, he was one of the architects of the Russian confrontation with Napoleon and carried out several diplomatic missions, including one to sway the Hohenzollern court to join the Third Coalition. Accompanying the czar to Olmutz, Dolgorukov extolled the Russian rear guard actions at as great victories and spoke with profound contempt of the Austrians, who had allowed themselves to be defeated at Ulm. His meeting with Napoleon, and subsequent report that the French emperor was weak and worried, contributed to the Russian emperor's decision to fight a battle at Austerlitz. 'If Your Majesty retreats, Napoleon will consider all of us cowards,' Dolgorouky told the czar, who responded, 'Cowards? Then it is better for us to die.' Bavarian chargé d'affaires Olry's Additional Bulletin, 31 December 1805, in 'Iz donesenii Bavarskago poverennago v delakh Olry v pervye gody tsartsvovanya (1802-1806) Imperatora Aleksandra I,' in *Istoricheskii vestnik* 147 (1917), pp.460–461.

11

Bergfried, Waltersdorf-Liebstadt, Hof and Heilsberg

On 20 January/1 February, in the morning, Lieutenant General Prince Bagration sent me some intercepted dispatches; Cossacks had found them on a French officer, whom they captured during a surprise attack on the town of Lautenburg, where nothing was less expected than the appearance of our Cossacks.[1] These dispatches contained order from the Minister of War, the Prince of Neuchâtel, speaking on behalf of Emperor Napoleon, to Marshal the Prince de Ponte-Corvo, which read as follows:

To M. Marshal the Prince de Ponte-Corvo
Prasznitz, 30 January 1807, midnight
The Emperor, *Monsieur* Marshal, has just arrived at Prasznitz; on February 1, he is taking the offensive via Willenberg. Wherever you are, concentrate your troops until you are assured that Marshal Lefebvre, with the *2e régiment* and the *15e d'infanterie légère française*, has arrived at Thorn. Until then have no other goal than to cover this town. When you know that these two regiments are at Thorn, do not concern yourself about this place anymore; if necessary, Marshal Lefebvre can hold out for eight days there. You must have surely sent there all the Hessians who took part in the blockade of Graudenz. Inform Marshal Lefebvre, when you will leave the fortress to his forces and tell him what the Emperor is doing; and then,

---

[1] Yermolov: 'Colonel Yurkovskii, who commanded our outposts, sent a captured courier to Bagration. Napoleon had sent him to Bernadotte with instructions to halt his retreat, the order stating that withdrawal had been necessary to lure us in the direction of Graudentz, while Napoleon planned to concentrate his entire army at Allenstein by 2 February [new style] and attack our extended forces. This capture was a stroke of luck because otherwise our main army would have advanced along a single road and would have been either defeated piecemeal or at least isolated and forced to retreat, abandoning its line of operations and magazines. In the latter case, only a small part of our troops would have survived; any remaining forces, isolated from Russia and pushed against the sea, would have suffered disaster and been forced to surrender. Although it was a well-conceived plan, Napoleon's enterprise could have succeeded only because of our total carelessness. We should not have attempted our movement on Preusissch-Eylau without precise intelligence on the location of the main French army. If our goal had been the destruction of Bernadotte's corps, then we had had our chance at Mohrungen, and should not have followed him afterwards.' Yermolov, *The Czar's General*, p.75.

Monsieur Marshal, in whatever position you are, concentrate all your forces. Send an intelligent officer to the Emperor at Willenberg, so that by his return you may find yourself at the rendezvous point. If, finally, by any circumstance whatsoever the orders did not reach you, you will act according to your experience in war and you will pursue the enemy who, in all likelihood, will be retreating before you by 2 February.

The Prince of Neuchâtel
Marshal Berthier
When I say that you will pursue the enemy, I meant that you will be observing him and, if he starts to fall back, only then you will follow him, prudently.

Based on the repeated news that we had received about the departure of Emperor Napoleon from Warsaw and the march of all the corps composing the *Grande Armée*,[2] I had, as you will have observed in my previous letter, deployed my forces on our left flank and taken a position that allowed me to move, with considerable forces, to any point where circumstances required it. After receiving this dispatch,[3] I therefore resolved to concentrate the army at Jonkowo and then march via Allenstein to confront the French army. As one can see on the map, I could have directed my march directly to Preussisch-Eylau and gained two days, but I hoped to avoid the enemy gaining too much ground before a general battle. You will soon learn the reasons that, two days later, made me choose however the battlefield of Preussisch-Eylau. The orders that I consequently sent to the generals were as follows:

Lieutenant General Sacken will move directly on Allenstein, with the reserve composed of the 3rd and 4th Divisions; he will place himself at Spiegelberg and its environs.

---

2   By the end of January, Napoleon perceived a chance to encircle and defeat his opponent. He acted with characteristic energy and determination to convert the enemy's unexpected advance into an opportunity: 'the emperor does not wish to return to winter quarters until he has annihilated the enemy,' wrote Berthier to Ney on 27 January. Napoleon anticipated that, by proceeding further westward, Bennigsen would inevitably expose his left flank and rear to the French main army. Accordingly, Napoleon conceived a brilliant manoeuvre sur les derrières. Keeping 10th Corps (16,000 men) at Thorn, Napoleon instructed Bernadotte to fall back to lure Bennigsen further west and into a trap. Bernadotte's retrograde movement would cover Napoleon's real intention of launching a bataillon carré along the Chorzellen– Willenberg axis to turn Bennigsen's left flank, drive the Russian army into a narrow spot between the Lower Vistula and the Frisches-Haff (or Vistula Lagoon), and destroy it. Thanks to his previous dispositions, Napoleon could concentrate some 115,000 men against the Russians for his counteroffensive. The 5th Corps received the separate task of containing Essen's corps between the Bug and the Narew Rivers. See *Correspondance de Napoléon*, vol.14, pp.354–355; Naulet, *Eylau*, p.132; Höpfner, *Der Krieg von 1806 und 1807*, vol.3, pp.193–194; Pierre Grenier, *Étude sur 1807: manoeuvres d'Eylau et Friedland* (Paris: Charles-Lavauzelle, 1901), pp.51–53.

3   Wilson: 'On the 1st [February] we reached General Bennigsen's headquarters at Mohrungen, and were received by him, as I expected, with all possible and pleasing consideration. We were lodged in his house and in the room where Bernadotte a few nights before had slept… During dinner, accounts came from all quarters of prisoners being brought in. Several French officers arrived, and a courier was taken bearing the whole plans of Bupnaparte.' *Life of General Sir Robert Wilson*, vol.2, pp.81–82. For details on the French side, see Berthier to Bernadotte, 31 January, in Dumas, *Précis des événemens militaires*, vol.18, p.380; Petre, *Napoleon's Campaign in Poland*, p.148n.

Lieutenant General Tuchkov will remain at Jonkowo. Lieutenant General Dokhturov with his division will leave Osterode and march via Bardungen and Detterswalde in order to place himself in the environs of Jonkowo.

Lieutenant General Essen III, with his detachment at Liebemühl, will march via Taberbrück, Lookken, Stenckienen, to occupy the village of Windtcken and its environs.

Lieutenant General Prince Bagration will leave Deutsch-Eylau and march via Taberbrück to Jonkowo.

These detachments, both those moving from Liebemühl and those from Deutsch-Eylau, saw no enemy on their marches. Marshal the Prince de Ponte-Corvo was supposed to follow them; but the second dispatch, sent to him from Willenberg, was also intercepted by our Cossacks. Besides, these detachments were too powerful for the French *1er corps d'armée* to engage and stop them alone.

Meanwhile, Lieutenant General Prince Golitsyn learned from his advance posts that Marshal Soult with his *corps* and the Grand-Duke of Berg [Murat] with his cavalry reserve were approaching Passenheim. He therefore ordered Prince Dolgorouky to retire from this post and join at Klein-Trinkhaus with Major General Baron Korff's cavalry brigade, which he did with the greatest order; although he was obliged to fight throughout the entire march, he lost only 16 men, as many killed as wounded.

Likewise, Major General Meller was ordered to evacuate Hohenstein and withdraw to Allenstein. This general, before leaving Hohenstein, pushed forward a strong patrol of Cossacks to gain certain news of the enemy's approach. The Cossack officer, who was tasked with leading this patrol, marched throughout the night, and arrived at daybreak at Neidenburg, where he surprised an advance-post of the French cavalry, which he defeated, capturing nine prisoners while losing not a single man from his small troop. From these prisoners we learned that Marshal Ney with his corps was marching on that route. From five prisoners, taken by Prince Bagration's Cossacks, we already knew that the Prince de Ponte-Corvo's *corps d'armée* was not moving.

That day Prince Golitsyn concentrated his *corps* in the environs of Allenstein in order to go to Jonkowo. He ordered Major General Baron Korff to cover his withdrawal with his brigade, Prince Dolgorouky's detachment, and the cuirassiers regiment commanded by Colonel Lindenbaum,[4] which this general executed with a great deal of prudence, despite superior enemy forces pressing him during this march. Prince Golitsyn left Major General Barclay de Tolly with his detachment at Allenstein, with instructions to occupy that post for as long as possible. Lieutenant General L'Estocq was similarly invited to retreat with his *corps* and to take the shortest route via Osterode to join the Russian army at Allenstein, where he could participate in a general battle.

During the night of 20 January/1 February to 21 January/2 February, Prince Bagration sent me a second dispatch that his Cossacks had captured with an officer who was sent from Willenberg by the Minister of War, the Prince of Neuchâtel, to Marshal the Prince de Ponte-Corvo, by the same route on which they had taken the first messenger. This dispatch revealed to us the intentions and the entirety of the enemy's plan of operations. Here is that dispatch:

---

4 Colonel Karl Lindenbaum commanded the Military Order (*Ordenskii*) Cuirassier Regiment in 1803–1809.

To His Excellency the Prince de Ponte-Corvo
Willenberg, 31 January 1807, six o'clock in the evening
The Emperor, Prince, orders me to inform you that the Grand-Duke of Berg [Murat] and Marshal Soult are moving tomorrow, with all of their forces, to Passenheim. Marshal Ney has orders to approach Allenstein, either by moving on Hohenstein, or by passing behind the lakes via Dembenofen. The Emperor desires, *Monsieur* Marshal, that you undertake a nocturnal march to mislead the enemy, and then form the left wing of the army. You will try therefore to reach Gilgenburg and maintain communication with Marshal Ney. But you will have to abandon the road to Thorn. In this case, a regiment of light cavalry, which should be charged with maintaining the fires in your bivouacs during your night movement, would move slowly on Thorn and keep turning back convoys, small detachments, and isolated individuals; upon arriving at Thorn, they would inform Marshal Lefebvre and the *commandant* of the place of the army's manoeuvre; you would, of course, have taken the care to inform them in advance. If the circumstances in which you find yourself would make you think that this manoeuvre is too difficult, the Emperor leaves you free to continue covering Thorn by remaining on the road that leads to it.

Of course, the Prince, informed as you are of the movement that the Emperor is intending to make, you will march vigorously against the enemy, from the moment that the necessity of weakening himself in front of you makes him execute his retreat. In the latter case, you will send orders to General Espagne's cavalry division, which is at Thorn, to join you. If that of General d'Hautpoul is with you, direct it to Marshal Ney's corps, of which it will follow the movements. In the first case, you will take with you General d'Hautpoul's division if it is with your *corps d'armée* and you will send orders to Espagne's division to join you in the rear. The two French brigades and the Poles that are currently at Thorn will suffice to hold that town.

I need not tell you, *Monsieur* Marshal, that His Majesty wishes to envelop the enemy and prefers to see you move on his left, but he does trusts in your zeal and knowledge, and is certain you would act in accordance with circumstances that you will find yourself in.

Marshal Davout with his *corps d'armée* is moving on the right of Marshal Soult; the [Imperial] Guard and Marshal Augereau are behind him. It is likely, *Monsieur* Marshal, that the Emperor will spend the entire day tomorrow at Willenberg.
The Prince of Neuchâtel
Marshal Berthier

These *coups de main* by our Cossacks gave new proof, if it was still necessary, of their utility to the army and of the great services that they render to it. The Cossacks protect our detachments from surprise attacks; they supply intelligence about the distant movements of the enemy; with great skill, they take prisoners every time new information is needed, and frequently intercept important enemy dispatches. They fatigue enemy's forces and wreck his cavalry with the continual alarms that they cause as well as through the activity, circumspection, and vigilance with which the enemy cavalry must act at the advance posts so as not to be surprised. They exploit any and every mistake and make the enemy regret each bit of negligence committed. How many interesting dispatches have they intercepted during this war! How many officers who were carrying verbal commands! I could cite a suitable number of examples of the Cossack agility and enterprise. You will also see that there are few days where I do not mention them and the essential services they rendered. It is unfortunate that during major actions they cannot serve with the same efficacy as in every other occasion of war. As much as their bravery renders them suitable to it so their irregular state renders them incapable of it. We have seen more than one example of when they attacked infantry with success in advance post actions, when the numbers were not too disproportionate. You will find the best testimony of the service of our Cossacks in many enemy dispatches as well.

On 21 January/2 February, I left Mohrungen with my headquarters and went to Jonkowo, where I learned from the reports from General Barclay de Tolly that the *Grande Armée* was approaching Allenstein and that the patrols that he had sent to scout the enemy's march had detected strong columns on the road coming from Passenheim via Klauckendorf, but the greatest enemy forces were on the main road from Willenberg, via Wuttrienen, to Allenstein. General Barclay de Tolly immediately sent the Military Order and Malorossiiskii Cuirassier Regiments, and the Kurlyandskii Dragoon Regiment to confront the enemy on the road from Klauckendorf. At the approach of this detachment, the enemy deployed his column of cavalry, which appeared to be 40 to 50 squadrons strong, behind which one could see a strong column of infantry deploying. Our cavalry had with it two horse artillery cannon against which the enemy mounted a battery of eight pieces of heavy calibre. After a minor skirmish, our men fell back to the Izumskii Hussar Regiment, commanded by Major General Dorokhov, who distinguished himself that day in covering our withdrawal with such a great deal of skill and orderliness that the enemy could not gain much. General Barclay de Tolly, seeing that he could no longer hold the post of Allenstein, given the superior forces of the enemy, retreated on Lykusen and Gettkendorf (on the road to Jonkowo). The detachment he left behind at Lykusen departed the following night; upon which the general, with the majority of his detachment, deployed three *verstas* [~3.2 kilometres] in front of our main position.

The day before a lieutenant-colonel of the Cossacks had been sent out with a detachment to reconnoitre the environs of Hohenstein. He went around that place and proceeded down the main road to Gilgenburg, where he encountered Marshal Ney's corps in full march. He shadowed it all day until reaching Hohenstein and then returned to the army to make his report, without having lost a single Cossack. Upon my arrival at Jonkowo, I sent orders to all generals to arrive, the next day in the morning, with their forces at the position at Jonkowo. To safeguard my left flank from being turned, I had infantry occupy the villages of Kaltfliess, Kainen and Bergfried on the Alle River, where the passage could be effected most easily.

The position at Jonkowo offered me no advantage as long as the enemy possessed Allenstein and was able to move his forces on both banks of the Alle. This position did not even cover Königsberg. Therefore, as I have already told you, I chose this position only to concentrate the army there and pass beyond the Alle, intending to confront the enemy in full forces on the plains on the other side of Allenstein. Yet the enemy had anticipated me, as we will see from the account of the next day.

Marshal Ney to the Minister of War
Hohenstein, 2 February 1807, six o'clock in the evening
I have the honour of informing Your Excellency that the *6e corps* has taken position: the *1re division* at Grieslienen, on the road to Allenstein; the *2e* [division] on the heights behind Hohenstein, the right having the direction toward Mispelsee and the left toward Sauden Farm. We encountered the enemy outposts, comprised of the Cossacks and hussars, at Lichteinen around one o'clock; after a minor skirmish, they retreated toward Hohenstein. Behind this town there was a detachment of some 300 cavalrymen but a few volleys of cannon fire made them swiftly retire too. The enemy was vigorously followed up to and beyond Grieslienen; he seemed to take the direction of Allenstein.

Yesterday, at three o'clock in the morning, two Russian regiments, one of dragoons and another of cuirassiers, departed from here for Allenstein. M. Steck, staff officer [*officier d'état-major*] of His Excellency the Prince de Ponte-Corvo, informed me from Soldau, dated today, that yesterday while approaching Lautenburg, at six o'clock in the afternoon, he learned that a fairly considerable party of Cossacks had penetrated this town and that, according to what the inhabitants of the area say, two officers of the headquarters of *1er corps* were taken prisoner, as well as an officer coming from the Imperial headquarters with dispatches for His Excellency the Prince de Ponte-Corvo. M. Steck adds that the *1er corps d'armée* retired to Strassburg and that a Russian *corps d'armée* of 15,000 to 20,000 men is encamped near Polischen, on the road to Neumark.

Your Excellency will note that it is impossible for me to communicate with the Prince de Ponte-Corvo's right wing. My two regiments of light cavalry, having furnished the necessary orderlies for the army headquarters, barely have 400 men remaining in their ranks. The active service that they are obliged to perform further reduces their numbers each day. Meanwhile, the enemy cavalry is numerous and present everywhere; barely had we left Gilgenburg that the Cossacks entered it. We had them on our rear, on the left flank and in front, throughout our march. It is rather disagreeable to be unable to conceal our movements from the enemy due to the disproportion between the size of our cavalry and the infantry.

On 22 January/3 February, our divisions entered, according to the orders received the day before, the position at Jonkowo.[5] Only Lieutenant General Prince Bagration was unable to arrive there that morning. I therefore sent him orders to halt with his detachment at Gottken and Wengaithen to cover our right wing. At the same time, I sent out strong reconnaissance detachments, made up of Cossacks, to scout the road from Hohenstein to Allenstein, where

---

5   Wilson: 'We went round the army, and never in my life did I behold such a martial spectacle. The countenances and figures of the men, and their habiliments, reminded me of the description of the Macedonian veterans: and when we looked at the ground covered with snow their only resting place, the sky driven with a fierce south-east blast their only canopy; when we recollected that these men had been gathered from the most remote regions of the globe, and had just performed a march of twenty-eight days without any interval of repose, I could not but admire and hope.' *Life of General Sir Robert Wilson*, vol.2, p.84.

I expected the approach of Marshal Ney with his corps. Major General Count Kamensky received orders to cover with the 14th Division, in reserve, our left wing, and to keep outposts at Kaltfliess, Kainen and Bergfried [along the Alle River]. General Barclay de Tolly was instructed to cover, with his detachment, the main road from Allenstein to Jonkowo, which led directly to the centre of our position.

By holding such a position, I only intended to ascertain the enemy's movements, which manifested themselves that same day and pointed to the enemy's intention to cross the Alle with all of his forces. [Napoleon] had already sent part of his army to Allenstein during the night and in the morning; he placed himself across from us and occupied with his left the distance from the village of Abstich to Gettkendorf, beyond which was his right wing.

Until one o'clock in the afternoon everything remained quiet, but then the enemy attacked on the Alle our outposts that were supposed to cover our left wing.[6] Count Kamensky, who had confided the post of Bergfried and the defence of the bridge there to Major General Gersdorf, with the Uglitskii Musketeer Regiment,[7] having recognized the importance of this post, sent him as reinforcements a battalion of the Tenginskii [Musketeer] Regiment. The enemy moved considerable forces against this post, and Marshal Soult's corps carried out this assault. A large detachment of cavalry first charged our infantry that was defending the bridge. The cavalry was sharply repulsed and retired in haste; but the attack was soon renewed by the enemy infantry. The bridge at this post was defended first by Major Guerkevitch with three companies and by Lieutenant-Colonel Dénissov[8] who had been sent to his aid with a battalion. These brave officers decided to charge the enemy with bayonets. They managed to cross the bridge and push the enemy back. Yet the French exploited the fact that the river was frozen in places and crossed it on the ice at a point where the bank was covered by woods, seeking to flank our position at Bergfried; Colonel Prince Urakov[9] attacked and forced them to retreat. Finally, the enemy moved such superior infantry and artillery forces against our position at Bergfried that General Gersdorf felt it necessary to abandon it and retreat. General Count Kamensky, who had noticed that both cannon and musket fire was growing ever

---

6   Wilson: 'Beningsen determined in the evening to face Allenstein, and move with the rest of the army to gain the right of the French and restore the communication with Essen. But as the advanced guard was moving for this purpose under Prince Galitzin [Golitsyn], the enemy advanced with a strong body of cavalry and infantry with several batteries, and began an affair by endeavouring to occupy in front a wood which divided the two armies. Soon afterwards they advanced, and twice gained a bridge which it was necessary to pass, over a deep ravine now filled with snow, and which lay in front and on the right of their line. Two battalions of the Russians stationed there charged the French and repulsed them with considerable loss, and finally maintained the bridge; but they suffered much in the charge from the fire of a battalion stationed to protect those that had passed the bridge. The action was very brisk in this quarter and lasted two hours. On the left of the French line, they advanced with their cavalry so far from the wood that the Russian hussars charged and drove them back; but from the fire of the artillery they themselves lost thirty men and one hundred horses. In this slight affair the Russian infantry and cavalry showed much spirit, and the cry of the former to the charge was highly animating.' Wilson to Lord Hutchinson, 4 February 1807, in *Life of General Sir Robert Wilson*, vol.2, pp.405–406.
7   Karl Maksimovich Gersdorf, the chef of the Uglitskii Musketeer Regiment in 1800–1813. In 1807, he commanded a brigade of the 14th Division.
8   Peter Denisyev, who later commanded the Uglitskii Musketeer Regiment in 1808–1810.
9   Colonel Ivan Afanasyevich Urakov, promoted to colonel in May 1806 and commanding the Uglitskii Musketeer Regiment in 1800–1802 and 1806–1808.

livelier, set off, on his initiative, with eight infantry battalions, a heavy artillery battery and the St Peterburgskii Dragoon Regiment to support this position, which was just five *verstas* [5.3 kilometres] from our left wing. On the way there, he received news that the French had already taken it with considerable forces and that not only the position at Kaltfliess was in their hands, but also that they had found a way to send even more troops across the ice. Count Kamensky, fearing that if he moved too far from our left wing he might be too exposed, wisely decided to halt his movement and content himself with covering General Gersdorf's withdrawal. During the enemy attacks at various points along the Alle

Karl Gersdorf. (State Hermitage Museum)

River we lost one major and five officers killed, while Colonel Prince Urakov, Major Tenishev and seven officers were wounded; almost 800 of our soldiers were killed and wounded.

In these circumstances, prudence dictated no longer holding the position at Jonkowo, all the more so as I expected that Marshals Ney and Bernadotte would march with their corps against my right wing, although the latter's movement should have been delayed since the orders given to him had been intercepted.[10] I therefore informed my division commanders that the army would set in march during the night and that it would only be at Preussisch-Eylau that I would accept battle. But to prevent the enemy from getting too close to our position and noticing our retrograde movement, I ordered that same night to attack the enemy forces closest to our right wing. General Barclay de Tolly was commanded to carry out this attack with his detachment, supported by a division, which he executed with the greatest effect. The enemy forces were forced to fall back with losses onto the first line of their main army. Our losses on that day amounted to 1,200 men, including the 800 that I mentioned

---

10 According to Wilson, '[Bennigsen] saw the impossibility of continuing at Yunkowo and regretted his movement from Mohrungen, since he now had to retire in presence of an enemy, and General Lestocq's corps was exposed to imminent hazard.' *Brief Remarks*, p.91. Also see his journal remarks: 'General Beningsen now finding from the reports of the prisoners that Buonaparte with his whole army was before him, determined to retire into a position where he could fight with advantage : but his object in the circumstances of the time was not to fight a decisive battle if it could be avoided. He therefore marched during the night; but the country only admitting of two columns, the great extension retarded the rearguard, five thousand men, and kept them until near nine o'clock on the ground: they then retired under the command of Prince Bagrathion, fighting the whole way, to their new position.' *Life of General Sir Robert Wilson*, vol.2, pp.84–85.

earlier. I was never able to learn the enemy casualties, but they must have certainly surpassed our own.[11]

I directed the first march from Jonkowo on Wolfsdorf, as much to take position there in the plains as to move closer to General L'Estocq's *corps* and protect his march. The first destination of this general had been, as I said before, to join the Russian army and to fight the enemy on the other side of Allenstein. But as the circumstances had changed, I invited this general to direct his march straight to Preussisch-Eylau and to arrive there by 27 January/8 February. Also, as the result of the reconnaissance conducted by our Cossacks, the next day I learned that Marshal Ney, with his corps, had moved left to get closer to the Passarge, which indicated his intention to harass General L'Estocq's *corps* and to prevent its junction with the Russian army.

The march of our army from Jonkowo was organized in three columns.[12] The first, which was supposed to serve as the advance guard, was under the orders of Lieutenant General Prince Golitsyn and included the 2nd and 14th Divisions, and the 7th and 24th Jager Regiments, along with the cavalry of the left wing; it was supposed to move via Blankenberg, Alt-Garschen, Ankendorf, Komalmen, Scharnick and Wolfsdorf. The second column, commanded by Lieutenant General Sacken, composed of the 3rd and 4th Divisions, the Pavlogradskii Hussar Regiment, and the Malorossiiskii Cuirassier Regiment, proceeded via Blankenberg, Alt-Garschen and Warlack to Wolfsdorf. This general was ordered to start his march at 11 o'clock in the evening. The third column, under the orders of General Tuchkov, was supposed to set off at midnight with the 5th, 7th, and 8th Divisions, as well as the heavy artillery and the cavalry from the right wing. It was instructed to march through Jonkowo, Pupkeim, Schlitt, Deppen, Waltersmühl, Kleinfeld and to arrive at Wolfsdorf as well. As for the rear guard, I let Lieutenant General Prince Bagration to act in accordance to the movements that the enemy would make to follow our columns. This general had under his command the detachments of generals Barclay de Tolly, Markov, and Baggehufvudt. I hoped that our rear guard would be able to begin its march at three or four o'clock in the morning.[13]

---

11 Wilson: 'In the evening a Frenchman was brought in with the most terrible sabre wound I ever beheld: his nose, cheeks, lips, and chin were actually shaved away: and yet the poor wretch lived; and was sensible of attention, as he expressed great gratitude for my obtaining him a room, and with much difficulty a surgeon, for they are scarce in the Russian army and the camp was at some distance.' *Life of General Sir Robert Wilson*, vol.2, p.85

12 Writing on February 4, Wilson enthused that 'at present I can only mention that I never saw a more martial army. Their discipline is good; their marching is regular; and, considering what they have gone through, their appearance is admirable. The infantry are all equal to what you saw in England. The cavalry are excellent, with truly warlike bearing, and even the infantry exult in their courage. The artillery is well appointed, and draws through *fossés* of snow that astonish me to look at. In short, I never saw better *mains*… How much I wish you could see this army! Report has done them wrong; even the Cossacks are more respectable than you have believed, and there is no more robbery and pillage than is always the practice of friends and foes. Instead of inhabitants flying, we have seen poultry of all kinds confidently strutting on the dunghills.' Wilson to Lord Hutchinson, 4 February 1807, *Life of General Sir Robert Wilson*, vol.2, p.407.

13 The immediate problem Bagration faced was the Russian stragglers and marauders. One of the participants recalled, 'The retreat was executed in relative order, in daylight and in view of the enemy… but there were still incidents of pillaging by the stragglers, especially in the tail end of the rearguard. It was impossible for [Bagration's] rear guard to be everywhere to detain these marauders, a large number of whom fell into enemy's hands.' Volkonsky, *Zapiski*, p.24.

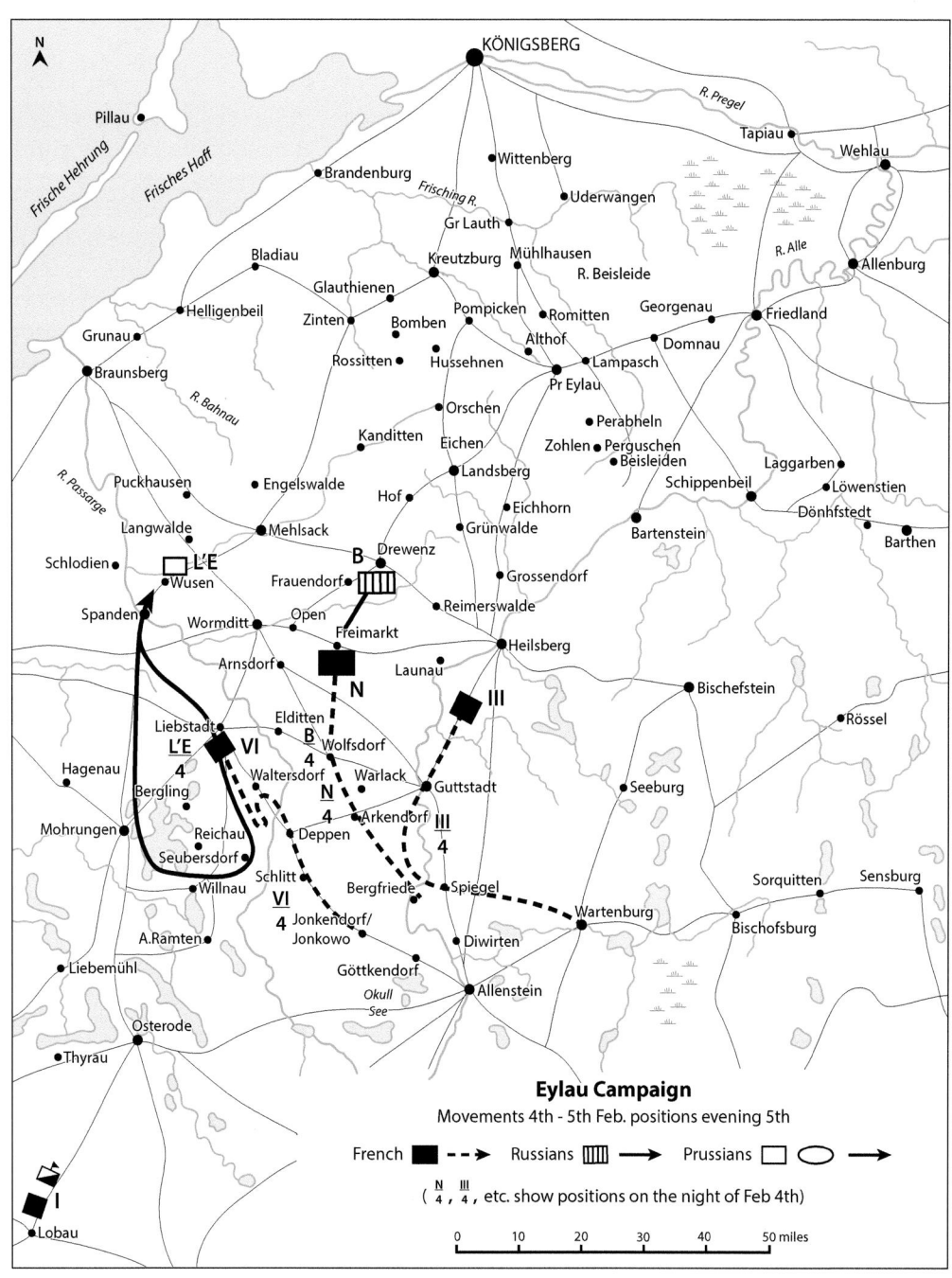

Situation as of 4-5 February 1807.

On 23 January/4 February, confusion and misunderstanding, which unfortunately too often occur while executing the orders of the army commander, delayed the march from Jonkowo to Wolfsdorf. General Sacken, who was supposed to start his march at 11 o'clock in the evening to make room for the troops that were supposed to move via Jonkowo on the same road, departed only at two o'clock in the morning. Consequently, our rear guard had to halt in the environs of Jonkowo until broad daylight and wait for our columns to move up the road.[14] Moreover, the heavy snows that covered the roads had rendered all movement very difficult.[15] Nevertheless, the good dispositions, the wise conduct and the presence of mind of the generals, who were at the head of the rear guards, made up for all of it. They managed to avoid grave losses that this delayed march could have caused us.[16]

Prince Bagration charged General Barclay de Tolly with covering the departure of the army from the position at Jonkowo and then the movements of the 1st and 2nd columns. Barely had Barclay de Tolly moved beyond Jonkowo when considerable enemy forces vigorously attacked him in front of a defile, where he stopped to allow the passage of the rest of the 2nd column of the army. He was forced to deploy his men into a battle order to confront the enemy; the Izumskii and Oliviopolskii Hussar Regiments, deployed in echelons and with a horse artillery in between, covered his flanks. None of the enemy efforts to turn or overwhelm this detachment succeeded, and the French were repulsed everywhere.[17] It was only at 10 o'clock in the morning that the tail of the second column passed through the defile, at which point General Barclay de Tolly began to move his echelons, beginning with the cavalry.

---

14 Bennigsen's charge against Sacken is unsurprising considering their prior animosity. Yermolov, meanwhile, thought that Bennigsen's dispositions were partly responsible for the confusion: 'The vanguard was ordered to cover the movement of our heavy artillery guns as well as the Prussian artillery. It was a surprising order since the column closest to enemy was that of the artillery; its horses were exhausted, and it slowed us down considerably. The vanguard thus soon caught up with this column and had to take up positions to allow artillery to move on.' Yermolov, *The Czar's General*, p.76.

15 One Russian participant noted: 'Often during a night march through a wood or a defile, the troops would be obliged to file past some trifling object, which blocked the way, because no one gave the order to remove the obstacle. What would I not have given to sleep on the snow for a few hours during these marches, but even that could not be … The weary soldier would sink instinctively to the ground, only to get up in a few minutes and do as many more paces. This went on for hours, whole nights indeed, until at last we came within sight of some broken down wagon, which had caused the jam … In our regiment, which has not seen the enemy and had a full complement when it marched across the frontier, the companies are reduced to 26 or 30 men. The grenadier battalion scarcely numbers 300 men, and the other two are even weaker.' The passage is cited in several German studies but the author remains unknown. See Colmar Goltz, *Jena to Eylau. The Disgrace and the Redemption of the Old Prussian Army. A Study in Military History* (New York: E.P. Dutton, 1913), p.236.

16 On 4 February, Wilson wrote, 'At present, I can only mention that I never saw a more martial army. Their discipline is good; their marching is regular; and, considering what they have gone through, their appearance is admirable. The infantry are all equal to what you saw in England. The cavalry are excellent, with truly warlike bearing and even the infantry exult in their courage. The artillery is well appointed, and draws through fosses of snow that astonish me to look at.' *Life of General Sir Robert Wilson*, vol.2, p.407.

17 Wilson: '[Russians] rallied behind barricades, formed with wagons, tumbrels, &c, and disputed the enemy's advance until the order of march [of the main army] was established, when they gradually retired, contesting desperately every inch of ground, in order to protect the army, whose columns moved very slowly.' *Brief Remarks*, p.92.

This general praised highly the conduct of General Prince Scherbatov,[18] commanding a brigade of infantry, and Colonel Prince Iachvill,[19] commanding a company of horse artillery; these two officers distinguished themselves so much during the war that I will have many more occasions to mention them.

General Barclay de Tolly then continued his retreat quietly until the environs of Ankendorf, where he had to pass a second defile and very dense woods. In traversing these woods, I had left behind five infantry battalions and five squadrons from Prince Golitsyn's column. Barclay de Tolly approached this detachment just as the enemy was pressing him strongly. Thanks to this reinforcement, he was able to repel all the enemy attacks and successfully arrived with his rear guard that evening on the left of our position, which he covered that night. The losses of this detachment were, in killed, one lieutenant of the 3rd Jager Regiment and 72 soldiers; in wounded, four officers and 104 soldiers.

Lev Iachvill (Yashvil/Iashvili). (State Hermitage Museum)

General Markov, who had held the distance between the two detachments of Generals Barclay de Tolly and Baggehufvudt, had moved directly on Heiligenthal; Prince Bagration was with this detachment which the enemy observed from afar throughout its march.

Major General Baggehufvudt[20] had received orders from Prince Bagration to move with his detachment, at one o'clock in the morning, to Pupkeim, on the main road from Jonkowo to Wolfsdorf, to await there the passage of the 3rd column and then to form its rear guard. The tail of this column only traversed Pupkeim at nine o'clock in the morning, which obliged General Baggehufvudt to choose a position on the heights behind the village. He was immediately attacked by the enemy with considerable forces, but he managed to stop the French ardour and to gain time for the 3rd column to move down the road and to separate

---

18 Major General Aleksei Scherbatov (1776–1848), the chef of the Kostromskoi Musketeer Regiment and brigade commander.
19 Lev Iachvill/Yashvil (1772–1836), Russian officer of the Georgian origin (Prince Iashvili), in charge of the 4th Artillery Brigade.
20 He commanded Sofiiskii, Belozerskii, Staroskolskii Musketeer Regiments, 4th Jager Regiment, Alexandriiskii Hussar Regiment, Sudakov's Artillery Company, and some Cossacks. In total, approximately 2,000 men.

itself from the rear guard by a few *verstas*; upon which General Baggehufvudt moved out his forces, having suffered inconsiderable losses. In his report on this affair,[21] this general told me that he had been perfectly supported by Major General Sukin II, with his Uglitskii Musketeer Regiment,[22] and by Major General Count Lambert, with his Aleksandriiskii Hussar Regiment.[23]

I had ordered Lieutenant General Golitsyn to reinforce our rear guard that was on the road to Deppen. This general dispatched there 18 infantry battalions and 20 squadrons. General Baggehufvudt, after falling back to this reinforcement, vigorously repulsed every enemy attack. The Aleksandriiskii Hussar Regiment, among others, did marvels that day; on several occasions it charged the enemy cavalry that threatened to outflank our detachment. Lieutenant-Colonel Efimovich, who covered the right flank of our first position behind Pupkeim, distinguished himself during one of the charges, but suffered a bad contusion from a cannonball.

In short, the good dispositions of the generals that commanded these rear guards and the bravery, of which our troops gave repeated proofs that day, greatly honoured the Russian army; they allowed our columns to arrive peacefully at the position of Wolfsdorf and diminished the losses to which we could have been exposed that day. Although the rear guards fought relentlessly from dawn to dusk, and even during the night, our losses were only about 600 killed or wounded. Those of the enemy, judging by the resolve with which he had attacked our rear guards and the resistance that he found everywhere, must have been equally considerable. Among the prisoners taken by the Aleksandriiskii Hussar Regiment on that day was Captain Robert, from Emperor Napoleon's entourage.

Our headquarters was established at Wolfsdorf. That evening General Prince Bagration re-united the detachments of generals Markov and Baggehufvudt at Warlack, the position that I had assigned to him to protect Wolfsdorf.[24] The troops that General Prince Golitsyn had sent to aid the rear guards returned to their divisions. To avoid the heavy artillery delaying the march of the columns and to have it follow a more frequented road, I diverted it, under a good escort during the night, to the main road from Wolfsdorf to Wormditt and Mehlsack, with orders to move as quickly as possible to Preussisch-Eylau, where it indeed arrived at a good hour on 26 January/7 February. I also sent orders to Guttstadt to evacuate from this place everything belonging to the army; but these orders did not arrive there in

---

21 The French first caught up with Bagration, who accompanied Baggehufvudt's detachment, at Waltersmühl, where the terrain was covered with thick forest, which prevented large-scale cavalry action. This helped Bagration to organize a fighting retreat. He moved Alexandriiskii Hussar Regiment to halt the French advance guard and repulse several French cavalry attacks. The French still managed to surround two Russian regiments but the Belozerskii and 4th Jagers kept up effective musket fire, repulsed cavalry charges, and cleared their way. Once the units got to the safety, Bagration deployed his infantry in three lines some 120 paces apart and brought up additional reinforcements, including His Majesty's, Military Order and Malorosiiskii Cuirassier, Pskovskii Dragoons and 7th Jager Regiments.
22 Bennigsen is mistaken – Major General Alexander Sukin II served as the chef of the Yeletskii Musketeer Regiment.
23 Major General Karl de Lambert, served as the chef of the Aleksandriiskii Hussar Regiment in 1800–1814.
24 Late evening on 4 February, Bagration deployed Elisavetgradskii Hussars and two Cossack Regiments (Malakov and Sysoev) with two horse artillery guns in front of the village of Warlack; the 4th Jager Regiment occupied Wolfsdorf, while the main forces were located on the hills behind the village.

time. That is why several regimental transports and a small hospital with sick and wounded fell into the hands of the enemy.

Lieutenant-Colonel Baron Rosen was sent with two squadrons of the Pavlogradskii Hussar Regiment to Heilsberg, with instructions to convey everything that he found belonging to the army from there to Insterburg.

On 24 January/5 February, at the break of dawn, the army set in march in two columns, from Wolfsdorf to a position behind Frauendorf, a distance of three *milles*. Prince Golitsyn, with his *corps*, constituted the advance guard of two columns, the first of which took the route via Lauterwalde, Sommerfeld, Benern and Bürgerswalde, the second via Diettrichsdorf, Arensdorf, Open and Kaschaunen. The march of the rear guard to cover these columns was again left to the discretion of Prince Bagration. General Barclay de Tolly covered, as on the day before, the march of the first column, that is, that of the right. This general made it more than halfway without having been followed by the enemy; small French detachments only observed his march from afar. But, having arrived in the environs of Freymarkt, he encountered a strong enemy column that was arriving from the direction of the village of Launau. According to the testimony of some prisoners, it was the advance guard of Marshal Davout's corps. Toward the evening, a lively musket fire broke out, but we saw from the direction that the enemy column was taking that it intended to turn our rear guard from the left and to occupy the woods behind Freymarkt before our troops could get there. Barclay de Tolly had, therefore, taken the measures to occupy it at once with the 13th and 20th Jager Regiments. At the approach of the enemy, a fierce musket fire erupted; our 10 battalions of jagers stopped the enemy and our entire rear guard then quietly traversed the defile and the woods of Freymarkt. Soon thereafter Barclay de Tolly reached the village of Bogen, where he was assigned to take position and to cover our left wing. The enemy also halted and only a few occasional musket shots were fired at the advance posts that evening.

Lieutenant General Prince Bagration, who was in person with the detachments of generals Markov and Baggehufvudt, covered the march of the second column. At the dawn he took position in front of Wolfsdorf, with the 4th Jager Regiment holding the settlement while the artillery deployed on the heights around it. His light cavalry remained in line that it had occupied during the night on both sides of Warlack. At eight o'clock in the morning the first French cavalry detachments approached Warlack. Major General Yurkovskii, who commanded our cavalry chain, quickly concentrated his men, and charged at the enemy cavalry, forcing it to retreat toward reinforcements that were behind it; the enemy lost a few soldiers in this fighting. Soon thereafter the enemy arrived in force. Receiving General Yurkovskii's report, Prince Bagration moved the entire rear guard through Wolfsdorf and ordered the 4th Jager Regiment to defend this place until our cavalry passed through; the jagers were instructed to then follow in the wake of our cavalry, under the protection of a few batteries placed on the other side of Wolfsdorf and directed by the skillful and brave Colonel Yermolov, of the horse artillery, who had served with the greatest distinction on all occasions of this war and of whom I will speak again often in my account.[25]

---

25 Yermolov: 'At dawn on 24 January [5 February], the enemy attacked us in superior numbers and we could hardly maintain order. At Wolfsdorf, the enemy struck our position and our left flank was only able to hold ground by charging with the bayonet, although that caused some casualties. The 7th Division of Lieutenant-General Dokhturov, whose retreat the rearguard now covered, moved in

Having captured Wolfsdorf, the French employed all of their means to occupy, with a strong infantry column, the woods on the road from Diettrichsdorf; but Colonel Gogel, with the 5th Jagers, and Colonel Vuich, with the 25th Jager Regiment, steadfastly resisted all such attempts. A fierce engagement ensued, and our men had to resort to bayonet charges.[26] At this moment, our artillery proved to be of a great help to us, as was the Aleksandriiskii Hussar Regiment, which distinguished itself by launching a charge against the French infantry and forcing it to retreat with considerable losses in killed, wounded or taken prisoner. Another enemy cavalry column, having turned the village of Wolfsdorf, threatened to turn Prince Bagration's left, but the brave Colonel Prince Michel Dolgorouky, with the Kurlyandskii Dragoon Regiment, attacked this column so well that it was obliged to retire.

Prince Bagration took full advantage of this moment to move the rear guard through the woods. General Markov received orders to cover this march. Part of our cavalry found a way of moving around this forest, which was traversed by a swampy stream with just one bridge across it, which greatly slowed down the passage of our troops.[27] Beyond this defile, the rear guard had to traverse a large plain. Describing events of that day in his report, Prince Bagration wrote that 'it is difficult for me to describe the great services rendered by General Yurkovskii and Colonel Prince Michel Dolgorouky with their cavalry, and by Colonel Ermolov with his horse artillery.' When the rear guard left these woods and arrived

---

complete disorder, its transports blocking the road and causing delay. We fell back slowly, fighting until late into the night. Passing through forests in the dark, we became so confused that the only way to distinguish an enemy from a friend was by shouting. Major-General Count Lambert, hoping to rally our dispersed skirmishers, approached the French lines by mistake and was almost captured. Our artillery was under fire the entire day, and if our hussars had not captured some French horses to replace our killed animals, I would have lost a few guns. I employed my horse artillery company more than others because of its flexibility. We had to use it even in the dark forest where it fired in the direction of enemy shouts or drumbeats.' Yermolov, *The Czar's General*, p.76.

26 Davydov: 'The edge of the woods between Wolfsdorf and Elditen was held by the men of the 5th Jager Regiment. A small cavalry detachment moved swiftly to keep the enemy under observation on our left flank. The French advance guard, preceded by a screen of skirmishers with the whole army behind it, sporadically fired from one or two cannon at our forward line. Masses of enemy troops were moving among the snow covered hills and were streaming downhill towards Wolfsdorf. [Colonel] Yurkovskii, under cover of the Cossacks closest to the enemy, alternately halted and advanced at an angle to the battle line of the reargaurd towards the right flank of the 5th Jager Regiment beyond the edge of the woods… Soon we were in the midst of attacking. The entire line gave a shout and hurled itself at the enemy flanquers. We got mixed up with the enemy. Swords clashed, bullets flew by and the fun began. I remember my sabre biting into live flesh and warm blood streaming from the blade. The fighting did not last very long. The French flanquers were mauled by our men and beat a hasty retreat. But in our eagerness to chase them we soon encountered their reserves that came quickly to their aid. These were dragoons with horsetails streaming from their helmets. They swooped on us hungrily, fresh blows were exchanged and we in turn were beaten back towards the woods…' Mikaberidze, *Russian Eyewitness Accounts of the Campaign of 1807*, p.132.

27 After the initial fight, Bagration remained at Wolfsdorf for another three hours before ordering to retreat in the wake of the main army. He moved his cavalry first because there was only one bridge over a deep ravine separating the Wolfsdorf valley. Yermolov recalled, 'We constantly changed positions and slowly retreated, fighting until late in night.' Bagration's troops suffered considerable losses in these actions, especially from the French artillery fire. Alexander Mikhailovskii-Danilevskii, *Opisanie vtoroi voiny Imperatora Aleksandra s Napoleonom v 1806 i 1807 godakh* (St. Petersburg: Tip. Schtaba Otd. Korpusa Vnut. Strazhi, 1846), pp.175–176; Yermolov, *The Czar's General*, pp.76–77.

at the plains of Diettrichsdorf, the enemy had received reinforcements and Prince Bagration vows that some 30,000 [French] troops followed him until Arensdorf and further still, to the village of Open.[28] At long last, the rear guard reached the great forest behind Open. Prince Bagration first ordered the artillery and cavalry to enter the woods while three jager regiments scattered as skirmishers. Yet they could not contain the advance of the enemy which kept following us closely and managed to enter the woods with such considerable forces that Prince Bagration was forced to reinforce the jagers with the Pskovskii Musketeer Regiment. It was only then that the enemy's steadfast advance was contained and, after the sunset, our rear guard arrived at Kaschaunen and Bürgerswalde. These two positions were assigned to Prince Bagration to cover the right and centre of our position at Frauendorf. Although the great forest remained occupied by both our and enemy parties, the night passed very peacefully. The day only cost our army 200 men killed and wounded.

The same day I sent Major General Warneck with two infantry regiments and five squadrons to Heilsberg to cover the right of our march the following day; I also instructed him to rejoin the army the next day by taking the main road via Neuendorf and Grünwalde.

Lieutenant General L'Estocq had meanwhile directed his march on Mohrungen where he arrived with his *corps* on 23 January/4 February. Marshal Ney, who had been detached from the French army with his corps to prevent the union of the Prussian *corps* with the Russian army, arrived, on 23 January/4 February, at Deppen, where he crossed the Passarge on 24 January/5 February and sent a cavalry detachment to Liebstadt. The majority of his corps found itself that day at Alt-Reichau and Horn, on the road to Mohrungen.

On 25 January/6 February, the Russian army, beginning with the left wing, marched from Frauendorf to Landsberg, a distance of two *milles*. The first column under the orders of Lieutenant General Sacken, composed of the 2nd, 3rd, and 14th Divisions, with the cavalry from the left wing, took the road from Sperwarten and Petershagen. The second column, under the orders of Lieutenant General Tuchkov, composed of the 5th, 7th, and 8th Divisions, and the cavalry of the right wing, marched via Stabunken and [Gross-]Glandau. The rear guard under the orders of Lieutenant General Prince Bagration covered this march in the same order as in the preceding days.

The position that I had the army take was in front of Landsberg, where I established my headquarters.[29]

---

28 Marshal Joachim Murat made another series of attacks on the Russian rearguard at Arensdorf and Open. Bagration again put up a resolute fight. At Arensdorf, he counterattacked with the Elisavetgradskii Hussars and Kurlandskii Dragoons supported by Yermolov's horse artillery company. As he retreated to Open, Bagration took advantage of the thick forest to spread his 4th, 5th and 25th Jager Regiments as skirmishers to harass the advancing French forces. Murat did not attack for the rest of the day, but sporadic fighting continued until late into the night, when Bagration reached Kaschaunen. That day, his troops covered 18 miles fighting the French.

29 Yermolov: 'The commander-in-chief thought it prudent to abandon this position as it was not broad enough to allow the troops to deploy. The second line was separated from the first by a stream with steep banks, which, despite the frost, had not frozen and complicated communications. The right flank was adjacent to a forest which covered part of the front, and this would have placed our skirmishers, whom the French surpass in skill, at a disadvantage. The proximity of woods also hampered the effective use of artillery and masked enemy movements. There were two roads for retreat and both were on the extreme left flank: one of them passed over a hill, which was very difficult to ascend because its steep elevation was frozen; the second road led through narrow gates

Prince Bagration, being with the detachments of generals Markov and Baggehufvudt behind the second column to cover the movement, was followed weakly by some light enemy troops and suffered few casualties. He arrived at five o'clock in the afternoon in front of the right wing of our position.[30] The enemy directed his principal forces down the road that our first column was marching on. I had ordered General Barclay de Tolly to take up positions with his detachment at the village of Hof and to stop the enemy there so as to gain the necessary time for our troops to deploy in a battle formation. Since the distance was rather short, the enemy would have been able to arrive at Landsberg in the afternoon to engage there in a general battle, which I wanted to avoid since our heavy artillery was sent by a different road to Preussisch-Eylau.

General Barclay de Tolly arrived at Hof, not having been followed closely by the enemy. But just an hour after he took up the position there, several large columns of French infantry and cavalry arrived to attack him. General Barclay de Tolly, having taken position in front of the village of Hof, moved the 1st Jager Regiment to his right to occupy a height covered in shrubs. Barely had it arrived there when a strong column of [French] infantry approached the height. Barclay de Tolly moved to his left flank the 5th Jagers, which encountered enemy battalions but forced them to retire. Yet, as the enemy received reinforcements, Barclay de Tolly found it necessary to also send there the 20th Jager Regiment and the Kostromskoi Musketeer Regiment, with a battery of horse artillery, while the Iliviopolskii Hussar Regiment was placed in reserve next to the village. Taking the Izumskii Hussar Regiment and a few cannon from the horse artillery, General Barclay de Tolly advanced closer to a bridge to defend the passage, which the enemy tried multiple times to force;[31] but the good direction of the fire of our horse artillery rendered these efforts fruitless until the French were able to bring into action a large battery of heavy calibre guns which forced our small battery to yield and retreat. The enemy exploited this opportune moment and sent his cavalry across the bridge, still under the protection of his batteries. Moments later, Colonel Prince Iashvil halted and deployed his artillery again, directing his fire so well against the enemy cavalry that it was forced to halt.

Just then General Dorokhov, who excelled at taking advantage of such opportune moments, rushed forward at the helm of his Izumskii Hussar Regiment and a regiment of Cossacks, attacked the enemy cavalry and forced it to re-cross the bridge. Dorokhov then crossed the bridge with his cavalry and took several prisoners. Despite the orders given, the Oliviopolskii regiment, which was in reserve, followed the Izumskii regiment into the defile, which was located after the bridge, and consequently prevented the Izumskii regiment from re-crossing the defile and the bridge fast enough. This unfortunate accident momentarily

---

into the twisting and constricted streets of Landsberg which would cause chaos and large casualties in our troops.' Yermolov, *The Czar's General*, p.78.

30 On 6 February, while on his march to Frauendorf, Bagration repulsed several minor French attacks before joining Barclay de Tolly, who, in previous two days, marched along a different road from Allenstein; he lost some 500 men in these actions but brought his detachment safely to Frauendorf.

31 Barclay de Tolly later reported, 'I would have withdrawn in time so as not to have my entire detachment annihilated for no purpose by a much superior enemy force. But some of my officers informed me that our army was still on the march and had not taken up final positions. Therefore I considered it my duty to sacrifice myself with my entire detachment to [halt] the enemy.' Cited in Mikhailovskii-Danilevskii, *Opisanie vtoroi voiny Imperatora Aleksandra s Napoleonom*, pp.178–179.

caused disorder and, to make matters worse, the worthy General Dorokhov received a contusion from a cannonball, which obliged him to leave the battlefield. General Barclay de Tolly personally intervened to address this critical situation. He ordered the Oliviopolskii regiment to return to its position immediately and placed Prince Iashvil's artillery so that it could cover the retreat of the Izumskii regiment, which, however, would have been impossible to carry out without losses if Major General Prince Scherbatov, had not advanced with two battalions from his Kostromskoi Musketeer Regiment to confront the enemy cavalry. The French tried three times to smash these two battalions but each time they were forced to yield with considerable losses due to our strong fire which was directed with notable *sang-froid*.[32] Each time the enemy was forced to retreat, Prince Scherbatov exploited the opportunity to move his men back for a certain distance. Just as the prince repulsed the enemy for the third time, our cavalry rushed forward at the adversary but, encountering several lines of cavalry ready to receive them, our cavalrymen wheeled about and beat a hasty retreat, during which they disordered two battalions of our infantry.

The enemy exploited this to assault one of these two battalions. This brave regiment, which covered itself in glory that day, had the misfortune to lose on this occasion a flag and four cannons, for which one cannot blame them in the least. General Barclay de Tolly, realizing then the impossibility of staying any longer on the other side of Hof, given the superior enemy forces, decided to pass through the village, all the more so as the 1st Jager Regiment, which was covering the right of his position, was already engaged by a strong enemy column and was able to re-join his detachment only after a great deal of trouble, having lost its commander, Colonel Arseniev of the Imperial Guard, and a few soldiers who were taken by the enemy cavalry during the retreat. The 3rd and 20th Jagers, who were covering the left wing of the detachment, were also attacked by considerable enemy forces but managed to execute an orderly withdrawal.

When General Barclay de Tolly informed me of the critical state in which he had found himself and that a part of the entire French army stood in front of him, I sent to him Prince Dolgorouky V, the commander of the Chernigovskii Musketeer Regiment,[33] with five infantry battalions. General Barclay de Tolly, having passed through the village of Hof, found these troops deployed in a plain. He placed his cavalry to the left of these five battalions and occupied with all of his jagers the brushwood that was also on its left; to observe

---

32   Yermolov offers a more realistic assessment: 'Hoff is in a valley surrounded by steep hills. As superior enemy cavalry engaged Barclay's exhausted cavalrymen, they would be forced to retreat through its narrow streets. His infantry, which should have occupied the town and enclosed gardens, was placed before the town and, because of the deep snow on the plain, would also have to fall back through the town. So it was – the French routed our cavalry and drove it onto our infantry and batteries. One of the batteries was captured and the commander of the second, Lieutenant Markov, fired canister against our own Olioviopolskii Hussars, although he also halted the enemy attack and forced it back with loss. The Russian infantry repulsed a charge, although the enemy cavalry reached its lines. The enemy made another attempt, and this time was more successful. The Dneprovskii and Kostromskoi Musketeer Regiments withstood the charge, but they were exhausted and did not retain formation for long. They were soon routed and at least half of them were cut down. The flags and the regimental guns were captured. Those who escaped sought the safety of the gardens to join the jager regiments already there. This action demonstrates how disastrous the deployment of infantry in the open can be.' Yermolov, *The Czar's General*, pp.77–78.
33   Vasilii Dolgorouky V served as the chef of the Chernigovskii Musketeer Regiment in 1802–1809.

the enemy's movements, he posted his Cossacks.[34] As Barclay de Tolly's second position was in view of the position occupied by our army, I sent to his aid part of our cavalry from the left wing. But before it arrived, the enemy strongly attacked Prince Dolgorouky V and forced him, despite his magnificent resistance, to fall back for some distance. Upon the arrival of our cavalry, it was the enemy's turn to retreat. The approaching darkness put an end to these persistent fights which had cost us 2,500 killed and wounded, as well as a few prisoners, among which were several brave officers, including Colonel Arseniev, as noted, and the Emperor's *aide de camp*, Kozhin; Prince Golitsyn, an officer of the Imperial Guard and a young man of great merit, was killed – he had only arrived at the army the day before. We also lost five cannons and two flags, the only ones that the Russian army lost during this war.[35]

The enemy losses must have been considerable. A few officers and 97 soldiers fell as prisoners into our hands, the majority of them the enemy cavalrymen captured by our Izumskii Hussar Regiment.

The chain of advance posts was placed, with the necessary support, along the length of our position; save for a few musket shots fired by skirmishers, the night passed peacefully.

General L'Estocq's march was at the same time becoming increasingly difficult. His rear guard was always closely pressed by Marshal Ney's corps. Upon leaving, on 24 January/5 February, Mohrungen for Pfarrersfeldchen, this general received the report that the enemy had strongly occupied the bridge at Kalckstein on the Passarge River. He therefore decided to direct his march to Spanden, where he crossed the river and went that same day still to Wuhsen. General Plötz's detachment dislodged the enemy from Liebstadt, which gave it an advantage over the direction taken by General L'Estocq. But as his rear guard was cut off from the route that L'Estocq's *corps* had taken on Wuhsen, he was obliged to move further to the left and reach Braunsberg, which he accomplished but with considerable losses.

The skill with which General L'Estocq removed himself from the critical situation in which he found himself with his *corps* during this march, testified to the wisdom and prudence of this general even in the most challenging moments of the war. Having received the invitation to go to Preussisch-Eylau to join the Russian army for the impending battle, General L'Estocq directed his march on that point.

The bloody events of 26-27 January/7-8 February, which will forever remain memorable in the annals of history, require particular explanations and I leave to the reader the care of judging the degree of importance that one can give to the consequences of those two days.

---

34 Yermolov: 'Barclay de Tolly had been reinforced by five battalions under Major-General Prince Dolgorukov, but this force was insufficient and the new battalions were routed as well, losing many men. Our troops, retreating through Hoff, suffered from terrible enemy artillery fire. Fearless Barclay de Tolly paid no heed to danger and appeared everywhere. However, this battle did not flatter his skill as a commander: it would not have been difficult to find a better way!' Yermolov, *The Czar's General*, p.78.

35 There are no official reports on the Russian losses because Barclay de Tolly and many of his officers were wounded or killed in the subsequent battle of Eylau. Estimates vary between 1,800–2,000 killed and wounded; the Kostromskoi Musketeer Regiment was virtually annihilated, losing two thirds of its strength and all its flags except one.

12

Eylau

On 26 January/7 February, at night, the army marched in two columns, in the same order as the day before, from Landsberg to Preussisch-Eylau (a distance of two *milles*). The 1st column moved via Woymanns, Zipperken, Gallehnen and Grünhöfchen while the 2nd column – via Kumkeim, Dultzen, Körnen and Storchnest.[1] Upon my arrival at Preussisch-Eylau, I ordered the army to take a position on the other side of the town, for two reasons: the first was to assure myself more perfectly, in any situation, of my march on the Pregel and on Königsberg, which held, as I have already said, a great many articles necessary for the army; and the second reason being because the terrain was more open there; no heights dominated it in either direction and the area was fairly suitable to cavalry action; still, the position offered few particular advantages in terrain and the wings were without assured support. Only the centre, commanded by Lieutenant General Dokhturov, was advantageously placed, holding the hills where batteries could be established directed opposite the town.[2]

---

1 Yermolov: 'On the night of 26 January [7 February], General Tuchkov (I)'s division began withdrawing over the hill in some disorder, thus delaying everyone else. The columns moving through Landsberg did not bother to maintain order and became confused in the narrow streets so, despite the long winter night, some forces remained in position because the units ahead of them had not moved. It is easy to imagine the position our rearguard was in: it faced the French but could only retreat a step at a time so that the main army could withdraw to a safe distance.' Yermolov, *The Czar's General*, p.78.

2 One of the participants left a vivid description of dreadful conditions in the Russian army. 'No army could suffer more than ours has done in these days. It is no exaggeration to say that for every mile between Jonkerndorf (Jankovo) and [Eylau], the army has lost 1,000 men, who had not come within sight of the enemy. And [Bagration's] rearguard! What terrible losses it has suffered in those perpetual fights!' The author criticized the poor organization of the march since 'the last divisions [had] to stand half a day or night with empty stomachs and wet feet. We left many dead and many sick men behind us on the road in this way. It takes a patient, healthy Russian to stand all this.' However, the troops suffered even more on the move in the cold weather: 'Often during a night march through a wood or a defile, the troops would be obliged to single file past some trifling object, which blocked the way, because no one gave the order to remove the obstacle. What would I not have given to sleep on the snow for a few hours during these marches, but even that could not be. We would hardly take 20 to 30 paces before the order to halt. Then the weary soldier would sink instinctively to the ground, only to get up in a few minutes and do as many more paces. This went on for hours, whole nights indeed, until at last we came within sight of some broken down powder wagon, which had caused the block. Mounted, dismounted, we tried each way in turn; but it was too cold for the one, and we had no strength left for the other. The poor soldiers glide about like ghosts. You see them asleep on the march

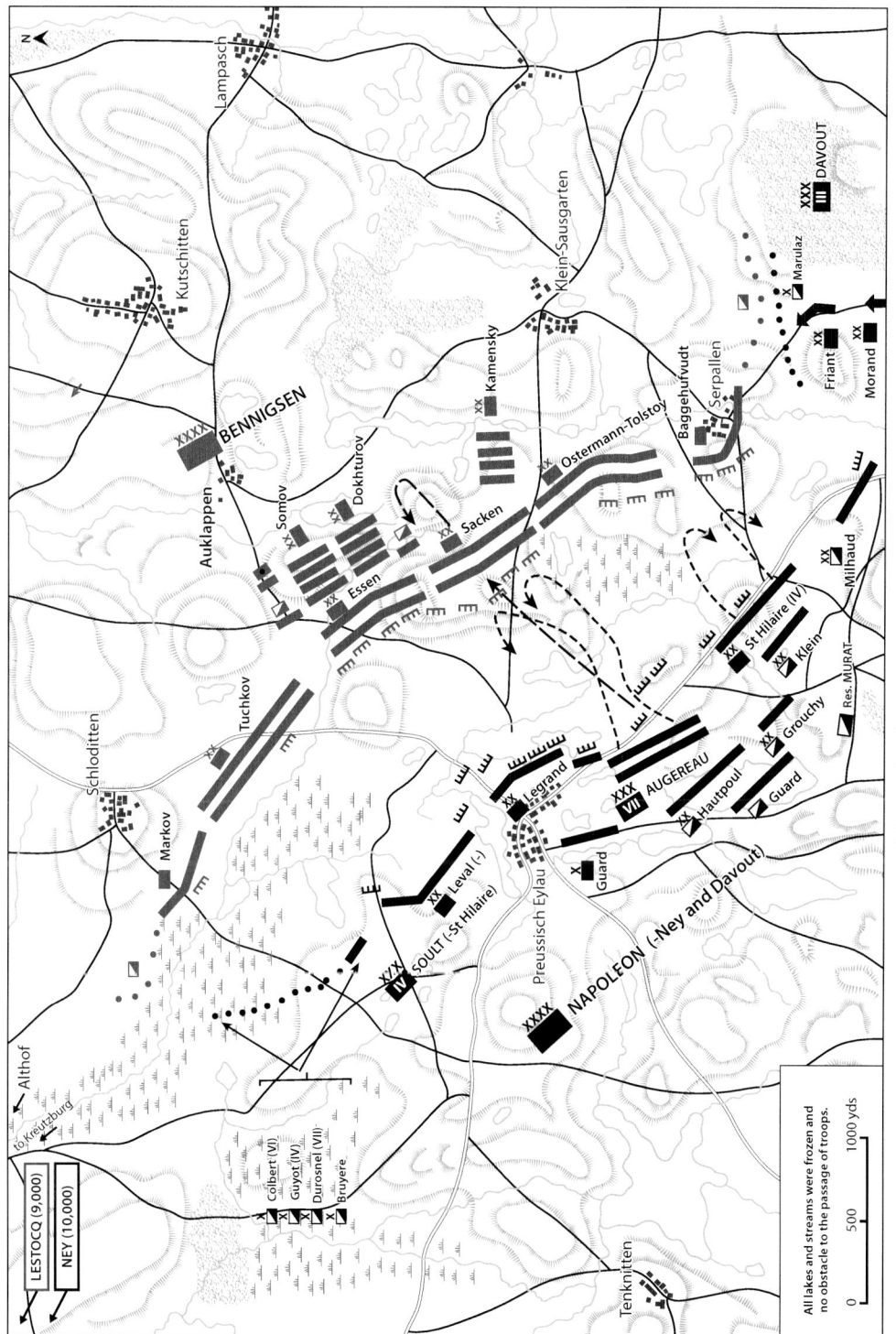

The Battle of Eylau: Starting Positions.

The right wing, commanded by Lieutenant General Tuchkov, forming an angle, supported itself on the village of Schloditten and was covered for a certain distance by a swampy stream, which, although frozen, posed nonetheless a serious obstacle to moving artillery across or utilizing cavalry in large numbers. The left wing, commanded by Lieutenant General Count Ostermann, extended to the village of Serpallen, upon which it rested. Major General Count Kamensky, with the 14th Division, made up the reserve of the left wing; Major General Somov, with twelve battalions from the 11th Division, formed the reserve for the centre, while Major General Markov, with his detachment, which was in the rear guard, was destined to be the reserve of the right wing.

My order of battle was as follows: in the 1st line, each regiment placed its 3rd battalion in reserve 100 steps behind the first two battalions; in the 2nd line, each regiment deployed in battalion columns [*bataillons déployés*]. In this way, the 3rd battalions of the 1st line, which stood in reserve, could quickly come to support the second line wherever the need arose, without breaking the line. Two or three regiments of the second line could very easily, and in little time, form itself into a strong column, and move where need be. In every battle I found the advantage of this order of battle against the system of these dense columns [*grandes colonnes*], which the French army employed in its attacks and against which one can only resist by maintaining a deep order in defensive positions. Because how can a simple line, which is only three ranks deep, resist and not be broken by columns in which, as I often have seen, the French involved 10,000 men and still more? Emperor Napoleon, this great captain, had so well calculated the advantage of strong columns against the system of thin three ranks deep lines that so many refused to give up on, that he had, with ease, crushed, overrun, and completely beaten every army which he had fought until this point. At the initial contact, these great dense columns must certainly lose men from enemy artillery fire but, as soon as a line is broken by these great masses, there is no longer a remedy; the columns move forward without giving time to the broken and dispersed lines to rally and reform; nothing can stop them and an army, once broken in this way and having no masses ready to contain these strong columns, will always be decisively beaten. It is also by this tactical system that Napoleon, in all the preceding wars, was able to beat the armies of his adversaries so completely upon the first encounter that a single battle sufficed for him to reduce them to imploring him for peace with enormous sacrifices, of which one can cite numerous examples. I therefore concluded that there is no other principle to adopt against the attacks of these great columns than to act in mass like the French did and to always have strong reserves at hand. At Preussisch-Eylau, the two armies met and gave battle on nearly the same principles. The Russian army was not broken at any point, despite the [French] great columns that relentlessly attacked it that day; instead, it [successfully] resisted the superior enemy forces, as you will see, General, by the account of that day.

---

with their heads resting on their neighbours… and the whole retreat seems more a dream than reality.' Oscar von Lettow-Vorbeck, *Der krieg von 1806 und 1807* (Berlin: Rittler, 1896), vol. 4, pp.88–90; Julius Hildebrand, *Die Schlact bei Preussisch-Eylau am 7 und 8 februar 1807* (Quedlinburg: Huch 1907), pp.5–6. The author of this passage remains unknown. According to Colmar, Lettow Vorbeck 'was not allowed to name the author, and, after his death, all efforts to trace the writer… remained unsuccessful.' Goltz, *From Jena to Eylau*, pp.234–238.

Our rear guard was barely challenged in this march by the enemy.[3] When it was three-quarters of a *mille* from Preussisch-Eylau, I sent word to Prince Bagration that it was necessary to halt the enemy as much as possible, given that the head of our heavy artillery only then reached the town of Preussisch-Eylau. At the same time I sent him reinforcements, composed of the Moskovskii Grenadier Regiment, Sofiiskii Musketeer Regiment from the 8th Division, and the St Petersburgskii and Ingermanlandskii Dragoon Regiments.

General, look at the map of this battle. I must point out that all the lakes that you see on the map were so frozen in that time of the year that they were no obstacle to manoeuvres and that there were even cavalry charges carried out on some of them. In consequence of the above-mentioned order, Prince Bagration ordered General Markov to take up with his detachment the position between the lakes of Tenknitten and Warschkeiten; the reinforcements that arrived at this time from the 8th Division were placed in the same area, a little to the rear. Just as we had taken this position, strong enemy infantry columns, preceded by *chasseurs à cheval* who were deployed as flankers,[4] advanced against us but were greeted by the fire of our skirmishers and artillery batteries. Yet, we were unable to stop their march.[5] General Markov then led the bayonet charge of the Pskovskii and Sofiiskii regiments and forced one enemy column to turn back. Meanwhile, the other column was attacked and overrun by the St Petersburgskii Dragoon Regiment,

---

[3] Yermolov disagrees: 'Bagration's rearguard was left at Landsberg. An hour after dawn, the rearguard marched through Landsberg and took up positions near the town, having left a strong infantry detachment and several guns at the gates. Some time later, a large body of French troops approached and, diverting our attention by its artillery fire, moved against our right flank. Taking advantage of the terrain, we fought back resolutely for a considerable time before quickly traversing a field that separated us from the forest. The enemy, following us, entered Landsberg and began deploying their forces on our former positions. It was obvious that we would have to engage not only the enemy vanguard but his main body as well; fortunately for us, the region between Landsberg and Preussisch-Eylau is mostly covered by dense forest. Prince Bagration dispatched his cavalry and part of his artillery for greater freedom of movement. All the jager units were combined and the line infantry was left in reserve. We effectively contained the French with light losses until 11:00 a.m.; however, numerous barrels of wine, abandoned by other troops in order to lighten the transports and save more valuable goods, were soon found along the road and it was impossible to restrain the troops, who were cold and hungry, from consuming alcohol. Before long, four jager regiments were so drunk it was impossible to rally them. The French noticed this confusion and made vigorous attacks, trying to cut our troops off they came from all directions. Artillery had to be committed to defend the drunkards and we were slowed down considerably. Generals Pahlen and Lambert used cavalry to protect these troops; but it was impossible to rally and withdraw these drunken soldiers and we lost plenty of them killed or captured.' Yermolov, *The Czar's General*, p.78.

[4] Around 2:00 p.m. Murat's cavalry, followed by Soult's corps, appeared at the edge of the woods around Grunhofchen. The French advanced in three main columns with the light cavalry in front. The central column was comprised of the 46th Line under Colonel Joseph-Pierre Richard. Second French column of the 18th Line under Colonel Jean-Baptiste-Ambroise Ravier was marching along the Landsberg road against Bagration's right flank. Finally, the third French column of the 24th Line under Colonel Jean-Baptiste-Pierre Semelle proceeded against the Russian left flank.

[5] Davydov: 'The artillery fired canister at the masses of the attacking [French] columns; their front ranks were mowed down in lines, but those following stepped over the corpses of their comrades and advanced forward, with remarkable heroism and impudence.' Denis Davydov, *Voennye zapiski* (Moscow: Gos. izd. khud. lit., 1982), p.211

commanded by its brave Colonel Balk.⁶ This column was routed and lost a flag. A third column, that was moving to help the first two, was also stopped by Colonel Yermolov's batteries. But these columns did not retreat far; they were soon joined by reinforcements from their army that was rapidly approaching the battlefield.⁷

The enemy brought to bear large batteries⁸ and renewed the attack with four columns. The Moskovskii

Mikhail Balk. (State Hermitage Museum)

---

6   Mikhail Balk (1764–1818) joined the St. Peterburgskii Dragoon Regiment in 1802 and was promoted to a colonel in May 1805. He served as a commanding officer of the regiment in 1806–1807.
7   Yermolov: 'Approaching Preussisch-Eylau, the rearguard came onto an open plain and was assigned positions covering the town behind which our army began deploying for battle. The rearguard was reinforced by several regiments from the 8th Division and cavalry units. We deployed on both sides of the road that ran through woods. I placed 24 guns on a steep plateau on the left flank. A small plain lay before this hill and the enemy would have to cross it to advance; our skirmishers were spread out there, concealed by the broken terrain. Part of the cavalry was on the right flank and the rest was moved behind our positions. The enemy soon deployed batteries on the opposite heights and subjected us to an intense bombardment; we rarely returned fire because I did not have a single heavy artillery piece. The French columns then came down at various points but were halted by the fire of 40 of our guns. Our canister fire routed some of them, inflicting considerable casualties. We maintained our position for almost two hours, but then the enemy advanced in superior numbers. Of their three columns, one marched on the main road, where we had fewer infantry, another moved against the Pskov and Sofia musketeer regiments and a third advanced against my 24-gun battery. The first column moved easily and threatened to outflank our strongest point, while the other columns advanced slowly because of the deep snow and they had to endure our canister fire for a prolonged time. Although disordered, one of them still managed to reach our position, where it was destroyed on the bayonets of the Pskov and Sofia regiments. Simultaneously, another column scattered its corpses before my battery. Meanwhile, Colonel Degtyarev led the St Petersburg Dragoons against the column on the main road; to evade our cavalry, the French veered away and moved into deep snow. The haste of their action led to confusion and our cavalry regiment took full advantage, capturing one eagle and 500 men after enduring light enemy musket fire. At least another 500 were killed, including the general who commanded this column. I have never witnessed a more decisive cavalry attack; I was equally surprised by how the St Petersburg Regiment came down a snow-covered slope without disorder. However, our success was short-lived, as the enemy brought up more troops; the French increased their batteries that now covered their columns and, being unable to contain them, we were ordered to pull back. The enemy immediately occupied our positions and followed us closely.' Yermolov, *The Czar's General*, p.79.
8   Yermolov, who commanded a 24-gun battery, lamented that he could not return fire because he had only light calibre cannon available.

Grenadiers, commanded by their chef, Prince Karl von Mecklenburg, and the skirmishers of the 24th Jager Regiment then entered the fray. Three of these enemy columns directed their march directly against Prince Bagration's position while the fourth one threatened to turn his right wing. General Bagration, noticing that General Markov's detachment was beginning to suffer as a result of the enemy's superiority in forces, ordered it to fall back.

By then my army was already deployed and ready to meet the enemy. Fearing that our rear guard might suffer considerable losses, I informed Prince Bagration that he needed to retire on Preussisch-Eylau and bring his troops into the position of our army, which he executed with the greatest order. Several regiments of French cavalry, wishing to profit from this retreat, charged but were once again repulsed with losses by His Majesty's Cuirassier Regiment, the Elisavetgradskii Hussar Regiment, and the Ingermanlandskii Dragoon Regiment. Colonel Yermolov once again distinguished himself a great deal on this occasion: he took full advantage of the terrain to skiluflly deploy his horse artillery and always brought it to bear so well that the enemy only followed our rear guard with great circumspection. Upon the arrival of Prince Bagration with the rear guard, General Barclay de Tolly was designated to occupy and defend the town of Preussisch-Eylau with the regiments of jagers from his detachment. The troops of our army were arranged for battle in the following order: the 5th, 8th, 7th, 3rd, 2nd, 4th, and 14th Divisions; General Baggehufvudt with his detachment; the cavalry on the two wings.

After four hours, the French army appeared in front of our position on the opposite side of the town and began to deploy into battle formation but still outside our artillery range. Nevertheless, one French corps soon approached and attacked the town so vigorously that General Barclay de Tolly, seeing himself pressed in on all sides, was obliged to yield and limited himself to taking positions in the gardens that abutted the town on the side of our position. But as I did not wish for the enemy to secure the area between the town and our position, which could have needlessly fatigued our troops from the continuous alarms during the night, I sent General Somov with nine battalions, from the reserve,[9] with orders to retake the town; the same order was also given to General Barclay de Tolly.

Major General Somov attacked the town near the cemetery leading his men in three columns: the left column was momentarily halted by the enemy but the two other columns broke into the town, fought their way with bayonets, and General Somov, with his nine battalions, succeeded in joining General Barclay de Tolly's detachment which had attacked from a different direction and penetrated up to the town's main square.[10] These two generals

---

9 Somov led the 4th Division.
10 Davydov, who witnessed the fighting, described soldiers following Bagration 'quietly, without any noise, but, when they entered the streets, everybody howled "Hurrah," charged with bayonets – and we captured Eylau again.' Davydov, *Voennye zapiski,* pp.211–212. The actual fighting lasted almost an hour and Yermolov offers more details on this affair: 'As soon as I passed through the city gates, the enemy launched assaults on the town. Its defence was entrusted to Barclay de Tolly, his detachment having been reinforced by fresh troops. The unequal ratio of forces did not allow us to take full advantage of the walls and fences that ringed the town; enemy skirmishers appeared, fired in the streets, and entered the nearest houses. Our infantry drove them out with bayonets on several occasions and the town was in our hands until Barclay de Tolly suffered a serious wound. Discouraged by this loss, his detachment abandoned the town to the enemy holding on to part of it. Major-General

had completely driven the enemy out the town and made him lose considerable number of killed, wounded, and prisoners. Unfortunately, General Barclay de Tolly was gravely wounded in the arm by a musket ball that shattered his bone. To the great regret of the entire army, this good and brave general was obliged to leave the battlefield and seek treatment in Königsberg. I informed General Somov, who had taken command of all of the troops in Preussisch-Eylau, about General Barclay de Tolly's departure and ordered him to hold the town until further orders. A very dark night, which descended upon us, ended the fighting of that day, which had already cost the enemy a considerable number of men, including more than 500 prisoners that fell into our hands.

After 10 o'clock in the evening, I sent an officer to General Somov with orders to evacuate the town as peacefully as possible, so as not to tip off the French army, and to deploy his 12 battalions, along with the Arkhangelogordskii regiment, between the town and our first line, and to stay there for the rest of the night. He executed this order perfectly after 11 o'clock in the evening.[11] Two battalions of the Moskovskii Grenadiers were placed with the same intention at Serpallen.

I must explain to you, General, what my intentions were in evacuating the town of Preussisch-Eylau, which was so close to our front and whose possession would have

---

Somov, who commanded a brigade of the 4th Division, arrived with reinforcements, stormed the houses, smashed the enemy, and recaptured the town.' Yermolov, *The Czar's General*, p.80.

11 In his journal, Osten-Sacken offers a different take: '26th [January, 7 February 1807]. We again marched at night and, by the morning, the army reached Preussisch-Eylau. The enemy was at our heels. Bennigsen made a mistake of not occupying the town with sufficient forces. The enemy immediately rushed into the town but was later driven out. Yet, Somov soon got scared, retreated and the enemy recaptured the town.' Osten-Sacken, *Diary*, p.172. But other participants point to a crucial mistake that Somov had made. Davydov recalled how 'the fires soon blazed in both army camps and it seemed that the fighting had ended until the next morning.' The soldiers of the 4th Division scattered in Preussisch-Eylau looking for some food and shelter. Somov was concerned not to lose control over his soldiers, so he decided to rally them. However, he had not specified the exact rallying spot, and ordered the drums to beat, sometime around 9:30 p.m., in the northeast part of the town, closer to the main Russian positions. It proved to be a huge mistake. Davydov recalled that 'it is difficult to fully convey confusion resulting from this misguided decision. As the drums sounded the signal, everyone rushed in disorder, leaving the main [city] gates, squares, and streets undefended.' The French then entered the town. Davydov, *Voennye zapiski*, pp.212–213. Yermolov agrees: '[Somov] tried to rally his troops in a remote part of town and when the drums beat the alarm the troops retired and did not have time to organize. The appearance of the enemy spread confusion, which was amplified by the darkness and French canister rounds. We had to abandon the town and, in addition to considerable casualties, we also lost a few artillery pieces. This incident forced the commander-in-chief to change the deployment of our army; during the night, our troops shifted to different positions. Bennigsen thought this necessary because the enemy, after it captured the heights defended by our rearguard, had made a reconnaissance of our positions.' Yermolov, *The Czar's General*, pp.79–80. Wilson briefly notes that Beningsen intended to deploy a division 'in the town to maintain it to the last extremity' but 'by a misconception of orders the troops destined for that service were withdrawn into the general alignment: when two French battalions instantly entered and posted themselves. General Beningsen being aware that his line might be considerably annoyed during the night from the houses, ordered two battalions to retake the town; and the troops so ordered instantly rushed with the bayonet through the streets putting to death many of the enemy. But as the suburbs were too extensive, the French still maintained a lodgment in two corners: their tirailleurs after dusk occasionally fired.' Wilson to Lord Hutchinson, 9 February 1807, *Life of General Sir Robert Wilson*, vol.2, p.408–409.

safeguarded our centre from any attack. But recall that I already said, at the beginning of this letter, that in our position only the centre was advantageously placed. Was I not supposed therefore to try to draw in the enemy there, still having ample time to prepare myself, and to profit from the advantage offered by the terrain to receive him there? You will judge, according to the relation of this battle, what would have happened to us if the enemy, instead of persisting in his attempts to break our centre, had contented himself with demonstrations there and employed on our left wing all of the forces that he had fruitlessly lost in the centre.

My headquarters was established that day at Auklappen. When I received the report that General Somov had evacuated the town, I sent the following order to the division commanders:

> General Dokhturov will immediately leave the centre with the 7th Division, which is 14 battalions strong, and this division, along with the 12 battalions under the orders of General Somov, will form the reserve of our centre, deployed directly across from the town. General Dokhturov, commanding all this reserve, will form it into two columns of deployed battalions. Lieutenant General Tuchkov commanding the right wing will shift to the left to fill, with his troops and General Markov's reserve, the distance that the 7th Division held in the first line; he will leave a strong detachment in the village of Schloditten; Cossacks and some cavalry from the right wing will take up positions in the plain before this village. This change in our position must be carried out without delay and as soon as the generals have received this order.'

The 14th Division, under the orders of Major General Count Kamensky, remained in reserve on the left wing. Two jager regiments from General Barclay de Tolly's detachment deployed as skirmishers in front of the centre of our position; the remainder of the troops from that detachment joined General Baggehufvudt on the left wing.

The French army remained during the night in the position that it had occupied at the end of the day.

On 27 January/8 February, between four and five o'clock in the morning, I went to the front of our position, directly across from the town, which due to the change that I had made in our deployment was then closer to our right wing. The fires lit by the enemy soon told me that a fairly considerable French *corps* had already passed through the town of Preussisch-Eylau. I therefore returned General Somov's reserve and the two battalions of the Moskovskii Grenadiers to their [original] places and, before daybreak, I moved forward our heavy artillery batteries to the heights I had chosen across from the town the day before.

At the break of day, some enemy *tirailleurs* and *chasseurs à cheval* advanced; a very lively fire soon ensued between them and our two regiments of jagers that had been dispersed as skirmishers.[12] As soon as it was light enough to be able to make out the enemy

---

12   Staff Captain Otroshenko commanded a company in the 7th Jager Regiment: 'On 27 January [8 February], the 7th Jager Regiment took up position on the right wing of our battle line at Preussisch-Eylau. We spread skirmishers in front of our line and immediately entered the fighting; we advanced towards the town but the French drove us back. We then received reinforcements and pushed the

French cavalry charge about to pierce the first line of the Russian infantry at Eylau. Copper engraving by Pierre Adrien Le Beau after Thomas Charles Naudet, published in Paris in late 1807. (Courtesy of Anne S.K. Brown Military Collection)

columns, which set in movement between our position and the town, and those that were debouching from it, I ordered the heavy artillery deployed in the battery across from the town to commence fire in order to prevent the enemy from reconnoitring my position and observing the changes I had made during the night. At first, the battery of Colonel Count Sievers fired with the greatest success.[13] We then discerned dense formations of enemy

---

    enemy back to the town, but were forced to retreat once more, the fighting continuing in this fashion until 10 o'clock in the morning. At that time a heavy snowfall commenced. Suddenly I heard shouts to the left of me – the French columns, under cover of the falling snow, attempted to strike our right wing. But our regiments held the line and charged at these columns with the bayonet, annihilating them. I was later told that at this time the enemy cuirassiers had penetrated our lines but the survivors barely managed to return. we have lost many men, even though there were over 400 men present in the morning. Now I had just two soldiers with me and one of them was already wounded. I could see no officers or non-commissioned officers around me and decided to retreat with these two jagers. Behind us we found a jager regiment which I warned that there were no longer any troops from my regiment in front of it. Just then a bullet wounded my last remaining healthy jager.' '*Zapiski generala Otroshenko*', in *Russkii vestnik* 9 (1877): pp.166–167

13 Count Jacob (Yakov) von Sievers (1773–1810). After the battle, Sievers received the Order of St George (4th Class) 'as a reward for the excellent gallantry and courage shown during the battle against the French troops on January 26 and 27 at Preussisch-Eylau, where, commanding part of the battery of the right flank, he demonstrated his knowledge and valour on multiple occasions; during the enemy

columns between the town and the elevation next to the town. Shortly thereafter our heavy artillery directed its fire against these columns as well as those infantry and cavalry forces that were marching out of the town and moving against our right wing commanded by Lieutenant General Tuchkov.[14] The enemy, which had been contained during his first attack in this direction, occupied the buildings in Stadt-Mühle, which were in front of this wing, in order to regroup and resume attacks from there. However, our skirmishers and the 24th Jager Regiment drove him out of there. Still, the enemy reinforced his troops in this direction; several columns of infantry and cavalry again came out of the town to attack our right wing, upon which General Tuchkov ordered Major General [Alexander von] Fock to move forward his infantry brigade, supported by the two dragoon regiments, Rizhskii and Liflyandskii. General Fock attacked these columns very vigorously at the bayonet, routed them, and partially destroyed them.

Three enemy columns, among which were the Imperial Guard, soon advanced against our centre. To confront them, General Dokhturov dispatched General [Andey] Zapolsky, with a column from the reserve; it deployed and the two fronts approached each other very closely, firing continuously. When General Zapolsky noticed that the enemy had been halted, he charged him at the bayonet, broke him, and pursued him for some distance. This enemy column lost a great many killed and wounded; it also lost an Eagle and 130 prisoners. At the same time, the other part of the enemy column, supported by yet another column, approached again the first line of our centre. Our closest regiments met it with lowered bayonets and routed it. A few regiments, that were in reserve behind the centre, profited from the moment and finished off the larger part of these columns. A few squadrons of enemy cuirassiers belonging to the *Corps des Gardes,* had managed to pass through a gap between two infantry regiments of our first line and to penetrate into the area between the first and second lines;[15] but despite the great valour with which they defended themselves and all the

---

    attack on the centre, the artillery that Sievers commanded inflicted a severe defeat on the enemy.' Entry no. 1776 in V. Sudravskii, *Kavalery ordena Svyatogo Velikomuchenika i Pobedonostsa Georgia sa 140 let (1769-1909)*, online version available at <http://george-orden.narod.ru/ordgrg4st1807.html>

14 Pavel Grabbe, serving in the artillery company of Fedor Schulman, witnessed the destruction of Marshal Pierre Augereau's corps: 'I was then an artillery officer commanding two cannon attached to the Vladimirskii Regiment in Dokhturov's corps, almost in the centre of our positions. So it was we who faced one of the columns of Marshal Augereau, whose corps was destroyed in the carnage… A strong blizzard blinded us with snow. Suddenly everything calmed down and directly in front of my cannon, no more than 30 paces away, we saw a column of Frenchmen, who were also startled by the proximity of our line. My cannon were loaded with grape-shot since I had no roundshot and only five rounds of grape shot per gun. The grapeshot had a devastating effect at such close range. The column veered right and charged the second battalion of the Vladimirskii Regiment; I stood in the interval between the 2nd and 1st Battalion. Our men received the enemy with bayonets but the [French] broke through in the middle. I was still firing the last remaining grape-shot rounds when the artillerymen behind me shouted 'Frenchmen' and made me look around. Several Frenchmen stormed into the battery from behind but they were soon followed by our men and were all stabbed with bayonets; I was able to save only a few them from the swords of my men. Our horses were wounded and all of the ammunition used. The bayonet melee ended up with the complete destruction of this enemy column. Mounds of corpses marked the sight of the carnage.' *Iz pamiatnykh zapisok…*(Moscow: Katkov, 1873), pp.47–50.

15 Wilson: 'A French regiment of cuirassiers had succeeded in penetrating through the line by an interval which a new formation had occasioned: but they had no sooner passed than they were pursued by some squadrons of dragoons and hussars entirely round and in a wide circuit to the rear of the camp,

efforts they had made to get out, they were unable to escape. We shouted at them multiple times to surrender, but they continued to fight in the hope of breaking through and re-crossing the 1st line, which, in the end, cost them the life of almost everyone. Among others, Captain Maret was wounded by a Cossack lance thrust that threw him from his horse. Despite the [medical] care we provided him, he died from his wound a few days later at Königsberg.

While these events were taking place [on the right flank and centre], another enemy column was repulsed with losses by the Moskovskii Grenadier and Schlüsselbourgskii Musketeer Regiments, commanded by Prince Karl of Mecklenburg. All of the repulsed enemy troops rallied into one column during their retreat and, having receive fresh reinforcements, including two columns of cavalry, they turned back for another assault. As soon as General Dokhturov realized this, he sent out General Somov with the entire column, which deployed in a battle formation. Our cavalry regiments, which had been until this moment in reserve behind the centre, formed into columns and General Zapolsky attacked with cavalry for a second time. The enemy cavalry, which was on the left side of these columns, was routed by Colonel Count O'Rourke,[16] who threw himself on it with three squadrons, broke it, and pursued it all the way back to the enemy batteries. The enemy infantry columns were also repulsed with considerable losses and pursued back to their line.[17] In each of these charges we took a number of prisoners.

Joseph O'Rourke. (State Hermitage Museum)

Since the break of day, the columns of the enemy light infantry had also attacked our left wing, where General Baggehufvudt's detachment stood in front of the village of Serpallen; we first sent our skirmishers against these columns. General Kakhovsky,[18] with the Polish

---

and finally by a corps of Cossacks who killed a great number of them.' Wilson to Lord Hutchinson, 9 February 1807, *Life of General Sir Robert Wilson*, vol.2, p.409–410.

16 Joseph O'Rourke (1772–1849), Russian officer of the Irish origin. He served in the Pavlogradskii Hussar Regiment until May 1807, when he was appointed the chef of the Volynskii Uhlan Regiment.

17 Wilson: 'The slaughter of the French was exceedingly great. In many places they lay in heaps upon each other.' Wilson to Lord Hutchinson, 9 February 1807, *Life of General Sir Robert Wilson*, vol.2, p.410.

18 Peter Kakhovsky, major general since 1803, the chef of the Polish Uhlan Regiment in 1803–1814.

Uhlan Regiment and the Malorossiiskii Cuirassier Regiment, was to the left of Serpallen. He moved through the village, attacked the enemy infantry column, overran it, and captured prisoners; the rest of this column retreated into the woods. General Kakhovsky then received orders to move with his cavalry regiments to our right, where he again attacked the enemy columns and forced them to retire as well.

General Count Pahlen, commanding the cavalry on the right wing, ordered Major General Baron Korff to attack with his brigade against the enemy columns, which were threatening General Sacken's division; the enemy was entirely defeated. Our cuirassiers, from the Military Order Cuirassier Regiment, took an Eagle and more than 100 prisoners. Also, the Izumskii Hussar and Kurlyandskii Dragoon Regiments made several successful charges on our right and repulsed the enemy with losses.

The enemy, having already lost a great deal of men and seeing the uselessness of his efforts to break our centre or our right wing, turned his attention to our left wing. Marshal Davout, with his corps of about 30,000 men, attacked our left wing and tried to turn it. He advanced in strong columns from Molwitten on Serpallen and Sausgarten against General Baggehufvudt who, too weak to resist it, set the village of Serpallen on fire and retreated on Sausgarten; our left wing cavalry, placed at Serpallen, also retreated and took position behind our left wing.

General Count Kamensky reinforced General Baggehufvudt with the reserve that was located behind Sausgarten. Yet as the reinforced enemy pushed forward with several new columns, Kamensky ordered General Prince Scherbatov to march with the Uglitskii and Kostromskoi [Musketeer] Regiments to Sausgarten while the Ryazanskii Musketeer Regiment was to hold the village of Sausgarten itself so that it could repulse the enemy if he had attacked from Molwitten.

Observing the advance of strong enemy columns on our left wing, Lieutenant General Count Ostermann considered it necessary to move his front to the left and leave Sausgarten. The enemy columns, supported by heavy artillery [on the Kreege Berge], vigorously attacked General Baggehufvudt and forced him to fall back, all the more so as the other columns were beginning to turn his left flank. Due to this movement, General Baggehufvudt placed himself to the south of Auklappen, on the left of General Count Ostermann's division against which the enemy now advanced rapidly. Very lively shooting broke out between the skirmishers on both sides. Count Ostermann then made the decision to send forward the 3rd battalions of each regiment standing in the first line of his division and, supporting them with his reserve, he had them attack these enemy columns. After a stubborn and bloody fight, the enemy was repulsed at this point. Yet soon thereafter we observed strong enemy columns advancing on our left with an intention to turn our flank. To prevent this, Count Ostermann considered it his responsibility to change his position first at Sausgarten and there, to move further to Auklappen. He felt all the more compelled to do this since Count Kamensky had already been forced to move his reserve to a position north of Auklappen in order to protect our left wing.

As soon as I noticed this movement on our left wing and the direction of Marshal Davout's corps advance to turn out flank at Kutschitten, I ordered a change in our position. General Steinheil, my chief of staff who went to execute this movement, pushed forward our horse artillery and placed three batteries [near Auklappen], which opened fire with great success; not only did they stop the march of the enemy columns, but they even forced one of them to retreat; as they retired, the enemy troops set fire to the farm of Auklappen.

A superb engraving by Johann Lorenz Rugendas, published in 1820, showing the panoramic battle scene of the fighting at Eylau. With the town on fire in the background, Napoleon, Murat and the rest of the entourage (on the left) closely observe the charge of the French cavalry while the Imperial Guard readies for the attack in the lower left corner. The Cossacks, on the right, are pursuing the retreating French cavalrymen while General Jean-Joseph Ange d'Hautpoul, grievously wounded, is about to fall off the horse at right lower edge. (Courtesy of Anne S.K. Brown Military Collection)

The enemy, after having forced General Count Kamensky to fall back, occupied the village of Kutschitten but was soon dislodged by General Czaplic's detachment, composed of three squadrons from the Pavlogradskii Hussar Regiment, the Moskovskii Musketeer Regiment, and a party of Cossacks. This detachment moved via Kutschitten, attacked the enemy column, and broke it.

The Don Cossack *ataman* and Lieutenant General Platov joined the army only on 26 January/7 February just when my troops were already in position behind Preussisch-Eylau and when the different corps and detachments were already distributed among the generals, which prevented me from giving him a command equal to his rank and capacities. He therefore took a temporary command of the Cossack regiments that were present with the army and that numbered about 2,500 men. But even with this small detachment, this general took an active part in the battle. He dispatched two regiments, those of Sysoev and Malakhov, to our right wing, and placed the regiments of Andronov and Kiselev within reach of the centre. He then went to our left wing with four regiments, those of Ilovaisky IX, Grekov XII, Efremov III and Popuzov. On the right wing, our Cossacks prevented on multiple occasions parties of enemy cavalry from crossing the marshes in front of the village of Schloditten. The Cossacks of the centre contributed greatly to the defeat of the French cuirassiers, who had penetrated between our first and second lines. Kiselev's regiment particularly distinguished itself on that occasion and captured an officer and 20 cavalrymen, the only ones from the enemy cavalry who had escaped death. The Cossack regiments were involved in every charge that took place that day and had captured 450 prisoners.

You will see, General, on the map of this battle, how much ground we had already lost by the third change in the front of our left wing, while our right wing had constantly held its first position.[19] Prudence had required that we refuse little on our left wing against superior enemy forces, which were manoeuvring to turn it. But, toward the evening, Lieutenant General L'Estocq arrived with the Prussian corps – in which was also a Russian infantry regiment and two regiments of Cossacks – on the road from Drangsitten and Althof, followed very closely by Marshal Ney and his corps.

We had left General L'Estocq at Wuhsen. After he had passed with his corps via Langwiese, Engelswalde, Schönfeldt, Tiefensee, Montitten, Rositten and Wackern, he encountered the head of Marshal Ney's corps. L'Estocq occupied this latter place with the detachments of generals Plötz and Prittwitz, who stopped the enemy, while he himself, with the main body of his corps, moved via Pompicken and arrived in the afternoon at Althof. The detachments of Generals Plötz and Prittwitz were no longer able to follow General L'Estocq, for they were forced to yield to the superior enemy forces and retreat to Kreuzburg, on the road from Königsberg, which procured a double advantage. First that town was covered on the main road and also that the enemy mistook these detachments for the entire Prussian corps and could no longer prevent L'Estocq from marching to Althof. The forces that this general brought us did not amount to more than 6,000 men under arms, including the Vyborgskii Musketeer Regiment and about 400 Cossacks that accompanied this corps. General L'Estocq had left a small rear guard on the road, which skirmished with Marshal Ney's advance guard in order to stop his march as much as possible. Lieutenant General L'Estocq, meanwhile, passed from Althof between Schloditten and Schmoditten, and moved to our left wing, the position I had assigned him in advance and where we had the greatest need of this reinforcement. But this reinforcement was not sufficient to render our forces even with those that the enemy had committed there.

General L'Estocq, upon his arrival on our left wing, attacked the village of Kutschitten, which the enemy had already occupied and from which he was dislodged with the loss

---

19 Writing three days after the battle, Wilson explained to Lord Hutchinson that 'in my letter of yesterday I probably omitted many interesting circumstances, but I really was too fatigued to pay that attention which is my duty and inclination. There is one circumstance, however, that requires an elucidation which I am happy to give. When the left [wing] was thrown back there was certainly some confusion, and the troops seemed unwilling to halt: but [the officer] who gives you this letter and who is aide-de-camp to the [Russian] emperor, will confirm my assurance that this retrograde march beyond the proposed alignment was in consequence of the standards being in the hands of young officers; who, conceiving the line to be forming for a charge, retired, as is the order in the Russian service (that the troops may rally upon them, after the dispersion of a charge), but did not halt, as they ought to have done, in one hundred paces. So the soldiers, on being accused of cowardice replied that they only followed their colours.' Robert Wilson to Lord Hutchinson, 11 February 1807, in *Life of General Sir Robert Wilson*, vol.2, p.413.

'The Prussians at Eylau on February 8, 1807,' an early twentieth-century painting by Richard Knötel embellishing the Prussian involvement in the battle. (Courtesy of Anne S.K. Brown Military Collection)

of four cannons. The enemy was then driven from a height behind Kutschitten. During these attacks, the following units distinguished themselves in particular: the Vyborgskii Musketeer Regiment under the orders of Colonel Pillar,[20] the Prussian infantry regiments of Schöning and Rüchel, and the grenadier battalion of Fabecky.[21]

General Count Kamensky also advanced and placed himself with his reserve and General Czaplic's detachment near Auklappen. General L'Estocq brought his heavy artillery into action against the enemy columns placed in a forest [the Birken Wäldchen]; he sent some

---

20 The future general of infantry and corps commander Vasilii Timofeyev was a 24-year-old captain when his regiment, the Vyborgskii Musketeers, went into battle at Eylau. When the Prussian corps reached the battlefield, he recalled, 'Lestocq initially dispatched only the Vyborgskii Regiment to join the fighting. The regiment deployed in front of Kutschitten which was occupied by the French. Our regimental commander, Colonel Piller, present with the regiment, asked for volunteers [okhotniki] and about 1,000 soldiers stepped forward, but not a single officer. As this was taking place in front of the Prussian forces, I found it rather embarrassing to let only rank-and-file, without any officers, to volunteer for this service. So even though I was just a company commander, I stepped forward and my entire company followed me.' His memoirs contain interesting details on the subsequent fighting around Kutschitten. See Mikaberidze, *Russian Eyewitness Accounts of the Campaign of 1807*, pp.158–161.
21 For interesting discussion of the Russian horse artillery's involvement in the fighting see Yermolov, *The Czar's General*, pp.83–84.

skirmishers against the enemy whom they dislodged from the woods; he then advanced, along with General Count Kamensky, toward Sausgarten and these generals forced the enemy columns, which had already turned our left wing, to retreat. The fast-approaching darkness halted the combatants in their attacks.

While all this was happening on the left wing, the 8th Division, under the orders of General Essen III, and General Markov's detachment were sent to the left wing of the 2nd Division. Their jagers and those of the 3rd Division made an attack to support that of General L'Estocq and General Count Kamensky. Lieutenant General Dokhturov having received a contusion that forced him to leave the battlefield, his *corps*, composed of the 7th and 8th Division, passed under the orders of Lieutenant General Prince Bagration; these two divisions took up positions [near Schloditten].

The 5th Division, forming our right wing [at Schloditten] and supported by a Prussian battery placed by General Fock in front of the village, repulsed the last attempts by the enemy against that wing.

Seeing that our troops were returning to their initial positions, I ordered the regiments of the 3rd Division, the day already dwindled, to once again dislodge the enemy from the village of Klein-Sausgarten, which they did after an intense but short fight. An overcast weather rendered that night very dark.

By the end of the battle, our cavalry gathered [near Kutschitten].

This battle, one of the bloodiest of our times, commenced at three o'clock in the afternoon on 26 January/7 February and ended at seven o'clock in the evening on the 27th/8th. During 15 hours of daylight, over these two days, we fought relentlessly. Columns or, more properly, masses of soldiers, after having been exposed to all the fire that the artillery brought to bear in an action, confronted each other with cold steel [*arme blanche*]. How many cavalry charges were repeated in this battle! The losses on both sides were enormous.[22] Our army

---

22 Mikhail Petrov, serving in the Yeletskii Musketeer: 'Our regiment, as all others, suffered heavy casualties in this battle: our earnest and fearless chef was shot in his right leg, above the calf; regimental commander Lieutenant-Colonel Tankachev was shot dead; all battalion commanders were wounded and only six officers out of 43 attended 370 rank-and-file that survived out of the almost full-strength three-battalion regiment that was now under the command of Captain Tikhonov I. In my company, I only had 47 men surviving. I was wounded in the right cheek by a bullet while my brother – just 19 – was injured in the head. During the night after the battle, many seriously and lightly wounded officers gathered around bonfires that were set up some five *verstas* behind the battle line, in the village occupied by the army and corps headquarters. I found my brother, [Staff Captain] Shenshin and other officers from our regiment laying with bandaged wounds on the straw scattered around a bonfire and joined their company. Looking back at the terrible whirlwind of bloodshed, I told my comrades, "I do not think one can envision any worse massacre between the offspring of Adam than the one that occurred today." Staff Captain Shenshin, who was lying next to me, raised his head and leaning on his good hand, he said, "If anyone had tried to surpass today's butchery, Satan himself would never allow him for he had exhausted all of his devilish skills today, and what a job he did!" "'That's true,' added Staff Captain Scheffler, "today's battle is the greatest undertaking of the infernal academy and we would not lie if we say that the imps themselves did not dare to stay in between the fighting columns but preferred to admire the sight from the distant hills and applaud the [murderous] play that they had prepared for us to perform. We are lucky that winter days are short, for they would have added another two-act play for us to perform.'" Petrov, 'Rasskazy...', pp.146–148.

General Jean-Joseph Ange d'Hautpoul leading the massive cavalry charge at Eylau. Hautpoul's cuirassiers broke through the Russian centre, wheeled and charged a second time but the general was severely wounded in the process and had to be carried to the French rear. Despite the best efforts of the French physicians, he died not long afterwards. Engraving by J.J. Wolff after Carle Vernet, 1810. (Private collection)

lost 9,000 killed and 7,000 wounded;[23] among them were 700 officers and nine generals wounded. With our losses so great, any soldier can easily imagine what must have been those of the French army and how much it must have lost while attacking in columns, which were repulsed everywhere. It is known that Marshal Augereau's corps, having crossed through the town, made the first attack against our centre; it was partially destroyed and the survivors of this corps were later distributed amongst other corps, especially into the 1st Corps or that of the Prince de Ponte-Corvo. Furthermore, we captured five Eagles and about 2,000 prisoners, amongst whom there were a few hundred wounded. The losses of the French army were never

---

23 Writing to Lord Hutchinson on 11 February, Wilson acknowledged that 'the loss of the Russians has been more considerable than I stated. Eight hundred officers, amongst which are seven generals, and near twelve thousand men, have been killed and wounded.' He also noted that, on 10 February, the French had sent a flag of truce asking the Russians if they would care to send medical assistance to the wounded who had been left behind. 'To ask the Russians such a question was neither humanity nor common sense, unless Buonaparte wished to sound the tone of the Russians as to their feelings relative to the battle and the measures they would adopt, for of all improbabilities that of the Russians having any superfluous surgeons is the most notorious. General Beningsen's answer was very proper. He said that he had many French wounded of whom he took care, and therefore that he expected the same treatment for his wounded.' *Life of General Sir Robert Wilson*, vol.2, p.416.

published, that is to say the truthful ones; but it is generally certain, and a great many people, who were in a position to know, confirm it that the French losses exceeded 30,000 men, which is very reasonable given the high number of generals and officers of all ranks that were killed and wounded; 16 generals, including Marshal Augereau, were wounded.

The following corps composed the French army at the battle of Preussisch-Eylau: 1st Corps, Bernadotte; 3rd, Davout; 4th, Soult; 6th, Ney; 7th, Augereau; the Imperial Guard, Marshal Bessières; the reserve of the Grand-Duke of Berg [Murat]. Part of the reserve, under Oudinot's command, took part in the battle, while the rest of this reserve faced General Essen on the Narew; neither of these corps, as you will see, took direct part in the battle. One could calculate the strength of these corps according to the rosters [*l'état*] and the losses that I cited in my previous letters. I refer you, General, to my fifth letter and you will see that at the beginning of this war these corps amounted to 151,200 men; then calculate the losses of the French army noted in subsequent letters, divide the losses among these corps, add 20,000 conscripts that arrived from the depots to their regiments in November and December, and you will see that the French army at the battle of Preussisch-Eylau must have been at least 100,000 men.

In my fifth letter you will have seen, General, that I entered Old Prussia with 70,000 men combatants and non-combatants; our losses from that time to the two days of Preussisch-Eylau were about 6,000 men; 4,000 ill were in the hospitals of Königsberg and Gumbinnen. Thus, there remained, on the day of the great battle, barely 60,000 men combatants and non-combatants. The loss of 16,000 combatants in those two days was therefore quite a bit more significant for the Russian army than the 30,000 men could have been for the French army. The reinforcement that General L'Estocq brought us amounted to only 6,000 men, as I have already noted, because this corps had been weakened by the losses that it had suffered on its march and by the dispatch of detachments that had directed their march on Kreuzburg.

So that you may, General, have a true and exact idea of the position of the French army, the evening following the action, and of the reasons that convinced me to move closer to Königsberg the next day, I will offer you here an abridged extract of Marshal Ney's report to the Minister of War, the Prince of Neuchâtel, of his march to the environs of Schlodittsen.

> Account of Marshal Ney of the Movements of February 7-8.
>
> The *corps d'armée* was on the march since the 7th from the positions at Liebstadt and Wormditt. It was ordered to assemble at Landsberg and then move to Kreuzburg. It took position, the 7th in the evening, as follows: General Lasalle's cavalry at Orschen, the route from Landsberg to Kreuzburg; General Marchand's 1st Brigade also at Orschen; the 2nd at Eichen. General Gardanne's division at Landsberg; the brigade of dragoons, the *20e* and *26e régiments*, commanded by General Delorme, also concentrated there.
>
> The enemy occupied Orschen with infantry and a little cavalry; they were attacked and dislodged from this post; we took some prisoners.
>
> On the 8th, the *corps d'armée* set in movement at six o'clock in the morning. Barely had the head exited from the forest behind Schlautienen than we observed General L'Estocq's Prussian column, marching by his left, heading to Preussisch-Eylau to make there its junction with the Russian army, which was in position at Schlodittsen and Auklappen.

I immediately ordered General Marchand's division to tighten the column, deploy the 1st brigade, and attack the enemy at Pompicken, behind which he was marching, and to support himself with the 2nd brigade. The rest of the corps followed this first movement; the dragoons in reserve behind Gardanne's division which was in battle formation on the right on the height and behind Schlautienen. General Lasalle's cavalry supported Marchand's division.

During his flank march [*marche de flanc*] the enemy left a detachment of 3,000 men on the road from Kreuzburg, between Soeben and Pompicken, to protect this movement. Another detachment sought to fix my attention on my left, near Waldkeim. Nevertheless, the cannonade could be heard from the direction of Pr.-Eylau. M. Montesquiou came at 10:30 to tell me, on behalf of the Emperor, to support the left of the *Grande Armée*. I immediately gave orders to follow the direction of the Prussian column via Leissen, Grawentien, Drangsitten and Althof. The enemy had burned the bridges of Drangsitten and Althof; we arrived soon enough to rebuild the crossings and move across at once…

It was eight o'clock in the evening when the 1st brigade of Marchand's division was in battle formation behind Schloditten…; the rest of the *corps d'armée* deployed in front of and behind Althof…. Finally, at 10 o'clock in the evening, this brigade moved to Althof, without any more losses than six wounded and a few dead.

General Roguet's brigade, still rather far in the rear, proceeded to Pompicken but, as it was already night-time, it made a mistake and directed its march to Kreuzburg instead. There [Roguet] found the enemy in force, that is to say around 3,000 men of infantry and 1,000 cavalry.[24] He immediately attacked and repulsed it; during this time, he received a second order to take up position behind the village of Drangsitten; only four companies of the *74e* [regiment] and a cavalry picket remained at Pompicken to ensure communications from Kreuzburg and Landsberg.

On 9 January, the *corps d'armée* set in march and placed itself in a battle formation of two lines. The right at Moulin-à-Vent, to the left of Eylau, and the left in the direction of Storchnest…

Note, General, that according to this report Marshal Ney had arrived with his corps at eight o'clock in the evening, which would have added 17,000 to 18,000 men to the enemy's forces at Althof. You can see on the map that he was less than a half-*mille* from Schloditten, on the main road from Königsberg, *behind our right wing*. A division of this corps was already, as you can observe, between Althof and Schloditten. The march of Lieutenant General L'Estocq with his *corps*, coming via the road from Pompicken, was executed via Leissen, Grawentien, Drangsitten, Althof and Schloditten, from whence he took up position on our left wing, as I have already said earlier. When I heard that evening cannon fire that the enemy fired *behind our right wing* against our skirmishers, which General L'Estocq's rear guard had left behind, I sent five infantry battalions and some Cossacks, under the orders of Prince Basil

---

24 Bennigsen's note: It is the detachment of about 2,000 men, which I mentioned, under the Prussian General Plötz, that marched on Kreuzburg.

The panoramic view of the epic charge of the French cavalry at Eylau on 8 February, painting by Jean-Antoine-Siméon Fort. (Public Domain)

[Vasilii] Dolgorouky, to take up a position between Schloditten and Althof and to cover our communications with Königsberg. Prince Dolgorouky attacked, at the bayonet point, this enemy brigade, which was still a truly short distance from Schloditten, and forced it to retire on Althof.

In addition to the arrival of Ney's corps behind our right wing, I had been informed, by prisoners, that they were expecting in the French army, on its right wing (therefore against our left), that the 1st Corps, that of the Prince de Ponte-Corvo, would soon join Marshal Davout's corps, which would have added another 13,000 men, even after the losses that it had suffered. These two corps, neither one of which had seen action on the days of the 26th/7th and 27th/8th, brought to the French army a reinforcement of about 30,000 men, which made up for the losses that the other corps had suffered and once again raised the overall strength of the French army to over 70,000 men, too unequal a number for what remained of mine to resist the enemy on the terrain that I occupied after the battle.

Adjudge now, General, and let every competent soldier assess the decision that prudence imposed upon me to take, either to remain in my position at Preussisch-Eylau and risk the next day a third engagement (because we had fought two days at that position), or to take the wiser path and, having repulsed the enemy at every point and inflicted heavy losses on him, to leave him in the snows in the region of Eylau, where he was deprived of any means of subsistence, of the means to care for his wounded, of repairing his artillery, etc., and to move with the army toward Königsberg, where I would find everything necessary to refresh our troops, to care perfectly for our wounded, to quickly repair our artillery, to replenish my ammunition caissons, etc. Incidentally, I found below Königsberg a position where I could

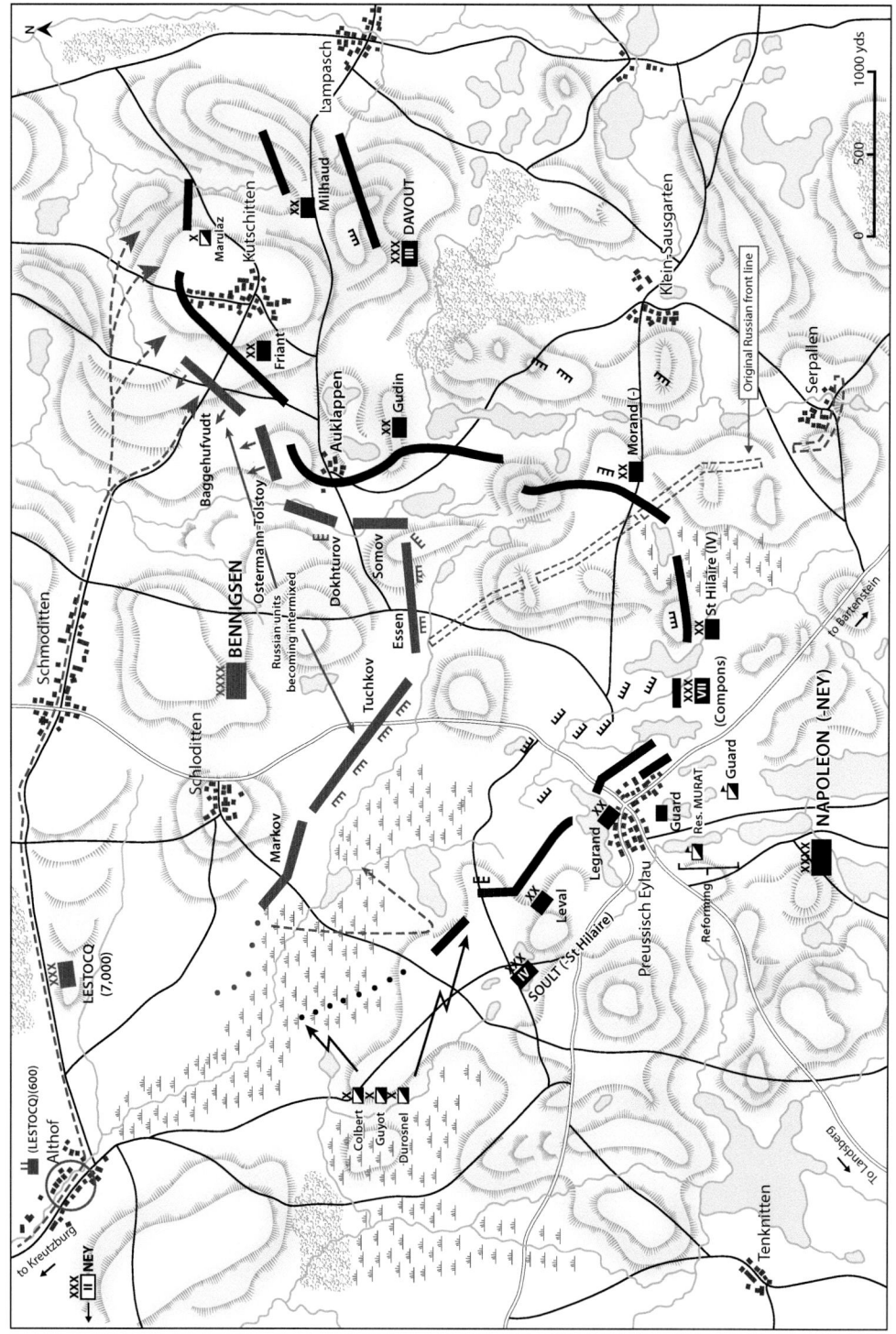

Battle of Eylau: Situation at the end of the battle.

support our two wings and render the position stronger by some works, as I did, and I still had a vast plain before our front, upon which our cavalry could act without impediments. It only remained for the enemy to choose to attack us in a position where we could fight against superior forces, or to retreat with the entire army. Napoleon, this great captain, who had never missed an opportunity where he could deliver a decisive blow to crush his enemy, however found it necessary to choose the latter. So subsequent events proved well that I had not been mistaken in my calculations.

By marching to Königsberg I obtained, without any losses, the same advantages that a new bloodshed would have procured for us. And even though I was confident of being able to repulse, for a third day, the enemy attacks on our position at Preussisch-Eylau, I had also to carefully consider if the army's circumstances permitted me to suffer losses similar to those of the day before, and if the forces that would have remained at my disposal after the battle would have allowed me to pursue the French army in its retreat, which I did do without equivocation after my movement to Königsberg, as you will see in my following letter. Can one even calculate the unfortunate consequences that would have resulted in the case of a setback, against which I could offer no guarantees? One cannot delude oneself in this respect if one wishes to reflect on this issue long and hard. Remember that all our efforts to support the army and the great preparations that had been made in the interior of the Empire to resist the enemy forces – under the direction of Emperor Napoleon himself, the man against whom no one had held in the field despite all the activity expended for it – had not advanced much since the time of the battle of Pultusk, when I had infinitely more resources than after the battle of Preussisch-Eylau. And we know well how impractical war preparations could become for a country if its field army is destroyed. When I reach the discussion of the peace negotiations at Tilsit, I will return to this matter and you will see that beyond the great sacrifices that Prussia was obliged to make, she would invariably also have lost Silesia if our armies had suffered a defeat. Careful reflections and calculations dictated by prudence therefore had to precede each step of my military operations.

The circumstances in which we found ourselves did not allow me to close my eyes to the dangers that we could run if I left even the smallest matter to chance. So in making my decision, I took an approach that was dictated by my sense of duty and desire to look after the interests of my Sovereign and the nation. Emperor Napoleon himself commended me about this and the manner in which he was willing to express his praise to me is all too flattering for me not to share it here. It was at Tilsit, during the peace negotiations, that one day, when I was passing before his residence, he had the kindness to send an officer after me, to tell me that he wished to see me at his residence. I had the honour of being brought into his office where he was alone. After a few gracious compliments, he said to me: 'Well! General, I witnessed your talents and your *prudence*,' emphasizing that last word as he looked at me.

So, General, do not reproach me of conceit in repeating these words of Emperor Napoleon. How could I be indifferent to a flattering testimony from such great a man?!

To show his satisfaction to the army for its conduct in this famous battle and to me in particular, the Emperor, my master, designed to decorate me with the Order of St Andrew the First Called. Moreover, His Majesty had the generosity to grant, by a decree to his Minister of Finances, me a perpetual pension of 12,000 *rubles*. All of my generals were rewarded as well.

Jean-Antoine-Siméon Fort's painting conveys the misery of fighting amidst the frozen cemetery for control of Eylau on 7 February. (Public Domain)

As were senior officers too. His Majesty granted, based on my report, to more than 1,200 officers a mark of distinction, consisting of a golden cross attached to the *boutonnière* and on which the date and year of the famous day of Preussisch-Eylau were marked. For those who earned it, this cross deducted three years of service out of the 25 that an officer must have served without reproach to receive the Order of St George of the 4th class. Moreover, the Emperor rewarded the non-commissioned officers [*sous-officiers*] and soldiers who had been in this battle with a monetary award in the amount of one third of their pay.[25]

---

25 To conclude this chapter Bennigsen later added a lengthy text from Emperor Alexander's 8/20 February letter, which was published in the Russian edition but was excluded from the French edition. The current editor and translator decided not to include the letter.

13

The Retreat to Königsberg

I have already explained, General, in my preceding letter all the reasons that compelled me to lead the army to Königsberg.[1] Consequently, I set it in motion, on 28 January/9 February, before daybreak, in two columns: the 1st or that of the right via Schloditten, Schmoditten, Leidtkeim, Knauten, Mühlhausen and Gross-Lauth, where it crossed the Frisching, and the 2nd via Gross-Sausgarten, Sossehnen, Romitten, Vierzighüben and Wetterckeim, where it also crossed that river. To cover our left wing and to prevent the enemy from being able to send across the Pregel light troops that would have harassed or forced us to divert detachments there, Lieutenant General L'Estocq moved with his corps, on 28 January/9 February, via Domnau to Friedland. Arriving at the former place, his rear guard was engaged by Marshal Davout's advance guard, leading to an inconsequential combat.

This march was executed with the greatest possible order. Lieutenant General Prince Bagration, not seeing any enemy troops pursuing him, arrived with the rear guard at Gross-Lauth at one o'clock in the afternoon.

On 29 January/10 February, the army marched in the same order from Wittenberg to the plains of Königsberg. Our left wing rested on the old Pregel, and our right wing extended to the fort of Friedrichsburg. We constructed a few earthworks on elevations that were located in front of our left wing; we did the same on our right, to dominate the small, swampy plain called Nasse-Garten, which was still frozen.

The majority of our light troops, forming the advance guard, under the orders of the Don Cossack *ataman* Lieutenant General Platov and Lieutenant General Prince Bagration, covered our position on the Frisching. The right of their chain rested on the shores of the Frische-Haff and the left extended to Friedrichsdorf, from which frequent patrols maintained our communications with Lieutenant General L'Estocq's *corps*, which had moved that day to Allenburg, to avoid a serious engagement with the few forces remaining to him

---

1   Wilson: 'Beningsen has been much blamed for leaving the field of battle. If he had consulted his own fame in preference to the real interests of the army he would not have retired: but in my opinion he acted wisely; not only because it was necessary to refresh his troops and obtain immediately the supplies he wanted by an approach to the stores, but because as [reinforcements were] within five days' march with twenty battalions and twenty-three squadrons, and as twenty-two regiments of Cossacks were also within that distance, any movement that might induce the French to advance nearer to Königsberg was an advisable measure.' Robert Wilson to Lord Hutchinson, 11 February 1807, in *Life of General Sir Robert Wilson*, vol.2, pp.413–414.

against Marshal Davout's corps, which had followed him closely. This General chose a position to defend the crossings between the Frisching and the Alle, as well as the forests of Astrawischken. General L'Estocq was invited to maintain secure communications with the Russian army and to remain ready to be able to rejoin it at the first signal.

You can see, General, roughly the position of the enemy at this time from the following report from Marshal Ney to the Minister of War, the Prince of Neuchâtel.

> Marshal Ney to the Minister of War
> Romitten, 10 February 1807, six o'clock in the evening
> I have the honour of informing Your Excellency that the troops of the *6e corps d'armée* are placed in the following positions: General Colbert, with his brigade of cavalry, the 2nd battalion of the *6e* [regiment] and two pieces of artillery, occupies Porschkam and Pompicken, on the road from Landsberg to Kreuzburg. There will be an observation post at Kreuzburg itself, if the enemy is not there in too great a force. This General will then take the head of the *corps d'armée* to the height of Schrombehnen, as soon as the troops of the Prince de Ponte-Corvo debouche onto the road from Kreuzburg, or when the army marches on Wittenberg.
>
> The 1st brigade of Marchand's division occupies Vierzighüben, Lewitten and Wetterckeim. The 2nd brigade, Mühlhausen, Schultitten and Schrombehnen. General Gardanne's 1st brigade occupies Knauten and Romitten. The 2nd brigade of this division occupies Kniepitten and Sossehnen.
>
> The general assembly point for the army is placed behind Mühlhausen, at the fork in the roads from Eylau and Domnau. A great portion of the Grand Duke's cavalry passed via Mühlhausen, moving on Gross-Lauth; I even believe that it crossed the Frisching. I heard a light cannonade and a skirmish that were fairly inconsequential.
>
> I am writing to the Grand Duke to inform him of the position of my troops so that should anything happen he can support himself...

> Other Report from Marshal Ney to the Minister of War
> Romitten, 11 February 1807
> His Excellency the Grand Duke of Berg [Murat] sent me one of his aides de camp yesterday evening, inviting me to place some infantry at his disposal, so as to take possession of Wittenberg. I noted to His Excellency that the passage of the Frisching, which he had effected with only cavalry and having the sole bridge at Gross-Lauth for retreat, seemed to be contrary to the instructions of Your Excellency and to the intentions of the Emperor. Nevertheless, so as not to compromise the Grand Duke, who was scuffling with the enemy, I ordered that the *69e régiment d'infanterie* to move immediately to the bridge at Gross-Lauth. I sent, before daybreak, one of my aides de camp beyond the posts occupied by the *69e régiment*, to reconnoitre the position of the cavalry corps of His Excellency the Grand Duke.
>
> General Colbert informs me that he was unable to occupy Kreuzburg with an observation post as dictated by my instructions from yesterday, because strong reconnaissance parties of hussars and Cossacks entering and leaving, day and night, Kreuzburg and that these patrols even came to Porschkam to attack our advance posts...

The French army was then in its position on two lines: the first was formed by Marshal Davout's corps, on the right wing; by that of Marshal Bernadotte, on the left wing. The other corps, forming the second line, were in the environs of Preussisch-Eylau.

I had ordered Lieutenant General Platov, as of our departure from Preussisch-Eylau, to employ the Cossacks night and day to harass the enemy advance posts wherever they could reach them. Our Cossacks acquitted themselves so well that in these three days they took from the enemy patrols and pickets two officers and about 200 soldiers, without having themselves lost a single man. You will soon see, in the continuation of my account, all the harm that they inflicted on the enemy, under the direction of their brave leader, by their activity in the position in which the two armies were. Beyond that nothing remarkable happened until 31 January/12 February. I ordered the general commanding the advance guard that when the enemy approached with forces that could indicate the march of his army on the Frisching, he would no longer defend the passage and instead retire with the entire advance guard onto our position, the work for the batteries of which I spoke earlier being almost completed. On this order, generals Platov and Prince Bagration moved with their headquarters to Ludwigswalde and pulled back the chain of our advance posts.

A large enemy cavalry detachment then crossed the Frisching at Gross-Lauth and approached the village of Jesau. As soon as Prince Bagration was informed of it by his advance posts, he sent there a reinforcement composed of the Oliviopolskii Hussar Regiment and a regiment of jagers with two pieces of horse artillery, with orders to hold this post. Besides the news that we had received of the march of this cavalry detachment, we also learned that the entire enemy army was advancing with an intention to attack our positions near Königsberg, which led me to invite General L'Estocq to join the Russian army and to receive battle there with all of our forces. The General moved, upon this invitation, with his *corps* between Genslacken and Wehlau, from where he could continue his march on the left bank of the Pregel and arrive in one march below Königsberg. However, two days later General L'Estocq returned to his original position at Allenburg, the French army having remained in the position that it had taken after the battle of Eylau.

On 1/13 February, everything still remained in the same order; a patrol of Cossacks captured 13 French soldiers from an outpost in front of the chain of our left wing. Lieutenant-Colonel Andronov, with his regiment of Cossacks, fell at the break of day on an enemy main advance guard and captured three officers and 50 cavalrymen. On 2/14 February, during the night, the Cossacks again captured on our left nine men from an enemy picket. Colonel Malakhov, sent on reconnaissance with his regiment of Cossacks, encountered, between Thomsdorf and Uderwangen, three enemy squadrons belonging to Bernadotte's corps; he overran them and took two officers and 72 cavalrymen prisoner. *Khorunzhiy*[2] Sysoev, with a [Cossack] party, captured six cavalrymen in a village.

Lieutenant General Platov received the report that a detachment of enemy cavalry had crossed the Frisching at Gross-Lauth and was advancing on the main road from Jesau and Wittenberg. You saw in the report from Marshal Ney to the Minister of War on 11 February/30 January that this was the Grand Duke of Berg himself, with part of the cavalry reserve,

---

2   Khorunzhiy ('chorąży' in Polish, derived from the Polish 'choragiew', or banner) was initially the name for a standard bearer but later become a junior officer rank in the Cossack forces, corresponding to the rank of cornet in regular cavalry.

that crossed the Frisching at Gross-Lauth with 12 regiments, according to the accounts of prisoners. Upon receiving this report, General Platov reinforced the post of Borchersdorf, so that there were eight squadrons of the Sumskii Hussars under the orders of Colonel Ushakov, and two regiments of Cossacks (those of Colonel Andreyev and Colonel Sysoev). The brave officers, who commanded this post, found the terrain – from the other side of Borchersdorf, where they saw this detachment of enemy cavalry appear in such superior force – too broken to be able to employ cavalry with advantage. They therefore retreated through this village to lure the enemy out into the open field that was on this side. The French cavalry did not hesitate to appear there in column, but our own did not give them the time to form entirely. They attacked the already deployed enemy front troops with such intrepidity that not only did they overrun it, but that all of the rest of the enemy column fell into a general route. The enemy cavalry was then followed with the greatest vigour up to the environs of Gross-Lauth, where it re-crossed the Frisching to fall back onto its infantry post. This affair, which earned the greatest honour for the Sumskii Hussars, the Cossacks, and the officers who led them, cost the enemy 400 men killed and wounded, not to mention an Eagle, 10 officers [*officiers majors* and *subalterns*] and 167 cavalrymen taken captive and brought back to Wittenberg, and from whence General Platov sent them to my headquarters at Königsberg. But what one could hardly believe is that we only lost in this action one man killed and four wounded. According to the accounts of prisoners, there were six regiments, under the orders of General Milhaud, that comprised the enemy detachment sent from Gross-Lauth.

Fedor von Korff. (State Hermitage Museum)

On the report from Major General Count Lambert that the enemy had sent across the Frisching a detachment of 2,000 infantrymen, with a few cavalry regiments, and that he had just occupied the villages of Wernsdorf and Lichtenhagen, I ordered Prince Bagration not to suffer the enemy's presence there, to dislodge him at once and, if the enemy forces were not too considerable, to push him back across the Frisching. Prince Bagration therefore sent Major General Korff with the 7th, 20th, and 21st Jager Regiments, the Izumskii Hussar Regiment, the Popov V Cossack Regiment, and two pieces of horse artillery to aid Count Lambert, with orders to attack the enemy and dislodge him from those villages.

On 3/15 February during the night, the enemy evacuated the village of Lichtenhagen, which Major General Korff immediately occupied with his jagers. At 10 o'clock in the morning, our generals set in march to attack the enemy, which had taken position near the villages of Mahnsfeld and Wernsdorf. General Count Lambert, having sent the Oliviopolskii Hussar Regiment directly to Wernsdorf, left Gollau with the Aleksandriiskii Hussar Regiment, while Major General Korff, with his detachment, moved from Lichtenhagen. Colonel Popov V, with his regiment of Cossacks who were sent on reconnaissance an hour in advance, soon reported that

Karl Lambert. (State Hermitage Museum)

the village of Mahnsfeld was still occupied by enemy infantry, but that the majority of his detachment was on the other side on some heights. On his arrival, General Korff attacked the village with the 7th Jager Regiment, supported by two squadrons of the Izumskii Hussars; the enemy was initially driven back but, having received infantry reinforcements on the other side of the village, he counterattacked. The 7th Jager Regiment was forced to retire in turn. General Korff then sent forward the 20th Jager Regiment. Then these two regiments [7th and 20th Jagers] renewed the attack, which succeeded entirely and the enemy was dislodged with considerable losses. During the attack on the village, an enemy cavalry detachment threatened General Korff's right wing, apparently to draw his attention there; but a squadron from the Izumskii Hussars, with Popov's regiment of Cossacks, smashed this cavalry and took several prisoners.

Meanwhile, General Korff moved his detachment through the village, and General Count Lambert also arrived at this time with the Aleksandriiskii Hussar Regiment. Then, these two generals forced the enemy to abandon his position and retreat. The cavalry was sent in pursuit up to the passage of the Frisching, on the road from Kreuzburg. At the same time, the Oliviopolskii Hussar Regiment drove the enemy out of the village of Wernsdorf. In these two places we took as prisoners four officers and 144 *sous-officiers* and soldiers; the enemy might have lost at least as many killed and wounded in the action and during the retreat. The Cossack regiments of Papuzin, Ilovaisky IX and Malakhov, sent by General Platov to harass the enemy advance posts, struck the road by which this same enemy detachment retreated after being repulsed at Mahnsfeld and Wernsdorf. The first regiment of Cossacks took prisoner two *sous-officiers* and 19 soldiers, and the latter – one Captain and 66 soldiers. Our losses were for the 7th Jagers – eight soldiers killed and 11 wounded, and seven that the enemy apparently captured during the fight, when this regiment was obliged to abandon the village after the first attack; for the 20th Jagers – one soldier killed, and one officer and 10 soldiers wounded. On hearing of this action, I ordered Lieutenant Generals Prince Bagration and Platov to engage directly all enemy troops that were still on the right bank of the Frisching and to establish a formidable post at Kobbelbude. On our left flank, the Cossacks again took on that day 10 men from various enemy pickets.

The Prussian Lieutenant General de Plötz who, after the battle of Preussisch-Eylau, had moved from Kreuzburg on our right, was invited to send a battalion to Brandenburg to occupy this place and to push reconnaissance parties to the other side of the river.

Marshal Ney reported that day the following to the Minister of War:

> Marshal Ney to the Minister of War
> Romitten, 14 February
> I moved my light cavalry to Abschwangen; it will also occupy Almenhausen, should this village be evacuated by Marshal Davout's troops. The goal of this disposition is to cover the army's right flank and to observe the enemy in Allenburg via patrols and reconnaissance; this cavalry will connect with the left of 3rd Corps. General Colbert received from Marshal Davout's chief of staff the news that the Prussian General L'Estocq, who had initially retired on Tapiau, returned to Allenburg, which he has occupied for 36 hours.[3] We heard a cannonade in the environs of Gollau and Weissenstein; I sent someone there to ascertain the cause and result.[4]

On 4/16 February, General Platov having ordered the day before that all Cossack regiments send parties down the various roads and attack at the break of day the entire chain of enemy advance posts, the Cossacks returned with 50 prisoners. General Platov himself went to the advance posts on the road from Ludwigswalde to Wittenberg. Upon his arrival, some enemy *tirailleurs*, supported by three squadrons, appeared and started a skirmish. Our General immediately attacked these three enemy squadrons with the Grekov XVIII and Efremov III regiments of Cossacks. The enemy was repelled and pursued beyond Wittenberg. Our Cossacks killed some and brought back 13 prisoners.

General Prince Bagration executed on that day the order that he had received the day before to securely occupy Kobbelbude; he sent there the Sumskii Hussar Regiment, which encountered an enemy cavalry detachment, which was defeated, and our hussars, having killed and wounded some enemy troops, took 98 more prisoners.

---

3 Bennigsen's note: See in the 12th letter the direction that General L'Estocq took after the battle of Preussisch-Eylau.
4 Bennigsen's note: The action of Mahnsfeld and Wernsdorf.

Report from Marshal Ney to the Minister of War
Romitten, 16 February
Monseigneur,
I received, this afternoon, at Gross-Lauth the general dispositions that the Emperor ordered today for the change of the army's position. I provisionally sent to generals Klein and Lasalle the necessary orders, so that tomorrow they move closer to Mühlhausen and cover the infantry. On my return here [Romitten], I sent the generals individual instructions for the whole of the operations confided to the rear guard and I neglected nothing to link all of the movements of the echelons. The Emperor can be certain that this movement will be executed steadfastly and that, if the enemy has the audacity to attack me, he will find resistance capable of making him repent of it.

I will always remain close enough to witness the conduct of the troops and that of the officers, and to give the orders that the circumstances might require.

I will take up position, on the 17th, on the plateau behind Eylau and will connect with the Prince de Ponte-Corvo at Schlautienen and, if it is possible, with Marshal Davout.

The enemy has made no demonstrations at my front and on my right, but he seems to want to move some cavalry forces on the left flank of the Prince de Ponte-Corvo.

Instructions from Marshal Ney to the generals of His Corps to Cover the Retreat of the French Army
Gross-Lauth, 16 February 1807
To General Lasalle
Charged by His Majesty to cover the retrograde movement of the *Grande Armée*, which is taking the direction of Osterode, I invite you, my dear General, to take, from this moment, the necessary dispositions to cross onto the left bank of the Frisching via Gross-Lauth. General Guyot's brigade will close the march. This movement will begin at nightfall. Reconnoitre the positions in which you will establish your echelons by brigade, in such a way as to support the tail if the enemy dares to attack it. General Colbert, established at Uderwangen, will hold this post until tomorrow morning and will withdraw on Lewitten and Vierzighüben. Be in active correspondence with this General, who passes under your orders; consequently send him a copy of my letter.

You will only leave General Guyot's brigade at Gross-Lauth, as well as the companies of *voltigeurs* of the *69e de ligne*; the remainder of your division will establish itself at Schrombehnen, Schultitten and Mühlhausen, where you will establish your headquarters.

The general assembly point of your three brigades will be, in case of pressing events, at Vierzighüben, for General Colbert, where General Guyot would anchor himself to cover the plain before Mühlhausen; no one must cross through this latter place if the retreat was forced, General Marchand's infantry being charged with its defence; the remainder of your two brigades, behind Mühlhausen.

General Klein's division will form your reserve echelon and will establish itself, as of this evening, behind Mühlhausen at Knauten and Romitten. I am writing to this General to support you as needed and to give him a general view of the preparatory movements of our light cavalry.

Communicate with the Prince de Ponte-Corvo, who is retreating via Kreuzburg on Porschkam.

I will have my headquarters at Romitten, from which I will send you final instructions.'

On 2/14 February General Bertrand, aide de camp to Emperor Napoleon, had sent through our advance posts a letter by which he informed me that he was charged with a mission by his master to the King of Prussia, and that he was requesting my permission to pass through to Memel. Persuaded that his mission could have no other goal than a [political] rapprochement while military operations continued unabated, I felt I should offer no obstacle to his voyage, all the more so as it was more advantageous than harmful to know the intentions of Napoleon on such an interesting subject. I therefore sent the necessary orders to our advance posts for him to arrive at Königsberg during the night, and I made my report to the King of Prussia, to inform His Majesty of his arrival.

General Bertrand did not stop long at Memel. On February 5/17, in the evening, he had already returned to Königsberg. Indeed, his mission was about general negotiations for peace. The King of Prussia charged himself with communicating to the Emperor of Russia and the other allied powers the pacific intentions of Emperor Napoleon, and to propose a congress to them. As these negotiations continued throughout our winter quarters, I will return to this matter in time. The King of Prussia, in a reciprocal act of civility, shortly thereafter sent his aide-de-camp general, Colonel Kleist, to Osterode, where Napoleon had taken up his headquarters after the French army retreated [from Eylau].

General Bertrand, on his passing through Königsberg, had the kindness to stop at my quarters. In our discussions, he told me among other things that the two armies needed some rest and that he believed that an armistice would be very salutary for both sides. I do not know if this General was authorized to engage in such discussions. I responded that I believed it would be difficult for us to be able to agree on [armistice] conditions, to which he replied: 'Worry not, General, you only need to wish it.' I again repeated to him that concluding a truce would be too difficult, and our discussion turned to some other trivial matters. He resumed his journey at night and returned to his master.

Two days before General Bertrand's return [from Memel], I had received a letter from General Guyot concerning the same subject [of armistice], which was delivered by a French emissary to our advance posts. I have copied it here with my response, convinced as I am that you will share my opinion that this proposal for an armistice was only made to conceal the French army's preparations for withdrawal, which followed soon after this correspondence.

To His Excellency the Commander-in-Chief of the Armies of His Imperial Majesty of all the Russias
Monseigneur,
One of the generals commanding the advance posts of your army yesterday proposed to one of our generals a sort of armistice. I therefore went to the advance posts and asked to contact the commanding general at Ludwigswalde, so as to conclude an agreement to cease all skirmishes at the advance posts

that achieve nothing but exhausting the troops of both armies. M. the Colonel, with whom I spoke, having responded to me that he had orders to receive no emissaries and still less any propositions, I had to turn back, telling him that I came only to respond to the proposal that had been made by one of your general officers. This evening, an emissary arrived and informed me that if I wished to make an offer of armistice to Your Excellency, we could immediately conclude some form of truce.

Quieting for the moment any pridefulness and listening only to the sense of forthrightness that is characteristic to the military men, I wish to revert to the norms that have been established between the Austrian army and others with which we were at war. I therefore have decided, Monsieur General, to propose to you to enter into an arrangement, by means of which we will agree respectively on the extent of time required to inform the other before attacking. I must nevertheless say to you, Monsieur General, that I have no specific authorization to conclude that which was proposed by your officers, but I am certain that I will obtain it from His Imperial Highness the Grand Duke of Berg [Murat], as long as Your Excellency designates someone furnished with the power to conclude the armistice.

I await Your Excellency's response. Please accept the assurances of my highest and most respectful consideration to you.

Commander of the light cavalry of the *Grande Armée*,
Guyot
15 February 1807

Response
To M. General Guyot, Commander of the Light Cavalry of the *Grande Armée*
Mon général,
I just received the letter that you were so gracious to write me and I am pleased to respond with the same military candour that you profess and that our side never abandons. No one is more convinced than me of the uselessness of these minor engagements, random and sporadic as they are, achieving nothing and needlessly exhausting the soldiers of both armies. For some time now I have forbidden our outposts and main outposts from troubling the troops that are before them; but I have not yet authorized anyone to offer to you the kind of armistice that you are, General, proposing to me. To respond to you more precisely, I would have liked to know who might have made this proposition to you but I am still unable to determine that. You speak of a general officer but such an individual is not assigned to the place that you have referred to.

As to the skirmishes that took place in these last days, they do not in any way contravene with the order that I referred above. They are only an inevitable result of the movement of one of your corps which had advanced on the right bank of the Frisching, which I occupy at this moment and which I intend to keep as it is, as you can see on the map, a natural line of demarcation.

Please accept, mon Général, assurances of my special consideration.
Bennigsen
Königsberg, 4/16 February 1807

On 5/17 February, the parties of Cossacks that were sent to harass the chain of enemy advance posts took at the break of day another 112 prisoners at various points. But they encountered infantry advance posts on the left bank of the Frisching and chose to return to the right bank, taking this change for a measure of prudence that the enemy shows so as not being willing to further expose his cavalry, which had been harassed daily ever since the battle of Preussisch-Eylau. That is why it was only in the evening that General Platov informed me that the entire French army was retreating on the road to Landsberg.

I had sent Lieutenant General Prince Bagration to St Petersburg with reports for the Emperor, my master, on the situation in which the army found itself at that moment.[5] General Platov, who consequently commanded the advance guard, immediately moved in pursuit of the enemy with all the light troops that were under his orders. That day General L'Estocq dislodged the enemy from Friedland and occupied that place with a detachment from his corps.

Here, General, I will momentarily fix your attention on the results of my march to Königsberg after the battle of Preussisch-Eylau, and upon the period when the two armies faced each other on the Frisching, that is from 28 January/9 February until 5/17 February, in such close proximity that a single march would have sufficed for them to reach each other.

All of the regular troops of our army had passed these nine days very quietly and thoroughly rested after the great fatigues that the soldiers had endured for more than two months in such a difficult time of the year. Here, near the town of Königsberg, they were well cared for in provisions, *eau-de-vie*, etc. Lieutenant General de Rüchel, Military Governor of Old Prussia, rendered us essential services and put everything in order so that nothing was lacking for us. This good general, who, after the wound he had received at the battle of Jena, had gone to Königsberg, was always very helpful to us there by his activity and his good measures in the conduct of affairs, which were his responsibility and that were often linked with the operations of the army, or other purposes, as you will see.

All the laborers necessary for rapidly repairing our artillery were requisitioned by the Prussian government; in the space of just eight days, the artillery was restored to the best possible state. The regiments that lacked shoes obtained them. Another essential article that we found at Königsberg was a very considerable magazine of hay and oats; it allowed us to furnish our cavalry and our artillery with as much supplies as was necessary to perfectly restore the horses, which, incidentally, had not been extremely worn out, despite the vigorous service in which our light cavalry had constantly been employed.

We also found at Königsberg all of the help imaginable to take good care of our wounded and our sick; spacious buildings were placed at our disposal for this use. The Prussian doctors and surgeons rendered great services in providing first care for the wounded.

I cannot refrain from saying here a word about the inhabitants of Königsberg. When they witnessed the difficulties experienced by those people who were in charge of the hospitals in procuring all that was necessary for such a substantial number of wounded and ill arriving all at once, the inhabitants did their best to contribute and assist in the relief for these poor

---

5   Sacken: '6th [18 February]. Prince Bagration, commanding our advance guard, left for St Petersburg. He despises the way of life many pursue here – everyone is involved in intrigue of some kind.' Osten-Sacken, *Diary*, p.173.

THE RETREAT TO KÖNIGSBERG 193

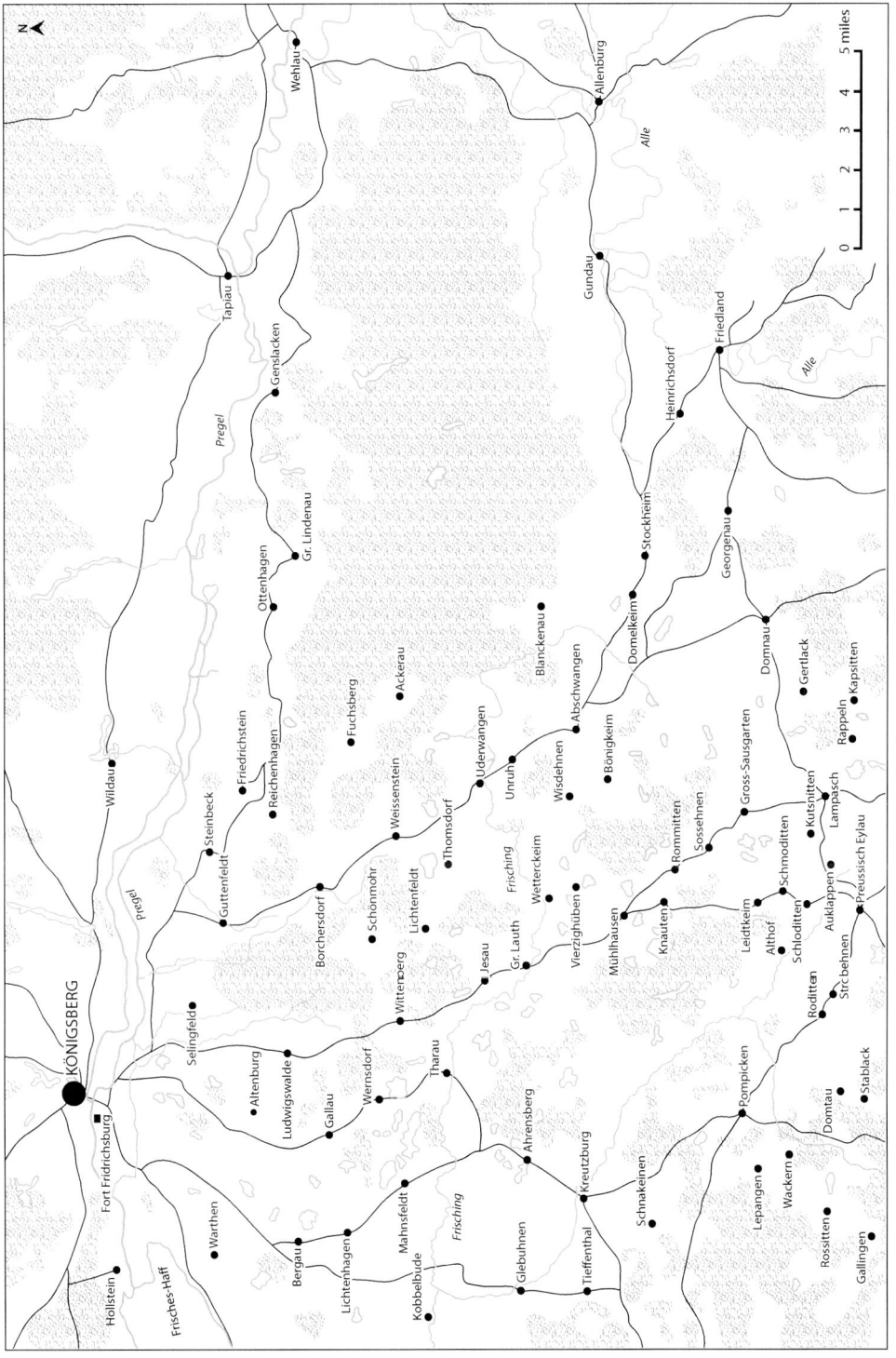

Area between Eylau and Königsberg.

souls.[6] Certain individuals, chosen amongst the most distinguished and the most respectable citizens of this town, namely the Duke of Holstein-Beck, Count Dona, Count Schlieffen, etc., placed themselves at the head of a commission to distribute among the various hospitals all types of aid that the inhabitants had offered. The enemy wounded, of which there were a few hundred, equally enjoyed the charitable deeds of the inhabitants; one of them was specifically charged with the care of the hospital designated for French prisoners. In short, the inhabitants of Königsberg sensed how much they owed at this time to the Russian army, and they tried to express their gratefulness as much as they could. I do not think the French army could not say as much about its stay in the environs of Preussisch-Eylau and on the Frisching. You will soon see it when I discuss its retreat and the despondent state of its cavalry horses.

> Marshal Ney to the Minister of War
> Preussisch-Eylau, 17 February 1807, six o'clock in the afternoon
> I have the honour of informing Your Excellency that, conforming with the dispositions that I ordered yesterday, the *corps d'armée* was under arms before six o'clock in the morning. The troops set in movement, marching, the left at the front, in the following order: General Gardanne's division, assembled behind Knauten, alongside the dragoons from Klein's division, opened the march. General Marchand's division, assembled behind Mühlhausen, with General Lasalle's light cavalry, began its retreat at noon. As of now, the troops hold the prescribed positions, which are:
> General Gardanne's division, on the heights behind Eylau, near Topprienen and Grünhöfchen. General Klein's dragoons, except for a regiment at Serpallen, are placed by echelons on the road from Landsberg to the height of Gallehnen. General Marchand's division occupies with its 1st brigade the position to the right of Eylau, the road from Domnau and by its 2nd the left of this town, near the windmill, the road from Kreuzburg. This division's *voltigeurs* hold Schmoditten and Schloditten.
> General Lasalle's light cavalry is placed behind Eylau, except for the brigades of generals Colbert and Guyot, which covered the movement of the army and occupy Goserken, Althof, Leidtkeim, Gross-Sausgarten, Kutschitten and Lampasch.
> The enemy did not follow the retrograde movement because I took the precaution of moving onto the left bank of the Frisching before midnight the cavalry advance posts, which were on the opposite bank, and to hold with infantry the fords and bridges, by which the enemy could debouche. It is to be supposed that the enemy feared an ambush, because he followed the cavalry to the Frisching without troubling it and, as soon as he saw the infantry, he retired in great haste. It was only at 12:30 p.m. that an officer of the Russian hussars and six men showed themselves on the height of Gross-Lauth. One of my *aides de camp*, who had stayed at the rear, observed him, and made it seem as though he was going to pursue him; then the observer retired. Since that moment, nothing has appeared to trouble our march.

---

6   Sacken: '5th [12 February]. I visited hospitals, which are in the most miserable condition. We have over 8,000 wounded, many of whom still have not been treated. Some 100 [wounded] are dying every day.' Osten-Sacken, *Diary*, p.173.

All of the wounded have been evacuated except for two men, who are too gravely wounded to be moved and who will probably die. The troops received here, through the care of my *ordonnateur*, two days worth of bread. Tomorrow, at five o'clock in the morning, the troops will be under arms and will move on Landsberg, observing the order of march that I established for today.

General Bertrand's *aide de camp* will leave tomorrow in broad daylight to transmit to His Majesty the reports that reach me on the enemy's movements. I do not think, after what happened today, that the enemy will dare follow me; the plain, due to the thaw, is absolutely impracticable for cavalry. This leaves only the main roads, which are in equally atrocious state…

6/18 February. I told you, General, in my relation from yesterday, that Marshal Ney, as you can see from his report, had fooled our Cossacks by the infantry that he had placed at every point of his advance posts, which gained the enemy rear guard an entire day and allowed it to retire without being followed. Moreover, due to the thaw which had begun, the roads were already so muddy and the lowlands on the plains so impassable that it would have been almost impossible for the infantry of our advance guard to make a forced march to support our light cavalry, especially with artillery, as you will soon see by a report from Marshal Ney himself. Nevertheless, General Platov occupied Preussisch-Eylau that evening with a detachment of Cossacks, which found in the town our wounded, gravely afflicted on the day of 27 January that could not be transported; there were three senior officers, four junior officers, and a few hundred soldiers. Our Cossacks, on the various roads they were sent down in pursuit of the enemy, took 90 men from Bernadotte's corps during the day.

The same day, I ordered all of the army's divisions to set in march and approach the Frisching. The cantonment quarters for the march of the army were assigned in the following manner:

> The 5th Division at Wernsdorf, the 8th at Wittenberg, the 3rd at Uderwangen, the 2nd at Abschwangen, the 7th at Schönfliess, the 14th at Neuendorf, the 4th at Ackerau. The advance guard, under the orders of General Platov, formed itself in two detachments, to follow the enemy down two paths; one crossed the Frisching early in the morning at Kreuzburg, the road that the Prince de Ponte-Corvo had taken with his corps, and the second, which General Platov personally commanded, crossed the Frisching at Gross-Lauth.

Marshal Ney to the Minister of War
Landsberg, 18 February 1807, five o'clock in the Afternoon
I have the honour of informing Your Excellency that the troops were under arms before six o'clock in the morning, and that they set in march from Preussisch-Eylau, in the same order as the preceding day to move to Landsberg. The enemy had not appeared. General Klein's division of dragoons, assembled on the heights behind Gallehnen, opened the march as soon as the head of the column of General Gardanne's infantry division left its position at Grünhöfchen. General Lasalle's light cavalry division [for the same reason] had assembled at Storchnest and followed on the left flank of Gardanne's division.

General Marchand was unable to move before 10 o'clock in the morning; the march was closed by General Colbert's light cavalry brigade, which still occupied Eylau and Schmoditten at noon. The troops, being extremely fatigued by the difficulty of the roads, will be in cantonments as of today in the following order:

> General Klein's dragoons at Drewenz and environs;
> General Lasalle's light cavalry division at Wotterlack, Paustern, Gross-Pehsten and Eichhorn;
> General Gardanne's infantry division, at Hof, Sienken and Gross-Glandau;
> General Marchand's division, at Landsberg;
> General Colbert's brigade of light cavalry and a battalion of *voltigeurs*, at Woymanns, Eichen, Worienen and Müggen.

Tomorrow the army will move on Freymarkt, to take cantonments there.

I will send Your Excellency the dispositions that I ordered to that effect.

I hope that we will retrieve the cannons and munitions caissons from the atrocious roads from Eylau to Landsberg.

I think that humanity requires that we leave at Landsberg part of the wounded brought from Eylau. The wagons, in which they are loaded, have broken down or become stuck in the mud. Several of these unfortunate souls died en route, and it is to condemn them to a certain death if we continue to lug them around in this way. We will take those who will be able to survive transportation.

Tomorrow I will leave a battalion of *voltigeurs* and General Guyot's brigade of line cavalry, who will relieve General Colbert from Landsberg to Bürgerswalde, so as to protect the removal of our munitions and wounded.

Four Cossacks arrived today at noon at Eylau, escorting General Bertrand, His Majesty's *aide de camp*. The enemy doubtlessly wished to profit from this occasion to confirm our retreat; nevertheless, he was unable to see anything concerning the evacuation of Eylau, which we still occupied fairly strongly at that time. The enemy was incidentally stopped at Schloditten and sent back immediately, escorted fairly far from there toward Mühlhausen.

P.S. – One of my *aides de camp* returning from the rear guard informed me that two *pelotons* of Cossacks appeared at Eylau, toward three o'clock in the afternoon, without firing a shot; they did not even follow the retrograde march of our troops.

We heard a light fusillade toward Orschen and Eichen, the route held by the Prince of Ponto-Corvo; I just sent one of my officers there. It seems that we will be obliged to abandon several caissons of munitions; in today's march alone, more than 50 transport horses died: they are collapsing from starvation and due to the lack of food. If the road is as horrible tomorrow, I fear I will be obliged to abandon my artillery.

Lieutenant General L'Estocq had received news that the brave General Rouquette, who had gotten himself out of a tight spot until this time with as much skill as prudence with his small detachment, which only consisted of a single infantry battalion and seven squadrons, being charged, with this handful of men, with the defence of the Niedrigung, after having had on multiple occasions success against Drouet's division in the environs of Preussisch-Holland, had been obliged to yield, on 11 February (new style), to the great superiority of the enemy forces that he met in the environs of Marienwerder, and to retire with losses on Danzig.

You will find, General, in the following letter the continuation of the events that took place until the two commanders of the hostile armies thought it necessary to give the troops some rest in winter quarters, after so much wear and spilled blood, and to gain time to repair their losses.

14

Return to the Offensive – Braunsberg

Before continuing the account of the operations of the two hostile armies, I think it necessary, General, to make you aware of the forces remaining to me at this especially important moment, so that you may judge more precisely if my forces allowed me to act with greater vigour. You know how greatly I respect the judgments passed on my operations whenever they are supported by judicious reflections and made with full knowledge of the facts. I think I can do no better than to communicate to you here the report that I received on the state of the army the day that it departed from the environs of Königsberg to pursue the French army in its retreat.[1] You will note that I found myself at the head of 37,000 regular troops and 2,500 Cossacks. Lieutenant General L'Estocq's *corps*, which was destined to cover the right of the main army and reinforce it if necessary, amounted to 9,000 men. I could therefore rally for a battle some 46,000 regular troops and 2,500 Cossacks.

As I told you in my twelfth letter, the French army was, once the corps of Ney and Bernadotte joined it, more than 70,000 men strong, its infantry almost double the size of my own. In cavalry, we had in every respect an advantage over that of the enemy, whose horses were in an extreme state of weakness, whereas those of our cavalry were still vigorous and in a good state. But with start of the thaw, the weather made the plains virtually impassable and the cavalry could only move on the roads; Napoleon then assembled everything that he actually had available in troops, behind his army, to reinforce it. The reserves received orders to join him. The divisions of Molitor and Boudet departed from Istria to reinforce the *Grande Armée*; some 20,000 conscripts were sent from France, in addition to the 20,000 already sent in the month of November.[2] Napoleon sent to the Senate, in Paris, a report from the Minister of War, accompanied by an Imperial Decree by which he requested the levy of the *conscription* of the year 1808. The Polish troops that were already formed received orders to join the army and to hasten the formation of the rest of the 30,000 men that the provinces belonging to the King of Prussia had offered to furnish at their expense. The princes of Germany, who formed the Confederation of the Rhine, received pressing communications to hasten the movement of their contingents. The princes newly accepted into in the League of the Rhine were also obliged to send their contingents, including: the Princes of Anhalt – 800 men; Schwarzenberg – 650 men;

---

1 Bennigsen's note: See the end of the letter.
2 Bennigsen's note: See the 12th letter.

Reuss – 450 men and Waldeck – 400 men. Finally, some 16,000 Spanish troops were sent to reinforce the French army.

You will find, General, in my following correspondence, an amazing state of forces to which Napoleon had raised his army for the second campaign.

For my part, immediately after the battle of Preussisch-Eylau, I had sent a report to the Emperor, my master, by which I demonstrated to him the necessity of sending everything that was still available in Russia. Lieutenant General Prince Bagration personally delivered a letter reiterating this request, after which His Majesty deigned to give the order that the 1st Division, which included the [Russian] Imperial Guard units, under the command of Grand Duke Constantine and 17,000 men strong, should march from St. Petersburg to reinforce the army. The most pressing orders were sent to the interior of the Empire, so as to hasten the formation of units and the recruitment of conscripts that were also destined to complete and reinforce the army.

When I was persuaded that the enemy no longer intended to fight a second battle for the moment, and foreseeing incidentally that the enemy would not be able to hold for long in his position between Preussisch-Eylau and the Frisching and would soon be forced to retreat, I dispatched Lieutenant General Count Tolstoy to Goniondz, on the river Bobr, to bring back to the army the *corps* that I had left there under the orders of General Siedmioraczki, for the reasons that I explained in my eighth letter. I could no longer do without this *corps*, given the circumstances in which the army found itself. To fulfil the responsibilities of the duty general of the army [*général de service de l'armée*], which Count Tolstoy fulfilled, I named Major General Fock, who had arrived the day before the battle of Preussisch-Eylau, where he distinguished himself greatly, as you will have noted in the account of that day, and who enjoyed the respect of the army, having always served with the greatest distinction.

Lieutenant General Essen I had detached 2,500 men (under the orders of Lieutenant General Prince Volkonsky) from his *corps,* which was stationed on the Narew and the Bug, and sent them to that of General Siedmioraczki. A detachment of 5,000 Don Cossacks was also close to joining the army. I instructed General Count Tolstoy to concentrate these forces and operate with this *corps* in the rear of the French army should it maintain its position, or, if it retreats, to harass its right flank and to open communications with Lieutenant General L'Estocq's *corps*.

On 7/19 February, my divisions executed the orders of the previous day and concentrated on the Frisching. I invited Lieutenant General L'Estocq to also move forward with his corps to pursue the enemy, and to proceed in the direction of Heilsberg, from where this General should take up position on the right wing of the army. General Platov continued to follow the enemy with light troops and harass his rear guard.

> Marshal Ney to the Minister of War
> Landsberg, 19 February 1807, 10 o'clock in the Morning
> I received Your Excellency's letter, which instructed me to halt my movement today, so that the artillery can follow me. I had, as of yesterday evening, ordered General Marchand to establish his division in echelons from here to Drewenz and to occupy, in concert with General Guyot's light cavalry brigade, Woymanns, Orschen, Worienen and Palassen; but General Gardanne's division, as well as

General Klein's dragoons and the remainder of General Lasalle's light cavalry, are marching to occupy cantonments in Freymarkt, Arensdorf and environs.

We spent the entire night withdrawing the artillery and the munitions caissons that were stuck in the mud; we will do everything possible today, tonight, and even all of tomorrow morning, so that the vast majority [of artillery] moves forward. All of our artillery has been saved; we only lost five caissons. My *sapeurs* repaired the road from here to Hof; two battalions had to be employed to repair the worst sections of the road. Everyone has redoubled their zeal to extricate us from the extreme predicament in which we found ourselves yesterday. I can assure Your Excellency that not one of the *corps d'armée*'s wagons would have remained in the rear if not for the great quantity of wagons and baggage, of convoys and caissons of the *1er Corps* and the Imperial Guard, which obliged our horses to remain for six hours in the mud without eating, after which they were without energy and falling from exhaustion at the slightest effort that had to be made to pull the artillery from the mud.

The Prince de Ponte-Corvo slept yesterday at Bucholtz; he informs me that only through incredible exertion would he be able to move his artillery and baggage on such bad roads. I informed him of my position and my firm resolve to wait for my artillery.

I thank Your Excellency for the care that he has shown us and for providing us with bread and *eau-de-vie* at Freymarkt. I will leave around noon to go to Freymarkt.

On 9/21 February, Lieutenant General Platov moved toward Landsberg, where he arrived at two o'clock in the afternoon, just as the last of the enemy troops were departing. During his march two regiments of Cossacks, which served as his advance guard, surprised an enemy dragoon regiment at daybreak and captured 134 prisoners after killing and wounding a fair number of men. In the town the enemy had abandoned four officers and 380 wounded soldiers, along with three surgeons; these men could not be transported any further given the lack of wagons and horses. That day our Cossacks also took a considerable number of carriages and munitions caissons that the enemy had abandoned, both on the muddy roads and in the town of Landsberg. Our army moved forward by divisions, which took the following cantonments:

Lieutenant General Prince Golitsyn, with part of the cavalry at Forst-Amt; the remainder of the cavalry was dispersed into the divisions forming the flanks of the army;

The 5th Division at Kreuzburg; the 8th at Jesau; the 3rd at Mühlhausen; the 2nd at Preussisch-Eylau; the 7th at Lichtenhagen; the 14th at Ludwigswalde; the 4th at Uderwangen; the general rallying point, in case of emergency, was set at Preussisch-Eylau. General L'Estocq arrived with his *corps* at Domnau.

Marshal Ney to the Minister of War
Freymarkt, 21 February 1807, seven o'clock in the Morning
I just received the letter from Your Excellency dated today at two o'clock in the morning, which instructed me to arrange my cavalry in such a manner as to be able to vigorously repel the parties of Cossacks that would dare to follow my rear guard.

Your Excellency will have noted in my letter from this morning that the sole brigade of light cavalry remaining to me is marching on Heilsberg, along with an infantry regiment, to prevent the capture of flour supplies that Marshal Davout gathered there. General Lasalle is also moving to Neidenburg as ordered by His Royal Highness the Grand Duke of Berg [Murat]. The enemy, after the defeat that he suffered yesterday,[3] has no longer appeared and probably will not dare to undertake anything against my infantry, which, far from fearing it, scorns all of the Cossacks [*cosaqueries*]. It is not the same with our light cavalry, and the reason lies not in a panicky terror, but in the exhaustion of the horses that have been deprived of food for six days and that are barely able to carry their rider, not to mention to gallop. Yesterday, the cavalry rested and found fodder in abundance in the cantonments that it occupied. Your Excellency must believe that I am in no mood to allow my rear guard to be harassed when there is the possibility of making the enemy stop it.

I am fully cognizant of the importance of Guttstadt and Your Excellency may rest assured that amidst my general dispositions I devote the utmost attention to this point and make sure to avoid any surprises and make the enemy regret it if he should dare to attempt to come after us. I will remain at Guttstadt and will go wherever the good of the service demands. The Prussians, according to what I was told this morning by one of Marshal Davout's aides de camp, occupy Bartenstein with cavalry and infantry. It is possible that they think that our retreat is decided. If they move further up the Alle, they will find the same soldiers that have beaten them everywhere and who will beat them again.

Other Report from Marshal Ney on the Same Date
21 February 1807, six o'clock in the morning
I received the general dispositions ordered by His Majesty for the emplacement of the corps of the *Grande Armée*. I have given the necessary orders for the execution of those concerning my corps. I will hold Arensdorf today with an infantry brigade; tomorrow, it will move toward its destination points at Quetz and Allenstein. General Marchand's division will approach Guttstadt today, which it will only be able to occupy this evening, since Marshal Davout, according to what he wrote me, can only evacuate it this afternoon.

I am also sending, at the suggestion of this Marshal [Davout], an infantry regiment and General Colbert's light cavalry brigade to Heilsberg, to safeguard the transportation of 50,000 rations of flour. Tomorrow these forces will return to the cantonments assigned them.

I have no news concerning the position of General Grouchy's dragoons.

I leave this morning for Guttstadt; I will have the honour of addressing within the day or tomorrow morning the dispositions that I made to fulfil the intentions of His Majesty relative to the positions ordered for the 6th Corps.

---

3 Bennigsen's note: This is an error! There was not a single man wounded on our side in the action of the day before, when our Cossacks took 134 prisoners from a French dragoon regiment that they had surprised.

On 10/22 February, I informed Lieutenant General Platov that having received reports on the difficulties that all of the artillery and even the supply wagons were experiencing due to the impassable roads, I had ordered, so as not to wreck the horses, that the divisions take a day of rest. At the same time, I ordered General Platov to continue to harass the enemy rear guard; but given that the infantry and cavalry were unable to follow closely to support him, I recommended all necessary prudence in this pursuit.

Unremitting thaw had made the roads increasingly impassable with each passing day. The artillery and especially the supplies, whose wagons got stuck in the mud at every step, slowed the march of the Russian army in pursuit of the enemy, whereas the latter found in his retreat the supplies sent to follow his army.

I had invited Lieutenant General L'Estocq to expedite his march so as to be able to cross the Alle before the arrival of the bulk of the Russian army and then to move between this river and the Passarge and take up a position with his *corps* on the right wing of the army. I had also instructed Prussian Lieutenant General de Plötz's detachment, which was at Brandenburg, to follow the banks of the Frische-Haff up to Heiligenbeil, from where he was supposed to occupy Braunsberg with his advance posts. As I have already told you, his detachment amounted to about 2,500 men, including the Russian troops, the Kaluzhskii Musketeer Regiment under command of Kazachkovsky,[4] and a few Cossacks. At the same time Plötz's detachment was instructed to establish communications with the 5th Division, commanded by General Tuchkov, until the arrival of Lieutenant General L'Estocq. The latter directed his march from Allenburg via Domnau to Bartenstein, from where he detached a Prussian detachment to attack the small town of Heilsberg. Lieutenant Colonel de Stutterheim was at the head of these troops and executed this mission with wisdom and intrepidness; he forced the enemy to abandon this town in haste and leave behind some of the supplies. Major d'Arnim, with a Prussian detachment, occupied Bischofstein, from which he dislodged the enemy and took a few prisoners. I invited General L'Estocq to direct the march of his *corps* to Heilsberg on the 11th/23rd and to Wormditt on the 12th/24th, so he can easily reunite with General de Plötz's detachment and cover the Russian army's right flank.

The French army made its retreat in a fairly concentrated order. When Marshal Ney, forming the centre of the 1st line, was at Freymarkt, Marshal Bernadotte formed the left wing at Bucholtz and Marshal Davout – the right wing at Guttstadt, while the rest of the army crossed the Passarge to approach Osterode.

> Marshal Ney to the Minister of War
> Guttstadt, 22 February 1807
> On my arrival here yesterday evening, I found Marshal Davout and some of his troops occupying Guttstadt. I stopped my own [corps] outside the town, except for an infantry regiment and General Colbert's light cavalry that moved to Heilsberg to relieve General Gudin's division. Today, the *3e Corps* moved to Allenstein;

---

4   Colonel Kirill Kazachkovsky, the chef of the Kaluzhskii Musketeer Regiment in 1806–1814. He was promoted to a major general in December 1807.

tomorrow, my troops will occupy the positions assigned in the general dispositions, of which a copy is attached.

The enemy made no movements today on the Alle, nor on my left by Landsberg. Nevertheless, the reports reaching me indicate that Prussian Lieutenant General L'Estocq's corps, to which a Russian battalion is joined, is marching to Bartenstein. Today I toured the various defensive positions around Guttstadt and I have determined to select the one on the heights behind this town, with the right wing in the direction of Knopen and the left in the direction of the lake of Sawanna, with the roads from Liebstadt and from Osterode via Quetz on my two flanks. I do not believe that the enemy can force me to evacuate Guttstadt. We will employ all means of surveillance and enterprise to make the enemy regret any attempt [to threaten us]. I will inform Marshals Soult and Davout of anything concerning the good of the service of His Majesty.

Marshal Ney's Order of the Day states the following:
By the orders of His Majesty [Emperor Napoleon], the *6e Corps* will occupy Guttstadt and Allenstein, and place its park, magazines, and ambulances at an intermediary point from Allenstein to Osterode. The troops will be in cantonments so as to be able to concentrate in two marches at Osterode, the general assembly point for the entire *Grande Armée*. Therefore, General Marchand's division will leave today from its position at Freymarkt and environs and move on Guttstadt. The light infantry brigade and the *3e de ligne* will occupy Lingnau, Altkirch, Gronau, Peterswalde and Zechern. Assembly point will be Altkirch, where General Belair will establish himself. This brigade will connect its left with Marshal Soult's troops at Elditten via Wolfsdorf and will push its patrols and reconnaissance on Heilsberg and Landsberg.

General Marcognet's Brigade, the *69e* and *76e* as well as the *1er Division*'s headquarters [*état-major*] will be at Guttstadt. Divisional assembly point – Guttstadt.

General Colbert with his brigade of light cavalry will continue to occupy Zechern, in concert with General Belair, until further orders.

The *1er Brigade* of the *2e Division*, the *25e légère* and *27e de ligne* will leave Sommerfeld and Reichswalde to march and spend the night at Quetz, Rosengarth and Münsterberg, occupying with posts all of the bridges on the Alle, from Knopen to the height of Münsterberg.

The *27e* [regiment] will take cantonments at Buchwalde, Jonkowo and Mondtken. General Roguet will establish himself at Rosengarth, indicated as the brigade assembly point.

The *2e Brigade*, the *50e* and *59e* [regiments] will leave Arensdorf, spend the night at Guttstadt and then proceed to Allenstein. The *50e* will occupy Unter- and Ober-Kapkeim, Süssenthal and Spiegelberg; the *59e* – Digitten and Allenstein. The brigades, according to the orders of General Gardanne, will take their own directions toward Osterode, if this movement becomes necessary; this division will link its right with Marshal Davout's corps at Hohenstein.

General Grouchy's division of dragoons will occupy Reichenberg, Klingerswalde and Eschenau. Assembly point for the *1er Brigade* is at Liebenberg; for the *2e* – Nosberg and the *3e* – Klingerswalde. Divisional assembly point – Klingerswalde.

You will soon see, General, that the enemy partially changed this disposition. On 11/23 February, General Platov remained with the headquarters of the advance guard at Landsberg; but the army moved forward and was placed in cantonments in the following manner:

> Lieutenant General Prince Golitsyn, with the majority of the cavalry, was at Orschen, to be able to support General Platov.
> In the 1st line: the 5th Division, under the orders of Lieutenant General Tuchkov, as the right wing, at Gross-Labehnen;
> The 8th Division, under the orders of Lieutenant General Dokhturov, as the centre, at Waldkeim;
> The 3rd Division, under the orders of General Sacken, at Forst-Amt;
> The 2nd Division, under the orders of Lieutenant General Count Ostermann, as the left wing, at Preussisch-Eylau.
> In the 2nd line: the 7th Division, as the right wing, at Ahrensberg;
> The 4th Division, as the left wing, at Mühlhausen;
> The 14th Division, under the orders of General Count Kamensky, in reserve, at Jesau.
> The general assembly point for the army was set at Preussisch-Eylau.

Lieutenant General Count Tolstoy arrived with his *corps* at Schippenbeil and Lieutenant General Prince Volkonsky's detachment moved via Rastenburg. General L'Estocq's headquarters arrived at Sperwarten.

An enemy detachment, which still occupied the forest before Wormditt, evacuated it, crossed the Passarge, and established itself behind the bridge below Sportehnen. Lieutenant General Platov reported that he was closely observing the enemy and that he was also following him with his Cossacks at each step of his retreat; that a few [Cossack] parties had slipped through as far as Guttstadt; that the various detachments of his advance guard had taken 106 prisoners; that the enemy had been obliged to abandon a cannon stuck in the mud on the bad roads, and that a great number of carriages had also fallen into the hands of the Cossacks.

I was obliged to halt, on 12/24 February, the march of our heavy artillery so as not to entirely wear out the horses on those bad roads. The extent to which the French suffered from the bad roads and lack of supplies can be gleaned from the following report that Marshal Ney submitted to the Minister of War [Berthier] 12/24 on February, in which he noted:

> We are having the greatest difficulty with supplies. It is hard to convey the gravity of the present situation. Bread is lacking entirely; there is barely any cattle remaining for meat; forage is equally wanting. If Your Excellency does not deign to transfer some basic necessities to us in Guttstadt, we will certainly starve to death. If I could spread my troops into cantonments other than those that I am forced to occupy at Guttstadt and its environs, we would certainly find sustenance to survive. But

as it is, due to the proximity of the enemy, there is nothing to be had here. Your Excellency knows that I would plead for supplies only in the extreme and that is truly where we are reduced to today.[5]

The enemy burned the bridges on the Passarge at Spanden and Alcken. The Prussian Lieutenant General Plötz's advance guard dislodged an enemy detachment from Braunsberg and forced it to retire via Zagern on Gross-Tromp. [Prussian] Majors de Roche-Aymon and de Szerdahelly and Lieutenant Koch distinguished themselves greatly in this action. The Prussians took some prisoners including two officers; they also brought back 32 horses taken from the enemy.

On 13/25 February, the army's headquarters was established at Landsberg; the advance guard's headquarters – at Arensdorf. Lieutenant General Prince Golitsyn, with most of the cavalry, advanced to Petershagen. The rest of the army also moved forward. The 1st line, whose right wing extended to Orschen, moved through Landsberg, Gross-Pehsten, Eichhorn up to Albrechtsdorf, where the left wing anchored itself. The 2nd line occupied the distance from Schönwiese to Zohlen and the reserve took up the quarters of Preussisch-Eylau and environs, which the 2nd line had just left. The point for a general assembly of the army was set near Landsberg.

Lieutenant General L'Estocq arrived with his corps in the environs of Wormditt. Lieutenant Colonel de Stutterheim, who had covered the march of this *corps*, moved into the environs of Sporthenen, to observe there the bridge on the Passarge. General L'Estocq took the necessary precautions to defend all crossings on the Passarge where the enemy would have been able to make attempts to harass his troops in the cantonment quarters.

On February 14/26, the army remained in the same position. General Platov reported that the day before, during the pursuit of the enemy, his Cossacks had taken in several engagements 150 prisoners and that they had again taken an enemy cannon stuck in the mud on the bad roads.

Upon my departure from Königsberg with the army, I had invited the Prussian Lieutenant General de Plötz to advance with his detachment, amounting to – as you will have observed – about 2,500 men including the Russian Kaluzhskii Musketeer Regiment, from Brandenburg to Heiligenbeil moving alongside the Frische-Haff; to establish himself there and to hold a post at Braunsberg and on the Frisching his chain of light troops whose right would anchor itself on the banks of the Frische-Haff, while the left would connect itself to the right of the main army; and to await in this position the arrival of General L'Estocq, with his *corps d'armée*. This general however judged it appropriate to act differently than indicated in my dispositions. He went with his small detachment to Braunsberg, from where he sent part to the other side of this town. Marshal Bernadotte, who had received orders not to permit enemy detachments to remain on the left bank of the Passarge, then attacked him with part of his corps and repulsed him with considerable losses. Major General Kazachkovsky,

---

5   According to Wilson, 'A French general, Thierry, with his aide-de-camp, has come over to the Russians. He describes the state of the French army as most deplorable from discontent and want of provisions. Indeed, there is every reason to believe that his accounts are not exaggerated. Without doubt, Buonaparte has been discomfited to a degree that he has never before experienced in Europe.' *Life of General Sir Robert Wilson*, vol.2, p.79.

commander of the Kaluzhskii Musketeer Regiment, reported to me the following details concerning this affair:

On 14/26 February, at two o'clock in the afternoon, the advance posts made known that the enemy was advancing and that the main outpost was already engaged. General de Plötz, upon this news, sent the remainder of his detachment to the other side of the town to meet the enemy and ordered the Russian Kaluzhskii Musketeer Regiment, which formed the left wing of his detachment, to deploy at two points: the battalion of grenadiers to the left and the two battalions of musketeers more to the right, so as to defend from the enemy the entrance to the town on this side, while strong French columns had already repulsed all of the Prussian advance posts which were retiring via the town.

General Kazachkovsky joined the action and, by means of a well-directed fire, not only stopped the enemy column, but also made it fall back for more than 300 paces. With that General de Plötz ordered the Russian regiment to advance, which it executed resolutely over a distance of 500 paces to the village of Stangendorf, which General de Plötz ordered General Kazachkovsky to take. The latter noted the inequality of his forces in comparison to those of the enemy, but General de Plötz insisted on the attack. His orders were executed immediately by Captain Bistrom, at the head of some skirmishers and volunteers. But behind this village were in fact the principal forces of Bernadotte's corps, hidden by a small wood that was in the vicinity and a fog that had covered the terrain. Barely had the Kaluzhskii Regiment penetrated the village when it came under fire from artillery and muskets on its right wing from an enemy column that tried to cut it off from Braunsberg. General Kazachkovsky, seeing the danger in which he was, being too far forward from the rest of the detachment that General de Plötz had formed in front of Braunsberg, decided to retreat to the Prussian line. But the enemy had already gained too much time. Marshal Bernadotte attacked with part of his corps the right wing of the small Prussian detachment which he broke and forced to retire in haste through the town. General Kazachkovsky was forced to halt for some time the superior enemy forces, which pressed him closely, in order to gain enough time for his battalion of grenadiers, under the orders of Lieutenant-Colonel Michelson, to rejoin him and save, if it was still possible, his artillery, whose horses were killed; the soldiers had to pull the cannon from the roads that had become impassable due to the thaws. But as the enemy directed all of his forces against the Kaluzhskii Musketeer Regiment, General Kazachkovsky could only with difficulty rejoin his grenadiers battalion, although with a great loss of men and of two cannon that got stuck in the mud. He retreated under constant fire and entered the town by the same gate by which he had left it.

At the same time the enemy penetrated the town by a different gate, so the Kaluzhskii Regiment and a Prussian battalion, then forming the rear guard, were obliged to break through the enemy in order to pass through the town. Having arrived at the bridge over the Passarge, they once again suffered a violent discharge of canister from an artillery battery that the enemy had had time to deploy on the Passarge itself, awfully close to the town, at the crossing of which the Kaluzhskii Regiment had been obliged to abandon another cannon. In the end, the casualties of Kaluzhskii Musketeer Regiment in killed, wounded and prisoners amounted to 10 officers and 502 non-commissioned officers and soldiers. The Prussians lost about as many, which reduced this small detachment to about half of what it had been before the combat. After this unfortunate affair, General de Plötz executed my first instruction; he retired with the remainder of his troops to Heiligenbeil and placed the chain of his advance posts before Braunsberg. The loss of these brave men, who perished so uselessly in this affair, was all the more notable as the circumstances required that we avoid as much as possible any action that could further weaken our army. Lieutenant General de Plötz shortly after this day retired from the army; H.M. the King of Prussia granted his retirement with a pension appropriate to his rank, in recognition of the great and honest services that he had previously rendered to the state.[6]

> Marshal Ney to the Minister of War
> Guttstadt, 26 February 1807, one o'clock in the Morning
> All reports confirm that the enemy continues his movements on my left; yesterday, at nightfall, a second infantry column, composed of a few Prussian battalions, defiled from Heilsberg toward Launau and Freymarkt. General Roguet, placed at Quetz, informs me that around 400 cavalrymen arrived before the night to attack for the second time the village of Scharnick. The infantry, after having repulsed the enemy as far as Wolfsdorf, found there greater forces and was forced to remain on the defence; we killed and wounded a great many enemy cavalry. The post of Lingnau, in pushing its reconnaissance on Petersdorf, noticed around 200 cavalrymen. General Roguet also informs me that he heard cannon fire from the direction of Liebstadt and that communications via Wolfsdorf and Elditten were completely cut off.
>
> The enemy, yesterday at nightfall, made a new reconnaissance along the entire length of my outposts on the right bank of the Alle. He showed around 1,200 horses between Heilsberg and Seeburg. The environs of Wartenburg and Allenstein were tranquil until then and our cavalry reconnaissance went as far as Passenheim without meeting anything.
>
> Lieutenant General L'Estocq arrived yesterday at Heilsberg, where he is with a few infantry regiments; the remainder of his *corps d'armée* is on the march from Bartenstein. I have been assured that this division, having received new reinforcements from Königsberg, amounts to 12–14,000 men and that it will serve to the left as support for the Russian columns, which must shortly return to the offensive and move on Wormditt and Mehlsack.
>
> We assume that the *aide de camp* Colonel de Kleist, sent by the King of Prussia to H.M. the Emperor, is charged with no important mission and that he is simply an observer. Your Excellency will no doubt know more in that respect than the reports that I am making to him.
>
> I have attached here the translation of a notification sent to the magistrates of the area in the name of the General Bennigsen to see to the subsistence of the Russian columns that, according to this piece, are in full march on Mehlsack. This notification was intercepted at General Colbert's advance posts; I do not know if the notification is a feint or real.[7] The enemy seems to be employing all stratagems to force us to cede terrain and to mislead us regarding his true designs; no doubt the reports

---

6 This account of the Russian setback at Braunsberg is missing in the Russian edition of the memoirs.
7 Bennigsen's note: I had indeed distributed this notification to make the enemy uncertain as to our march.

from Marshal Soult and the Prince de Ponte-Corvo will provide Your Excellency the degree of confidence merited by the notification in question, that I join here in the original with the translation.[8]

On 15/27 February, the army remained in the same position. Lieutenant General Platov reported that on the 14th/26th Major General Baron Korff,[9] finding himself at the advance posts with two battalions from his jager regiment in the village of Peterswalde, had dropped his guard so much so that the enemy had managed to surprise him and take him prisoner, as well as his *aide de camp* as he was leaving his quarters to join his troops. The imprudence this general demonstrated on this occasion is simply unheard of. The assembly of his troops was set at one end of the village, while he, to obtain better lodging, decided to take his quarters on the other side of the village. Two Cossacks arrived one after the other to inform him of the approaching enemy, but found him still in bed. He barely had time to dress and leave his quarters when the enemy took him prisoner along with his *aide de camp*.

Encouraged by this success, the enemy passed through the village with superior forces, advancing against our two battalions of jagers, who were already at arms, thanks to the alarm and the news that 30 or so Cossacks had given them by their retreat from the advance posts. Instead of seeing their commander arrive, which they expected, these troops were vigorously attacked by the enemy. Our detachment defended itself bravely; but, unable to resist the superior enemy forces, it decided to retire along the road to Zechern, where there was a more considerable detachment of our advance guard. These two battalions made an orderly retreat and, although they were not closely followed, they still lost, as a result of General Korff's unpardonable negligence, in killed, one officer, one non-commissioned officer, and 43 jagers; in wounded, two staff officers, two junior officers, and 151 jagers. The enemy losses were certainly no less considerable thanks to the bravery with which our detachment defended itself.

You will soon see, General, in Marshal Ney's report to the Minister of War, the Prince of Neuchâtel, concerning this affair, just how much General Korff[10] again rendered himself culpable by his unheard-of and indecent conduct during his captivity.

Lieutenant General Platov again reported that Major General Ilovaisky V, with three regiments of Cossacks, newly arrived from the Don, moving ahead of the *corps* that General Count Tolstoy was bringing back from the river Bobr to the army, had approached Guttstadt, on the right bank of the Alle, and Major General Denisov, with a few regiments of Cossacks from General Platov's *corps*, from the left side of this river; that the remainder of Marshal Ney's rear guard had abruptly left this town at their appearance; that these two generals had jointly followed the enemy for a distance of more than a *mille* on the road from Allenstein and that they had killed several men and took 55 prisoners.

---

8 Ney's letter is missing in the Russian edition of the memoirs.
9 Nikolai Fedorovich Korff, the chef of the 7th Jager Regiment in 1806–1807.
10 Bennigsen's note: One must not confound this Major General Korff, commander of a jager regiment, with Major General Korff of the cavalry, commander of the Pskovskii Dragoon Regiment, who distinguished himself so well at the battle of Preussisch-Eylau, where he was wounded, and who served throughout the entire war with the greatest distinction.

Upon this report, I informed General Platov that the enemy's evacuation of Guttstadt seemed suspect and that I thought that this move was only a ruse to deliver a more painful blow against one of our advance detachments, the majority of our army still being quite distant by five *milles* from this place. At the same time, I advised General Platov to give the most precise orders to the detachment that he would send to occupy this place to keep guard forcefully [*garder militairement*] and, as soon as the enemy approached in force, to immediately evacuate and retire on the bulk of our advance guard, or to retreat onto the right bank of the Alle and occupy the great forest of Guttstadt, on the main road from Heilsberg. I took these measures, given the impossibility of holding in this place without being master of the left bank, across from the town, and which dominated it. General Platov occupied Guttstadt with a single battalion of jagers, adding a regiment of Cossacks for the forward outposts. At the same time he detached Major General Prince Scherbatov with three infantry battalions, six artillery pieces, two squadrons and 150 Cossacks on the road from Guttstadt to Schmolainen, between Gronau and Altkirch, to be ready for all eventualities.

Lieutenant General L'Estocq and his *corps* occupied cantonment quarters between Mehlsack and Heiligenbeil, across from Marshal Bernadotte's corps, who had established himself on the left bank of the Passarge, his left extending to the mouth of this river or Frische-Nehrung and his right to the village of Boarden, where he linked up with Marshal Soult's corps. General L'Estocq's *corps* having been weakened again by the latest events, I supported him with the 5th Division under the orders of Lieutenant General Tuchkov.

> Marshal Ney to the Minister of War
> Guttstadt, 26 February 1807, nine o'clock in the Morning
> This morning, before daybreak, the *6e Regiment* attacked the village of Peterswalde; the enemy had a great many more troops there than we thought; nonetheless the village was taken. The Russians who were occupying it with three battalions were chased out with great losses. We took as prisoners Major General Baron de Korff, his aide de camp, several other officers,[11] and a few hundred soldiers.
>
> The enemy retired onto Zechern, where he revealed greater forces. We continue to skirmish with him and I would not be surprised if we were forced to cede terrain in turn. Nevertheless I have given the most concrete orders to maintain for today the positions ordered by my dispositions from yesterday; but, as there is no longer any doubt that the notification that I had the honour of addressing at one o'clock this morning to Your Excellency merits the greatest confidence, I thought it necessary in order to save the army to retire tomorrow on Allenstein, conforming to the attached dispositions.
>
> Major General Korff told me that he had passed the day before yesterday through Landsberg with four infantry regiments and one of hussars, and that he formed the left flank of the advance guard.
>
> For two days, I have found myself so boxed in on Guttstadt that it would be dangerous to direct my march to Quetz and from there to Osterode, because the

---

11 Bennigsen's note: The Russians only lost General Korff and his *aide de camp* as prisoners.

roads are impassable. Moreover, my communications with Liebstadt are cut and the enemy seems to have directed a fair number of forces on that point.

The Prussians seem to wish to follow the movements of the Russians in going back up the left bank of the Alle and moving on Liebstadt. They have only shown little infantry from Heilsberg to Seeburg, but enough cavalry to exhaust extremely the troops. I would infinitely prefer to be in camp than to be thusly on the lookout from dusk till dawn.

I am sending the Russian general prisoner of war to Osterode. He is disposed to give up all information that he knows provided that we do him no harm. That is the expression he used; I have reassured him greatly in that respect.[12]

On 16/28 February, based on the news that we received from the inhabitants of various places on both banks of the Passarge that the enemy was concentrating to move forward once more, I had the army occupy more tightly grouped cantonments, as such:

> The centre of the advance guard at Freymarkt, its right at Open and its left at Langwiese;
> Lieutenant General Prince Golitsyn, with the majority of the cavalry, before the centre of the army at Frauendorf and environs;
> The 5th Division formed the right wing at Lichtenau, and the 7th Division at Eschenau;
> The 8th Division formed the centre at Stabunken;
> The 2nd Division, or the left wing, at Grossendorf;
> The 3rd and 4th Divisions, forming the second line, occupied the distance from Petershagen to Sieslack;
> The 14th Division, or the reserve, at Gross-Pehsten and environs.

The news that the inhabitants had given was not borne out; the movement of a few enemy troops had apparently given rise to speculation about a concentration and offensive intentions. The movements, made at this time by the two opposing armies, manifested the desire of both parties to give to the troops the rest of which they had such urgent need, given the great fatigues to which both had been exposed during the entire winter. Besides, the roads were becoming more impractical and rendered movement essentially impossible for the moment. Thus, it was only a matter of determining the area that one wished to occupy to protect the troops from any surprises in their quarters of cantonment or rest. The circumstances compelled me to make another march forward the next day with the entire army.

> Marshal Ney to the Minister of War
> Allenstein, 27 February 1807, one o'clock in the Afternoon
> I have just received the letter from Your Excellency dated yesterday at midnight. Guttstadt was evacuated this morning at four o'clock precisely, as I noted in my

---

12   The Russian edition is missing Ney's letter and Bennigsen's early commentary on the events of 27 February.

letter from yesterday. The enemy remained in force in the forest of Schmolainen, in front of the *6e légère*, until two o'clock in the morning; after which this regiment retired on Guttstadt, in closing the march of the column that was moving on Allenstein.

I just ordered General Roguet with the *25e légère* and *27e de ligne*, which was supposed to go to Detterswalde and then move back onto Deppen and Heiligenthal.

The *2e Brigade* of Gardanne's division will move tomorrow on Schlitt and Blankenberg, so that this division will be able to arrive at Guttstadt, via Quetz and Glottau in one day.

General Lasalle, with his three brigades of cavalry, will move tomorrow into the same position that General Roguet will occupy at Deppen, to scout the routes to Elditten, Wolfsdorf and Guttstadt.

General Grouchy's dragoon division, which is today at Wuttrienen, will come tomorrow to Allenstein and environs.

Tomorrow General Marchand's division will occupy Gettkendorf up to Wadang and Nickelsdorf. By this disposition, if His Majesty insists that I retake Guttstadt, I will be in a position to capture it from the 1st to 2nd of March, in concentrating my forces on Quetz, with the exception of an infantry regiment that I will leave at Allenstein.

Nevertheless, as it is to be presumed that the enemy will harass my left during this enterprise, it would be, I think, necessary to support me in the direction of Elditten and Wolfsdorf with some troops from Marshal Soult. If it is true that the enemy has absolutely nothing but light troops to form an observation cordon along the Passarge and the Alle, it is probable that he will easily be forced to retreat and that the blow that we will be able to give him will render him circumspect in his later attacks.

The town of Guttstadt, as I have had the honour of observing to Your Excellency, is completely denuded of all kinds of resources to live there and it is not by holding cantonments far from there that we will be safe there. It would be better perhaps that my *corps d'armée* be in column from Quetz to Taberbrück, keeping Allenstein with a regiment of infantry.

The illness that ravages in the army continues to diminish daily the forces of the regiments in a horrifying manner. In just four days, while we were in the enemy's presence, more than 800 men had to be sent to the hospital, all due to exhaustion and lack of decent food. I only really have 10,000 to 11,000 men at arms; as for the cavalry, the regiments are, on average, reduced to just 120 horses. If we do not gain a few days of rest, not only will the corps diminish still more, but it will not be able to make any repairs of armaments and clothing, of which they have the greatest need.[13]

I await the orders of His Majesty to execute them with all the zeal with which I am animated for his service.

13　The Russian edition reproduces only this paragraph.

You will have observed, General, that the enemy had chosen the position of Osterode as the general assembly point for the army so as to receive battle there, if I had wished to follow it relentlessly. I even learned since then that it was expected that I would direct my march on Osterode to attack the French army there. But if the map had not shown me the advantage of this position and the difficulties that I would have had in penetrating there, in passing between lakes and through considerable forests, which would have forced me to descend with the army to the environs of Hohenstein to avoid these forests, I already knew the importance of this position from the defensive plan that Frederick II had prepared against the Russians back in 1776.[14] It is the 13th position that he indicates, that of Schmigwalde. The king says: 'If the Russians approach this position, we must attack them, etc.' Incidentally, I would have been obliged to considerably reinforce General L'Estocq's *corps* with Russian troops to place it in a state to be able to resist the efforts that the two corps of Soult and Bernadotte combined would have been able to undertake on Königsberg during this operation.

---

14   In the Russian edition – 1753.

15

Launau – Winter Cantonments

On 17 February/1 March, the army set in march at the break of day and occupied the following cantonments:

The advance guard, under the orders of Lieutenant General Platov, formed a cordon, of which the right wing extended to Wormditt, from which that of the Prussian *corps* continued to the Frische-Haff, and the left wing to Guttstadt. General Platov's headquarters was at Arensdorf. The quarters of Lieutenant General Prince Golitsyn, commanding the cavalry of the left wing, at Benern. The right wing, or the 5th Division, under the orders of General Tuchkov, at Mehlsack, from which he linked up on his right with the Prussian *corps* under the orders of General L'Estocq, with orders to support him in case of an attack. The 8th Division was at Frauendorf; the 4th Division – at Amt-Heilsberg; the 3rd – at Raunau; the 2nd Division, forming the left wing, at Reichenberg; the 14th, in reserve, at Stabunken.

So as to be closer to events that could have taken place after this march, I moved my headquarters to Heilsberg, where the general assembly point of the army was set. The same day I received a report that General Count Tolstoy had arrived with his *corps* at Bischofstein and that his communications with the left wing of the main army were open. This reinforcement of 6,000 men placed me in a position to assure the tranquillity of the cantonment quarters for the army and to assure my communications with General Essen's corps on the Narew. Major General Knorring, with a detachment of light troops belonging to Lieutenant General Count Tolstoy's *corps*, moved into the environs of Allenstein, where he surprised an enemy convoy, which was transporting 200 Russian prisoners; they killed part of the escort, freed the prisoners, and also took 50 prisoners from the enemy.

> Marshal Ney to the Minister of War
> Schlitt, 1 March 1807, five o'clock in the Morning
> I just received the orders from Your Excellency from yesterday at six o'clock in the evening. By the dispositions of my cantonments of February 28, Your Excellency will note, in calculating the distances and time necessary to send out the orders, that it is impossible for me to concentrate all of my troops today in order to execute the dispositions of the Emperor which are: to occupy Guttstadt as an advance guard, to place my line in such a way as to anchor my right on the heights behind this town, to extend my left to the Passarge in the vicinity of Elditten and to equip with infantry posts the left bank of the Alle up to Allenstein. I am giving the necessary orders to concentrate the troops; tomorrow or the day after tomorrow at the latest, I will attack the enemy and do my best to fulfil in every respect the intentions of His Majesty.

Following are the dispositions of Marshal Ney for the march of his corps.

Order of Movement for 1 and 2 March
Schlitt, 1 March 1807
General Marchand's division – General Bélair's brigade with the *6e légère* and *3e hussards*, will occupy today with the 1st battalion at Allenstein and with the 2nd battalion maintaining the posts on the left bank of the Alle, from Allenstein to Schwuben. It will send out frequent patrols to reconnoitre the opposite bank in the direction of Guttstadt, as well as on Wartenburg, Passenheim and Hohenstein. If General Bélair is forced to abandon his position, he will rally at Deppen.

General Colbert's brigade, the *39e de ligne* and *10e de chasseurs*, will leave its position on the Wadang to go to cantonments at Schlitt and Blankenberg, moving via Allenstein, Gettkendorf and Jonkowo.

General Marcognet's brigade will leave Allenstein to go to occupy today Steinberg and Blankenberg.

General Gardanne's division – General Roguet's brigade will occupy today Quetz, Ankenau and Heiligenthal.

General Labassée's brigade will assemble at Deppen; it will nevertheless leave posts at the bridges of Redikainen, Bergfried and the one between Schwuben and Münsterberg on the Alle, until the 2nd battalion of the *6e* relieves them.

General Lasalle's division – General Lasalle's light cavalry will occupy the same positions as those indicated for General Roguet's brigade.

The Division of Dragoons – General Grouchy's dragoons will concentrate at Gallinden.

All of the troops of the *6e corps d'armée*, with the exception of General Bélair's brigade, which will remain in observation at Allenstein and along the left bank of the Alle, will take up arms tomorrow at three o'clock in the morning and will move on Quetz, the general assembly point, marching via Deppen in the following order: [General Lasalle's cavalry]; Gardanne's division, Roguet's brigade, [Labassée's brigade]; Marchand's division, General Colbert's brigade, General Marcognet's brigade; finally General Grouchy's dragoons will close the march.

The generals will give the necessary orders so that the troops are provided with two days of supplies and that they carry 50 cartridges per man.

Generals Lasalle and Roguet will take all possible measures so that the enemy cannot notice the assembly of troops that is taking place at Quetz; they will redouble surveillance in the service and will communicate with the troops of Marshal Soult.

The reserve park of the army will leave today from Dittrichswalde for Looseker; tomorrow it will establish itself until new orders at Gallinden. The generals will receive new orders for tomorrow's subsequent movements.

The park for Marchand's division and that of General Gardanne will remain at Deppen until new orders. The main headquarters will be at Deppen tomorrow.

Marshal Ney[1]

---

1   This letter is missing in the Russian edition.

On 18 February/2 March, the Russian army and advance guard remained peacefully in the same positions.

> Marshal Ney to the Minister of War
> Deppen, 2 March 1807, 4:30 in the Morning
> I received the new dispositions ordered by His Majesty for the simultaneous attack of the *Grande Armée* for tomorrow. I am perfectly ready to march on the enemy at such time in the morning as is judged suitable. Unless ordered otherwise, I will attack shortly before daybreak, so that the enemy may not observe the whole of my operation. The enemy occupies Quetz, and maintains a double chain of *vedettes* on the heights that dominate Ankendorf via Komalmen and Waltersmühl. I had scouted out an assembly point behind Ankendorf, so as to fall suddenly on Quetz and from there on Glottau so as to take possession of Guttstadt.
>
> I think it necessary not to take some prisoners today, as this attempt would give place to a cavalry action, for which I am infinitely inferior in forces to those of the enemy. As soon as an officer appears to make observations, one sees the *vedettes* triple in number and one sees up to 150, placed four to six paces from each other. The heights that they occupy prevent seeing what is behind them.
>
> I am ordering General Bélair's brigade to establish itself today at Münsterberg and at Schwuben, but nevertheless to leave some men at Allenstein until the arrival of the infantry regiment from Morand's division.
>
> General Bélair will attack the enemy tomorrow on the flank between Glottau and Guttstadt as soon as he hears that I am in measure to move on Quetz with the principal column.

On 18 February/2 March, a patrol from Blücher's Prussian hussar regiment met near the village of Alt-Passarge a French Colonel[2] with a trumpeter and four soldiers that it took prisoner. The Colonel insisted that he was sent as an envoy; but as he was found with weapons with his small troop and he had nothing to say that could give credence to his declaration, we sent him as a prisoner to Königsberg.

On 19 February/3 March, the Russian army again remained in the same position. General Platov reported to me that Marshal Ney had approached Guttstadt with his entire corps and had once again rendered himself master of the town. You no doubt recall that I told you earlier that this town was only occupied by a single battalion and a few Cossacks. At the same time I explained to you the apprehensions that caused me to only keep there that weak detachment. My orders were executed punctually. The commander of this battalion of jagers, seeing that the enemy was pushing superior forces against the town, abandoned it in an orderly fashion, after a minor skirmishing action and retired on the right bank of the Alle into the woods of Guttstadt which he kept occupied. Marshal Ney then moved against the weak detachment of Prince Scherbatov, posted at Schmolainen, and attacked him vigorously. But our General knew how to manoeuvre so well and to profit from the terrain that the enemy, despite his great superiority in forces, found an imposing resistance in the retreat

---

2 Colonel Boudinhon.

of the Prince, who arrived with his detachment almost without losses at Peterswalde, where he joined with General Markov's advance guard. You will soon see in a report by Marshal Ney the praise he had for Prince Scherbatov's retreat.

This movement by Marshal Ney was supposed to make me suspect offensive intentions on his part, combined and supported by the other French *corps d'armée,* to make us give up territory. But I decided to cede none and to hold my position on the Alle and, in parts, on the Passarge, pushing forward the 3rd, 4th, 7th, and 14th Divisions, with the majority of Prince Golitsyn's cavalry (or that of the left wing), all under the orders of General Sacken, the most senior Lieutenant General of the army. I ordered this general to support the advance guard and to cede no terrain to the enemy, unless he was forced to do so by superior forces; his own forces amounted to at least 20,000 men, including the advance guard, which was certainly double that of all the concentrated forces of Marshal Ney's corps. We will soon see that General Sacken, with a little more skill and a little determination, would have been able to deliver a decisive blow against Marshal Ney's corps, make him retrace his steps with notable loss, and gain for us territory for the rest of the winter, because the enemy, after a good lesson, would have been quite hesitant to return to the offensive with so few forces, all the more so as the commanders of the two armies wished to put their troops into winter quarters. But our general had allowed a handful of enemy soldiers to halt him and had lost as many men as he would have in a serious but well directed action. You will soon be convinced of this truth by Marshal Ney's report about this affair to the Minister of War, the Prince of Neuchâtel.

In the morning, Marshal Ney attacked Zechern and Peterswalde. General Sacken pulled our advance guard back into the forest between Launau and Zechern, and concentrated the rest of his troops near Launau. Our chain of light troops moved across to Peterswalde, from where it continued via Sommerfeld, Petersdorf, Schwendt up to the Passarge and from there, holding to the right bank of this river, up to the Prussian advance posts.

I ordered Lieutenant General Count Tolstoy, who had already arrived at Bartenstein, to move with his *corps* on Heilsberg via the right bank of the Alle, while also giving him the 2nd Division, under the orders of Lieutenant General Count Ostermann. Lieutenants Generals Tuchkov and Dokhturov received at the same time the order to move to Heilsberg with their 5th and 7th Divisions via the left bank; part of the cavalry of the right wing also moved there. In this way, I could vigorously repulse any serious attacks by the enemy. Lieutenant General L'Estocq informed me that the enemy, with a detachment from the Prince de Ponte-Corvo's corps, had crossed the Passarge at Braunsberg and that it had occupied Neustadt, but that he would take measures to dislodge it immediately.

On 20 February/4 March, General Sacken was with his *corps* so close to the enemy that it would have sufficed for him to leave his position at Launau with his 20,000 men in order to roll back the detachments of Marshal Ney one after the other and finally topple the rest of his corps without him being able to recover from it. Having 2,000 Cossacks and all of the cavalry of the left wing at his disposal, General Sacken could, in employing them well, have made the enemy pay dearly in his retreat. He also had the advantage that Marshal Ney could not know the superiority of his forces, thanks to the forests that covered his position. Also we will soon see from Marshal Ney's account that in fact he did not suspect having so close to him a *corps* that was so formidable and that could be supported by the rest of the Russian army. In the morning, General Sacken ordered the attack or, to be more accurate, he commanded uselessly alarming the enemy advance posts before Zechern. He sent out from the forest a few battalions of jagers across from Peterswalde, but without any dispositions to support this attack. The result was that these brave battalions were soon repulsed with losses. Marshal Ney, as one sees from his report, had at the two points of Zechern and Peterswalde only the *50e, 27e* and *59e régiments de ligne* with two companies of *voltigeurs* and two companies of *carabiniers* from the *25e légère*. All these troops, as we will see from primary documents, were not even concentrated, and amounted to, at most, 4,000 men, against whom General Sacken could act with 20,000 men who had been concentrated for action. And yet he got himself repulsed twice on that same day. Marshal Ney also said, as we will see later: 'I was not in a position to support my troops, while the enemy continued to reinforce his own. I ordered my reserves to remain in defensive positions and limit themselves to sporadic musket fire, supported by artillery. The enemy, manoeuvring very poorly, advanced seven to eight times in the greatest disorder and with dreadful cries, up to 15 paces in front of my battalions, but everywhere he found death, etc…'

After the lesson that he had just received from the enemy and after having uselessly sacrificed his own men, General Sacken, rather than rallying his troops and exploiting a mistake that the enemy had just made before his eyes, had bungled another opportunity. By the order of General Gardanne,[3] the *6e régiment légère* had entered the woods, close to our right, between Zechern and Peterswalde. General Sacken could very easily have cut off the two French detachments; but he limited himself to attacking this wood with some cavalry which was, as it should have been expected, repulsed with losses; then he continued a useless fusillade throughout the entire day. Finally in the evening, with the sun already set, General Sacken decided to make a serious attack. Around nine o'clock, he moved various detachments out of the woods of Launau. The heads of these detachments were too weak and unsupported and so were repulsed once again at the first clash before Zechern, even though the entire Russian *corps* was in arms and deployed in columns a short distance away, ready march upon the enemy. In this disorder, General Sacken got muddled up in his plan of attack and ended up ordering the retreat to the great surprise and utter indignation of all the troops under his orders, upon which he returned his *corps* to the position it had occupied before in the middle of the forests of Launau. Such was the result of this fatal day, which cost us 500 victims among our brave soldiers, while the enemy only lost 262 men killed and wounded, as is mentioned in the detailed report by Marshal Ney to the Minister of War.

General Platov sent to the headquarters two officers and 74 soldiers, which his Cossacks had taken prisoner in several encounters.

Lieutenant General L'Estocq informed me that he had sent a detachment to dislodge the enemy from Neustadt, that the latter had abandoned this post, and that he had retired beyond the Passarge upon the approach of the troops. I had invited General L'Estocq not to lose from view in his positions the security of Königsberg. Consequently, this general placed his *corps* behind the Bahnau, a position by which he perfectly covered this town. His advance posts occupied a chain on the right bank of the Passarge, from Braunsberg to the right of the Russian army.

---

3   Bennigsen's note: One will find this action in a letter from Marshal Ney to the Minister of War on 6 March.

On 21 February/5 March, the troops remained in the same position. That evening my chief of staff, General de Steinheil, who had gone to the advance guard, began work on a battery for six pieces of 6-pounder cannon (to our left in front of Launau, on a height across from Zechern), which was so well placed that as soon as it came into action, on 22 February/6 March, in the morning, the enemy abandoned that place. But the enemy remained close enough to be able to prevent our troops from occupying it immediately; the enemy retired onto the heights before Gronau, upon which some detachments bivouacked to support the pickets and the chains of advance posts. The rest concerning the position of Marshal Ney's corps is found in the reports of this Marshal from 5 and 6 March, as follows.

> Marshal Ney to the Minister of War
> Guttstadt, 5 March 1807
> I have the honour of informing Your Excellency that the enemy continues to occupy the position of Launau with around 10,000 infantry and cavalry; but I cannot discern what is in place toward Heilsberg, although the smoke of bivouacs announces the presence of a reserve. The advance posts border the forest, from the road from Launau to Freymarkt, until across from Peterswalde and Zechern. The sentinels on both sides and the mounted *vedettes* are within half a pistol shot from each other. I can crush all of these troops with canister rounds but I have forbidden firing a shot by cannon or musket, because if Marshal Soult was supporting my attack on Launau, I do not believe that the enemy could save either infantry or cannon.[4]
>
> Yesterday, the enemy, sensing how critical his position was and thinking that I only had at Zechern a few companies of infantry, began, at seven o'clock in the morning, an attack on this post with great impetuosity and was repulsed with great losses. The fusillade continued without halt; he manoeuvred by his right and acted as though he wished to break into the forest between Zechern and Peterswalde, to cut off the retreat of the *50e* regiment, but the two companies of *voltigeurs* and the two of *carabiniers* of the *25e légère* and the *27e de ligne*, supported by the *59e*, moved so suddenly on the column of Russian infantry that dared to move for an instant from the forest, seconded by a swarm of Cossacks, that the enemy retired in a dreadful disorder.
>
> A general engagement was going to occur and I was not in a position to support my troops, while the enemy continued to reinforce his own. I ordered my reserves to remain in defensive positions and limit themselves to a sporadic musket fire supported by the artillery. The enemy, manoeuvring very poorly, came seven to eight times in the greatest disorder and with dreadful cries up to 15 paces in front of my battalions; but he found death everywhere and such firmness, particularly in the *50e* regiment, that he retired in disorder, leaving the ground strewn with corpses.

---

4   Bennigsen's note: One sees how little Marshal Ney suspected having in front of him such considerable forces of the Russian army.

Around three o'clock in the afternoon, the shooting stopped across from Peterswalde and the enemy began to concentrate all of his forces to attack Zechern; he was constantly repulsed. Finally, at 7:30 in the evening, he made another attack, as fruitless as the previous ones. A battalion of the *59e* reinforced the *50e*, which was exhausted from fatigue and had lost a great many men wounded and killed. Finally, at 10:30 in the evening, the enemy attacked for the last time, and managed to get up the height and penetrate up to 40 paces from the *50e* regiment. General Labassée pulled back all of the sentinels and set the trap for the enemy. The fire of two ranks began immediately and the Russian battalions were broken and left the ground strewn with their dead. The entire night passed tranquilly.

This morning, our soldiers made a gesture of generosity and humanity that merits mention. Several Russian wounded remained on the battlefield. Insofar as we had means of evacuation, we took one Russian and two other wounded French soldiers. With broad daylight, there were still 15 wounded Russians soldiers. After having been bandaged, they received from our soldiers some potatoes and were taken to the line of Russian sentinels, while shouting out to them that we were giving them wounded men, as we lacked the means of evacuation, so that these unfortunates would not be killed, being without defence, in case the battle recommenced. Some Russian officers arrived to receive the wounded and spoke with the greatest respect for the conduct of the French soldiers, telling them: 'Brave Frenchmen, it is unfortunate that two nations honourable enough to admire each other for their valour, are instead at each other's throats; let us hope for peace.'

The enemy losses during yesterday's combat were at least 2,000 killed or wounded.[5] On our side, we had around 150 killed and wounded from the *50e* regiment; 12 from the *59e*; 80 from the *27e de ligne* and 20 from the companies of *voltigeurs* and *carabiniers* from the *25e légère*.

These are the dispositions I took this morning to concentrate myself more and to be in a position to repulse any act of aggression on the enemy's part.

- The *59e* has replaced the *50e*, which I placed in the second line behind Zechern and Peterswalde;
- The *6e légère* took position at the head of the wood to fill the interval from Zechern to Peterswalde. The *76e* replaced this regiment at Schmolainen;
- The *27e de ligne* at Peterswalde;
- The *25e d'infanterie légère* at Mawern, Rosenbeck and Gronau, supported by the *39e* at Altkirch;
- The *69e*, at Guttstadt;
- General Lasalle's light cavalry at Zechern and Peterswalde; there are also two regiments of *dragons* in the latter place; the two others are in reserve at Schmolainen;
- The *3e hussards* and *10e chasseurs* at Mawern, Rosenbeck and Gronau, linking up with Marshal Soult's troops at Benern.

I await His Majesty's orders and the men are ready to march on the enemy.

---

5   Bennigsen's note: Our effective losses were about 500 men.

Other Report from Marshal Ney to the Minister of War
Schmolainen, 6 March 1807

I already had the honour of writing to Your Excellency that General Gardanne was incapable of fulfilling his duties as *Général de division*. Yesterday, he nearly compromised the troops with the outrageous dispositions he took, an instant after my departure from Zechern.

I had placed the *6e d'infanterie légère* in reserve; at the first musket shots that the enemy fired on the troops at Peterswalde, he summoned this regiment to throw it into the forest and to act against the enemy. Happily Colonel Laplane noted that he was from another division and that he had received from me explicit orders to move only to support the post at Zechern. The *27e régiment* was also thrown for no reason into the forest in the pursuit of an infinitely superior enemy. It is only by the good conduct of Colonel Bardet and the dispositions of General Roguet that we retired with honour from such a failed gambit, which could have ruined this regiment.

Today, I ordered General Gardanne to go to Thorn. He asked to go to the Imperial headquarters to protest my conduct. I will declare to Your Excellency that I am unable to serve with a general of this type. The luck of war has favoured me up till this point; nevertheless I can be wounded or killed in an action; then it would be General Gardanne, as the most senior divisional general, who would replace me, while waiting for His Majesty to decide on the commander of the troops.

I do not complain at all about General Gardanne's bravery; I am satisfied with him in this respect. But it is in my opinion the least important quality of a general.

The following report from Marshal Ney to Emperor Napoleon was intercepted by our Cossacks; it was carried by Marshal Ney's *officier de correspondance*, M. de Montesquiou, whom they sent to me at the headquarters at Heilsberg.

Marshal Ney, to H. M. the Emperor and King
Zechern, 6 March 1807, seven o'clock in the Morning

Sire! I have the honour of informing Your Majesty that the enemy appears to have chosen the position of Launau to anchor the left of his army and that his right extends in the direction of Raunau. Enemy forces have grown since yesterday, at least judging by the camp fires.

The enemy worked over the night on the construction of a fortified battery [*batterie à embrasure*], placed across from the Zechern windmill, behind the road from Launau. Five pieces of *calibre de 7* are in battery there. We were obliged to withdraw our own behind and to the right of Zechern.

The enemy extends into the forest at Mawern, and I have just learned that he is making an infantry movement on that position. He does not cease to provoke me to fight; but I will remain on a respectable and formidable defensive, until Your Majesty supports me and gives his orders for the entirety of operations.

Some intelligence, albeit indirect, suggests that General Tolstoy, who was at Bischofstein, has concentrated on Bartenstein, as of the 3rd, and should be at Heilsberg and Langwiese.

I have the honour to be, Sire, of Your Imperial and Royal Majesty the very humble and loyal subject.

Ney

On 23 February/7 March, Marshal Ney relieved with fresh troops those that had been at the advance posts for a few days. Our own outpost, established on the right bank of the river Alle, reported that the enemy had just placed posts from the same *corps*, fairly numerous on the opposite bank, from their position behind Zechern up to Guttstadt. At the same time I received from our advance posts, that were in the plain, across from Peterswalde, the report that the enemy had placed artillery in front of his infantry between this place and Zechern and that he was working on the construction of several batteries. Other reports from our advance posts on the Passarge informed me that the troops of the corps of Marshals Soult and Bernadotte, whose advance posts held the left bank of this river from Deppen to Braunsberg, were making no movement that could indicate offensive intentions. I again received similar reports from parties of Cossacks, sent into the environs of Allenstein, concerning the establishment of advance posts for Marshal Davout's corps on the left bank of the Alle and the dispersion of the troops of this corps into cantonments.

Through secret agents I learned that the other corps composing the French army were also continuing to disperse into winter quarters in the environs of Osterode. All of these reports and this news convinced me that the French army considered the winter campaign over; that it needed, perhaps still more than us, rest to heal the wounds of the first campaign and that all of the movements they made had no other goal than to establish a few bridge heads on the right bank of the Passarge, the better to protect his cantonments from any surprise. I only asked to be able to also give rest to the troops who also needed it after so many fatigues, all the more so as bivouacs, given the damp weather, daily increased the number of ill in the regiments. An armistice offered the means of buying time to bring to the army the reinforcements necessary to be able to resist the French army, whose forces grew every day via reinforcements that Emperor Napoleon brought in from all directions; a consideration that indispensably had to make me await the arrival of some reinforcements before exposing the army to losses, which would have been able to further diminish its strength and which I had to carefully avoid for the moment. Incidentally I dared not overextend my left wing in order to avoid giving the enemy a hold on my right, occupied by General L'Estocq with the Prussian *corps*, which amounted to barely 9,000 men, too weak to be able to resist two enemy corps, that of Marshal Soult and that of Marshal Bernadotte, occupying the distance from Liebstadt to Braunsberg, or up till the banks of the Frische-Haff. These two corps, each one of which was a great deal stronger than that of General L'Estocq and the latter of which had been reinforced by the remains of Marshal Augereau's corps after the battle of Preussisch-Eylau, could very easily rally and act against the Prussians to menace Königsberg, if I had overextended my forces on my left. Also, since my arrival on the river Alle, I had no other goal for the moment than to establish the left of my army at Guttstadt, which I would have managed perfectly without the error committed by General Sacken, on 20 February/4 March.

We will easily agree, in carefully examining the map, that the position of the French army was a little bit weak; Marshal Ney's corps was too exposed. Also, when I saw that the enemy was making no change to this position, I formed a plan to deliver a decisive blow to this corps by turning it at different points, as soon as the first reinforcements arrived for my army. The execution of this plan however was postponed until the beginning of the second campaign, and the reader will be informed of it when we reach this period in my account. One will see that it was again the same General Sacken who led to the failure of this plan.

The reasons and circumstances that I have just discussed made me decide to put the army, on 24 February/8 March, in winter cantonments, as follows: Lieutenant General Tuchkov with the 5th Division as the right wing at Landsberg and environs; The 8th Division at Albrechtsdorf; the 4th Division at Loyden; the 3rd Division at Heilsberg. The cavalry of the right wing, between Wormditt and Heilsberg. The advance guard remained in its first position on the left bank of the Alle. On the right bank of this river, the 2nd Division at Roghausen and environs; the 14th Division, at Lauterhagen; the 7th Division at Gallingen. The cavalry of the left wing, at Amt-Heilsberg and environs. General Count Tolstoy's *corps* remained between Heilsberg and Guttstadt, on the right bank, and his headquarters was at Heilsberg. Seeburg was occupied by a cavalry detachment from Count Tolstoy's *corps*, under the orders of Major General Knorring; his reconnaissance and patrols were supposed to observe the enemy over the distance from Guttstadt to Allenstein, on the right bank of the Alle.

Major General Czaplic with his Pavlogradskii Hussar Regiment was sent to Bischofstein to support the post of Seeburg, should that be needed.

Major Selivanov had already been sent with his Cossacks regiment to Bischofsburg, to serve as a warning outpost should the enemy have wished to turn our left to disturb our cantonments on that side.

Based on these positions, the location of my headquarters at Heilsberg, being too close to the advance posts, would have been too exposed to alarms. I therefore moved myself that same day still, with my entire entourage, to Bartenstein where my headquarters was established for the rest of the winter.

The position of Heilsberg on both banks of the Alle remained set as the first assembly point for the troops in case of enemy movements requiring the concentration of our army and, in case it was able to be forced in this position, the army was supposed to direct its march on Schippenbeil, where it should occupy a position, the right wing anchored on the Alle and its front covered by the small river Zaine. Part of our heavy artillery was for that reason already placed in the environs of Gerdauen; I then placed it in the position of Heilsberg when the army was stronger.

Lieutenant General L'Estocq remained in the position that he had already occupied and his headquarters was also at Mehlsack. He was supposed to be supported, in case of attack, by Lieutenant General Tuchkov, with his troops in cantonments at Landsberg.

> Marshal Ney to H. M. the Emperor and King
> 7 March
> The enemy has made no changes to his position at Launau. We are noticing a great many troop movements, which are relieving the advance posts. The news from the locals and prisoners indicates that the enemy has constructed earth works in which to place his infantry and his artillery, as well as numerous abatis in case of battle.[6]

---

6 Bennigsen's note: This is an error. At that time we were only working on a single battery before Launau; the enemy took for abatis the trees we were cutting for heating the troops in bivouac.

Yesterday passed without a musket shot; the enemy redoubt in front of Launau fired a hundred cannon shots without doing harm. This morning the troops of the *1er Division* relieved those of the second, following the dispositions of which I sent a copy to His Excellency M. the Minister of War. The enemy is holding everywhere in arms and has not troubled the execution of these dispositions.

Similarly nothing new is happening on the right bank of the Alle. The enemy from his position of Sparlingen is observing the defensive, like all the rest of the Russian army. I am connected to Marshal Soult's right; but it would be most essential that the *1er corps d'armée*[7] can show infantry before Benern and Freymarkt. This movement would force the enemy to retreat or to show his hand, if he continues to hold his position at Launau and Raunau, [his intention] to wish to accept battle. This resolution seems strange to me, because at that time he would renounce his communications with Königsberg and his retreat could only move on Grodno or Insterburg, in descending the lower Alle.

Marshal Ney to the Minister of War
Schmolainen, 8 March 1807
I have returned from the reconnaissance of the posts that I just made on Zechern, with General Mouton, His Majesty's *aide de camp*. The enemy seems less numerous than yesterday; nevertheless it is very difficult to judge his forces due to the forests that cover the entirety of the right of the position of Launau. We see a great deal of smoke and all of the officers posted at Zechern insist that, last night, the enemy fires appeared infinitely more considerable than the night before.

We noted a fairly considerable gathering of cavalry, but in bivouac, on the Launau height; a column of several squadrons seemed to arrive from the right and marched on Launau. The greatest tranquillity reigns everywhere.

I had sent one of my *aides de camp* toward Benern, to ascertain the results of the reconnaissance that Marshal Soult was supposed to make. He met General Bertrand, His Majesty's *aide de camp*, who went to the enemy advance posts as an envoy; he gave him a note for me in which this General tells me that Marshal Soult's reconnaissance was cancelled; that it seemed as though the enemy was making a movement on Willenberg and that Marshal Davout had received orders to march on Osterode; that he thought that I had received this news.

Nevertheless, if Marshal Davout is leaving the Alle, I will be obliged to send men there to cover my rear. I would ask to the contrary that a regiment or two of that *corps d'armée* might establish itself from Guttstadt to Allenstein, so as to be able to augment my reserves in case of an attack on my front.

M. Montesquiou, whom I sent from Zechern the day before yesterday, with a letter for His Majesty, seems to have been taken prisoner between Benern and Freymarkt. That is the direction that I had him take believing, according to what Marshal Soult told me, that he held this latter place; but I have since learned that the

---

7   Bennigsen's note: It is to be assumed that Marshal Ney wished to say the *4e corps* or that of Marshal Soult, as the *1er corps* was too far away.

enemy holds that post. I am attaching here a copy of that letter, which incidentally cannot be of any importance to the enemy.

Marshal Ney to the Minister of War
Schmolainen, 11 March 1807
I have the honour of informing Your Excellency that the enemy has made no movement on the front of his camp of Launau. The advance posts are still watching each other as closely as the preceding days.

Tomorrow, at five o'clock in the morning, I will proceed with the dispositions contained in the order of movement of which a copy is attached here.

I do not think it at all prudent to extend myself any further for the moment, until the enemy's designs are known definitively, because the goal of His Majesty is to cover Guttstadt. Although I have nothing to fear on the front of this position any more than on the right bank of the Alle, it is not so on my left flank. The enemy could arrive in force at Lingnau and Wolfsdorf and menace my rear.[8] I will do in all events that which depends on me to conserve this point to the last extremity, if I were attacked, just as I have already said to Your Excellency…

The changes made in the position of our troops and the events that occurred during winter quarters will be discussed later.

---

[8] Bennigsen's note: We will subsequently see that it was at precisely this point that Marshal Ney's corps was attacked at the beginning of the second campaign.

Select Bibliography

Anon. (ed.), *Zhurnal voennykh deistvii imperatorskoi Rossiiskoi armii s nachal do okonchaniya kampanii* (St Petersburg: Imperial Academy of Sciences, 1807)

Arnold, James R. and Ralph R. Reinertsen, *Crisis in the Snows. Russia Confronts Napoleon: The Eylau Campaign 1806–1807* (Lexington: Napoleon Books, 2007)

Benckendorff, Alexander, 'Vospominaniya…', in M. Sidorova and A. Litvin (eds), *Rossiiskii arkhiv* (Moscow: TRITE, 2012)

Bennigsen, Levin August Theophil von, (Jean Jules Cazalas (ed.)), *Mémoires du Général Bennigsen* (Paris: Charles-Lavauzelle, 1907). Russian edition: 'Zapiski grafa L.L. Bennigsen o voine s Napoleonom 1807 goda,' P. Maikov (ed.), *Russkaya starina* 12 (1896), pp.481–518; 1 (1897), pp.81–110; 2 (1897), pp.253–272; 4 (1897), pp.73–102; 5 (1897), pp.299–316; 7 (1899), pp.205–224; 8 (1899), pp.453–466; 9 (1899), pp.675–693; 10 (1899), pp.213–229; 12 (1899), pp.697–712; 1 (1900), pp.259–272; 2 (1900), pp.501–516; 3 (1900), pp.745–767

Bennigsen, Levin August Theophil von, *Gedanken über einige dem Officier der leichten Cavalerie nothwendige…* (Leipzig: W. Rein et Comp., 1805)

Bulgarin, Faddei, *Vospominaniya Faddeya Bulgarina* (St Petersburg: M. Olkhin, 1847)

Davydov, Denis, *Voennye zapiski* (Moscow: Gos. izd. khud. lit., 1982) English edition: Gregory Troubetzkoy (trans. & ed.) *In the Service of the Tsar against Napoleon: The Memoirs of Denis Davidov, 1806-1814* (London: Greenhill, 1999)

Dumas, Mathieu, *Précis des événemens militaires, ou, Essais historiques sur les campagnes de 1799 à 1814* (Paris: Treutell, 1826)

Goltz, Colmar, *Jena to Eylau. The Disgrace and the Redemption of the Old Prussian Army. A Study in Military History* (New York: E.P. Dutton, 1913)

Grabbe, Paul, *Iz pamiatnykh zapisok grafa Pavla Khristoforovicha Grabbe* (Moscow: Katkov 1873)

Eduard von Höpfner, *Der Krieg von 1806 und 1807* (Berlin: S. Schropp, 1850)

Foucart, Paul-Jean, *Campagne de Pologne. Pultusk et Golymin* (Paris: L. Militaire Berger-Levrault, 1882)

Jackson, George, *Diaries and Letters of Sir George Jackson, KCH* (London: R. Bentley, 1872)

Landmann, Karl Ritter von, *Der Krieg von 1806 und 1807: auf Grund urkundlichen Materials sowie der neuesten Forschungen und Quellen* (Berlin: Voss, 1909)

Löwenstern, Eduard von, *Mit Graf Pahlens Reiterei gegen Napoleon: Denkwürdigkeiten des russischen Generals Eduard von Löwenstern, 1790-1837* (Berlin: Mittler, 1910)

Mikaberidze, Alexander (ed.), *Russian Eyewitness Accounts of the Campaign of 1807* (London: Frontline Books, 2015)

Mikhailovskii-Danilevskii, Alexander, *Opisanie vtoroi voiny Imperatora Aleksandra s Napoleonom v 1806 i 1807 godakh* (St Petersburg: Tip. Schtaba Otd. Korpusa Vnut. Strazhi, 1846)

Naulet, Frédéric, *Eylau: La campagne de Pologne, des boues de Pultusk aux neiges d'Eylau* (Paris: Economica, 2007)

Obolenskii, A., 'Vosponinaniya Knyazya A.P. Obolenskago (1780-1812)' in *Khronika nedavnei stariny: iz arkhiva Knyazya Obolenskago-Neledinskago-Meletskago* (St Petersburg: Tip. Vtorogo Otdel. Sobst. E.I.V. Kantselyarii, 1872)

Osten-Sacken, Fabian von der, 'Iz zapisok feldmarshala Sackena', *Russkii arkhiv*, vol.101 (1900), pp.168–174

Otroshenko, Jacob. '*Zapiski generala Otroshenko*', in *Russkii vestnik*, 9 (1877), pp.160–183

Petre, F. Lorraine, *Napoleon's Campaign in Poland, 1806-7* (London: Low & Marston, 1901)

Petrov, Mikhail, 'Rasskazy sluzhivshego v 1-m egerskom polku polkovnika Mikhaila Petrova o voennoi sluzhbe i zhizni svoei i trekh rodnykh brat'ev ego, zachavsheisya s 1789 goda' in F. Petrov, A. Afanasyev, et al. (eds), *1812 god. Vospominaniya voinov russkoi armii* (Moscow: Mysl, 1991), pp.112–355

Plotho, Carl von, *Tagebuch während des Krieges zwischen Russland und Preussen einerseits, und Frankreich andrerseits, in den Jahren 1806 und 1807* (Berlin: Braunes, 1811)

Sherbatov, Aleksey, (A. Shiryaeva (ed.)) *Moi vospominaniya* (St Petersburg: Nestor-Istoria, 2006)

Shishkov, Alexander, *Zapiski, mneniya i perepiska…* (Berlin: B. Behr's Buchhandlung, 1870)

Volkonskii, Sergei, *Zapiski Sergeya Grigorievicha Volkonskago (dekabrista)* (St Petersburg: Sinodalnaya Tip., 1902)

Wilson, Robert, (H. Randolh (ed.)), *Life of General Sir Robert Wilson, From Autobiographical Memoirs, Journals, Narratives, Correspondence, etc* (London: John Murray, 1862)

Wilson, Robert, *Brief Remarks on the Character and Composition of the Russian Army and a Sketch of the Campaigns in Poland in the years 1806 and 1807* (London: T. Egerton, 1810)

Yermolov, Aleksey, (A. Mikaberidze (trans. & ed.)), *The Czar's General: The Memoirs of a Russian General of the Napoleonic Wars* (Welwyn Garden City: Ravenhall Books, 2005)

Index

Alexander I, Emperor of Russia 21, 24–26, 28, 32, 34–35, 37, 39–40, 53, 57, 95, 101, 109–110, 140, 169
Alle, river 103, 107, 109, 112–113, 145, 147–148, 184, 193, 201–203, 207–211, 213–216, 221–224
Allenstein 75, 100, 112–113, 117, 119, 133–134, 136, 139, 142–147, 149–150, 201–203, 207–211, 213–215, 221–223
Alt-Bestendorf 127
Alt-Ramten 117, 124–125, 127
Anrep 54, 75, 78–79, 82, 84, 105, 121, 123, 139
Arensdorf 117, 154, 156, 200–201, 203, 205, 213
Auerstädt 20, 35, 54, 56
Augéreau, Marshal Pierre 55, 64, 90, 96, 102, 129, 134, 137–138, 144, 176–177, 221
Auklappen 167, 171, 174, 177
Austerlitz 20, 38–39
Austria 20, 24–29, 35–36, 38–39, 43, 50, 67

Baggehufvudt, General Karl Gustav von 76–77, 80–82, 84, 105 106, 111 113, 115, 117, 127, 133, 136, 149, 152–154, 157, 165, 167, 170–171
Bagration, Lieutenant General Prince Peter 127, 132–133, 141, 143, 146, 149, 151–157, 163, 165, 175, 183, 185–186, 188, 192, 199
Baltic Sea 30–31, 47–48, 103, 109
Barclay de Tolly, Major General Mikhail 59–60, 63, 67, 69, 75 76, 80, 83 84, 105, 112, 116–117, 128, 131–133, 136, 143, 145, 147–149, 151–152, 154, 157–159, 165–167
Barthen 100, 107, 109, 113, 150
Bavaria 27, 40
Bergfried 145, 147, 214
Berlin 34, 37–38, 51, 58, 140
Bernadotte, Marshal Jean, Prince de Ponte-Corvo 38, 55, 73, 96, 98, 102, 105, 113–117, 119–121, 124–125, 127–136, 138–139, 141, 143–144, 146, 148, 176–177, 179, 184–185, 195, 198, 200, 202, 205–206, 208–209, 212, 221
Berthier, Marshal Louis-Alexandre Berthier, Prince de Neuchâtel 63, 102, 109, 141–144, 177, 184, 208, 216

Bessières, Marshal Jean-Baptiste 55, 102, 177
Bischofstein 111–112, 114, 119, 202, 213, 220, 222
Bischofswerder 61, 70
Black Sea 23, 26, 41, 47, 52
Blonie 59, 61, 67
Braunsberg 75, 116–117, 119, 134, 150, 159, 202, 205–207, 216–217, 221
Bug 59, 63, 67, 70, 72, 74, 199
Buxhöwden, General Fedor von 36, 54, 59, 65, 68, 70–71, 78–80, 84, 86, 89, 91, 97–99, 101

Catherine II, Empress of Russia 24, 26, 42, 48–49, 51, 71
Colbert, Brigadier General Auguste François-Marie de 103, 106–110, 112, 114, 119, 132, 184, 188–189, 194, 196, 201–203, 207, 214
Constantinople 24–26, 29
Cossacks 59–60, 67, 69, 75, 102, 105–106, 109, 111, 116, 128–131, 133, 136, 139, 141, 143–146, 149, 157, 159, 167, 172–173, 178, 184–188, 192, 195–196, 198–202, 204–205, 208–209, 215–218, 220–222
Czaplic, Major General Yefim 89, 91–92, 94, 172, 174, 222
Czarnowo 61, 69, 72, 74–75, 101

Danzig 29–34, 60, 63, 65, 70, 75, 80, 103, 105, 117–119, 128–129, 133, 197
Davout, Marshal Louis-Nicolas 55, 57, 67–68, 72–73, 81, 102, 129, 131, 144, 154, 171, 177, 179–180, 183–185, 188–189, 201–203, 221, 223
de Ponte-Corvo, Prince of, see Bernadotte
Deutsch-Eylau, see Eylau
Digitten 117, 203
Dokhturov, Lieutenant General Dmitri Sergeevich 54, 75, 78, 82, 89, 91–92, 94–95, 106, 136, 143, 160, 167, 169–170, 175, 180, 204, 216
Dolgorouky General Prince Peter 37–38, 83, 125
Dolgorouky Colonel Prince Michel 139–140, 143, 155, 158–159, 179

Dolgorouky V, Major General Vasilii Yurievich 83, 158–159
Drewenz, river 58, 69, 102, 129, 133, 135, 137–138, 150, 196, 199

Essen I, Lieutenant General Ivan Nikolaevich von 37, 55, 59, 65, 68, 101–102, 134, 136, 199, 213
Essen III, Lieutenant General Peter Kirillovich von 75, 78–79, 99, 143, 175, 177
Eylau 28, 32, 61, 75, 80, 103–109, 113, 117, 128, 133–134, 136–137, 142–143, 149–150, 153, 157, 159–163, 165–168, 172, 174, 176–182, 184–185, 188–190, 192–196, 199–200, 204, 221

Fock, General Alexander von 169, 175, 199
France 20–21, 24–25, 27–29, 31–32, 34–52, 198
Frederick II, King of Prussia 212
Frederick William III, King of Prussia 36, 39, 54, 58
French army, regiments of: **Hussars**; 3e 103–14, 111–113, 214, 219; **Chasseurs à Cheval**; 10e 103–104, 112, 214, 219; **Line Infantry**; 27e 112–113, 128, 131–132, 137, 203, 211, 217–220; 39e 112, 214, 219; 50e 112, 203, 217–219; 59e 112–113, 203, 217–219; 69e 112, 184, 189, 203, 219; 76e 112, 203, 219; **Light Infantry**; 6e 112, 132, 220; 25e 104, 112, 211, 217–219
Freymarkt 115, 154, 196, 200, 202–203, 207, 210, 218, 223
Friedland 21, 75, 103, 107, 109, 134, 150, 183, 192
Frisching, river 75, 104, 134, 183–189, 191–195, 199, 205

Galicia 36, 51, 66–68, 73
Georgenthal 120, 125
Gersdorf, General Karl Maksimovich 147–148
Gogel, Colonel Fedor Grigorievich 120, 122, 155
Golenischev-Kutuzov, General Mikhail, see Kutuzov
Golitsyn, Lieutenant General Prince Dmitri 53, 60, 74–75, 85–86, 89–95, 97, 106, 111, 125, 127–128, 130–133, 136, 139, 143, 149, 152–154, 159, 200, 204–205, 210, 213, 216
Golymin 28, 61, 75, 87, 89, 91–92, 101, 134
Goniondz 61, 100–102, 136, 199
Grand Duke of Berg, see Murat
Grodno 38, 53–54, 58, 101–102, 223
Gross-Lauth 104, 183–186, 189, 194–195
Grouchy, General of Division Emmanuel de 75, 112, 114–115, 118, 134, 201, 204, 211, 214

Guttstadt 75, 101, 107, 112–115, 117, 119, 134, 136, 150, 153, 201–204, 207–211, 213–215, 218–219, 221–224

Halle 54, 56
Hautpoul, General of Division Jean-Joseph Ange d' 128–129, 144, 172, 176
Heiligenthal 152, 211, 214
Heilsberg 75, 103–104, 112–113, 115, 134, 150, 154, 156, 199, 201–203, 207, 209–210, 213, 216, 218, 220, 222
Hely-Hutchinson, Lieutenant General John 29–30, 117
Hof 157–158, 196, 200
Hohenstein 61, 75, 112–115, 117–119, 129, 131–136, 138–139, 143–146, 203, 212, 214

Iachvill, Colonel Prince Lev 60, 152

Jena 20, 35, 54, 56, 109, 192
Johannisburg 61, 75, 102, 106, 115, 134, 136
Jonkowo 75, 134, 136, 142–143, 145–152, 203, 214
Jurburg 38, 58

Kakhovsky, Major General Peter 139, 170–171
Kalkreuth, Friedrich Adolf Graf von 59–60, 66
Kamensky, Field Marshal Mikhail 71, 74, 77–78, 86, 89, 91, 97–98, 102, 106, 117, 147–148, 162, 167, 171–172, 174–175, 204
Kerwienen 113–115
Kiselev 172–173
Knorring, General Bogdan von 213, 222
Knorring, Colonel Karl Bogdanovich von 77, 101
Kolozomb 69, 90, 96
Königsberg 33, 98, 100, 102–109, 145, 150, 160, 166, 170, 173, 177–179, 181, 183, 185–186, 190–194, 198, 205, 207, 212, 215, 217, 221, 223
Korff, Major General Fedor von 94, 143, 171, 186–187, 208–209
Kozhin, Major General Sergei 81, 159
Kreutz, Major General Cyprian Belzig von 90, 126
Kreuzburg 75, 104, 134, 173, 177–178, 184, 187–188, 190, 194–195, 200
Kutschitten 171–175, 194
Kutuzov, General Mikhail Golenischev- 36, 38

L'Estocq, Major General Anton Wilhelm von 34, 60, 64–66, 68–70, 75, 96, 100, 104–114, 116–117, 127–128, 130–134, 136, 143, 149, 156, 159, 173–175, 177–178, 183–185, 188, 192, 196, 198–200, 202–205, 207, 209, 212–213, 216–217, 221–222

Lambert, Major General Count Karl 75–76, 153, 186–187
Landsberg 75, 107, 109, 114, 134, 150, 156–157, 160, 177–178, 184, 192, 194–196, 199–200, 203–205, 209, 222
Lannes, Marshal Jean 55, 57, 60, 64, 67–68, 73, 81–82, 102, 129, 134
Lasalle, General of Division Antoine-Charles-Louis 75, 134, 161, 177–178, 189, 194–196, 200–201, 211, 214, 219
Launau 117, 150, 154, 207, 216–218, 220, 222–224
Lefebvre, Marshal François Joseph 55, 135, 141, 144
Liebstadt 102, 113, 115–116, 118–119, 124, 127, 136, 150, 156, 159, 177, 203, 207, 210, 221
Löbau 61, 102, 128, 133, 135–138
Lopaczyn 88, 90

Makow 61, 75, 78, 84, 86, 91–92, 95, 134
Markov, General Yevgeni Ivanovich 105, 112–114, 116, 120–125, 127, 149, 152–155, 157, 162–163, 165, 167, 175, 180, 216
Mecklenburg 165, 170
Miastkowo 61, 98
Michelson, General Ivan 54, 66, 206
Mohrungen 102, 117–120, 124–125, 127–130, 145, 150, 156, 159
Moldavia 23–26
Mühlhausen, 75, 116–117, 134, 150, 183–184, 189, 193, 196, 200, 204
Murat, Marshal Joachim, Grand Duke of Berg 57, 67–68, 73, 81, 90, 102, 143 144, 172, 177, 184–185, 191, 201

Napoleon I, Emperor of France 20, 23, 29, 35, 38, 40, 44, 50–51, 53, 62, 65, 70, 72–74, 78, 80, 86–87, 94, 96, 98, 101–103, 105, 108, 119, 128–129, 131, 141–142, 147, 153, 162, 172, 181, 190, 198–199, 203, 220 221
Narew, river 28, 59, 61, 63, 66, 69–70, 72, 74–75, 78–82, 84–87, 91, 98–99, 102, 136, 177, 199, 213
Nasielsk 75–77, 134
Neidenburg 61, 75, 100, 102, 112–114, 117–118, 129, 131–133, 135, 137–139, 143, 201
Neuchâtel, Prince de, see Berthier
Ney, Marshal Michel 55, 73, 96, 98–103, 105–107, 109–110, 112, 114–119, 128–132, 134–136, 138, 143–149, 156, 159, 161, 173, 177–180, 184–185, 188–189, 194–195, 198–204, 207–210, 213–218, 220–224
Niémen, river 35, 51
Nowe Miasto 69, 72, 74–75, 78, 89–90, 96

Oder, river 30, 58, 65
Ostermann, Lieutenant General Count Alexander 53, 60, 69, 72, 74–76, 81–83, 106, 113–114, 131, 162, 171, 204, 216
Osterode 58–59, 61, 64–65, 67, 75, 102, 114–115, 117–119, 127–129, 131–138, 143, 150, 189–190, 202–203, 209–210, 212, 221, 223
Ostrolenka 58, 60–61, 68, 75, 80, 85, 87, 89, 95, 97–98, 115, 134
Ottoman Empire, the 23–27, 29, 41, 52, 66
Oudinot, General of Division Nicolas-Charles 56, 102, 177

Pahlen, Major General Peter Graf von der 73, 88–89, 125, 139, 171
Passarge, river 107, 109, 115–116, 119, 149, 156, 159, 202, 204–206, 209–211, 213, 215–217, 221
Passenheim 112, 115–119, 133, 139, 143–145, 207, 214
St Petersburg 25, 27, 29, 32, 42, 46, 54, 58, 62–63, 108, 127, 140, 192, 199
Pillar, Colonel Yegor 111–112, 174
Platov, Lieutenant General Count Matvei Ivanovich 172, 183, 185–188, 192, 195, 199–200, 202, 204–205, 208–209, 213, 215, 217
Plock 59–61, 63, 72, 75, 128, 134
Plötz, Lieutenant General Franz Heinrich Christian de 188, 202, 205–207
Pogone 61, 88
Poland 24, 41, 43–44, 49–52, 61, 64, 87, 103
Poniatowski, Prince Józef Antoni 64, 67
Posen 59, 67, 70
Praga 59, 61–62, 64, 66–68, 75
Pregel, river 109, 150, 160, 183, 185, 193
Preussisch-Eylau, see Eylau
Prussia 20, 27, 29, 33–40, 44, 50, 53–54, 56, 58, 64, 67, 98, 100, 102–103, 105–106, 108–111, 127, 140, 177, 181, 190, 192, 198, 207
Pultusk 28, 60, 62, 64–70, 72–82, 84–91, 96–98, 101–102, 131, 134, 181
Pupkeim 149, 152–153

Rastenburg 75, 100, 106, 109–111, 113, 115, 119, 134, 204
Rhine, river 40, 43–44, 51–52, 55, 103, 198
Rozan 61, 68, 75, 85, 87, 97–98, 134
Russian army, regiments of: **Cuirassiers**; His Majesty's 139, 165; Malorossiiskii 91, 145, 149, 171; Military Order 89–90, 94, 171; **Dragoons**; Ingermanlandskii 91, 163, 165; Kargopolskii 81, 139; Kurlyandskii 125, 145, 155, 171; Moskovskii 92, 94; Pskovskii 89, 93–94; **Hussars**; Aleksandriiskii 59, 69, 153,

155, 187; Elisavetgradskii 120, 165; Izumskii 81–82, 116, 131, 145, 151, 157–159, 171, 186–187; Oliviopolskii 151, 157–158, 185, 187; Pavlogradskii 81, 91, 94, 149, 154, 172, 222; Sumskii 88, 90, 94, 125–126, 186, 188; **Cossacks**; Andronov's 172, 185; Efremov III's 172, 188; Grekov XII's 128, 172; Grekov XVIII's 69, 111, 188; Ilovaisky IX's 112, 139, 172, 187; Kiselev's 172–173; Malakhov's 91–92, 120, 172, 185, 187; Popov V's 186–187; Sysoev's 172, 185–186; **Other cavalry**; Tatar Light Horse 77, 80, 101; **Grenadiers**; Ekaterinoslavskii 92, 120–121; Moskovskii 163–165, 166–167, 170; Tavricheskii 91, 93; **Jagers**; 1st 157–158; 4th 69, 80–81, 154; 5th 120–122, 155, 157; 7th 120, 187–188; 20th 80, 154, 157–158, 187–188; 21st 88–89, 186; 24th 111, 149, 165, 169, 25th 120–121, 155; **Musketeers**; Chernigovskii 83, 158; Kaluzhskii 202, 205–206; Kostromskoi 89, 93, 95, 157–158, 171; Moskovskii 92, 172; Pskovskii 120, 122, 156, 163; Starooskolskii 80–81; Tenginskii 80, 147; Tulskii 81–82; Uglitskii 147, 153, 171; Vyborgskii 111, 173–174
Rypin 61, 73, 75, 134–135

Saalfeld 56, 60, 131
Sacken, Lieutenant General Fabian von Osten- 53, 60, 75–76, 83, 127–128, 130, 136, 142, 149, 151, 156, 171, 204, 216–217, 221–222
Sausgarten 171, 175, 183, 194
Saxony 35, 49–50, 103
Scherbatov, Major General Prince Aleksei 93, 152, 158, 171, 209, 215–216
Schloditten 162, 167, 173, 175, 177–180, 183, 194, 196
Seeburg 75, 104, 112–114, 116–117, 119, 134, 136, 150, 207, 210, 222
Serpallen 162, 166, 170–171, 180, 194
Sierock 61, 69, 76, 80
Silesia 35, 39, 50, 54, 58, 67, 117, 181
Slubowo 89–90
Sochaczew 61, 67
Soldau 58–61, 80, 100, 114, 135, 137–138, 146
Somov, Major General Andrei 82, 106, 162, 165–167, 170, 180
Sonnenborn 130, 132
Soult, Marshal Nicolas 55, 73, 102, 109, 113, 115, 118, 128–129, 131–132, 134, 137, 143–144, 147, 161, 177, 203, 208–209, 211–212, 214, 218–219, 221, 223
Spiegelberg 142, 203
Steinheil 53, 84, 99, 171, 218
Stettin 21, 58
Stralsund 31, 34
Strassburg 61, 69–70, 75, 100, 102, 129, 134, 146
Strzegocin 61, 74–76, 89–91, 134
Sweden 20, 31–35, 40–42, 140
Sysoev 172, 185–186

Thorn 60–61, 64, 66, 69–70, 73, 75, 100, 117, 128–132, 135, 137–138, 141, 144, 220
Tilsit, Treaty of 19, 31, 44, 49–51, 63, 75, 109, 134, 181
Tolstoy Lieutenant General Count Peter 73, 84, 199, 204, 208, 213, 216, 220, 222
Tuchkov I, Lieutenant General Nikolai Alekseevich 54, 75, 84, 91, 106, 127–128, 130, 132–133, 136, 143, 149, 156, 162, 167, 169, 180, 202, 204, 209, 213, 216, 222
Tykoczin 97–99, 101

Ulm 20, 66

Vienna 27–29, 38–40
Vistula, river 20, 28, 46, 51–52, 54, 56, 58–61, 63–69, 72–73, 75, 80, 100, 102, 105, 117, 128, 131, 133–134
Vuich, Colonel Nikolai 121–122, 155

Wallachia 23–26
Warsaw 28, 38, 41, 43, 49–50, 55, 59, 61–68, 70, 72–73, 75, 102, 117, 130–131, 138, 142
Wernsdorf 186–187, 195
Willenberg 112–114, 118, 129, 131, 133, 135–136, 141–145, 223
Wittenberg 150, 183–186, 188, 195
Wkra, river 28, 61, 69, 72–74, 76, 80, 86, 88–91, 96, 101
Wolfsdorf 149–155, 203, 207, 211, 224

Yermolov Colonel Aleksei (Alexis) 92, 120, 154, 164–165
Zakroczyn 69, 75
Zapolsky, Major General Andrei Vasilievich 92, 169–170
Zechern 203, 208–209, 216–221, 223

From Reason to Revolution – Warfare 1721-1815

http://www.helion.co.uk/series/from-reason-to-revolution-1721-1815.php

The 'From Reason to Revolution' series covers the period of military history 1721–1815, an era in which fortress-based strategy and linear battles gave way to the nation-in-arms and the beginnings of total war.

This era saw the evolution and growth of light troops of all arms, and of increasingly flexible command systems to cope with the growing armies fielded by nations able to mobilise far greater proportions of their manpower than ever before. Many of these developments were fired by the great political upheavals of the era, with revolutions in America and France bringing about social change which in turn fed back into the military sphere as whole nations readied themselves for war. Only in the closing years of the period, as the reactionary powers began to regain the upper hand, did a military synthesis of the best of the old and the new become possible.

The series will examine the military and naval history of the period in a greater degree of detail than has hitherto been attempted, and has a very wide brief, with the intention of covering all aspects from the battles, campaigns, logistics, and tactics, to the personalities, armies, uniforms, and equipment.

Submissions

The publishers would be pleased to receive submissions for this series. Please contact series editor Andrew Bamford via email (andrewbamford@helion.co.uk), or in writing to Helion & Company Limited, Unit 8 Amherst Business Centre, Budbrooke Road, Warwick, CV34 5WE

Titles

No 1   *Lobositz to Leuthen: Horace St Paul and the Campaigns of the Austrian Army in the Seven Years War 1756-57* (Neil Cogswell)

No 2   *Glories to Useless Heroism: The Seven Years War in North America from the French journals of Comte Maurès de Malartic, 1755-1760* (William Raffle (ed.))

No 3   *Reminiscences 1808-1815 Under Wellington: The Peninsular and Waterloo Memoirs of William Hay* (Andrew Bamford (ed.))

No 4   *Far Distant Ships: The Royal Navy and the Blockade of Brest 1793-1815* (Quintin Barry)

No 5   *Godoy's Army: Spanish Regiments and Uniforms from the Estado Militar of 1800* (Charles Esdaile and Alan Perry)

No 6   *On Gladsmuir Shall the Battle Be! The Battle of Prestonpans 1745* (Arran Johnston)

No 7   *The French Army of the Orient 1798-1801: Napoleon's Beloved 'Egyptians'* (Yves Martin)

No 8   *The Autobiography, or Narrative of a Soldier: The Peninsular War Memoirs of William Brown of the 45th Foot* (Steve Brown (ed.))

No 9   *Recollections from the Ranks: Three Russian Soldiers' Autobiographies from the Napoleonic Wars* (Darrin Boland)

No 10 *By Fire and Bayonet: Grey's West Indies Campaign of 1794* (Steve Brown)

No 11 *Olmütz to Torgau: Horace St Paul and the Campaigns of the Austrian Army in the Seven Years War 1758-60* (Neil Cogswell)

No 12 *Murat's Army: The Army of the Kingdom of Naples 1806-1815* (Digby Smith)

No 13 *The Veteran or 40 Years' Service in the British Army: The Scurrilous Recollections of Paymaster John Harley 47th Foot – 1798-1838* (Gareth Glover (ed.))

No 14 *Narrative of the Eventful Life of Thomas Jackson: Militiaman and Coldstream Sergeant, 1803-15* (Eamonn O'Keeffe (ed.))

No.15 *For Orange and the States: The Army of the Dutch Republic 1713-1772 Part I: Infantry* (Marc Geerdinck-Schaftenaar)

No 16	*Men Who Are Determined to be Free: The American Assault on Stony Point, 15 July 1779* (David C. Bonk)
No 17	*Next to Wellington: General Sir George Murray: The Story of a Scottish Soldier and Statesman, Wellington's Quartermaster General* (John Harding-Edgar)
No 18	*Between Scylla and Charybdis: The Army of Elector Friedrich August of Saxony 1733-1763 Part I: Staff and Cavalry* (Marco Pagan)
No 19	*The Secret Expedition: The Anglo-Russian Invasion of Holland 1799* (Geert van Uythoven)
No 20	*'We Are Accustomed to do our Duty': German Auxiliaries with the British Army 1793-95* (Paul Demet)
No 21	*With the Guards in Flanders: The Diary of Captain Roger Morris 1793-95* (Peter Harington (ed.))
No 22	*The British Army in Egypt 1801: An Underrated Army Comes of Age* (Carole Divall)
No 23	*Better is the Proud Plaid: The Clothing, Weapons, and Accoutrements of the Jacobites in the '45* (Jenn Scott)
No 24	*The Lilies and the Thistle: French Troops in the Jacobite '45* (Andrew Bamford)
No 25	*A Light Infantryman With Wellington: The Letters of Captain George Ulrich Barlow 52nd and 69th Foot 1808-15* (Gareth Glover (ed.))
No 26	*Swiss Regiments in the Service of France 1798-1815: Uniforms, Organisation, Campaigns* (Stephen Ede-Borrett)
No 27	*For Orange and the States! The Army of the Dutch Republic 1713-1772: Part II: Cavalry and Specialist Troops* (Marc Geerdinck-Schaftenaar)
No 28	*Fashioning Regulation, Regulating Fashion: Uniforms and Dress of the British Army 1800-1815 Volume I* (Ben Townsend)
No 29	*Riflemen: The History of the 5th Battalion 60th (Royal American) Regiment, 1797-1818* (Robert Griffith)
No 30	*The Key to Lisbon: The Third French Invasion of Portugal, 1810-11* (Kenton White)
No 31	*Command and Leadership: Proceedings of the 2018 Helion & Company 'From Reason to Revolution' Conference* (Andrew Bamford (ed.))
No 32	*Waterloo After the Glory: Hospital Sketches and Reports on the Wounded After the Battle* (Michael Crumplin and Gareth Glover)
No 33	*Fluxes, Fevers, and Fighting Men: War and Disease in Ancien Regime Europe 1648-1789* (Pádraig Lenihan)
No 34	*'They Were Good Soldiers': African-Americans Serving in the Continental Army, 1775-1783* (John U. Rees)
No 35	*A Redcoat in America: The Diaries of Lieutenant William Bamford, 1757-1765 and 1776* (John B. Hattendorf (ed.))
No 36	*Between Scylla and Charybdis: The Army of Friedrich August II of Saxony, 1733-1763: Part II: Infantry and Artillery* (Marco Pagan)
No 37	*Québec Under Siege: French Eye-Witness Accounts from the Campaign of 1759* (Charles A. Mayhood (ed.))
No 38	*King George's Hangman: Henry Hawley and the Battle of Falkirk 1746* (Jonathan D. Oates)
No 39	*Zweybrücken in Command: The Reichsarmee in the Campaign of 1758* (Neil Cogswell)
No 40	*So Bloody a Day: The 16th Light Dragoons in the Waterloo Campaign* (David J. Blackmore)
No 41	*Northern Tars in Southern Waters: The Russian Fleet in the Mediterranean 1806-1810* (Vladimir Bogdanovich Bronevskiy / Darrin Boland)
No 42	*Royal Navy Officers of the Seven Years War: A Biographical Dictionary of Commissioned Officers 1748-1763* (Cy Harrison)
No 43	*All at Sea: Naval Support for the British Army During the American Revolutionary War* (John Dillon)
No 44	*Glory is Fleeting: New Scholarship on the Napoleonic Wars* (Andrew Bamford (ed.))
No 45	*Fashioning Regulation, Regulating Fashion: Uniforms and Dress of the British Army 1800-1815 Vol. II* (Ben Townsend)
No 46	*Revenge in the Name of Honour: The Royal Navy's Quest for Vengeance in the Single Ship Actions of the War of 1812* (Nicholas James Kaizer)
No 47	*They Fought With Extraordinary Bravery: The III German (Saxon) Army Corps in

- No 47 *the Southern Netherlands 1814* (Geert van Uythoven)
- No 48 *The Danish Army of the Napoleonic Wars 1801-1814, Organisation, Uniforms & Equipment: Volume 1: High Command, Line and Light Infantry* (David Wilson)
- No 49 *Neither Up Nor Down: The British Army and the Flanders Campaign 1793-1895* (Phillip Ball)
- No 50 *Guerra Fantástica: The Portuguese Army and the Seven Years War* (António Barrento)
- No 51 *From Across the Sea: North Americans in Nelson's Navy* (Sean M. Heuvel and John A. Rodgaard)
- No 52 *Rebellious Scots to Crush: The Military Response to the Jacobite '45* (Andrew Bamford (ed.))
- No 53 *The Army of George II 1727-1760: The Soldiers who Forged an Empire* (Peter Brown)
- No 54 *Wellington at Bay: The Battle of Villamuriel, 25 October 1812* (Garry David Wills)
- No 55 *Life in the Red Coat: The British Soldier 1721-1815* (Andrew Bamford (ed.))
- No 56 *Wellington's Favourite Engineer. John Burgoyne: Operations, Engineering, and the Making of a Field Marshal* (Mark S. Thompson)
- No 57 *Scharnhorst: The Formative Years, 1755-1801* (Charles Edward White)
- No 58 *At the Point of the Bayonet: The Peninsular War Battles of Arroyomolinos and Almaraz 1811-1812* (Robert Griffith)
- No 59 *Sieges of the '45: Siege Warfare during the Jacobite Rebellion of 1745-1746* (Jonathan D. Oates)
- No 60 *Austrian Cavalry of the Revolutionary and Napoleonic Wars, 1792–1815* (Enrico Acerbi, András K. Molnár)
- No 61 *The Danish Army of the Napoleonic Wars 1801-1814, Organisation, Uniforms & Equipment: Volume 2: Cavalry and Artillery* (David Wilson)
- No 62 *Napoleon's Stolen Army: How the Royal Navy Rescued a Spanish Army in the Baltic* (John Marsden)
- No 63 *Crisis at the Chesapeake: The Royal Navy and the Struggle for America 1775-1783* (Quintin Barry)
- No 64 *Bullocks, Grain, and Good Madeira: The Maratha and Jat Campaigns 1803-1806 and the emergence of the Indian Army* (Joshua Provan)
- No 65 *Sir James McGrigor: The Adventurous Life of Wellington's Chief Medical Officer* (Tom Scotland)
- No 66 *Fashioning Regulation, Regulating Fashion: Uniforms and Dress of the British Army 1800-1815 Volume I* (Ben Townsend) (paperback edition)
- No 67 *Fashioning Regulation, Regulating Fashion: Uniforms and Dress of the British Army 1800-1815 Volume II* (Ben Townsend) (paperback edition)
- No 68 *The Secret Expedition: The Anglo-Russian Invasion of Holland 1799* (Geert van Uythoven) (paperback edition)
- No 69 *The Sea is My Element: The Eventful Life of Admiral Sir Pulteney Malcolm 1768-1838* (Paul Martinovich)
- No 70 *The Sword and the Spirit: Proceedings of the first 'War & Peace in the Age of Napoleon' Conference* (Zack White (ed.))
- No 71 *Lobositz to Leuthen: Horace St Paul and the Campaigns of the Austrian Army in the Seven Years War 1756-57* (Neil Cogswell) (paperback edition)
- No 72 *For God and King. A History of the Damas Legion 1793-1798: A Case Study of the Military Emigration during the French Revolution* (Hughes de Bazouges and Alistair Nichols)
- No 73 *'Their Infantry and Guns Will Astonish You': The Army of Hindustan and European Mercenaries in Maratha service 1780-1803* (Andy Copestake)
- No 74 *Like A Brazen Wall: The Battle of Minden, 1759, and its Place in the Seven Years War* (Ewan Carmichael)
- No 75 *Wellington and the Lines of Torres Vedras: The Defence of Lisbon during the Peninsular War* (Mark Thompson)
- No 76 *French Light Infantry 1784-1815: From the Chasseurs of Louis XVI to Napoleon's Grande Armée* (Terry Crowdy)
- No 77 *Riflemen: The History of the 5th Battalion 60th (Royal American) Regiment, 1797-1818* (Robert Griffith) (paperback edition)
- No 78 *Hastenbeck 1757: The French Army and the Opening Campaign of the Seven Years War* (Olivier Lapray)

No 79   *Napoleonic French Military Uniforms: As Depicted by Horace and Carle Vernet and Eugène Lami* (Guy Dempsey (trans. and ed.))

No 80   *These Distinguished Corps: British Grenadier and Light Infantry Battalions in the American Revolution* (Don N. Hagist)

No 81   *Rebellion, Invasion, and Occupation: The British Army in Ireland, 1793-1815* (Wayne Stack)

No 82   *You Have to Die in Piedmont! The Battle of Assietta, 19 July 1747. The War of the Austrian Succession in the Alps* (Giovanni Cerino Badone)

No 83   *A Very Fine Regiment: the 47th Foot in the American War of Independence, 1773–1783* (Paul Knight)

No 84   *By Fire and Bayonet: Grey's West Indies Campaign of 1794* (Steve Brown) (paperback edition)

No 85   *No Want of Courage: The British Army in Flanders, 1793-1795* (R.N.W. Thomas)

No 86   *Far Distant Ships: The Royal Navy and the Blockade of Brest 1793-1815* (Quintin Barry) (paperback edition)

No 87   *Armies and Enemies of Napoleon 1789-1815: Proceedings of the 2021 Helion and Company 'From Reason to Revolution' Conference* (Robert Griffith (ed.))

No 88   *The Battle of Rossbach 1757: New Perspectives on the Battle and Campaign* (Alexander Querengässer (ed.))

No 89   *Waterloo After the Glory: Hospital Sketches and Reports on the Wounded After the Battle* (Michael Crumplin and Gareth Glover) (paperback edition)

No 90   *From Ushant to Gibraltar: The Channel Fleet 1778-1783* (Quintin Barry)

No 91   *'The Soldiers are Dressed in Red': The Quiberon Expedition of 1795 and the Counter-Revolution in Brittany* (Alistair Nichols)

No 92   *The Army of the Kingdom of Italy 1805-1814: Uniforms, Organisation, Campaigns* (Stephen Ede-Borrett)

No 93   *The Ottoman Army of the Napoleonic Wars 1798-1815: A Struggle for Survival from Egypt to the Balkans* (Bruno Mugnai)

No 94   *The Changing Face of Old Regime Warfare: Essays in Honour of Christopher Duffy* (Alexander S. Burns (ed.))

No 94   *The Changing Face of Old Regime Warfare: Essays in Honour of Christopher Duffy* (Alexander S. Burns (ed.)

No 95   *The Danish Army of the Napoleonic Wars 1801-1814, Organisation, Uniforms & Equipment: Volume 3: Norwegian Troops and Militia* (David Wilson)

No 96   *1805 – Tsar Alexander's First War with Napoleon* (Alexander Ivanovich Mikhailovsky-Danilevsky, trans. Peter G.A. Phillips)

No 97   *'More Furies then Men': The Irish Brigade in the service of France 1690-1792* (Pierre-Louis Coudray)

No 98   *'We Are Accustomed to do our Duty': German Auxiliaries with the British Army 1793-95* (Paul Demet) (paperback edition)

No 99   *Ladies, Wives and Women: British Army Wives in the Revolutionary and Napoleonic Wars 1793-1815* (David Clammer)

No 100 *The Garde Nationale 1789-1815: France's Forgotten Armed Forces* (Pierre-Baptiste Guillemot)

No 101 *Confronting Napoleon: Levin von Bennigsen's Memoir of the Campaign in Poland, 1806-1807, Volume 1 Pultusk to Eylau* (Alexander Mikaberidze and Paul Strietelmeier (trans. and ed.))